THE ASQ AUDITING
HANDBOOK

Also available from ASQ Quality Press:

Quality Audits for Improved Performance, Third Edition
Dennis R. Arter

The Internal Auditing Pocket Guide: Preparing, Performing, Reporting and Follow-up, Second Edition
J. P. Russell

Auditing Beyond Compliance: Using the Portable Universal Quality Lean Audit Model
Janet Bautista Smith

Process Driven Comprehensive Auditing: A New Way to Conduct ISO 9001:2008 Internal Audits, Second Edition
Paul C. Palmes

AS9101D Auditing for Process Performance: Combining Conformance and Effectiveness to Meet Customer Satisfaction
Chad Kymal

Lean Acres: A Tale of Strategic Innovation and Improvement in a Farm-iliar Setting
Jim Bowie

Lean ISO 9001: Adding Spark to your ISO 9001 QMS and Sustainability to your Lean Efforts
Mike Micklewright

The Quality Toolbox, Second Edition
Nancy R. Tague

Mapping Work Processes, Second Edition
Bjørn Andersen, Tom Fagerhaug, Bjørnar Henriksen, and Lars E. Onsøyen

Root Cause Analysis: Simplified Tools and Techniques, Second Edition
Bjørn Andersen and Tom Fagerhaug

The Certified Manager of Quality/Organizational Excellence Handbook, Third Edition
Russell T. Westcott, editor

To request a complimentary catalog of ASQ Quality Press publications, call 800-248-1946, or visit our website at http://www.asq.org/quality-press.

THE ASQ AUDITING HANDBOOK

PRINCIPLES, IMPLEMENTATION, AND USE

Fourth Edition

ASQ Audit Division

J. P. Russell, Editor

ASQ Quality Press
Milwaukee, Wisconsin

American Society for Quality, Quality Press, Milwaukee 53203
© 2013 by ASQ
All rights reserved. Published 2012
Printed in the United States of America
18 17 16 15 14   5 4 3

Library of Congress Cataloging-in-Publication Data
The ASQ auditing handbook : principles, implementation, and use / ASQ
Quality Audit Division ; J.P. Russell, editor.—4th ed.
    p. cm.
  Rev. ed. of: The quality audit handbook. 3rd ed. c2005.
  Includes bibliographical references and index.
  ISBN 978-0-87389-847-8 (alk. paper)
  1. Auditing—Handbooks, manuals, etc. I. Russell, J. P. (James P.),
1945– II. ASQ Quality Audit Division. III. Quality audit handbook.
  HF5667.Q35 2013
  657'.45—dc23
                                    2012039493

Publisher: William A. Tony
Acquisitions Editor: Matt Meinholz
Project Editor: Paul Daniel O'Mara
Production Administrator: Randall Benson

ASQ Mission: The American Society for Quality advances individual, organizational, and community excellence worldwide through learning, quality improvement, and knowledge exchange.

Attention Bookstores, Wholesalers, Schools, and Corporations: ASQ Quality Press books, video, audio, and software are available at quantity discounts with bulk purchases for business, educational, or instructional use. For information, please contact ASQ Quality Press at 800-248-1946, or write to ASQ Quality Press, P.O. Box 3005, Milwaukee, WI 53201-3005.

To place orders or to request a free copy of the ASQ Quality Press Publications Catalog, visit our website at http://www.asq.org/quality-press.

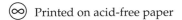 Printed on acid-free paper

Quality Press
600 N. Plankinton Ave.
Milwaukee, WI 53203-2914
E-mail: authors@asq.org
The Global Voice of Quality™

Contents

List of Figures and Tables

Foreword

Change is the only constant, and changes to the audit profession continue in order to improve effectiveness and efficiency and to adjust to changes in technology. We are no longer just process and system auditors—rather, members of our profession are valued teammates, adding fresh eyes and organizational expertise to the wealth of tools available to management. Management system standards such as ISO 9000–based management systems are now viewed as starting points for organizational excellence. ASQ Audit Division members are no longer considered compliance police. Rather, our membership has evolved to meet the challenges of the new millennium, just as Norm Frank predicted in his foreword to the second edition of this handbook. We are no longer just auditors—we are assessors, and our chosen discipline has grown to include advising management on best practices. We are teachers in the true sense of the word.

This edition of *The ASQ Auditing Handbook* reflects those changes. Subject-matter experts skilled in the audit profession have grown the Body of Knowledge (BoK), working in tandem with the ASQ Certification Department, and this book reflects the latest revision. Teams of ASQ Certified Quality Auditors (CQAs), working on your behalf, met at ASQ headquarters and volunteered long hours to ensure that the BoK, reflected herein, represents generally accepted, world-class audit practices. Contributors to this book, also subject-matter experts, volunteered their time to ensure that the excellence of the new BoK is scholastically available to audit professionals the world over.

The words *thank you* don't begin to express my appreciation to the ASQ Certification staff, the CQAs involved in updating the BoK, the Audit Division members who volunteer to manage the certification program, the CQAs who meet every year to write test questions, and the fine authors who contributed to the latest edition of this book. This book has become the text of choice for candidates sitting for the CQA examination. The exam is written such that the handbook is a major source of information needed to attain the CQA credential.

Enjoy our latest edition, and use the information to grow your expertise. The path leading from compliance auditing to system assessing is great, but the rewards are worth the effort. I think you'll find this book to be an invaluable resource to help you along that path.

George Callender
Chair, ASQ Audit Division

Notes to the Reader

This handbook supports the quality auditor BoK, developed for the ASQ CQA program. The quality audit BoK was revised in 2012. The fourth edition addresses new and expanded BoK topics, common auditing (quality, environmental, safety, and so on) methods, and process auditing. The handbook is designed to provide practical guidance for system and process auditors. Practitioners in the field provided content, example audit situations, stories, and review comments as the handbook evolved.

New to the fourth edition are the topics of common and special causes, outliers, and risk management tools. Besides the new topics, many current topics have been expanded to reflect changes in auditing practices since 2004 and ISO 19011 guidance, and they have been rewritten to promote the common elements of all types of system and process audits (quality, environmental, safety, and health).

The text is aligned with the BoK for easy cross-referencing. We hope that use of this handbook will increase your understanding of the auditing BoK.

THE USE

The handbook can be used by new auditors to gain an understanding of auditing. Experienced auditors will find it to be a useful reference. Audit managers and quality managers will use the handbook as a guide for leading their auditing programs.

The handbook will also be used by trainers and educators as source material for teaching the fundamentals of auditing. It is not designed as a stand-alone text to prepare for the ASQ CQA exam. As with all ASQ certification activities, you are encouraged to work with your local section or the Quality Audit Division for preparation. *The ASQ Auditing Handbook*, when used in conjunction with other published materials, is appropriate for refresher courses, and we hope that trainers will use it in that manner.

The handbook contains information to support all aspects of the CQA BoK and is not limited to what new auditors need to know. Hence, the amount of material in each part of the handbook is not directly proportional to exam emphasis. The CQA exam is designed to test a candidate's basic knowledge of quality auditing. All the information in the handbook is important, but those preparing for the CQA exam should spend more time on their weakest areas and on those parts of the BoK receiving more emphasis on the exam. The number of questions and the percentage of CQA exam questions are indicated at the start of each part of the handbook.

THE CONTENTS

The handbook is organized to be in alignment with the CQA BoK. We have included the BoK at the back of the handbook as an appendix. Since many concepts and practices of process and system auditing are still evolving, the BoK will be revised from time to time. As changes occur, the handbook must also be revised to be current.

Terms and definitions are addressed throughout the text. Definitions are taken from ISO 19011:2011 and ISO 9000:2005, with definitions from the former superseding the latter. Definitions have undergone extensive peer review and are accepted worldwide. However, even the definitions of audit terms continue to evolve in order to meet the needs of the users of the standard.

The ASQ Auditing Handbook represents generally accepted audit practices for both internal and external applications. Thus, it may not depict the best practice for every situation.

The handbook uses generic terms to support broad principles. For clarity, specific industry examples and stories from CQAs are sometimes used to explain a topic in the BoK. The stories, depicted as sidebars, are a way for auditors to share their experiences. Industry examples incorporated into the text and presented in the appendices are not intended to be all-inclusive and representative of all industries. We are pleased to incorporate examples shared by audit practitioners as a means to add value to the text. Needless to say, this work cannot address the most appropriate practice for every industry or organization.

In some cases CQA information needs are the same as other certified professional needs. Several sections in Part V, "Quality Tools and Techniques," are the same as similar sections for certified manager of quality. All sections and chapters are clearly marked and referenced.

This publication, which describes audit methods and their application, is not intended to be used as a national or international standard, although it references many existing standards. The conventions for writing standards and using the term *shall* to mean a requirement and *should* to mean a guideline do not apply to *The ASQ Auditing Handbook*.

WHO WROTE IT

The CQAs who supplied information for the handbook represent a broad spectrum of organizations in the United States and around the world. More than 120 individuals contributed material for the first, second, third, and fourth editions. Input from members and a number of published texts were also used to create and develop *The ASQ Auditing Handbook*. It represents internal and external audits in a variety of product and service industries, regulated and nonregulated.

For each edition, a developmental editor gathered material to address the BoK topics and issued a manuscript to be reviewed by audit experts and practitioners in the field. Extensive peer review further strengthened the manuscript. The editor sorted, culled, augmented, and refined the manuscript to be turned over to the publisher.

WHY THE HANDBOOK

The ASQ Audit Division sponsored the development of this handbook to promote the use of auditing as a management tool—our primary mission. We believe that the Audit Division's members possess the greatest concentration of theoretical and practical auditing knowledge in the world. In *The ASQ Auditing Handbook*, we have tried to give you the benefits of this collective expertise.

J. P. Russell, Editor

Acknowledgments

ASQ Audit Division members and experts have contributed to all editions of the handbook as contributors, reviewers, and handbook project leaders. For a list of our first, second, and third edition contributors and reviewers, please see Appendix K. For the fourth edition, we relied on expert input from the developmental editor, other proven expert sources, and peer review. The auditing BoK has evolved since the first edition of the handbook, published in 1997, and needs more refinement than creation. Over the years, the quality of the feedback from day-to-day practitioners has significantly improved the content applicability and value to users of the handbook.

Reviewers of the fourth edition of the handbook are:

Nancy Boudreau, ASQ CQA, CQPA, RABQSA QMS PA

Mary Chris Easterly, ASQ CQA, ASQ CMQ/OE

Anita McReynolds-Lidbury, ASQ CQA

Lawrence Mossman, ASQ CQA

Sandra Storli, ASQ CMQ/OE, CBA, CQA, RABQSA-LA

J. P. Russell, Editor

Overview

This handbook is organized in the same way as the ASQ Certified Quality Auditor BoK, starting with Part I and ending with Part V. This section was written as an overview of auditing to better prepare readers for Part I of the handbook and is not meant to be an explanation of the BoK.

The word *audit* is associated with formal or methodical examining, reviewing, and investigating. Professional groups such as ASQ and the Institute of Internal Auditors (IIA) define preferred methods for conducting examinations and investigations (to audit). For product, process, and system audits, the Audit Division of ASQ has developed the BoK for auditing. ASQ also certifies individuals who meet the criteria for Certified Quality Auditor, Quality Auditor–HACCP Certification, and Quality Auditor–Biomedical. This handbook explains the topics listed in the BoK issued by ASQ.

Auditing is a prescribed work practice or process. There is a preferred sequential order of activities that should be performed to conduct a proper audit. Part II of the BoK ("Audit Process") follows the same preferred order. Audits must be prepared for (planning ahead), then performed (conducting the audit), the results reported (let everyone know what was found), and then the results responded to (feedback on what is going to happen next) by the organization that was audited. It is common to refer to these as phases of an audit: preparation, performance, report, and follow-up and closure. As with most service jobs, the outcome is influenced by how the service provider performs the job. That is why Part I of the handbook is about audit fundamentals, ethics, and conduct. Auditing is considered a profession; therefore, individual auditors need to know how to conduct themselves in a professional manner.

In the late 1980s the Quality Auditing Technical Committee (now the Audit Division of ASQ) defined *audit* as:

> A planned, independent, and documented assessment to determine whether agreed-upon requirements are being met.

For now, let us think of a quality audit as an assessment to determine whether agreed-upon quality requirements are being met and will continue to be met (whereas an environmental audit may be related to environmental requirements, a financial audit related to financial or accounting requirements, and so on). A distinguishing attribute of an audit is objectivity. The individuals performing audits must be able to evaluate the area being audited in an objective and unbiased manner. The degree of objectivity varies depending on the situation and type of audit (purpose and scope). For example, auditors can audit within their own department, but they cannot audit their own jobs.

There are several groupings or classifications of audits, depending on the relationships (external and internal), the need for objectivity, and the reason for the audit (verification of product, process, or system). In Figure I.1, the circle represents an organization. Outside the circle are the organization's customer(s) and supplier(s). All organizations have customer-supplier relationships. Any audits done inside the circle are *internal* audits, and audits done outside the circle are *external* audits. We further classify the audits as first-, second-, or third-party audits based on relationships. *First-party* audits are ones within the organization itself (the same as internal audits or self-assessment) and are inside the circle. *Second-party* audits are audits of suppliers or of customers crossing into the circle to audit the organization (their supplier). *Third-party* audits are totally independent of the customer-supplier relationship and are off to the right in the diagram. Third-party audits may result in independent certification of a product, process, or system.

Auditors can focus the audit (examination and investigation) on different areas, depending on the needs. A product or service audit determines whether product or service requirements (tangible characteristics or attributes) are being met. The process audit determines whether process requirements (methods, procedures) are being met. A system audit determines whether system requirements (manual, policy, standards, regulations) are being met. The handbook discusses all types of audits, but most of the discussion is focused on system audits (being the most complex and having the greatest potential influence). A system can be thought of as a group of processes providing a product or service.

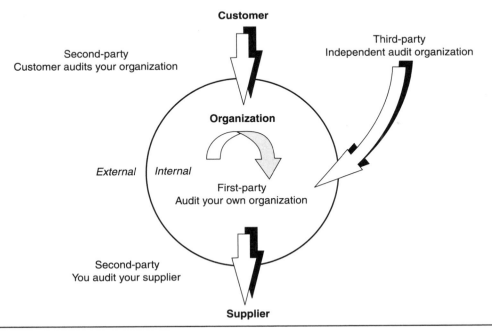

Figure I.1   Types of audits.

Source: J.P. Russell & Associates training materials. Used with permission.

When auditors are auditing, they are making observations and collecting evidence (data). They are seeking to verify that requirements are being met. They do this by collecting hard evidence, not hearsay or promises. Evidence produced as a result of the activity may be tangible objects or records, or personal observations.

Auditors must be familiar with auditing techniques and the criteria they are auditing to. What auditors observe is not always straightforward or obvious, so they must be able to judge whether the intent (reason for the requirement) is being met or addressed. The audit evidence and the method of collecting the evidence form the basis of the audit report.

The primary participants needed for conducting an audit are the auditor, the auditee, and the client. The person conducting the audit is called the auditor, lead auditor, or audit team leader. The organization being audited or investigated is called the auditee. There is also a client, the person or organization that has requested the audit. Audits are conducted only when someone requests one; they do not happen by accident. There has to be a sponsor or client with the authority to call for an audit.

Any type of organization can be audited against a set of standard requirements. The organization can produce a product or provide a service, such as government agencies or retail stores. An organization can be audited against almost any type of standards or set of criteria. The criteria or standards can be government regulations, ISO 9001 or ISO 14001 requirements, TS 16949, Malcolm Baldrige National Quality Award criteria, customer requirements, and so on. If there is a set of rules, auditors can compare actual practice with the rules.

While auditors are comparing actual practice with the rules or standards (determining conformity or compliance to requirements), they may also observe that certain practices and trends are not in the best interest of the organization being audited. Hence, auditors may report compliance and noncompliance as well as areas that are not effective or areas that can be improved as input for management consideration. Auditors may also include best practices or good practices as part of an audit report so that they can be shared with other areas of the organization.

Findings are the results of the investigation. They may be reported as nonconformities/conformities, findings, noncompliances/compliances, defects, concerns, and so on. The audit results can include both positive and negative issues identified. It is important for everyone to agree on the terminology that will be used in the audit report.

Recently there has been more emphasis on looking beyond conducting the audit steps, to management of the audit process. It is important to understand the objectives of the audit function and the potential benefits to the organization. This understanding and clarification has resulted in some audit programs being strictly limited to auditing for compliance and other audit programs seeking information about the effectiveness and efficiency of internal controls.

Auditing is a management tool used to verify that systems and processes are compliant/conformant, suitable to achieve objectives, and effective. For additional background information on auditing, continue on to Part I.

AUDITS ARE NOT INSPECTIONS

All too often the term *audit* is used to describe an inspection activity. Inspection is a tool to detect errors or defects before a product is approved for release or distribution. It is normally part of the manufacturing or service approval process. An organization may form a quality control department to manage and conduct the inspections.

In other cases, some organizations may use the word *inspection* to describe an audit. Audits conducted by the government (such as the FDA) may be described as inspections in regulatory documents. For the purposes of this handbook, we will differentiate between audits and inspections on the basis of national and international standards such as the ISO 19011 guideline standard regarding management system audits.

As organization sectors (other than manufacturing) attempt to apply auditing principles, they may become frustrated due to some initial misunderstandings. One of these misunderstandings is the way they use the term *audit*. For example, in the insurance industry, claims (such as medical, property, and liability) are processed as a case file. This file contains the insured party's claim, the evidence, the adjuster's report, the offered compensation, the accepted compensation, and the closing statement. All this paperwork is subject to error and omission. So the managers will audit these case files before they are ultimately closed. Sometimes the audit is performed before a check is cut. In reality, this is an inspection and not an audit.

The general public associates quality with conducting an inspection. The irony is that using inspections to ensure quality has proved to be too costly and ineffective compared to using other quality tools and techniques.

For more information on the history of quality control and auditing, see Appendix E, "History of Quality Assurance and Auditing."

Part I

Auditing Fundamentals

[27 of the CQA Exam Questions or 18 percent]

The purpose of Part I is to present audit purpose, types, and criteria as well as auditor roles and responsibilities. The last chapter addresses professional conduct and consequences for auditors. Ethics affect professional conduct, and professional conduct affects liability and audit credibility.

Chapter 1
Types of Quality Audits/Part IA

1. METHOD

An *audit* is a "systematic, independent and documented process for obtaining audit evidence and evaluating it objectively to determine the extent to which audit criteria are fulfilled."[1] Several audit methods may be employed to achieve the audit purpose. There are three discrete types of audits: product (which includes services), process, and system. However, other methods, such as a desk or document review audit, may be employed independently or in support of the three general types of audits. Some audits are named according to their purpose or scope. The scope of a department or function audit is a particular department or function. The purpose of a management audit relates to management interests such as assessment of area performance or efficiency.

Product Audit

A *product audit* is an examination of a particular product or service (hardware, processed material, software) to evaluate whether it conforms to requirements (that is, specifications, performance standards, and customer requirements). An audit performed on a service is called a *service audit*. Elements examined may include packaging, shipment preparation and protection, user instructions, product characteristics, product performance, and other customer requirements.

Product audits are conducted when a product is in a completed stage of production and has passed the final inspection. The product auditor uses inspection techniques to evaluate the entire product and all aspects of the product characteristics. A *product quality audit* is the examination or test of a product that had been previously accepted or rejected for the characteristics being audited. It includes performing operational tests to the same requirements used by manufacturing, using the same production test procedure, methods, and equipment. The product audit verifies conformance to specified standards of workmanship and performance. This audit can also measure the quality of the product going to the customer. The product audit frequently includes an evaluation of packaging, an examination for cosmetics, and a check for proper documentation and accessories, such as proper tags, stamps, process certifications, use of approved vendors, shipment preparation, and security. Product audits may be performed on safety equipment, environmental test equipment, or products to be sent to customers, or they can be the result of a service such as equipment maintenance.

A product audit is the examination of the form, fit, and function of a completed item after final inspection. It is technical; it may involve special (sometimes periodic) examination, inspection, or testing of a product that previously passed final inspection and has been accepted for characteristics being audited to ensure that it has not degraded over time; and it can be customer oriented. The reference standard for a product quality audit is the product quality program and the product performance specification. One of its characteristics is a complete examination of a small sample of finished product. Sometimes a product audit includes the destructive test of sample products.[2]

A service audit is one type of product audit. For many services an auditor can verify physical attributes of the service that was performed. For example: Was the label added? Is the area clean? Have records been completed? Are tools organized? For other services there are few or no traces of the service that was performed and therefore it must be verified by a process audit, for example, tuning an engine, performing repairs, receiving education or training, and receiving some personal services (a haircut can be checked and verified, but not a massage).

Process Audit

The process audit is performed to verify that processes are working within established limits. "The process audit examines an activity to verify that the inputs, actions, and outputs are in accordance with defined requirements. The boundary (scope) of a process audit should be a single process, such as marking, stamping, cooking, coating, setting up, or installing. It is very focused and usually involves only one work crew."[3] A process audit covers only a portion of the total system and usually takes much less time than a system audit.

A *process audit* is verification by evaluation of an operation or method against predetermined instructions or standards to measure conformance to these standards and the effectiveness of the instructions. Such an audit may check conformance to defined requirements such as time, accuracy, temperature, pressure, composition, responsiveness, amperage, and component mixture. It may involve special processes such as heat-treating, soldering, plating, encapsulation, welding, and nondestructive examination. A process audit examines the resources (equipment, materials, people) applied to transform the inputs into outputs, the environment, the methods (procedures, instructions) followed, and the measures collected to determine process performance. A process audit checks the adequacy and effectiveness of the process controls established by procedures, work instructions, flowcharts, and training and process specifications.

Auditors conducting process audits by their nature follow a process. The audit method of following process steps is a *process audit technique*. The process audit technique is an effective audit method and offers a good alternative to auditing by clause element or department or function. System auditors may use process audit techniques to the extent possible when auditing a management system.

System Audit

An audit conducted on a management system is called a *system audit*. It can be described as a documented activity performed to verify, by examination and evaluation of objective evidence, that applicable elements of the system are appropriate and effective and have been developed, documented, and implemented in accordance and in conjunction with specified requirements.

A *quality management system audit* evaluates an existing quality program to determine its conformance to company policies, contract commitments, and regulatory requirements. It includes the preparation of formal plans and checklists that are based on established requirements, the evaluation of implementation of detailed activities within the quality program, and the issuance of formal requests for corrective action where necessary.[4] Similarly, an *environmental system audit* examines an environmental management system, a *food safety system audit* examines a food safety management system, and *safety system audits* examine the safety management system.

Criteria contained in the American Society of Mechanical Engineers (ASME) codes, nuclear regulations, good manufacturing practices, or ISO standards, for example, may describe a management system. Normally these descriptions state what must be done but do not specify how it must be done. The "how" is left up to the organization being audited. An auditor looks at the management systems that control all activities from the time an order comes into a company (that is, how the order is handled, processed, and passed on to operations, and what operations does in response to that order) through delivery of the goods, sometimes including transportation to the site.

A system audit looks at everything within the system (that is, the processes, products, services, and supporting groups such as purchasing, customer service, design engineering, order entry, waste management, and training). It encompasses all the systems of the facility that assist in providing an acceptable product or service that is safe and conforms to applicable local, regional, national, and international requirements.

Desk Audit or Document Review

A *desk audit* or *document review* is an audit of an organization's documents. It can be conducted at a desk since people are not interviewed and activities are not observed. If auditing a new area, function, or organization, a desk audit must be conducted prior to a process or system audit to verify that documents meet requirements specified in the audit criteria or standards. The document review verifies that there is an adequately defined process or system prior to the full process or system audit. Findings from a desk audit or document review help ensure that audit program resources are used efficiently. It would be very costly if an audit team arrived to do a system audit, only to find out that the established system was not adequate. Also, a desk audit or document review may be conducted periodically or when documents (processes) are changed to verify the adequacy of the changes.

2. AUDITOR-AUDITEE RELATIONSHIP

Internal and External Audits

An audit may be classified as internal or external depending on the interrelationships that exist among the participants. Internal audits are first-party audits, while external audits can be either second- or third-party audits. *Internal audits* are audits of an organization's product(s), processes, and systems conducted by employees of the organization. *External audits* are audits of an organization's product(s),

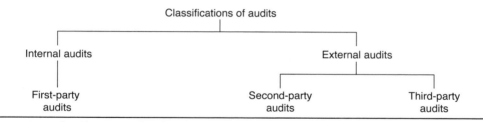

Figure 1.1   Classifications of audits.

processes, and systems conducted by individuals who are not employees of the organization. Figure 1.1 illustrates the classifications commonly used to differentiate between types of internal and external audits. The figure is provided as a guide to classifications, but there is no absolute rule, because there are exceptions. The types of audits depicted in Figure 1.1 are not mutually exclusive. An audit can be a blend of the different types of audits. Third-party auditors (certification) could be joined by second-party auditors (customer auditors), or internal auditors could be joined by external auditors (customer).

First-, Second-, and Third-Party Audits

First-Party Audit

A *first-party audit* is performed within an organization to measure its strengths and weaknesses against its own procedures or methods and/or against external standards adopted by (voluntary) or imposed on (mandatory) the organization. A first-party audit is an internal audit conducted by auditors who are employed by the organization being audited but who have no vested interest in the audit results of the area being audited. The auditing management systems standard ISO 19011 states that the independence of the audit team members from the activities to be audited should be considered, and to avoid conflicts of interest when selecting audit team members. Companies may have a separate audit group consisting of full-time auditors, or the auditors may be trained employees from other areas of the company who perform audits as needed on a part-time basis in addition to their other duties. One of the benefits of using part-time auditors is that the auditor learns the requirements by evaluating the objective evidence to determine conformance with the requirement beyond their normal work assignment.

In some cases an organization may hire (outsource) an audit organization to conduct its internal audits. The benefits of hiring an external auditing organization are that internal employees do not have to take time from their day-to-day jobs, auditors may be more objective and impartial, and the organization may benefit from employing more experienced auditors.

A multisite company's audit of another of its divisions or subsidiaries, whether it is local, national, or international, is often considered an internal audit. If, however, the other locations function primarily as suppliers to the main operation or location, audits of those sites would be considered second-party audits.

Second-Party Audit

A *second-party audit* is an external audit performed on a supplier by a customer or by a contracted organization on behalf of a customer. A contract is in place, and the goods or service is being, or will be, delivered.[5] Second-party audits are subject to the rules of contract law, as they are providing contractual direction from the customer to the supplier. Second-party audits tend to be more formal than first-party audits because audit results could influence the customer's purchasing decisions. A *survey*, sometimes called an assessment or examination, is a comprehensive evaluation that analyzes such things as facilities, resources, economic stability, technical capability, personnel, production capabilities, and past performance, as well as the entire management system. In general, a survey is performed prior to the award of a contract to a prospective supplier to ensure that the proper capabilities, controls, and systems are in place. The scope of the survey may be limited to specified management systems such as quality, environmental, or safety systems, or it may include the entire organization management system.

> An auditor told of one case in which an organization wanted to acknowledge a supplier for the perfect product it had been receiving. However, during the award process it was discovered that the supplier had absolutely no quality system in place! The supplier was able to ship an acceptable product simply because its employees were good sorters.

Third-Party Audit

A *third-party audit* is performed by an audit organization independent of the customer-supplier relationship and is free of any conflict of interest. Independence of the audit organization is a key component of a third-party audit. Third-party audits may result in certification, registration, recognition, an award, license approval, a citation, a fine, or a penalty issued by the third-party organization or an interested party. Third-party audits may be performed on behalf of an auditee's potential customers who cannot afford to survey or audit external organizations themselves or who consider a third-party audit to be a more cost-effective alternative. Government representatives perform mandatory audits on regulated industries such as nuclear power stations, airlines, and medical device manufacturers to provide assurances of safety to the public.

3. PURPOSE

It is also common to refer to an audit according to its purpose or objectives. An auditor may specialize in types of audits based on the audit purpose, such as to verify compliance, conformance, or performance. Some audits have special administrative purposes such as auditing documents, risk, or performance or following up on completed corrective actions.

Certification Purposes

Companies in certain high-risk categories—such as toys, pressure vessels, elevators, gas appliances, and electrical and medical devices—wanting to do business in Europe must comply with Conformité Europeëne Mark (CE Mark) require-ments. One way for organizations to comply is to have their management system certified by a third-party audit organization to management system requirement criteria (such as ISO 9001).

Customers may suggest or require that their suppliers conform to ISO 9001, ISO 14001, or safety criteria. The U.S. Federal Acquisition Regulations (FARs) 48 CFR 46.202-4 replaced references to government specifications with higher-level contract quality requirements. Cited higher-level contract quality requirements include ISO 9001, AS9100, ANSI/ASQC E4, and ANSI/ASME NQA-1. However, this does not preclude other federal government entities, such as the Department of Energy (DOE) or the Department of Defense (DOD), from having additional requirements for the specific work they do (for example, nuclear facility stan-dards/regulations such as Federal Register 10 CFR 830 Subpart A). Many national standards have been canceled, and users have been referred to the U.S.-adopted ISO 9001 standard. A third-party audit normally results in the issuance of a certifi-cate stating that the auditee organization management system complies with the requirements of a pertinent standard or regulation.

Third-party audits for system certification should be performed by organi-zations that have been evaluated and accredited by an established accreditation board, such as the ANSI-ASQ National Accreditation Board (ANAB). As the U.S. accreditation body for management systems, ANAB accredits certification bodies for ISO 9001, ISO 13485, ISO/TS 16949 QMSs, and ISO 14001 EMSs, as well as for several other conformity requirements standards.

What's the difference between certification, registration, and accreditation?

The terms *certification* and *registration* are used interchangeably to refer to verifying the conformance of an organization's management systems to a standard or other requirements. The term *accreditation* is used when validating or verifying the conformance of a certifica-tion body to the requirements of national and/or international crite-ria. *Certification* also refers to the process of validating and verifying the credentials of individuals such as auditors.

A *certification body*, also known as a registrar, is a third-party company contracted to evaluate the conformance of an organiza-tion's management systems to the requirements of the appropriate standard(s) and issue a certificate of conformance when warranted.[6]

Performance versus Compliance/Conformance Audits

There has been increased emphasis on how audits can add value. Various authors use the following terms to describe an audit purpose beyond compliance and con-formance: value-added assessments, management audits, added value auditing, and continual improvement assessment. The purpose of these audits goes beyond traditional compliance and conformance audits. The audit purpose relates to orga-nization performance. Audits that determine compliance and conformance are not focused on good or poor performance. Yet performance is an important concern for most organizations.

A key difference between compliance/conformance audits and audits designed to promote improvement is the collection of audit evidence related to organization performance versus evidence to verify conformance or compliance to a standard or procedure. An organization may conform to its procedures for taking orders, but if every order is subsequently changed two or three times, management may have cause for concern and want to rectify the inefficiency.

All types of audits—including product, process, and system and first-, second-, and third-party audits—can include a purpose to identify and report performance observations. However, audits with an objective to identify risks and opportunities for improvement are more likely to be first-party, process, or system audits.

If an organization's audit program has an objective for audits to be a management tool for improvement, performance may be included in the audit purpose. The mission of the ASQ Audit Division is "to develop the expectations of the audit profession and auditors. To promote to stakeholders auditing as a management tool to achieve continuous improvement and to increase customer satisfaction."

Follow-up Audit

A product, process, or system audit may have findings that require correction and corrective action. Since most corrective actions cannot be performed at the time of the audit, the audit program manager may require a follow-up audit to verify that corrections were made and corrective actions were taken. Due to the high cost of a single-purpose follow-up audit, it is normally combined with the next scheduled audit of the area. However, this decision should be based on the importance and risk of the finding. An organization may not be willing to risk a fine due to a repeat sampling equipment failure or risk sending customers a nonconforming product.

An organization may also conduct follow-up audits to verify preventive actions were taken as a result of performance issues that may be reported as opportunities for improvement. Other times organizations may forward identified performance issues to management for follow-up.

4. COMMON ELEMENTS WITH OTHER AUDITS

Regardless of the scope of a system or process audit, they all have some common elements. ISO 19011:2011 defines an audit as a "systematic, independent and documented process for obtaining audit evidence [records, statements of fact, or other information relevant to the audit criteria and verifiable] and evaluating it objectively to determine the extent to which audit criteria [set of policies, procedures, or requirements] are fulfilled."

Audits can address almost any topic of interest where activities or outputs result from defined plans. The scope of the audit might be product or service quality; environmental, marketing, or promotional claims; financial results and statements; health and safety conditions; equal opportunity compliance; internal controls for operations (Sarbanes-Oxley); postproduction sales and service with feedback for improvement; and the like. Basically, if an activity or status is subject to planning or reporting, it can be audited.

> The universality of auditing extends to most sectors of our society, including the American Civil Liberties Union (ACLU), local building or fire inspectors, the Environmental Protection Agency (EPA), the Occupational Safety and Health Administration (OSHA), union representatives, critical customers, and the Internal Revenue Service (IRS), to assess and report how well the organization is performing.

Audit-like inquiries that do not fulfill all the technical requirements of an audit (such as an audit plan or avoiding conflicts of interest) are known as an evaluation or an assessment. Commonly, evaluations are fairly subjective audit-like activities that compare current performance with some potential status, like theoretical capacity or capability of a system or process, for example. Evaluations are judgments. Similarly, assessments are activities that more closely align with the definition of an audit but lack satisfying some known and identified requirement. Assessments are estimates or determinations of significance or importance.

> A common type of assessment is termed "statutory and regulatory compliance audit." While the auditors may be trained and informed in the relevant materials and documents, they need to be careful to avoid going beyond their competence in their reporting. For statutory issues, interpretation of laws is often required and can be viewed as the domain of lawyers who are members of the bar. Typically, determination of regulatory compliance lies solely in the domain of persons who are formally recognized by the regulatory agency as being competent to interpret regulations developed by statutory authorities, for example, OSHA, the EPA, the Department of Transportation (DOT), the Federal Aviation Administration (FAA), and the Food and Drug Administration (FDA). Auditors may be qualified as technical subject matter experts (SMEs) but lack appropriate recognitions by interested bodies.

The key concept is that audits, regardless of form or name, are processes. Processes consist of a set of resources (materials, labor, finance, and so on) called the inputs being transformed through interactions to create outputs. Outputs of processes are typically not just the desired product or service but also the nonconforming product or service, waste, pollution, and worn equipment or tooling. In most cases, unless management specifically requests the associated negative or less positive results, only the desired positive outputs are emphasized, and management is provided with less than the total available data or information necessary to manage the organization and avoid risks.

For the audit process, we have inputs of competent auditors; an authorizing, supportive client; cooperative auditee personnel; defined auditee plans and procedures for satisfying requirements and accomplishing objectives; an identified audit purpose and scope; reference documents; and appropriate administrative and infrastructure support. These inputs, along with a planned sequence of audit activities, provide an output of accumulated data that are transformed into useful actionable information and presented to the auditee and the client in a formal report. Appropriate follow-up corrective and preventive actions are implemented to support improvements and mutual benefits.

Some common elements of audits include:

1. Purpose and scope: "Why are we doing this?" The answer will provide the purpose of the audit and lead to the proper scope (extent) of inquiry.

2. Document review: Documents are reviewed during the audit preparation phase to determine whether the auditee has developed a suitable (adequate and appropriate) set of comprehensive documents for the audited area or activities to satisfy all relevant goals and requirements.

3. Preparation for review: Details of who will be interviewed, at what location, and which aspects of the operations should be scheduled. Data collection plans are finalized.

4. On-site or remote data collection (the audit): Actual data collection activities may vary somewhat (for example, a shorter opening meeting) in internal and external audits due to the familiarity of auditor(s) and auditee, and auditor's knowledge of auditee's processes, products, services, and infrastructure. External audits are generally more formal. Collection of data, however, is the same for both internal and external audits.

5. Formal audit report: While most audit reports follow a prescribed format, sometimes the client (or an applicable standard) may require a unique format for the audit. Audit reports normally include an introduction, an overall summary, findings, and conclusions.

6. Audit follow-up: The auditee is responsible for implementation of the corrective action and its verification. An auditor may be assigned to perform a follow-up audit (an independent verification that the corrective action was implemented and effective).

The auditing community continues to move toward establishing common audit practices. The ISO 19011 provides guidance on all management system audit types, such as quality, environmental, and occupational safety and health. The main differences among audits are the standards against which the organization is audited and the emphasis on certain techniques over others, depending on whether it is a quality, environmental, or safety audit.

Chapter 2
Purpose and Scope of Audits/Part IB

The type of audit to be performed may be described by its scope or purpose. An auditor may conduct system audits of a department or function such as manufacturing, operations, or a laboratory. Process audits can be described as machining, cutting, testing, extinguishing, welding, loading, packaging, and sealing audits. Similarly, product or service audits can be described by the name of the product or service, such as X cable, ready room, package, and tire audits. An audit may also be described by its purpose, such as a verification, management, or compliance audit.

AUDIT REASON

An audit can provide management with unbiased facts that can be used to:

- Provide input to management so that they can make informed decisions

- Keep management informed of actual or potential risks

- Identify areas of opportunity for improvement

- Assess personnel training effectiveness and equipment capability

- Provide visible management support of the quality, environmental, safety, and other programs

- Ensure ongoing compliance and conformity to regulations and standards

- Determine system and process effectiveness

- Identify system and process efficiencies

The purpose of most audits is to determine compliance or conformity of a system, process, or product to requirements. An auditor may determine whether the documented system conforms to requirements and whether it has been implemented by the users. Auditors can also determine effectiveness based on the ability of the organization to achieve stated objectives. Management has a need to ensure ongoing compliance and conformance.

Management also needs factual information to stay competitive and to allocate resources. The need for system and process audits may also include:

- Monitoring risk treatments

- Identifying risks

- Improving organization performance

The words *effectiveness, efficiency,* and *performance* are related because they are linked to management's interests to stay competitive and achieve budgetary goals. Public sector organizations are interested in effectiveness, efficiency, and performance so that they can meet budget requirements and use resources efficiently, whereas determination of compliance and conformity is more closely linked to meeting requirements and maintaining the status quo.

Experts state that if a process is meeting output objectives, it is an effective process. Management determines the goals and objectives. Audit evidence should indicate whether the process owners are measuring results against the stated objectives/ goals. They should know whether the process objectives are being achieved.

A first-party audit may be needed by management to ensure that procedures are adequate and utilized, and to provide for early detection of a problem, which gives management the opportunity to identify root causes of problems and take corrective action.

> The tasks of management at whatever level in the organization are to identify possible sources of problems, to plan preventive action in order to forestall the problems, and to solve them should they arise. If this were not the case, managers would not be needed. When reduced to fundamentals, the vast majority of the problems are, in essence, quality problems. They are problems concerning the quality of work being performed, the quality of work that has been performed, the quality of items being received, the quality of information being communicated, the quality of available equipment, the quality of decisions made. All quality problems have a cost associated with them. It, therefore, follows that the avoidance, prevention, and resolution of these problems equates to the prevention and reduction of unnecessary costs.[1]

Second-party supplier audits may be needed to help eliminate the shipping of nonconforming products and reduce costs and waste. Audits of suppliers may promote partnerships that ensure a better understanding of customer expectations or provide a means for technology transfer between the customer and the supplier. Second-party quality audits help ensure a better final product by verifying that there are appropriate controls for inputs into the system. Second-party environmental or safety audits are not the norm; however, if a customer-supplier relationship included environmental and safety requirements, they could be audited as well.

The reason for most third-party audits is to verify compliance or conformance to specified regulations or standards. The regulations and standards may be required by law, such as in the FAA, FDA, and Department of Energy (DOE) regulations, or they may be voluntary, such as ISO 9001, TS 16949, or AS9100. Some organizations seek third-party audits to improve their competitive position, for recognition in the form of a certificate, or for an award.

1. ELEMENTS OF PURPOSE AND SCOPE

Audit Purpose

It is the client's responsibility to determine the purpose of an audit. Usually, this statement is specific. However, a client may state the purpose in general terms with the understanding that the lead auditor will specify the particulars to fit the situation. In the case of an audit performed on a regular basis, the purpose may have been defined and known well in advance of the audit by all parties.

First-party audits may be performed to assure management that the audited area is in compliance with particular standards and that the goals and strategies of the organization are being met. The following list provides example purpose statements for first-party audits.

The purpose of the first-party audit is to:

- Ensure continued compliance or conformance (readiness) of the management system, to evaluate the effectiveness of the system in meeting the stated goals and objectives, and to identify opportunities for improvement in the product, process, and system

- Review the mechanical assembly area's compliance with procedures and to evaluate the procedures for opportunities for improvement

- Confirm that project engineering, document control, and procurement activities performed in support of basic design are being accomplished in accordance with the Quality Assurance Manual, selected integrated execution procedures, and governing project procedures, including, as appropriate, client requirements

- Assess the progress of the management system toward meeting the requirements of a management system standard such as ISO 9001, ISO 13485, ISO/TS 16949, ISO 22000, and ISO 14001

- Identify opportunities for improved system/process effectiveness to achieve objectives

- Identify process efficiencies for the delivery of products and services

- Report organizational risks to management for evaluation

As auditing has evolved, management also expects management risks to be identified. Risk exists in all processes; however, the kind and degree of risk must be managed. There may be safety (worker or customer injury), environmental (pollution, fines), financial (loss of revenue, excessive cost), and customer goodwill (loss of future sales) risks. Management needs to be informed of risks to the organization as input into the decision-making process.

Example objectives of a process performance audit may be to:

- Determine if the system design is adequate to achieve organization objectives

- Identify performance weaknesses and strengths

- Verify process responsiveness to customer and organization needs

- Identify process risks and areas to be optimized[2]

Some audit programs may allocate resources specifically to areas that have been problematic or that are high risk. This could include product characteristics, product or process hazards, personnel or process safety, and environmental controls. This is often called risk-based auditing. A starting point for risk-based auditing is for the organization to identify and quantify its risks.

Internal auditors and some external auditors should be aware of the existence of risk and that effectiveness, efficiency, performance, and risk are important factors when determining the purpose of the audit or when planning the annual audit schedule.

In this section we have discussed organizational risk as a purpose of an audit. Later we will discuss audit program risk and audit process risk.

For a second-party audit, the audit program, the engineering and technology departments, or the purchasing department normally determines the purpose of the audit and communicates it to the auditee. The primary purpose of a second-party audit is to either assess a supplier to verify that contract requirements are being followed or assess a potential supplier's capability of meeting specific requirements for a product or service. By determining that the supplier is meeting the requirements specified in a contract, the purchaser gains confidence in the quality of goods and services being delivered. The following list provides example purpose statements for second-party audits.

The purpose of the second-party audit is to:

- Assess the capability of XYZ Company to meet contract requirements by a review of the available resources and by obtaining objective evidence of management's commitment to the quality requirements of its product

- Verify that the materials, equipment, and work being performed under Contract 12345-P-001 are in accordance with the procurement documents, as specified in Section 6 of this contract, and that the work is being executed by qualified personnel

- Identify the possible cause of recent nonconformities by conducting a comprehensive assessment of the tasks, procedures, records, and system documentation related to the production of the wireless widget

- Verify that the supplier has an active environmental abatement and safety improvement program that meets customer requirements

Most third-party audits are performed by auditing organizations to determine the compliance or conformance of the auditee's systems with agreed-upon criteria. In the case of an audit for certification, an auditor examines an auditee's systems for conformity with a specific standard (for example, ISO 9001 or ISO 14001) or current good manufacturing practices. The purpose statement for most third-party audits is very specific, as shown in the following examples.

The purpose of the third-party audit is to:

- Determine the degree of conformity to the requirements of the standard (ISO 9001, ISO 14001, AS9100) for the purposes of certification of the company management system

- Assess the conformity of the system to all requirements of the international standard (ISO 9001, TL9000, ISO/TS 16949) for the purpose of recommending the organization for certification to the standard or approval of a license

- Assess the compliance of the organization to all requirements of Regulation 123 for the purpose of recommending approval or disapproval as a supplier

Third-party audits performed for regulatory purposes determine the compliance of the auditee's systems with regulations or laws. These audits have penalties associated with them (fines, jail, or both), so they are very serious. The purpose of the audit is determined by the regulatory agency and is normally specified in the regulation or law. These audits focus on detailed compliance with regulations or laws to ensure that companies are protecting the environment, the public, and their employees.

Audit Scope

According to ISO 19011 the audit scope is the extent and boundaries of an audit. The audit scope normally includes a description of the physical locations, organizational units, activities and processes, and the time period covered.

The audit scope indicates or fixes a limit or extent of the audit. The scope has been described as the breadth of the audit and may specify areas not to be included in the audit.

The scope or criteria of an audit can include:

- Physical locations

- Departments, areas, or units

- Products, processes, or systems

- Areas excluded from the audit

- Timeline for audit activities or events

- Relevant system and process policies, procedures, instructions, and plans

- Applicable standards, contracts, regulations, codes, and other legal documents

The following list provides examples of audit scope. The scope of the audit includes:

- Processes performed in the raw material storage, fermentation and purification suites, bulk filling area, final product storage, and the product testing laboratory.

- Policies and procedures for IT security for financial computer systems. Quality-related computer systems will not be addressed during this audit.

- The confined space entry and lockout/tagout safety systems for process vessels.

- Controls in place at supplier XXX Container Company for the manufacture, testing, and release of bottles and caps during the past two years.

If the scope or audit criteria must be changed before or during the audit, the audit participants should be informed of the change and it should be documented in the audit plan.

If two or more management systems of different areas or disciplines (e.g., quality, safety, environmental) are audited together (a combined or integrated audit), it is important that the audit objectives, scope, and criteria be compatible with the objectives of the relevant audit programs.

2. BENEFITS OF AUDITS

The benefits of an audit are numerous. Audits can verify ongoing conformance to requirements and promote improvement of the organization's effectiveness and efficiency. Management can utilize the objective data to make informed decisions regarding the achievement of organization objectives.

Auditing benefits include:

- Verification of conformance to requirements such as a management system, regulatory and contractual

- Identification of risks and monitoring of risk treatments

- Identification of opportunities for improvement

- Verification that projects were implemented according to plan

- Determination of readiness of new products and processes

- Verification of system effectiveness

- Identification of inefficiencies and ineffective controls

- Verification of corrective actions and their effectiveness

- Identification and reporting of best practices

- Advancing the achievement of organization objectives

Auditors have a broad perspective of an organization and analyze evidence reported to management. Management can use this information to evaluate the organization and implement measures necessary to meet its objectives.

> A new auditor received lots of complimentary feedback from an auditee who was very close to the process he managed. A staff auditor had coached the new internal system auditor to ask reporter-type questions, explaining that the "why" question was not philosophical. The answer to "why" gives the reason or driver for an activity. After the audit, the manager said that he had learned more from attempting to answer and document the driver for the activity than from any previous audit experience. It reinforced the actions needed for an activity and surfaced unnecessary actions.

Management review should consider recurring nonconformities (for example, at a particular location or with a particular procedure) as possible evidence that the plans and procedures should be changed. Even more useful is a management review of potential inefficiencies.

When audit results are being viewed as added system information, auditing starts to provide the information needed for the "Check" step in the Deming (also known as "Shewhart") Plan-Do-Check-Act (PDCA; also known as the PDSA: Plan-Do-Study-Act) cycle. With the kind of information that process and system audits provide, management is better prepared to move forward with more-informed decisions. Elevation of nonconformity resolution to the PDCA paradigm requires the use of more contemporary tools for problem solving, improvement, and overall management. The universe of opportunities expands as new knowledge and theories are developed. System and process auditing can provide this new knowledge, if understood and properly applied.

Chapter 3
Criteria to Audit Against/Part IC

DISCUSSION

Audit criteria is a universal term that describes the reference used by an auditor against which the evidence collected during the audit can be compared. The ISO 19011, clause 3.2 states that audit criteria are a set of policies, procedures, or requirements used as a reference against which audit evidence is compared. The ISO 9000 vocabulary standard explains that requirements may be generated by various stakeholders or interested parties. Requirements may be specified or they may be generally implied, such as customs or common practice. This definition recognizes that not all requirements can be specified. For example, we expect new products to arrive clean, services to be performed in a timely manner, reports to be legible, and service persons to practice good hygiene, even though such requirements may not be specified in a document, contract, or standard.

The audit criteria may be referred to as system or process requirements, rules that the auditee follows, or a specific named standard or regulation. The audit principle is that auditors audit against criteria, a set of rules or specified controls, and not their own opinion of what the auditee should be doing. The evidence collected, which is used as a basis for findings and the audit report, should be relevant to the audit criteria.

Assigned auditors must be knowledgeable of the audit criteria, document, or standard that the organization is being evaluated against. Auditors must be competent, and part of that competency is knowledge of the audit criteria and their interpretations.

AUDIT REQUIREMENTS

Audits of programs (such as quality or environmental programs) normally require reference standards against which to judge the adequacy of the plans. These are normally external documents that may include:

- National and international standards
- Customer and corporate specifications
- Contract and customer requirements
- Local and national statutes and regulations

- Industry codes and standards

- Guides, handbooks, and so on

Standards, codes, and regulations . . . are issued by related industrial or professional associations, by national standards writing organizations concerned with the intended marketplace, by local/state/national legislative bodies and by international bodies.[1]

Performance standards are the documents that contain the norms or criteria against which an activity is measured. There are four levels of performance standards:

1. *Policies:* Examples include corporate policy statements, international and national quality system standards, regulatory standards, and business sector standards.

2. *Manuals:* Examples are corporate manuals and plant manuals. One may exist for each function, department, or division.

3. *Procedural documents:* These include the step-by-step requirements for doing a job.

4. *Detailed documents:* These documents, such as drawings, purchase orders, product specifications, and inspection plans, contain specific requirements or instructions.

Audit Basis

To perform an audit, an auditor must be aware of the audit basis, sometimes called reference standards, audit criteria, or performance standards. The compliance or adequacy of a system cannot be measured until those requirements are defined. Regardless of the requirements, an audit must be performed against a basis for reference (for example, organization performance standards and/or national standards such as ISO 9001). These reference documents may include the following: (1) management system, product, or process standards, (2) contracts, (3) specifications, (4) organization policies and objectives, and (5) laws or regulations.

Standards

Certain international, national, and industry standards are mandated for many organizations. Audits verify compliance/conformance with the applicable management system standard, whether it be ISO 9001, AS9100, TL 9000, or ISO 14001. An organization may voluntarily adopt certain standards by incorporating them into contracts or policies even though there is no requirement to do so. An organization may adopt certain standards because it is in its best interests, such as for external marketing or providing an internal structure for managing the organization.

Contracts

In a second-party audit, the purchase order or other contract between two parties states the specific requirements that must be met, and an audit is performed to verify that the supplier is meeting those requirements. A contract may include references to a specific standard, such as American National Standards Institute (ANSI), American Society for Testing and Materials (ASTM) International, FAA, DOE, or FDA standards.

Contracts may specify that a supplier establish and maintain a management system standard such as ISO 9001 or ISO 13485. A third party may verify that the supplier conforms to the management system standard. However, the customer may have additional requirements, referring to them as "ISO 9001 plus" audits. Other suppliers may not have a management system in place and may be subject to an "ISO 9001 minus" audit (not all ISO 9001 controls are required).

Specifications

Specifications are normally used when conducting product or service audits. An auditor examines physical dimensions, placement or arrangement of items, or chemical compositions, for example, to see if they are in compliance with the specified requirements.

Policies and Objectives

Internally, many companies regularly assess compliance/conformance and effectiveness with their own policies or policy statements. These policies are often stated in manuals and are the basis for a quality, environmental, or safety program. Most companies publish specified objectives. Objectives may relate to cost, safety, stewardship, health, efficiency, effectiveness, optimum use of resources, and so on. Auditors can verify the progress of departments, functions, and projects toward the achievement of objectives.

Laws and Regulations

Many companies perform internal audits to ensure that they are meeting all the requirements imposed by various laws and regulations, whether general or industry-specific. Third-party auditors within a regulatory agency use the laws and regulations, case law, and their internal requirements/guidelines as the basis for the audit. Auditors verify mandatory governmental standards such as FDA current good manufacturing practices (cGMPs), FAA, 10 CFR 830, or Sarbanes-Oxley.

The audit criteria must be stipulated as part of the audit plan. There is no minimum or maximum limit to the amount or kinds of audit criteria. However, for an audit to be performed, there must be audit criteria. If there are no criteria to compare the organization with, the investigation may be called a survey or review.

Chapter 4
Roles and Responsibilities of Audit Participants/Part ID

AUDIT PARTICIPANTS

An audit involves three key participants who may interrelate in a number of ways. Described by function, these participants are the client, the auditor, and the auditee.

The *client* is the person or organization that has requested or commissioned the audit. The client is usually a member of senior management, and the audit is typically conducted of an organizational unit under the client's jurisdiction, of independent suppliers, or to support an application for third-party certification.[1]

The *auditor* is the person who plans and carries out the audit. An auditing organization, which employs auditors to carry out audits, may be internal to a company or an independent organization, such as the auditing group of a quality or environmental program certification body or consulting organization.

The *auditee* is the organization to be audited. The auditee may be a division of the client's organization or an entirely separate entity, such as a supplier. In internal audits, the client is the top management and the auditee is the function or area to be audited.

The following are examples of external audits:[2]

Situation: Organization desires recognition or approval of its capability to meet a particular standard such as ISO 9001

Client: The top management of an organization desiring certification/registration

Auditee: The organization desiring certification/registration

Auditing organization: The organization granting certification/registration using an auditor employed by the auditing organization or hired to conduct the audit

Situation: Customer organization desires to evaluate a supplier

Client: The interested purchasing agent, purchasing manager, or engineer

Auditee: The potential or existing supplier

Auditing organization: Member(s) of the customer organization staff or auditors under contract to the customer organization

Situation: Regulatory organization verifies that supplier or operator is in compliance with requirements

Client: The regulatory agency

Auditee: The potential supplier or operator

Auditing organization: Employee(s) of the regulatory agency or auditors under contract to the agency

The following is an example of an internal audit:[3]

Situation: Organization desires to determine the degree of conformity of its own organization elements to a predefined management system

Client: Upper-management team of the organization desiring to use auditing as a management tool

Auditee: The department/function(s) of the organization to be evaluated

Auditing organization: Employee(s) of the organization or individuals hired to conduct the audit

In the internal audit example, the client can be the organization's own top management.

The origin of the term *audit client* comes from the very first application of audits in the United States (external financial audits). After the Great Depression, laws were passed requiring a financial audit of the books of companies subject to securities and exchange regulations. In order for the audit results to be creditable, the audits had to be performed by outside certified public accountants (CPAs). These CPA auditors were hired by a client. Today, we call them the auditee. The CPAs delivered their report to the client, who gave it to the audit committee on the board of directors.

ROLES AND RESPONSIBILITIES

The audit process involves several participants. By its nature, an audit can cause stress between participants. Therefore, it is in everyone's best interest if the participants work together to ensure a successful and effective audit. The more contentious the relationship between participants (such as the auditor and the auditee), the more difficult it will be to achieve compliance, conformity, or improvement.

The following are audit process participants:

- Client: Person or organization that requested the audit

- Auditor: Person carrying out the audit

- Lead auditor or audit team leader: Auditor responsible for managing the audit

- Auditee: Person or organization to be audited

  — Escort: Person assigned to escort the audit team members

  — Coordinator: Person in contact with the lead auditor or the audit program manager in order to arrange for the audit

- Audit program manager: Person responsible for the audit program

List of Responsibilities and Duties

Client

1. Determines the need for an audit
2. Determines the audit organization to be used
3. Determines the audit purpose
4. Determines overall audit scope and may confer with the audit program manager or lead auditor to define specifics
5. Addresses budget issues
6. May determine the audit team leader or delegate the responsibility to the audit program manager
7. May choose to attend audit process meetings such as the exit meeting
8. Receives the audit report
9. Determines and directs the distribution of the audit report
10. Determines the need for follow-up actions
11. Supports the audit initiative
12. Follows organizational procedures regarding the audit process

Auditor

1. Understands the purpose and scope of the audit
2. Understands the audit criteria being audited against
3. Prepares for the audit
4. Performs the audit to collect evidence to verify conformance or nonconformance to the audit criteria
5. Records the results of the investigation (perhaps on a checklist)
6. Attends the opening and exit meetings
7. Reports findings to the lead auditor
8. Cooperates with the lead auditor
9. Verifies the correction of previous nonconformities if directed to do so
10. Provides input to the formal report if directed to do so by the lead auditor or client
11. Maintains confidentiality of the audit information
12. Reports conflicts of interest to the lead auditor
13. Is ethical and adheres to an organization code of conduct or the principles of auditing as listed in ISO 19011, section 4

Lead Auditor/Audit Team Leader

1. Is responsible for communication with the client, auditor program management, and the auditee representative

2. Provides audit team selection input if requested to do so

3. Communicates audit plan and requirements to auditee

4. Ensures that necessary resources are available to audit team

5. Ensures the team has the appropriate working papers

6. Plans the audit and directs the audit team

7. Conducts audit process meetings

8. Prepares audit report

9. Manages the audit process and resolves conflicts of interest or other personnel issues

10. Ensures reports and records are properly filed and safeguarded

Auditee

1. Coordinates audit with the lead auditor

2. Informs employees of the pending audit purpose and scope

3. Addresses logistical issues with the lead auditor

4. Provides adequate space and privacy for the opening and exit meetings

5. Attends the opening and exit meetings

6. Provides area for auditors to work and meet if requested

7. Cooperates with the auditors

8. Provides access to areas included in the audit scope

9. Acknowledges audit results

10. Takes corrective action on audit findings

Audit Program Manager

1. Assigns auditors to scheduled audits

2. Ensures availability of resources (budgeting)

3. Establishes a reporting relationship that ensures objective and impartial audits

4. Qualifies auditors (knowledge, experience, and skills)

5. Establishes controls (procedures, criteria, plans, and objectives) for an effective and efficient audit program

6. Creates, distributes, and maintains audit program schedules

7. Reports audit program progress to management

8. Monitors auditor performance

9. Determines audit program objectives and creates plans to accomplish the objectives

10. Keeps and safeguards audit program information

11. Promotes ethical behavior on the part of auditors and those involved in managing the audit program[4]

The audit participant's role and involvement will be discussed further as topics are presented.

Part ID

Chapter 5
Professional Conduct and Consequences for Auditors/Part IE

E thics affect professional conduct, and professional conduct affects credibility. Ethics are basic philosophical conclusions about whether conduct and behavior are right or wrong. Ethics are also moral principles by which an individual is guided. It is imperative that auditors be ethical (objective and impartial) and behave appropriately (with professional conduct) in carrying out their responsibilities.

Professional conduct is the manner in which auditors conduct themselves. Objectivity, courtesy, honesty, and many other character attributes combine to make up the particular conduct of any auditor during an audit.

Liability is the degree of legal responsibility an individual or company has in a given situation. Liability issues are beginning to surface with the increase in third-party auditing and certification/registration. The audit participants must provide the audit service in such a manner as not to cause harm or injury, for which the law gives a remedy to the auditee (as damages, restitution, specific performance, or injunction).

1. PROFESSIONAL CONDUCT AND RESPONSIBILITIES

Codes of Ethics

A *code of ethics* is a standard for conduct. An auditor's ethical and moral principles should be compatible with a formal set of ethical standards. The American Society for Quality (ASQ) developed a code of ethics that each ASQ certified individual must pledge to uphold. The content of the ASQ code of ethics is included in certification examinations. Acceptance of the code of ethics by the examinee is required prior to certification. ASQ's code of ethics is shown in Figure 5.1.

Many companies and professional organizations have developed a code of ethics to guide them in the performance of their work. The Institute of Internal Auditors (IIA) developed its code of ethics in 1974. The IIA took a slightly different approach than ASQ in the content of its code of ethics. Although these codes of ethics represent different perspectives, they both have the same basic principles described in their standards of conduct. Figure 5.2 presents the IIA code of ethics.

Fundamental Principles
ASQ requires its members and certification holders to conduct themselves ethically by:

   I. Being honest and impartial in serving the public, their employers, customers, and clients.
  II. Striving to increase the competence and prestige of the quality profession, and
 III. Using their knowledge and skill for the enhancement of human welfare.

Members and certification holders are required to observe the tenets set forth below:

Relations with the Public
Article 1—Hold paramount the safety, health, and welfare of the public in the performance of their professional duties.

Relations with Employers, Customers, and Clients
Article 2—Perform services only in their areas of competence.
Article 3—Continue their professional development throughout their careers and provide opportunities for the professional and ethical development of others.
Article 4—Act in a professional manner in dealings with ASQ staff and each employer, customer, or client.
Article 5—Act as faithful agents or trustees and avoid conflict of interest and the appearance of conflicts of interest.

Relations with Peers
Article 6—Build their professional reputation on the merit of their services and not compete unfairly with others.
Article 7—Assure that credit for the work of others is given to those to whom it is due.

Figure 5.1   ASQ code of ethics.
Source: ASQ. http://www.asq.org/about-asq/who-we-are/ethics.html.

A code of ethics serves as a guideline for performance for both the auditor and the auditee. According to Charles A. Mills:

> A formal code of ethics allows quality auditors to approach audit performance uniformly. A formal code provides a benchmark against which an auditee and client can measure an auditor's activities, establish an auditor's independence, and recognize potential conflicts of interest.[1]

Ethical standards serve as a general behavioral guide for auditors. Auditors often rely on personal judgments and past experiences to determine ethical conduct in specific situations, however. Auditors' personalities, temperaments, auditing styles, and basic perceptions can vary tremendously. By incorporating a set of ethical principles into their daily audit activities, auditors can maintain the high standards of conduct, honor, and character needed for audit results to be received as an unbiased and accurate product.

Conflict of Interest

The subject of conflict of interest often arises during audits. Conflict-of-interest situations sometimes encountered prior to and during audits include:

- Previous employment of the auditor (or close relative) by the auditee or a major competitor of the auditee, regardless of the reason for separation

- Holding of significant amounts of stocks or bonds in the auditee's business or that of a major competitor

Code of Ethics
The Code of Ethics states the principles and expectations governing the behavior of individuals and organizations in the conduct of internal auditing. It describes the minimum requirements for conduct, and behavioral expectations rather than specific activities.

Code of Ethics—Principles
Internal auditors are expected to apply and uphold the following principles:

1. **Integrity**
   The integrity of internal auditors establishes trust and thus provides the basis for reliance on their judgment.
2. **Objectivity**
   Internal auditors exhibit the highest level of professional objectivity in gathering, evaluating, and communicating information about the activity or process being examined. Internal auditors make a balanced assessment of all the relevant circumstances and are not unduly influenced by their own interests or by others in forming judgments.
3. **Confidentiality**
   Internal auditors respect the value and ownership of information they receive and do not disclose information without appropriate authority unless there is a legal or professional obligation to do so.
4. **Competency**
   Internal auditors apply the knowledge, skills, and experience needed in the performance of internal audit services.

Rules of Conduct

1. Integrity—Internal auditors:

1.1. Shall perform their work with honesty, diligence, and responsibility.
1.2. Shall observe the law and make disclosures expected by the law and the profession.
1.3. Shall not knowingly be a party to any illegal activity, or engage in acts that are discreditable to the profession of internal auditing or to the organization.
1.4. Shall respect and contribute to the legitimate and ethical objectives of the organization.

2. Objectivity—Internal auditors:

2.1. Shall not participate in any activity or relationship that may impair or be presumed to impair their unbiased assessment. This participation includes those activities or relationships that may be in conflict with the interests of the organization.
2.2. Shall not accept anything that may impair or be presumed to impair their professional judgment.
2.3. Shall disclose all material facts known to them that, if not disclosed, may distort the reporting of activities under review.

3. Confidentiality—Internal auditors:

3.1. Shall be prudent in the use and protection of information acquired in the course of their duties.
3.2. Shall not use information for any personal gain or in any manner that would be contrary to the law or detrimental to the legitimate and ethical objectives of the organization.

4. Competency—Internal auditors:

4.1. Shall engage only in those services for which they have the necessary knowledge, skills, and experience.
4.2. Shall perform internal audit services in accordance with the International Standards for the Professional Practice of Internal Auditing (Standards).
4.3. Shall continually improve their proficiency and the effectiveness and quality of their services.

Figure 5.2   The Institute of Internal Auditors code of ethics (selected sections).

Source: Institute of Internal Auditors, https://na.theiia.org/standards-guidance/mandatory-guidance/Pages/Code-of-Ethics.aspx.

- Previous or current close working relationship (for example, teaming partner, major supplier) with the organization
- Prior involvement by the auditor in developing the quality program or procedures used by the group being audited
- Desire to be hired by the group being audited
- Close friendships within the group being audited
- Offer by auditee of money, goods, or services in the nature of a bribe, kickback, or secret commission
- Acceptance of a gift (money, gratuity, or other thing of value) with more than a nominal value, or involvement in auditee-sponsored sales promotions or other activities that may represent or be construed as a conflict of interest
- Performance of outside work for the auditee that might adversely affect the auditor's performance or judgment on the job

The auditor should be aware of the different types of conflicts of interest. Prior to accepting an audit, auditors should examine their activities and relationship with the auditee and determine whether an actual or potential conflict of interest exists. For example, if after the start of an audit an auditor realizes that one of the department managers of the auditee organization is a past personal friend or mentor, the auditor should immediately report a potential conflict of interest even though the audit of the on-site activities has already started.

When a Conflict of Interest Exists

When there is an actual or potential conflict of interest with the organization or people being audited, the auditor must relay this information to audit program management or decline to conduct the audit, whichever is more appropriate. Actions that management and the audit team leader can take include:

- Ensuring that sufficient time has passed to eliminate the conflict
- Assigning a different auditor to cover the specific area of conflict
- Removing the auditor or the audit team leader from the team

> During an internal audit, the auditor may face a situation where he or she was involved in the development of the process or system under evaluation. If the auditor developed the process or wrote the procedure, it will be difficult to maintain objectivity when the process or procedure is audited for acceptability against a reference standard.

By avoiding conflicts of interest, an auditor upholds the standards of independence, fairness, objectivity, and impartiality of the audit process.

Confidentiality

With processes, formulas, and equipment being developed by individual companies, the question of confidentiality of proprietary information has become a major concern during audits. Businesses could suffer great financial loss if customers or competitors were to gain access to proprietary processing knowledge, formulas, and trade secrets. The auditor must maintain confidentiality, but not to the point of performing an inadequate audit. Each auditor needs to be prepared to sign agreements or utilize techniques for working around a proprietary area.

Confidentiality and Security Concerns

Auditees can use a confidentiality agreement or a nondisclosure agreement to protect their interests. Both serve the same purpose—to keep proprietary information within the control of the auditee.

Confidentiality Agreement

An auditor is often expected to sign a confidentiality or nondisclosure agreement before an audit begins. In general, these agreements require that the auditor not disclose any proprietary information gained during the audit. They may be extended to the auditor's company, family, assigns, and so on, through legal language. Some confidentiality agreements that auditees expect the auditor to sign before being allowed to perform an audit of proprietary areas have become particularly onerous. Often these are written in legal language and are understandable only by someone familiar with the legal definitions of the words used. Auditors are normally not authorized to obligate their organizations. Agreements should contain a release that takes effect if proprietary information becomes public. An auditor should receive the agreement in advance so that it can be reviewed and approved by the auditing organization's legal counsel or designated authority before the auditor signs it.

> An auditor was asked to sign a four-page confidentiality agreement before being allowed to perform an audit of a supplier. The agreement was written in legal language and obligated the auditor, the auditor's heirs, the auditor's assigns, and the auditor's company to pay for any damages that might come about if the information was obtained by the supplier's competitors. There was no time frame for the agreement, so if the information was disclosed at any time and by any person, they were all liable for the damages. The audit organization's attorney advised against signing this agreement, and the audit team used alternate techniques to determine whether the process was adequate.

Conduct

Discussing proprietary information with others destroys the integrity of the audit function. While it is acceptable for an auditor to discuss actual audit experiences with other auditors, the discussion should be generic so that the auditee cannot be identified. Proprietary information should never be divulged in a sharing situation with other auditors.

Even body language could disclose proprietary information. For example, when asked a question about a proprietary process, auditors who shrug their shoulders, roll their eyes, or raise their eyebrows could signal the answer even if no words are spoken.

Techniques

Several techniques are available to the auditor to ensure that proprietary information remains proprietary. When auditing in an undisclosed area, the auditor can rely on memory and not write audit notes. Any notes could become accessible to the public and would be discoverable in litigation.

An auditor can "audit around" an undisclosed area. The auditor needs to be very flexible to be able to accomplish audit objectives when the auditee erects barriers. A company may be in the process of getting a patent on a new method, for example, and may flatly refuse to allow the auditor to view a certain portion of that system. In these instances, the auditor must respect the auditee's wishes and audit around the undisclosed area. If the inputs going into the undisclosed area appear to be correct and the outputs are likewise acceptable, then the auditor may assume that the undisclosed process is doing its job correctly. Another technique is to remove personnel from the undisclosed area for interviews.

The auditor can view parts of a document or have the auditee certify it. A company sometimes will refuse to allow an auditor to look at the procedure for a certain process even though a written procedure is required. To verify that the procedure exists, the auditor can ask the auditee to certify that the procedure does exist and that it covers the relevant process. The auditee may allow the auditor to view nonconfidential sections of the document. The auditor may never actually view all the details but should do as much as practical to ensure that a procedure does exist and is approved for use.

Such situations often resolve themselves on subsequent audits involving the same parties. As an auditee becomes more comfortable with the audit team and places greater trust in the ethics of the team members, the need to limit access to certain areas often becomes nonexistent.

Security

Companies in certain highly sensitive industries, such as those involved in national defense, may require that auditors have or obtain security clearances. This requirement should be determined well in advance of the audit to permit sufficient time for processing the request. Without the proper security clearance, an auditor may be restricted from certain areas of a company.

One way to work through the lack of a security clearance is to be constantly escorted, with classified areas, equipment, and activities shielded from view. This way, the auditor can evaluate part of the process and interview the people on the line.

> Some products may be adversely impacted by the presence of audi-
> tors or by the auditor's health. For example, some pharmaceutical
> products may be sensitive to people with certain medical condi-
> tions. Medical tests may need to be performed and results evaluated
> before the auditor is permitted to enter the processing facility. Wear-
> ing appropriate personal protective equipment such as gowning to
> limit human exposure may be sufficient to protect the product from
> humans.

Trust

The auditee must be confident that the auditor will conduct the audit professionally and that the auditor possesses the integrity and technical knowledge to
successfully complete the audit. Auditors are expected to exercise due care while
performing their activities. This means that an auditor should be sufficiently competent to arrive at conclusions similar to those that another auditor would reach in
the same or similar circumstances. Since an audit only samples a particular product, process, or system at a particular point in time, an auditor cannot be held
responsible if an audit fails to recognize all deficiencies or irregularities in a system, as long as that auditor has used theoretically sound sampling techniques, has
complied with applicable standards, and has adhered to the code of ethics.

In addition to the usual responsibilities, an auditor may need to address difficult situations that require careful handling for successful resolution. Possible
conflicts of interest should be recognized and reconciled before an audit begins.
The detection of unsafe, unethical, or even illegal practices during an audit may
rapidly change the planned course of the audit.

Discovery of Illegal or Unsafe Conditions or Activities

Auditors are in a unique position to observe illegal or unsafe conditions during the
course of an audit because of their access to almost any area necessary for successful completion of the audit. Auditors must know what to do when these activities
are observed.

When Unsafe Activities Are Observed

In some industries, an auditor may need to access potentially hazardous areas in
a company during the course of an audit. Auditors are usually provided with personal protective equipment such as goggles or hard hats. Normally, auditors face
no physical danger as long as regulations are enforced and the process is functioning properly. Sometimes, however, negligence or inexperience on the part of the
auditee's employees, a deficiency or malfunction of equipment or a process, or a
combination of these may result in potentially dangerous situations.

When an unsafe practice (such as open containers of hazardous chemicals
near work areas, release of controlled chemicals, or flammable materials near a
welding station) is observed, whether within or outside the scope of an audit, an
auditor must not ignore it. In an internal audit, an auditor should immediately
inform an auditee representative and the audit team leader, who will inform the

auditee manager so that the problem can be resolved. In an external audit (second- or third-party audit), the auditor must immediately inform the auditee and create a record of the situation. If anyone on the audit team is endangered, the audit must be stopped and the auditors returned to a safe area. In most situations, management welcomes information about liability risks or other potential dangers.

When Illegal or Unethical Activities Are Detected

An auditor finding evidence of wrongdoing, whether within or outside the scope of an audit assignment, has an ethical duty to bring the matter to the attention of the client and appropriate management for action. The auditor should keep a record of such matters, safeguard the evidence, and obtain copies of pertinent documents and records (if necessary). The auditor must be aware of and apply the ethics of the profession and the law in this regard. An auditor may ask the client about the company's ethics policy and ethics department prior to accepting the audit. If an ethics department exists, it may be a valuable resource if potentially unethical situations surface before, during, or after an audit.

> One example of an unethical practice was noted during a supplier audit. A check of the material certification provided by the supplier revealed some similarities to another certification received from another supplier. The certificates were identical, including the names of the people and the dates signed, except that the supplier's logo and name were now at the top. Further investigation found that the supplier simply pasted its logo and name over the logo and name of another company, made a copy, and sent it out as its own material certification. The company was caught only because the auditor had seen both certifications.

Management will take appropriate action on illegal or unethical activities within the company. This may involve legal action of some type and the involvement of the auditor. Auditors should be aware of their legal responsibilities and rights under the law, including whistle-blower laws.

If management sponsors allegedly illegal activities, either internally or externally, the auditor's employment may be threatened. An auditor should have access to legal counsel to resolve questionable issues. Often that legal counsel is best if it comes from outside the company. The U.S. Congress and various states have passed laws protecting people who report incidents of wrongdoing, including waste, fraud, and abuse (see a list of these laws at http://www.ncsl.org/issues-research/labor/state-whistleblower-laws.aspx). These whistle-blower statutes (see Figure 5.3 for examples) protect auditors and others. Questions about specific laws should be directed to the appropriate federal, state, or local authorities (see Figure 5.4 for an example of a local regulation). Please note that Figures 5.3 and 5.4 are provided as examples and may be dated. An auditor faced with a potential whistle-blower situation should seek the latest information available. It is sufficient to say that whistle-blowers have some protection under both federal and some state laws; however, the amount of protection and how it is applied depend on each situation.

The following are selected statutes relevant to the whistle-blower programs adjudicated by the Office of Administrative Law Judges (OALJ), U.S. Department of Labor:

Clean Air Act, 42 U.S.C. § 7622

Comprehensive Environmental Response, Compensation and Liability Act of 1980, 42 U.S.C. § 9610

Consumer Product Safety Improvement Act of 2008, Section 219

Dodd-Frank Wall Street Reform and Consumer Protection Act, 12 U.S.C. § 5567

Energy Reorganization Act, 42 U.S.C. § 5851

FDA Food Safety Modernization Act, Section 402, 21 U.S.C. 399d

Federal Water Pollution Control Act, 33 U.S.C. § 1367

National Transit Systems Security Act of 2007, P.L. No. 110-053, § 1413

Pipeline Safety Improvement Act of 2002, 49 U.S.C. § 60129

Safe Drinking Water Act, 42 U.S.C. § 300j-9

Sarbanes-Oxley Act of 2002, 18 U.S.C. § 1514A

Seaman's Protection Act, 46 U.S.C. § 2114

Solid Waste Disposal Act, 42 U.S.C. § 6971

Surface Transportation Assistance Act, 49 U.S.C. § 3110

Toxic Substances Control Act, 15 U.S.C. § 2622

Wendell H. Ford Aviation Investment and Reform Act for the 21st Century (AIR 21), 49 U.S.C. § 42121

Figure 5.3 Whistle-blower statutes.

Source: Office of Administrative Law Judges, http://www.oalj.dol.gov/public/whistleblower/references/statutes/whistleblower_statutes.htm (accessed on October 8, 2012). OALJ makes no representation that the documents linked here are the most up-to-date versions.

University of California Business and Finance Bulletin G-29, Procedures for Investigating Misuse of University Resources, Appendix C, Whistle Blower Policy

Figure 5.4 Example of other whistle-blower laws.

The 1863 False Claims Act was enacted by Congress to protect the government from fraudulent suppliers of faulty war equipment during the Civil War. This law remained in effect until 1974, when it was narrowed in scope. It was expanded and strengthened in 1986. The 1986 amendment brought new attention to the whistle-blower as a key to enforcement. The Whistleblower Protection Act of 1989 is a U.S. federal law that protects whistle-blowers who work for the government and report agency misconduct. The act supersedes any restrictive language in a gag order. Anti-gag statutes protect employees who sign a secrecy pact prior to government employment, agreeing to never discuss certain subjects, usually related to national defense issues. In the past, these whistle-blowers would be stripped of their clearances and, in most cases, their jobs, due to their violating the secrecy pact. Anti-gag statutes allow such whistle-blowers to go around their management if management does not respond when given the information.

An auditor may encounter illegal or unethical situations during the course of an audit, such as when an auditee is knowingly shipping defective products, exposing personnel to unsafe conditions or dumping waste. The auditor should verify the situation and then inform the audit team leader, who will inform the auditee. If the problem is caused by an oversight, it should be corrected immediately. However, an auditee who knowingly ships a defective product, bypasses safety rules, or allows unauthorized discharges of pollution may be unwilling to correct the problem. In this case, the auditing organization should refuse to return to that company or internal group. If a third-party audit is being performed, the auditor should immediately report the situation to the client. If the auditee is a supplier, the auditing organization may delay or stop shipments (if given the authority to do so) until the appropriate management function can resolve the issue. The auditing organization may advise its management to cancel any existing contracts or agreements and find more reputable and socially responsible sources for the item or service.

> An auditor reported that one of the most blatantly unethical activities he observed was by a supplier who knowingly shipped empty outer casings for a particular device. The casing had a sticker over the edge stating, "Warranty void if sticker broken." The sticker would be broken if the customer opened the casing to look inside. After verifying what he had discovered, he discussed the situation with the audit manager, who in turn discussed it with auditee management. The auditor's company ended up pulling its order from the supplier.

An auditor who detects illegal or unethical activities within the auditing organization must tell the audit team leader, who will inform the manager. If the same or similar illegal or unethical activities recur often, the auditor's principles are probably not compatible with those of the organization, and new employment should be considered. Unethical activity that is in violation of internal company policy should be reported directly to management, whether it is unethical behavior of another employee, a customer, or a supplier. Illegal or unethical behavior on the part of an ASQ member that violates the ASQ code of ethics should be reported to the ASQ Ethics Committee at ethics@asq.org.

Although not commonplace, bribery is another example of an illegal or unethical situation that an auditor may encounter. An auditor encountering obvious bribery should flatly refuse the offer and stop the audit. The client and auditing organization management must be alerted and give the matter immediate attention. Gift-giving could be a less obvious form of bribery. Many public agencies and private companies have specific regulations and policies on ethical behavior. For example, a limited dollar amount may be specified for gifts that the auditor may ethically accept. An auditor has an obligation to refuse or return any gift that exceeds the stated amount, along with the option of refusing any item. Many auditors will accept an offer of an inexpensive meal since they feel that both parties benefit from the rapport established in a casual setting, while others will refuse even the offer of a soft drink.

> During the course of an audit, an auditor happened to mention that she was an avid tennis player. Several weeks later she received a case of tennis balls from the auditee. She wrote a polite note and sent it to the auditee, along with the case of tennis balls.

Social and Cultural Considerations

In the international auditing arena, an auditor must be familiar with local customs so that potentially unethical situations can be interpreted correctly and responded to appropriately. For example, in the United States it is considered a breach of ethics for an auditor to accept a gift or favor from a person in the audited organization. The custom in Japan is that gifts are given to visitors from foreign countries as a sign of friendship or as a memento of their visit to the factory. However, accepting gifts is not permitted for auditors. Government auditors in Japan are strictly prohibited from accepting any gift or meal. Some companies allow acceptance of gifts to avoid offending the auditee but require the person to turn in the gift (for possible donation to a charity). As quality auditing becomes increasingly global, organizations and individuals must be aware of such differences to prevent serious cultural misunderstandings from undermining the audit process.

The need to be familiar with different cultures and norms is not limited to international auditing. Auditors should also be aware of cultural differences and expectations in each individual workplace where the audit is being conducted. The auditor's awareness and willingness to work with different cultures will help avoid misunderstandings and ensure the effectiveness of the audit.

Overcoming Language and Literacy Barriers

Audit personnel must either be fluent in the language in which the audit is to be conducted or have the support of a technical expert with the necessary technical language skills. When necessary, the auditing organization should employ a skilled interpreter to assist with the audit.

> One technique that can be used when the auditor does not speak the language of the auditee is for the auditor to observe the process, take detailed notes, and then have someone in the audit room walk the auditor through the related procedure (even if it is in the native language) so that he or she can compare it with his or her notes. This practice can highlight issues with following the written procedure.

Even if all primary participants in an audit speak the same language, the auditor may encounter language or literacy barriers when attempting to interview individual employees. These same barriers may prevent the employee from understanding or performing assigned tasks. A written procedure may solve the problem, but if the employees are unable to read or understand the procedure, then the problem has not been addressed. If an auditor understands the physical process before going into an audit and then focuses on the work, some of the literacy issues may be overcome with the aid of flowcharts and other simple diagrams. At times, an auditor may need to ask extremely simple questions to overcome a lack of language skills. If it is necessary for personnel to be able to follow procedures and complete records to perform their job and they are not able to do so, they may not be competent. Competency issues may lead an auditor to determine how personnel were trained and competency needs addressed.

> An auditor was shown documented instructions that were available to guide the operators in their work. The instructions were written in English. However, the auditor noticed that a number of the operators were unable to read or speak English, and no translated instructions were available for this portion of the workforce. Were the non-English-speaking operators more competent than the English-speaking operators, and therefore instructions were unnecessary? Or, did the instructions include pictures and diagrams to overcome the language barrier? Literacy questions or understanding documentation in another language can be very sensitive issues. The auditor should be very cautious in phrasing questions on these topics.

Avoiding Internal Conflict-of-Interest Problems

Selecting an auditor from within an organization (for a first-party audit) can cause problems, especially in the case of a one-site operation. The objectivity of an auditor working in an area of previous employment may be questioned. Former peers may be intimidated or uncooperative, or they may use the auditor as a sounding board for complaints, making it difficult for the auditor to obtain objective information. They also may think that the auditor will not report procedural violations. Furthermore, the auditor's knowledge of how a product, process, or system functions may be outdated, and time may be wasted as the auditor follows the wrong path using incorrect criteria.

Ideally, an auditor will not be assigned to audit an area of previous employment. For internal audits, though, such assignments cannot always be avoided, especially for small organizations. The negative effects must be weighed against the benefits that selecting an auditor from within the organization may offer. Such benefits may include a superior understanding of the organization's product or service and the processes involved in production, along with a strong familiarity with the applicable quality requirements or standards. Negative effects may include hidden agendas, perceived bias on the part of the auditee, and the possibility that the auditor will try to solve problems using past knowledge rather than auditing the current system.

During an audit, some auditees will request to be notified of nonconformances so that they can take immediate action. In many cases, immediate action would be remedial action (also called containment action or correction) and not corrective action. Remedial action addresses only the symptom and does not eliminate the underlying cause of the problem as corrective action would. The auditor may discuss with the auditee the pitfalls of taking only remedial action. The auditor should also explain that even though remedial action was taken, it would be unethical not to include the observed nonconformance in the final report.

Besides acting professionally at all times, the auditor must maintain the confidence of the auditing organization by never divulging proprietary information to the auditee, by refraining from speaking negatively about the auditing organization or previous auditees, and by refraining from discussing the performance of previous auditees with people in the organization currently being audited. When facing one of these problems or other more difficult ones, the auditor must remain focused and in control of the audit process.

2. LEGAL CONSEQUENCES

Personal and Corporate Liability

This handbook is not a primer on law as applied to auditing and should not be considered a source of legal advice. If questions arise, auditors must consult their own lawyers for information.

Liability issues have become more apparent with the advent of the quality management system (QMS) and environmental management system (EMS) registration/certification programs. Each company and each auditor accepts liability for the decisions made regarding whether to grant registration/certification. There are appeal processes, but in the end, a court of law could be called in for the final decision. A key liability consideration is whether a company relies on audit information as the basis for making a decision.

Illegal Activities

As an auditor collects information throughout the audit process, the auditee may disclose certain kinds of information. This information can lead to illegal activities by the auditor, unless the auditor is aware that the use of this information is illegal. Figure 5.5 provides a general explanation of each type of information and the illegal activity that the auditor can inadvertently engage in.

The Auditor as an Agent

As a representative of a company, an individual auditor can unknowingly acquire legal liability in several areas. First, the auditor might make statements that an auditee uses to make decisions. If these statements are later shown to be untrue, the auditee might have recourse against the auditor's company for damages. For example, if a third-party auditor told the auditee that the auditee's company would get a discount on insurance if it were compliant with ISO 9001, and the auditee used that information as a reason for deciding to implement ISO 9001, then the auditee might recover damages if no discount was forthcoming.

An auditor also has to be careful not to tell the auditee how to do his or her work or what decisions to make. If an auditee relies on the auditor's words and subsequently fails to provide a good product or service, ensure compliance to governmental regulations, or obtain registration, the auditee might recover damages.

Liability	Explanation	Auditor example
Violation of securities laws	If someone learns information that is important to investors but not available to the public and proceeds to act on it or tells someone who then acts on it, it is a violation of securities laws.	During an audit interview, a senior manager accidentally reveals acquisition plans to an auditor. The auditor uses the information to make personal investments in the stock market.
Violation of antitrust laws	If someone learns information and uses it to restrict competition in a particular market, it is a violation of antitrust laws.	An auditor comments to the auditee that another supplier with the same quality system realizes far fewer gains. The auditee uses the information to produce negative advertisements against the supplier.
Violation of due care	If someone fails to exercise reasonable care or competency in the course of providing guidance for others in their business transactions, it is a violation of due care.	An auditor grants a supplier ISO 9001 certification despite the audit team's failure to follow correct accrediting procedure (not exercising due care) during the audit. Based on the certification, a company purchases faulty product from the supplier for commercial distribution.
Aiding and abetting	If someone willfully causes an act to be done and the same act would be an offense against the United States if directly performed by him or her, it constitutes aiding and abetting.	An auditor discovers that an auditee is using materials against contractual requirements but does not include the information in the final audit report.

Figure 5.5   Illegal auditor activities.

Source: ASQ's Foundations in Quality: Certified Quality Auditor, Module 1: Ethics, Professional Conduct, and Liability Issues (Milwaukee, WI: ASQ Quality Press, 1998), pp. 1–16.

Also, if an auditor provides guidance, even if the guidance fixes the problem, the auditor still owns the solution. If the recommended solution is not the best, there may be malicious compliance that will reflect back on the auditor.

> An auditor discovers that the auditee is shipping defective products. After verifying and investigating the incident, the auditor records 10 product deficiencies that should be corrected before shipping resumes. The audit team prioritizes the deficiencies and includes them in the final report.[2]
>
> The fact that the audit team prioritized the deficiencies means that it accepted partial responsibility for the solution. This makes the audit team and its company at least partially liable should a problem involving the defective products surface in the future.

Registrar/certification organizations and their auditors face a special liability during the audit and after registration/certification. An organization certifying that others meet a set of standards must use reasonable care or competency in certifying.[3] The auditor must follow the procedures of the certification body during the audit process and base the certification recommendation on the results of the audit. The certification body must have specific procedures and requirements for certification, and these must be equally applied to all companies.

Proprietary Information

Disclosure of proprietary information can come about because of the legal process itself. An auditor completes audit checklists, makes notes of the results of the audit, and often makes copies of information supporting the findings of the audit. These notes, completed checklists, and copies find their way into the audit record and are kept for a specified period of time. If a lawsuit is initiated during that time, the contents of the file may become available for "discovery" by the parties to the lawsuit.

Records of both internal and external audits are subject to discovery by parties in a lawsuit. For example, if a supplier to your organization is party to a lawsuit and your organization conducted an audit (external) of the supplier, your records are subject to discovery. The same rights of discovery are true for both civil and criminal legal proceedings.

Through discovery, these records can become public. This is one of the main reasons an auditor should not make copies of or take notes on proprietary information when auditing a company. It is also a major reason for keeping extraneous comments out of the audit record. Such comments can come back to haunt an auditor at the most inappropriate time.

> During an FAA audit of an organization, the FAA regulator asked to review the completed internal audit checklists. On one checklist, an auditor had written "This procedure is terrible" in the margin. The auditor and the lead auditor spent the next three hours explaining why the comment was on the checklist even though the auditor evaluated the procedure as satisfactory.

Audit Record Disclosure

Because most management systems require records indicating that each step is performed by following documented procedures or methods, there are many documents and records available for both the defense and the prosecution in the event of a lawsuit.

> *Discovery* is a pretrial device used by one party to obtain facts and information about the case from the other party in order to help prepare for trial. Under federal rules of civil procedure and in states that have adopted similar rules, tools of discovery include deposition to oral and written questions, written interrogatories, production of documents, permission to enter land or other property, physical and mental examinations, and requests for admission. In criminal proceedings, discovery emphasizes the right of the defense to obtain access to evidence necessary to prepare its own case.[4]

Copies of the audit report must be sent to the client. Clients either designate other organizations and individuals to receive copies or do the distribution themselves. In most cases, it is agreed that the auditee will receive a copy of the audit report.

The audit records should be treated as confidential information and should not be disclosed to internal or outside entities without prior approval of the client and the auditee. Accidental or deliberate disclosure of negative audit information that other companies can use as a basis for making decisions that adversely affect the auditee may make the auditor and the auditor's company liable for damages. These damages can be considerable if a major contract is canceled or awarded to another company on the basis of the audit information.

> For FDA audits of organizations, the FDA typically will not request to see internal audit reports but will ask to see evidence that scheduled audits were performed. In some cases where there is a serious issue, the FDA may require review of the internal audit report content to evaluate whether the issue had been found during internal audits. The potential audiences of the reports should be kept in mind when the reports are written.

3. AUDIT CREDIBILITY

Auditor Conduct

Professionalism is defined as the aims and qualities that characterize a profession or a professional person. Auditors must comply with high standards of honesty, integrity, work ethic, diligence, loyalty, and commitment.[5] Auditing is a profession that requires individuals to conform to certain behaviors for maximum job proficiency.

The book *Standards for the Professional Practice of Internal Auditing*,[6] published by the IIA, defines and amplifies five general standards:

1. *Independence*—Internal auditors should be independent of the activities they audit

2. *Professional proficiency*—Internal audits should be performed with proficiency and due professional care

3. *Scope of work*—The scope of the internal audit should encompass the examination and evaluation of the adequacy and effectiveness of the organization's system of internal control and the quality of performance in carrying out assigned responsibilities

4. *Performance of audit work*—Audit work should include planning the audit, examining and evaluating information, conducting interviews, communicating results, and following up

5. *Management of the internal auditing department*—The director of internal auditing should properly manage the internal auditing department

These general standards could also apply to product, process, and system auditing. People in the auditing field should be aware of standards of performance in other professions. A broader knowledge allows the auditor to quickly understand different and difficult situations as they arise.

Communicating with the Auditee

An auditor's temperament is often the key to a successful audit. A sullen or unfriendly attitude could lead to resistance or malicious compliance. Overly friendly or garrulous behavior could lead to the impression that the audit is not serious. The auditor should find an acceptable balance.

By approaching an auditee in a diplomatic and objective manner, the auditor can set a tone of success for an audit. The auditor must be aware that each auditee views the audit process differently, on the basis of individual management style, culture, personality, and opinions. Many auditees are reluctant to welcome auditors into their world. Resentment, fear, and anxiety are obstacles that must be overcome. By diplomatically presenting and maintaining the audit program, the auditor can influence the auditee's perception of the audit function as well as the overall success of individual audits.

The auditor can establish good rapport with an auditee early in the audit by being respectful, courteous, and appreciative of any special arrangements made for the auditor's comfort and convenience. By demonstrating that the audit has been adequately planned and prepared for, and by making every effort to maintain the audit schedule, the auditor projects an image of efficiency and professionalism.

Maintaining open communication channels throughout an audit is essential. An auditor must listen attentively during interviews, allow the interviewee adequate response time, and refrain from asking leading questions. Frequent and timely communication of findings, questions, and concerns gives both the auditor and the auditee opportunities to request clarifications, address corrective action, examine the scope of the situation, and discuss the progress of the audit.

Additionally, an auditor can set a positive tone for an audit by highlighting commendable findings and observations. The auditor's ability to communicate effectively with management sets the tone for the entire audit and may influence the auditee's response to the audit findings. Auditors should avoid naming names and should emphasize the purpose of the assessment of the product, process, or system.

> In a closing meeting at a supplier audit, the auditee asked the name of the person involved with every negative finding. These individuals were brought to the meeting room by the auditee management. It was a very uncomfortable situation for the auditor and for those being singled out as having caused the nonconformances, some of which were minor issues. The auditor should make every effort to emphasize that a negative finding is not meant to point fingers at a specific person but to identify a gap in conformance with a requirement.

However, exemplary conduct by an auditor does not prevent an auditee from making false claims of theft, discrimination, sexual misconduct, or other forms of unprofessionalism. No one is immune from false accusations, but disgruntled auditees may target auditors who issue unfavorable reports. Grievance procedures can be abused by the auditee to "get even" with the auditor for finding problems in the auditee's area of responsibility.

> While performing an audit, an auditor found several points where a specific auditee was not following procedures. The auditee was informed during the interview that these would show up in the audit report. Unknown to the auditor, the auditee immediately filed a formal written complaint against the auditor, claiming unprofessional conduct and lack of objectivity. After an extensive investigation (one that was not kept confidential and that damaged the auditor's professional reputation), the end result was that there was no basis for the complaint, and so it was dismissed. Because of this investigation, none of the auditor's concerns were allowed to be included in the audit report.

All audit organizations should have grievance or complaint procedures. The procedures should include the protection of the rights of the accuser and the accused. For audits that represent a high risk of false claims, or when the auditor feels uncomfortable with a situation, one of the following options should be considered:

1. A second person should be scheduled to work with the auditor

2. The auditor should use some type of recording device (for example, a digital voice recorder)

3. An escort should be present to witness interviews between the auditor and the auditee

Audit Ethics

Audit ethics is perhaps the area that demands the most skill from an auditor. Training is available for enhancing skills in checklist development, interviewing techniques, audit documentation, follow-up methods, and almost all other phases of an audit. On the other hand, very little information is available on the topic of audit ethics. An auditor's use of questionable or unethical methods during or following an audit can quickly erase any favorable impressions and be detrimental to the auditor and the auditing organization as a whole.

ISO 19011 contains six principles of auditing that are "prerequisite for providing audit conclusions that are relevant and sufficient for enabling auditors working independently from one another to reach similar conclusions in similar circumstances."[7] These principles are:

1. *Integrity:* the foundation of professionalism

   Auditors and the person managing an audit programme should:

   — Perform their work with honesty, diligence, and responsibility;

   — Observe and comply with any applicable legal requirements;

   — Demonstrate their competence while performing their work;

   — Perform their work in an impartial manner, i.e. remain fair and unbiased in all their dealings;

   — Be sensitive to any influences that may be exerted on their judgement while carrying out an audit.

2. *Fair presentation:* the obligation to report truthfully and accurately

   Audit findings, audit conclusions and audit reports should reflect truthfully and accurately the audit activities. Significant obstacles encountered during the audit and unresolved diverging opinions between the audit team and the auditee should be reported. The communication should be truthful, accurate, objective, timely, clear and complete.

3. *Due professional care:* the application of diligence and judgement in auditing

   Auditors should exercise due care in accordance with the importance of the task they perform and the confidence placed in them by the audit client and other interested parties. An important factor in carrying out their work with due professional care is having the ability to make reasoned judgements in all audit situations.

4. *Confidentiality:* security of information

   Auditors should exercise discretion in the use and protection of information acquired in the course of their duties. Audit information should not be used inappropriately for personal gain by the auditor or the audit client, or in a manner detrimental to the legitimate interests of the auditee. This concept includes the proper handling of sensitive or confidential information.

5. *Independence:* the basis for the impartiality of the audit and objectivity of the audit conclusions

   Auditors should be independent of the activity being audited wherever practicable, and should in all cases act in a manner that is free from bias and conflict of interest. For internal audits, auditors should be independent from the operating managers of the function being audited. Auditors should maintain objectivity throughout the audit process to ensure that the audit findings and conclusions are based only on the audit evidence.

For small organizations, it may not be possible for internal auditors to be fully independent of the activity being audited, but every effort should be made to remove bias and encourage objectivity.

6. *Evidence-based approach:* the rational method for reaching reliable and reproducible audit conclusions in a systematic audit process

Audit evidence should be verifiable. It will in general be based on samples of the information available, since an audit is conducted during a finite period of time and with finite resources. An appropriate use of sampling should be applied, since this is closely related to the confidence that can be placed in the audit conclusions.[8]

These principles should help make the audit an effective, credible, and reliable tool in support of management policies and controls by providing information on which an organization can act in order to improve its performance. The principles provide a foundation for the conduct of auditors and persons managing an audit program.

Audit Function Credibility

A credible audit is a meaningful audit. Competent individuals who gather and handle all information pertaining to the audit in an unbiased and ethical manner provide a credible audit. An audit group should be structured so that it does not report directly to the manager of the function being audited. Management must use the audit results appropriately to establish and maintain the credibility of the program. The misuse of audit results or failure to initiate corrective actions will erode the credibility of the audit program, regardless of the performance of the auditors. Misuse of audit results includes using results as the sole basis for disciplinary action against individuals in a department, evaluating personnel performance against goals and objectives, and deciding pay raise, bonus, or perk.

Using a knowledgeable, experienced, skilled, capable, and well-trained auditor is the most effective way to enhance the credibility of the audit function. Becoming an ASQ Certified Quality Auditor is one way for an auditor to demonstrate knowledge. Many organizations have their own auditor qualification and/or certification process to ensure auditors are knowledgeable and capable. The use of unqualified auditors who possess little knowledge or who do not have the ability to assist management in making good decisions or improving a process can discredit the entire audit process.

> I am familiar with the attitude of one company in choosing members for its internal audit group. Rather than selecting its best employees and training them as auditors, this company uses the audit group as a means of relieving its worst employees from critical areas in the organization. These people are completely wrong for this position.

A good auditor does not have to be an expert in the area being audited, but the auditor does need to be knowledgeable in the discipline of auditing. The auditor needs to have an understanding of what is being observed. At times, an auditor must be able to grasp that understanding in minutes. When auditors need help, they should ask another member of the audit team to verify an observation or to assist in other ways.

Auditors need to be able to communicate effectively, both orally and in writing. A large part of the job consists of interviewing. A good auditor must ask intelligent, proper questions and listen attentively.

An auditor needs to be tactful and offer feedback in a positive, nonintimidating manner. An auditor needs to be especially considerate of an auditee's employees. The audit process is disruptive to daily operations and can inconvenience employees. The auditor shows respect for and sensitivity to those being audited by sticking to the proposed audit schedule and not retaining employees through their meal or refreshment breaks. If people see the audit process as a nuisance, they are less likely to cooperate, and the auditor runs the risk of being unable to complete the assignment well or on time.

> As an auditee, I had received an audit agenda for a third-party audit. The first item on the agenda was a quick plant tour. However, as we started the tour, the auditor requested to see a certain area of the plant not scheduled for that audit. As we were about to leave the area, he said, "I know it's not on the agenda, but I would like to ask a couple of questions here. It won't take long; I don't want to get off schedule, but I'd like to start here." A day and a half later, the auditor was still in that area asking questions. He never audited another department in the entire facility.

An auditor aims to keep the credibility of the audit function on a high plane. The auditor does this by looking at information objectively and avoiding ethical conflicts. An auditee must trust that an auditor will not divulge proprietary information to competitors or other outsiders who can use it to their benefit. Even internally, auditors must be careful to maintain confidentiality. This is especially true when the locations or departments report to different management.

Following a code of ethics is not the sole responsibility of the auditor. Everyone involved in the process must practice and promote ethics. Audit program managers and audit functions/departments should be responsible for promoting and monitoring ethical behavior throughout the audit function and requiring auditors to adhere to a code of ethics.

Higher levels of ethical conduct can be achieved only when management actively promotes this conduct and when auditors are supported instead of being left to fend for themselves. The credibility of the audit function is enhanced when the role of the audit function is communicated and understood by all stakeholders, when the auditors act professionally, and when the program is professionally managed. Fear of the audit function will reduce its credibility. The audit function should be managed and made accountable in the same way as other functions within the organization.

Part II

Audit Process

[42 of the CQA Exam Questions or 28 percent]

Audit preparation consists of everything that is done in advance by interested parties, such as the auditor, the lead auditor, the client, and the audit program manager, to ensure that the audit complies with the client's objective. The preparation stage of an audit begins with the decision to conduct the audit. For our purposes, preparation ends when the audit itself begins.

For a third-party audit (or when an outside organization conducts a first- or second-party audit), the client selects and contracts with an auditing organization. For regulatory agency audits of an organization, the agency either contacts the organization to schedule an audit or, in some cases, arrives at the organization to conduct the audit without prior notice. For a first- or second-party audit, the client and/or employer of the auditing organization usually initiates the audit either by request or by approval of an audit schedule. The client and/or the employer of the auditing organization should define the purpose and scope of the audit as well as the criteria against which the audit is to be conducted. The auditing organization personnel, in return, prepare the audit plan and other working papers, select or participate in the selection of the audit team members, and notify the auditee in writing of the impending audit. For a contracted audit, the client should notify the auditee.

For a first-party internal audit that is not contracted out, the preparation stage may be less formal. Since internal audits are often scheduled on a regular basis, such as semiannually or quarterly, an interoffice memo may suffice for notification. In some companies, a phone call followed by an e-mail message or memo may be acceptable because the lead auditor and the manager of the area to be audited are likely to have greater contact prior to the actual audit.

An auditing organization must carefully prepare for an audit. A well-planned audit is likely to progress according to schedule, earn respect for the auditor, secure the full cooperation of the auditee, efficiently utilize the time and other resources of the auditee and the auditor, and produce results that management can use to guide the organization.

When preparing to be audited, an auditee organization has certain responsibilities, such as ensuring that the audit team will have adequate working space and that necessary personnel and documents will be made available as needed. The auditee often assigns an escort to the audit team to function as a liaison with employees, management, and the audit team.

If preparation for an audit has been inadequate, the audit team risks wasting time during the performance stage of the audit or performs a mechanical audit following a canned checklist. An unprepared auditor may focus on trivial matters or personal areas of interest or knowledge (pet peeves), or spend more time in a conference room than in work areas. Such an audit is of limited value since it fails to properly assess the product, process, or system, and it wastes resources.

Chapter 6
Audit Preparation and Planning/Part IIA

U pon receiving an audit assignment from a client, an audit manager assigns a lead auditor, who will be responsible for all phases of the audit. The lead auditor is responsible for preparing an audit plan, generally a one- to two-page document (see Figure 6.1) that serves as a link between audit planning and audit execution. An audit plan identifies:

- The purpose (objectives) and scope (boundaries) of the audit

- The auditee and the organizational units to be audited

- The audit team members

- The criteria being audited against (such as a standard, contract, or procedure)

- Logistical information such as the audit date(s), place of the audit, the expected duration of the audit, interview schedule, and meetings with auditee

In addition, when applicable, the audit plan may list confidentiality requirements, transportation requirements, required health and safety permits, or security clearances.

ISO 19011, clause 6.3.2.2, Preparing the audit plan, states that the following additional items should be covered or referenced as part of an audit plan:

- The roles and responsibilities of audit team members and accompanying persons such as guides and observers

- The allocation of appropriate resources to critical areas of the audit

- The audit methods to be used, including the extent to which audit sampling is needed to obtain sufficient audit evidence and the design of the sampling plan, if applicable

- As appropriate, the audit plan should include:

  — The identification of the auditee's representative for the audit

  — The working and reporting language of the audit when this is different from the language of the auditor and/or the auditee

  — The audit report topics

— Logistics and communication arrangements

— Any specific measures to be taken to address the effect of uncertainty on achieving the audit objectives

— Matters related to confidentiality and information security

— Any follow-up actions from a previous audit

— Any follow-up activities to the planned audit

— Coordination with other audit activities, in the case of a joint audit

---

Audit Plan—2/2/XX

Audited Organization: ABC Industries, ABC Fla.

Purpose:
To assess conformance (compliance) and effectiveness of the management system against internal and external performance standards and to report findings.

Scope of the audit:
The ABC production facility and support activities will be included in the audit. The audit includes all departments that support the production of gizmos that are responsible for meeting ISO 9001 requirements. The areas of interest include the purchasing, quality assurance, laboratory, distribution, order entry, scheduling, production, and training departments.

Requirements:
As specified in ISO 9001 and existing ABC company policies and procedures.
Other regulatory requirements and industry standards

Applicable documents:
The Quality (policy) Manual(s)—QM9001
Unit procedures and records that address the ISO 9001 requirements

Overall schedule (detailed interview schedule to follow):
March 23, 20XX

8:00 A.M.	Orientation for auditors (safety and environment)
9:00 A.M.	Opening meeting (for auditees)
9:30 A.M.	Tour/review documents
10:30 A.M.–4:00 P.M.	Interviews and observations
4:00 P.M.–5:00 P.M.	Audit team meeting

March 24, 20XX

8:00 A.M.–8:30 A.M.	Daily briefing with ABC coordinator
8:30 A.M.–1:00 P.M.	Interviews and observations continued
1:00 P.M.–3:00 P.M.	Audit team meeting, preparation of report
3:00 P.M.–4:00 P.M.	Exit meeting

Team members:
John Smith, lead auditor, ASQ CQA
Jane Doe, ASQ CQA

Approved: _____   Approved: _____
                    Audit Organization   ABC Industries

Figure 6.1   Audit plan.

During the audit preparation phase, the auditing organization must ensure that the audit's purpose and scope are defined and identify the needed resources and applicable reference standard. The audit team is selected based on these criteria. The lead auditor then secures the appropriate documents, prepares (or ensures that other members of the audit team prepare) applicable checklists and other working papers, and determines the proper data collection methods. The written audit plan should be signed by the lead auditor and approved by the audit program manager, the client, or the auditee. The plan should be reviewed, approved, and presented to the auditee before the on-site audit activities begin.

The following topics are discussed in this chapter:

- Elements of the audit planning process
- Auditor selection
- Audit-related documentation
- Logistics
- Auditing tools and working papers
- Auditing strategies
- Communication and distribution of the audit plan

1. ELEMENTS OF THE AUDIT PLANNING PROCESS

Identification of Authority

A very important step is to verify the authority to perform the audit. "By specifying the authority for the audit to all involved parties (including your audit boss and other users of the audit), you confer legitimacy to the audit and remove (or minimize) those adverse feelings. Of course, another reason to verify your authority is to avoid wasting time preparing for something not authorized."[1]

The authority to perform an audit may come from a single source or a combination of sources. The important thing is not where the authority comes from but that it does indeed exist. Without a specific authority source that permits an audit, an auditor has no right to perform one. The authority to perform an audit may come from inside or outside the auditee organization. Internally, authority may come from an organization's chain of command, such as the president, the director, or a department manager. Externally, authority may reside in purchase agreements approved by an officer of the company, industry standards adopted by the organization, or government regulations enacted by elected officials. Authority to conduct an audit comes from a person. If the authority does not come directly from a person, it may be in documents approved by persons of authority.

Internal Sources

Internal sources of authority are either organizational or hierarchical. The term *organization* describes functions or groups but does not rank them. The word *hierarchy* refers to status, particularly among individuals. Internal audit authority can come from either source or a combination, depending on the company's structure.

Part IIA

Organization

The source of authority for the performance of internal audits usually resides in an approved document—often called a quality, environmental, or safety manual—that describes the organization's management system. This document should define the authority of certain groups or individuals to perform audits.

At other times, a company's policy defines and authorizes audits. If, for example, an organization agrees to meet certain industry standards voluntarily, then the organization policy specifies that those standards will be met. In this case, an audit is a planned group of activities to assure management that the organization is meeting those industry standards, which are usually promoted as voluntary, but which are often required of organizations to be competitive in the industry.

Sometimes an organization decides to adopt or adapt certain criteria even though it is not required to do so. For example, an organization may elect to meet ISO 9001 or ISO 14001 standards even though it has no intention of applying for registration/certification. Likewise, criteria for national, state, or regional quality awards may be used as a basis for business improvement even when an organization has no intention of applying for the award.

Hierarchy

Hierarchy is the chain of command that controls how work is delegated and how responsibilities are assigned within an organization. Rather than being driven by approved documents, as in the case of organizational authority, the decision to conduct an audit is driven by the people who have the authority to do so. The audit authority must be higher in the organizational structure than the functions being audited. For example, it would be extremely difficult for a division or department of a company to commission an audit of corporate headquarters. But the vice president of operations might request a quality or environmental audit of department operations. A department manager may request a series of process audits to be conducted on a new or existing manufacturing step or service. This kind of audit is not normally defined or required by the organization's policies and procedures, and it is usually requested at a higher level to address a specific need. The client in these cases would be the vice president of operations or the department manager.

External Sources

At times, the authority for an audit is external to the auditee organization, as in the case of authority specified by a contract, standard, or regulatory body.

Contract

The authority to perform external second-party audits should reside in the purchasing agreement (a contract or purchase order) between an organization and its suppliers. Sometimes this authority is not readily visible; it may be included in a section on rights of access. A *rights-of-access clause* gives a customer or regulatory body the right to inspect or audit a supplier facility, product, or service. The clause usually specifies reasonable access during normal business hours. In the United States, the Federal Acquisition Regulations (FARs) require federal agencies to include this authority in most procurement documents.

A contractual audit source is common in second-party audits. The source of authority is the signed contract between two parties—the supplier and the customer. Proprietary processes, such as research and development projects or processes that are being conducted for a competitor, are defined and are excluded from the concern of the auditor. Access to plant locations is restricted in these circumstances but should be defined in advance.

Standards

National and international management system standards such as ISO 9001 require internal audits to be performed. These standards may be followed voluntarily or may be imposed by contract or regulation.

Industry standards are written to clarify, amplify, and, in some cases, limit federal regulations. For example, in the pharmaceutical industry, voluntary industry associations such as the Advanced Medical Technology Association (AdvaMed) have developed standards that may be used as the basis for internal audits. After an industry has demonstrated that voluntary standards are working, the best practices may be incorporated into federal regulations. However, industry standards are not regulatory documents.

Normally, the requirements of the standards are incorporated into or interpreted by the company's internal documents. The policies and procedures might include the authority to audit the organization and a reminder to managers that they are to cooperate with the auditors. Also, procedures implemented as a result of a national/international standard may provide guidance on how the audit program will be managed and how audits are conducted.

Regulatory

International, federal, or state law may be the source of requirements in certain regulated industries. Within the United States, these regulations are derived from laws passed by Congress and interpreted by the Code of Federal Regulations promulgated by the authorized agency. The courts have enforced and reinforced the rights of regulatory bodies to conduct inspections and audits of organizations to monitor their compliance with the law. Regulatory bodies include organizations that oversee safety, health, and environmental laws, such as OSHA, the FDA, the FAA, the DOE, and the EPA.

Determination of Audit Purpose

The client or the person or organization designated by the client determines the purpose and/or objectives. The purpose sets the tone of the audit, such as determination of compliance or identification of opportunities for improvement.

The auditors may verify, determine, or confirm auditee actions for the purposes of approval, certification, renewal, and so on. The audit process may be used to identify weaknesses, opportunities for improvement, or ineffective or inefficient processes for the purpose of informing management who can make improvements. See Chapter 2 ("Purpose and Scope of Audits/Part IB") for a list of example purpose statements. Purpose statements should be concise and clear. The audit conclusion should address the purpose of the audit.

Part IIA

Everyone involved in the audit process should be informed of the audit purpose. The audit purpose will affect most aspects of the audit process, such as the selection of auditors, sampling plans, auditing time, type and extent of the exit meeting, and so on.

An example of an audit purpose may be to determine conformity to ISO 9001 (quality), ISO 14001 (environmental), JCAHCO (health care), AIB (baking), or AABB (blood) requirements.

Determination of Audit Type and Scope

The scope of an audit is developed in conjunction with the purpose statement. The scope establishes the boundaries by identifying the exact items, groups, and activities to be examined. The auditor and the client must agree on the scope, which is then documented and communicated in the audit plan to confirm a common understanding.

By looking at the specific circumstances surrounding an audit, and by examining the auditee's audit history, an auditor can confirm that required corrective actions have been implemented and make judgments about which areas might require less attention. Areas that involve less risk and areas with excellent audit histories may require less sampling.

The following are examples of scope statements for first-, second-, and third-party audits:

First-party: To audit the purchasing activities for wireless widget production

Second-party: To audit the heat-treatment facility as it relates to contract number 95-003

Third-party: To audit the design and manufacture of gaskets, seals, and other compounded elastomer products for commercial and automotive applications at Plant Number 1, 123 Main St., Anytown, USA

Determining the scope of an audit keeps the auditor focused and keeps the audit from becoming a witch hunt or fishing expedition. An auditor should not seek to uncover problems in areas outside the audit's stated scope. However, if such problems emerge in the course of an audit, the auditor must be prepared to address them. For example, if an auditor observes equipment that is overdue for its calibration check, this should be recorded and reported even though the equipment might not pertain to the process being audited or fall within the audit scope. However, taking the time to investigate problems outside the scope will affect the planned sample time inside the scope. Therefore, the auditor should record his or her observations, point out the problem to management of the area, and continue with the planned audit within the scope. Problems found outside the scope should be considered when future audit schedules are being developed.

The scope of an audit significantly affects resources and time requirements. If the scope is immense, a large audit team will be needed to complete the audit in a reasonable time frame. If the scope is too large for the available resources, the audit may have to be scheduled for a time when adequate resources are available, or the scope may have to be narrowed. However, too narrow a scope wastes valuable resources. Clarifying the scope makes audit planning and execution efficient since the availability of resources directly bears on achievement of audit objectives.

System and Process Audit Scopes

A *system* is a collection of processes or elements linked to achieve a common purpose. In the book *After the Quality Audit*, the authors define a system as a collection of processes supported by an infrastructure to manage and coordinate its function.[2] The scope of an audit may be the entire management system of a facility or a portion or subsystem. Process-based management system standards such as ISO 9001 and ISO 14001 require that the processes that make up the system be defined, along with the sequence and interaction. Some processes may be grouped and identified with names such as operation processes, administration processes, management processes, support processes, core processes, measurement processes, and so on. An audit scope may be one of the support processes of the management system, such as the purchasing department.

Auditors are encouraged to use process audit techniques when auditing management systems. The process audit technique includes following the defined process sequential steps and interactions with other processes. In the book *How to Audit a Process-Based QMS*, the authors explain, "As auditors, we must both understand and then measure those processes [the QMS processes]. Since there are too many possible processes to examine, boundaries must be set. These boundaries are called the scope of the audit. They serve a practical need by limiting the investigation to something that can be accomplished within the allotted period of time."[3]

The scope of a process audit is normally limited to activities that can be observed during the audit. In the book *The Process Auditing Techniques Guide*, the author states, "One of the main differences between a process and system audit is scope definition and expansion. A process audit could be a singular process or part of a process such as filling, washing, reacting, drilling, cutting, treating, transporting, informing, ordering, and so on."[4]

As depicted in Figure 6.2, a process audit may be the drilling operation, or if there are several drilling stations, a process audit could be all the drilling stations.

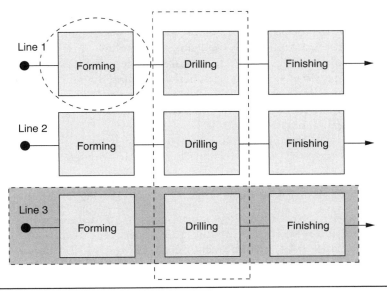

Figure 6.2   Process audit scope.

Source: Modified from QualityWBT training materials.

Part IIA

If drilling is one of three steps to make a part, a process could be auditing all three steps: forming, drilling, and finishing.

A process audit could be a single process, such as Line 1 Forming; the same process for Line 1, Line 2, and Line 3, such as Drilling; or all three processes for a specific line of operations, such as Line 3.

Observing Problems outside the Stated Scope

As indicated earlier, while auditors should remain within the scope stated in the audit plan, they may discover problems beyond that scope. An auditor has an obligation not to ignore problems outside the stated scope. An auditor's reaction to such a discovery will depend on the severity of the problem, its effect on the system, and the type of audit being performed. Conditions outside the scope of the audit may not be included in the formal report as a finding or violation for that particular audit. Conditions should be reported directly to the client and the auditee if there is a serious condition adverse to quality, to safety, or to the environment, or if there is a possibility of litigation. However, minor process problems need be reported only to the auditee. For example, an unsafe practice or one with serious legal ramifications cannot be ignored, while a minor process problem may not be acknowledged in the formal audit report. A minor problem may be communicated to the auditee as feedback for improvement actions.

In internal audits where management's goal is to improve the management system, problems that interfere with that goal are usually not ignored since improvement of the management system cannot be promoted if an auditor intentionally overlooks obvious problems. Therefore, the audit team may expand the stated scope and look into the problem. In an internal audit, problems within or outside the scope need to be identified so that appropriate corrective action can take place.

Sometimes an auditee will want to expand the scope of an audit. Expanding the scope is permissible before the audit begins, as long as the team has time to prepare for the modified scope. If an auditee asks to have the scope expanded once the performance stage has begun, the lead auditor should suggest that the next audit encompass the additional area, since the team will not have done the necessary preparation. Additionally, the team may not have adequate time or the team members with the appropriate technical skills to conduct a thorough investigation. There may be fewer obstacles when expanding the scope of an internal audit, because the auditor's time is not constrained by a contract, external management approvals are not required, and all parties internal to the organization should have the same organizational objectives.

In summary, auditors should stay within the scope of the audit and use their judgment to address problems encountered outside the scope.

Requirements to Audit Against

The requirements to audit against (audit criteria) are discussed in Chapter 3. The specified requirements make up the audit basis and normally do not change. ISO 19011, clause 6.4.4, Communicating during the audit, states, "Any need for changes to the audit plan which may become apparent as auditing activities progress should be reviewed and approved, as appropriate, by both the person managing the audit programme and the auditee."

Requirements to audit against can be very formal, such as government regulations. Formal requirements or contractual standards are normally written using the words *shall*, *must*, or *will* to designate a mandatory requirement. A common auditor technique for identifying auditable requirements is to create a checklist where each auxiliary verb *shall*, *must*, or *will* is used in the documents to cite a mandatory requirement. Other optional requirements, suggestions, and guidance normally use the auxiliary verbs *should*, *may*, or *might*.

Requirements are also found in organization documents. Internal organization documents may create their own style or follow the same "shall"/"should" style used in formal documents or the style of the individual author of the procedure, instruction, or guide. One auditor technique is to review internal documents for promises to keep records, follow a schedule, or complete a task in a specific order or time period. Organizations can be audited against self-imposed requirements or promises made in documents as well as statements made by managers of the area being audited.

Sometimes an auditor may be required to audit against requirements that are not in an external standard, internal procedure, or other document. It will be the auditor's job to determine whether there are predetermined methods for a particular process or activity. One of the elements needed to establish control over a process or activity is the existence of predetermined methods. The predetermined methods are normally found in procedures but not in all cases. Some may be established by word of mouth, in a flowchart or picture, or as a result of training. An auditor may need to search for the established method, verify its existence, and then audit the organization against it.

In the book *How to Audit the Process-Based QMS*, the authors explain that "without requirements [criteria] to match against the evidence, there can be no audit." The authors go on to explain that requirements may be either external or internal. "External requirements originate from outside the location or site being audited. Internal documents tell how to apply the external requirements to specific processes, site, and functions."[5]

Examples of Internal Requirements

- Written policies, procedures, and work instructions
- Training procedures and materials
- Stated objectives in the budgets, programs, contracts, and so on
- Defined process requirements as stated by managers of areas audited
- Company (internal) product or service specifications

Examples of External Requirements

- Customer (external) specifications
- Industry handbooks, published guides
- A contract that includes references to a specific standard, such as ANSI, ASTM, FAA, or FDA standards
- ISO 9001, AS9100, ISO/TS 16949, ISO 13485, or ISO 14001

Determination of Resources Required

Once an audit's purpose, scope, and criteria are confirmed, an audit team must be assembled. Often, a lead auditor has already been selected and has completed some of the planning activities. The audit team leader or the lead auditor usually participates in the selection of audit team members and may help determine the size and composition of the audit team. Each member of the audit team must be independent of the functions being audited. As noted in Part I, total independence may not be possible for internal audits, especially in very small organizations.

When selecting an audit team, the auditing organization must determine the number of auditors needed to complete the job. Often, the scope of an audit, the time frame in which it is to be completed, and budgetary concerns will determine whether a single auditor or an audit team is needed. The multiple-auditor or audit team approach allows depth of inquiry and breadth of examination. In addition, it encourages balance since no single individual can possess all the technical knowledge and personality traits necessary in all audit situations. However, one experienced, well-trained auditor may be all that is required to conduct a meaningful and effective audit.[6] In some cases, subcontract personnel may be added when the audit team does not have the expertise needed to accomplish the audit purpose and scope. This may be done for technical knowledge as well as for quality assurance and environmental or safety knowledge.

An audit team may break into mini-teams or subteams to perform portions of an audit. Each mini-team consists of two persons—one to interview personnel, the other to listen and take notes during the interviews. Seldom does the availability of personnel permit such luxury, except when members of an audit team are accompanied by auditors-in-training. A second way of forming mini-teams is to pair a technical specialist with an auditor. The auditor can explore the system and management controls while the technical specialist observes the work being done to provide a product or service.

When scheduling an audit, the lead auditor should calculate the estimated number of personnel hours needed to complete each portion of the audit and then determine the total number of team hours required for the audit. For example, if the sum of interview and data collection hours is 10, then one auditor should be able to conduct the interviews and data collection in 10 hours; two auditors working as a team but in different areas should be able to complete the interviews and data collection in 5 hours. Time for common audit process activities such as the opening, exit, and team meetings also needs to be added to the overall audit time calculated.

For third-party certification audits, the International Accreditation Forum (IAF) has issued a guidance document for determination of number of auditor days. The latest version of IAF guidance for quality and environmental systems is available on the internet.[7]

Determining the proper number of on-site audit days can be complicated when all variables are considered. Given a particular audit purpose and scope, the primary factors influencing the number of auditor days include (1) the number of employees in a company, (2) the maturity of the existing management system, and (3) the criteria being audited against. Complex operations and labor-intensive organizations may increase the number of auditor days. Yet, auditor days could be reduced for large yet simple or single-production-line operations.

The lead auditor ensures that the size of the audit team is appropriate on the basis of the amount of work to be performed, its complexity, the availability of personnel and other resources, and the desired time frame in which the audit is to be completed. Additionally, the lead auditor should consider the physical size and layout of the space in which the auditors will be working.

The following factors may be considered when determining the number of auditors needed on the audit team based on time constraints:

- On-site time restrictions or allocation

- If remote audit or eAudit, communication delays or technical difficulties

- Average expected interview time per interviewee

- Number of interviews (percentage of employees to be sampled)

- Time in meetings (opening, exit, auditee briefings, and audit team meetings)

- Data analysis and report preparation time

- Observation of work time for single or multiple shifts or weekends

- Records review time

- Meal and break times

- Lost time due to inefficiencies such as distance from department to department

The amount of pre- and postaudit work could also affect the number of auditors needed on the team. Examples include previsit communication (written and verbal), review of documents, preparation of checklists and collection plans, reporting, and follow-up actions. Many factors affect the total amount of labor needed to conduct a system or process audit, but a general guideline is that the pre- and postwork time (labor hours) equals the on-site or performance phase time (labor hours). Therefore, two on-site days for a team of two auditors (four labor days) would require a total of eight labor days to complete the necessary pre- and postaudit work. Though there is no set rule comparing pre- and postwork to the time performing the audit, it is important to ensure that adequate resources are scheduled for an effective audit. Independent of the audit process labor needs, travel time to the audit site could be a significant factor.

2. AUDITOR SELECTION

An audit team is accountable to the client (the person or organization that hired or directed them to perform the audit). An audit team also has responsibilities to assess the organization or process so that the auditee knows what is working, what is nonconforming, and where opportunities for improvement exist. The members of an audit team are also accountable to the audit program manager or certification body for whom they are working. Therefore, their actions must reflect the audit organization's operating procedures and standards.

Part IIA

Selection

This section assumes that there is a pool of qualified auditors to choose from. Auditor competence will be covered in Part III, and auditor training will be covered as part of audit program management in Part IV. Following clearly defined qualifications, the audit program manager must select competent auditors. The authors of *After the Quality Audit* stress that the people selected to perform quality audits should be the organization's best people.[8] Who the best people are, however, may differ from one audit work assignment to another, depending on the auditors' backgrounds.

> In a DOE nuclear facility, the contracting operations company used senior managers from other nuclear facilities as management self-assessment auditors. These senior operations managers were extremely skilled at identifying significant safety issues facing the operations managers of the facility, and company management addressed them in a very timely manner. The operations managers performing the management self-assessment were on temporary assignment from their normal operational duties.

Audit management must consider a variety of factors for a particular audit assignment to secure an auditor with the most appropriate skills. Figure 6.3 summarizes some of the key factors.

Even with well-defined auditor criteria and a well-defined work assignment, selection of individuals to be auditors may become arbitrary without additional structure. Figure 6.4 outlines features within sample procedures that may be used to evaluate particular auditor qualifications. The results of the evaluation and selection should be recorded and communicated to auditor candidates as quickly as possible.

Work assignment–related
- Audits conducted against management system standards for hardware, software, or process or service industries
- Service or product type and its associated regulatory requirements (for example, health care, food, or nuclear devices)

Audit team–related
- Audit team size
- Audit team skill composition
- Audit team leadership requirements
- Training needs for new auditor or lead auditor

Auditor-related
- Professional qualifications or technical expertise required in a particular discipline
- Personal skills required to deal with a specific auditee
- Language skills required
- Real or perceived conflict of interest

Figure 6.3   Assignment considerations.

To evaluate knowledge
- Review the candidate's written work
- Obtain evidence (such as an examination) that the candidate has the required knowledge
- Administer a separate competency exam using a company scenario

To evaluate experience
- Seek outside confirmation of the candidate's experience level
- Interview the candidate to assess experience in detail

To evaluate personal skills and traits
- Consider information from the candidate's previous employers and colleagues, if available
- Seek feedback from auditee organizations the candidate has audited
- Interview the candidate to assess work style and personal style
- Perform role plays
- Observe the candidate working under actual audit conditions
- Administer a personality/personal attribute examination

Figure 6.4   Evaluation considerations.

Team Member Roles

Lead Auditor Selection and Duties

Every audit team has a lead auditor or audit team leader. Large teams may have a lead auditor as well as audit team leaders who lead small auditing groups and who report to the lead auditor. When the audit team consists of only one auditor, that auditor is the lead auditor. When more than one auditor is needed for an assignment, the lead auditor, usually an individual with supervisory experience or management capabilities, is identified prior to the other team members and participates in their selection. A lead auditor whose duties include auditing, directing, and monitoring team members usually has more auditing experience than other team members and is more familiar with the standard being audited against.

The lead auditor has ultimate responsibility for the satisfactory performance of all phases of the audit as well as for the professional conduct of the audit team members. As the representative of the entire audit team, the lead auditor is responsible for initiating and maintaining communication with the auditee. The lead auditor prepares the audit plan, conducts the opening and exit meetings, reviews the findings and observations of the auditors, and prepares and submits an audit report. The lead auditor may also conduct daily briefings with team members throughout the audit.

Just because an auditor has considerable auditing experience and expert knowledge of the audit criteria does not mean he or she would be an effective lead auditor or audit team leader. In fact, many experienced auditors have worked alone for many years, are self-motivated, and may feel uncomfortable with lead auditor responsibilities. Lead auditors need to be able to deal with people issues and adjust to social climate changes within the audit team and the auditee organization. A lead auditor that lacks people and project management skills can be a detriment to the auditing organization. Audit organizations may have senior or principal auditor job titles to recognize highly skilled auditors but not force them into the role of lead auditor, which requires higher levels of communication, project management, and social skills.

Audit Team Selection and Assignments

When preparing an audit plan, the lead auditor (and/or client or audit program manager) should assess the complexity of the activities to be audited and select team members who possess the qualifications or expertise needed to perform the audit. Qualified auditors must be knowledgeable in audit criteria such as ISO 9001, ISO 14001, the organization's quality assurance manual, cGMPs, and so on. Auditors should be familiar with the industry of the organization they are auditing. It is common for auditors to claim industry-sector experience based on prior work experience. System audits will be more effective if auditors understand the industry jargon and common processes for that type of organization.

When conducting system audits, auditors are not required to have specific job experience (for example, auditors are not required to have scheduling experience in order to audit the scheduling department). In the book *How to Audit the Process-Based QMS*, the authors state that "the audit team should be a balance of technical and management system knowledge. They must understand the processes used to produce the goods and services. They must also understand the business processes used to manage the organization so as to achieve quality objectives. They must know the interrelationships of the functional departments within the enterprise. This combination is best obtained by using people who have broad experience in both technical and administrative processes of the organization."[9] However, for process audits (versus system audits) it is important that auditors have related process experience.

If the area to be audited is highly specialized, the auditing organization may need to outsource or subcontract a specialist or expert experienced in that area. Some organizations may issue guidelines for the use of subject matter experts (SMEs) (see Appendix C, "Example Guide for Technical Specialists"). To avoid misunderstandings, an outside specialist, technical expert, or SME must be briefed as to his or her expected role prior to an audit. An audit team may be made up of qualified auditors, auditors-in-training, and support personnel as needed. Support personnel can include SMEs, administrative assistants, clerks, and translators.

Personnel are selected for specific auditing assignments on the basis of experience or training that indicates qualifications commensurate with the complexity of the activities to be audited.[10] The lead auditor is responsible for determining auditor assignments and communicating the assignments prior to the audit. The lead auditor should consider an auditor's work experience and education when making assignments. An audit team member's work experience and education may benefit the audit team and improve the effectiveness of the audit. For example, if a design group is being audited and one of the audit team members is an engineer, the lead auditor may consider assigning the engineer to audit the design group. Each auditor is responsible for preparing suitable working papers for his or her portion of the audit.

The responsibility of an audit team is to gather factual evidence of conformance or nonconformance (compliance or noncompliance) of the audited area to the audit criteria. Since the audit function intrudes on daily operations, an auditor has a duty to gather information promptly, objectively, and considerately. After comparing and analyzing observations, an audit team should be able to draw conclusions about the systems and report those findings in a timely manner.

Additionally, audit team members should be free from biases or conflicts of interest, comply with standards of ethical conduct, and exercise due care in the performance of their duties. To ensure an effective audit, audit team members must be able to report the audit results objectively and impartially.

The audit team members are listed in the audit plan. The plan should include individual auditor certifications, such as ASQ CQA. The plan may include individual assignments if the lead auditor thinks it is appropriate for communication purposes. If included in the audit plan, area assignments may represent specific experience or expertise such as purchasing, engineering, testing, piloting, IT, nondestructive testing, and so on. The audit interview schedule serves as a record of audit team assignments.

In addition to selecting qualified auditors who will be impartial and objective, a lead auditor or audit program manager must consider the demeanor of the auditor and audit team dynamics. According to ISO 19011, clause 5.4.4, Selecting the audit team, when selecting the audit team, the person managing the audit program should consider the ability of the audit team members to interact effectively with the representatives of the auditee and to work together. The lead auditor's awareness of team dynamics is an important consideration in ensuring an effective audit. As professionals, all auditors should be able to work together; however, there may be situations where strained relationships between auditors impede the effectiveness and efficiency of the audit process.

In summary, the number of personnel needed and their experience and qualifications depend on the amount of material to be covered, the availability of personnel and other audit resources, the amount of time available to perform the audit, and the subject of the audit.[11] For instance, a management system audit of a bank will require different auditor skills than an audit of technical areas for a chemical processing operation or a robotics or software company.

3. AUDIT-RELATED DOCUMENTATION

Examination of Audit-Related Documentation

Before performing an audit, an auditor must secure documentation of the policies or practices and procedures of a company so that conformity of a product, process, or system with the requirements specified in the documents may be assessed. The lead auditor should contact the auditee to determine the availability of documents related to the audit criteria and to request copies or online access. Proprietary material contained in the documents may be removed before the documents are sent to an auditor, or online security programs may block access. Historically, paper has been the conventional form of documentation, but documentation may be in any medium that can be recorded, reviewed, and retrieved. For instance, computer files and audio and video recordings are all acceptable forms of documentation. Many companies have placed their controlled documents on an intranet for use and downloading by employees. The auditor may be asked to visit the organization's website and obtain the documents independently. If the audit is a second-party or third-party audit, it may be necessary for the auditee to brief the audit team on how to access, review, and retrieve online documents.

> For second-party audits where the relationship is subcontracted man-
> ufacturing or testing, the subcontractor would likely provide manu-
> facturing or testing records (or the auditor may already have access
> to them) but may not want to share procedures until during the audit.

Auditors observe, examine, and report compliance and conformance by assessing systems, processes, and products against documents related to the requirements making up the audit criteria. Processes are compared with objectives and
standards, while products are tested and inspected to determine conformance to
specifications or standards. The following documents specify requirements.

Manuals and Procedures

- Quality, environmental, safety, and health management manuals
- Procedures
- Work instructions
- Workmanship standards or models
- Service standards
- Software operating manuals
- Industry practices/methods
- Trade practices

Forms

- Completed forms such as purchase orders, failure modes and effects
  analysis (FMEA) forms, and so on
- Blank forms used to record data

Plans

- Management system plans
- Strategic plans to identify objectives
- Control plans
- Project plans
- Quality plans
- Inspection plans
- Preventive maintenance plans
- Emergency plans
- Contingency plans
- Risk management plans

Documents for Each Project/Order

- Specifications

- Blueprints and drawings

- Detailed instructions

- Routing cards

- Schedules

- Batch records

- Testing records

Other Documents

- Flowcharts

- Process maps

- Process flow diagrams (PFDs)

- Certificates of compliance

Written procedures, if available, are reviewed before an audit starts, because the policies, specifications, and standards drive the audit preparation. In an audit with a scope limited to training in an organization, for example, the appropriate part of the standard that describes the training requirements becomes part of the documentation for that audit, along with the corporate training policy, the records of training for the individuals involved, and the plan for training.

Sufficient documentation is secured before an audit so that the auditor can determine whether the system is properly designed. The data collection phase (on-site or remote) of the audit will then determine whether the system is functioning satisfactorily. Information contained in documents must be appropriate, adequate, and current if the documentation is to be used in decision making. A manual may contain a master list of documents or other similar documentation information to instruct the auditor how to locate and obtain applicable documents. Reviewing these documents before the audit helps an auditor prepare working papers and determine where to concentrate effort during the performance stage.

Documentation should meet minimum expectations in identifying the organization's requirements and what the policy of the organization is relative to meeting those requirements. The audit team should review the documentation to ensure that it meets and complies with the requirements of the applicable standards and laws/regulations. A matrix or table relating each requirement to the location in the company's documentation where it is addressed will greatly help the audit team make this determination as well as help the company ensure that all requirements have been adequately addressed.

A key consideration during this phase is whether the bits and pieces of a system noted in procedures and instructions compose a cohesive, integrated set of interconnected activities—interconnected in the sense that the outputs of one activity constitute the inputs to the subsequent activities—and whether adequate and appropriate intrasystem controls and feedback provide for prompt response to activities not accomplishing their desired outputs.

Auditors must safeguard and protect any documents or information they are given access to. Documents and information must be safeguarded against damage, loss, or unauthorized access. Auditors must never remove documents from their storage location or delete files online without permission to do so. Copies of documents, information, or data must be authorized.

Review Performance History

The auditee organization will have a performance history unless the audit is an initial audit or qualification survey. Knowledge of the auditee organization performance history will help ensure that positive practices continue and problems are corrected.

When prior audit information exists, it should be reviewed as part of an auditor's checklist to ensure that corrective action has been implemented effectively. Sometimes a prior observation may be reported that was not a violation but an emerging trend. During audit preparation, an auditor may examine data to see if this trend has continued or if action has been taken to reverse it.

Another reason to review past audit records is to identify specific areas that are likely to have continuing or repeat problems and to determine the status of actions taken earlier to resolve any noncompliance/nonconformance. The audit team should verify that the corrective actions implemented following previous audits have remained in effect and that they have prevented the problem or noncompliance from recurring.[12]

For internal audits, performance data may already be available to the auditor. For second- and third-party audits, the performance data may need to be requested before or during the audit. Performance data may relate to the product, process, or system.

One of the most common performance records reviewed by auditors is the prior audit report. The review may be for the auditor's professional benefit, or the client may request that the auditor verify corrective actions from prior audits as part of the audit purpose. If the client has a concern about the objectivity of the prior audit, the client may instruct the current audit team not to review the prior audit.

Performance records to be reviewed may include:

- Prior audit reports

- Customer feedback

- Corrective and preventive action records

- Product returns

- Product warranty claims and complaints

- Product quality levels

- Process and unit performance compared to goals

- Organization and business performance

- Customer surveys

- Field reports

- Regulatory citations (if not confidential)

- Risk assessments (product, service, versus objectives)

Auditors should be especially interested in product, process, and system changes since the last audit. Changes represent both desirable improvements and potential risks that should be avoided. Continual improvement of a management system or process is a good thing that auditors should encourage. However, auditors can provide a value-added service by ensuring that changes achieve objectives and that other system elements are not at risk.

4. LOGISTICS

Logistics Planning

Audit logistical planning is necessary for both audit team coordination and establishing auditee communication links. Good planning will result in a smooth, seamless audit performance. Poor planning will make the audit team appear less professional and might jeopardize meeting the audit objectives. Auditors need to arrive at the right place at the right time, with the right equipment and information and a suitable duration of time to get the job done right. To help the auditor think through what is necessary to start the audit process, it is prudent to outline a detailed logistical plan.[13]

The logistics of an audit are a crucial part of the planning process anytime the auditor must travel to the audit location. The following items should be included in the logistical plan:

- A timeline for arrival, meetings, and interviews.

- Location and time of the opening and exit meetings.

- A request for an audit team meeting place, such as a conference room, for team debriefings and discussions of observations. It should be equipped with a telephone or cell phone access, electrical outlets, table and chairs, and any other equipment needed to conduct audit activities (for example, computers with internet access [wireless or hardwire], printer, scanner, fax machine, and a data projector).

- For remote or e-audits, a room needs to be identified for virtual meetings and interviews. Equipment includes audio and video hardware and software. Internet access speeds for uploads may need to be specified to ensure adequate video streaming.

- A request for facility layout maps, office locations, confidential areas, and so on, and any special requirements such as safety, environmental, or health equipment, including steel-toed shoes, hard hat, lab coat, hair net, head cover, grounding devices, hearing protection, and safety glasses.

- Travel plans, possibly identifying an audit team rendezvous prior to the opening meeting and including extra time to meet at a nearby hotel and become familiar with the area.

- Hotel arrangements and requirements such as table space, wireless high-speed internet access, printer-scanner-fax facilities, room service for late-night meetings, and transportation service to the airport.

An auditor who must travel to the audit location should ask the auditee about suitable lodging in the area so as to avoid expensive hotels, fleabags, and hotels requiring a long commute to the audit site. The auditee may make the hotel reservation in order to receive a corporate discount. The auditor should request a map to the location of the audit (including travel times). If the audit site is large, a facility or building map may be needed as well.[14]

Confirmation of Audit Logistics

The logistics plan should be sent to the auditee well in advance of the audit. The audit team leader should then contact the auditee to confirm that the timing is acceptable and that meeting space will be available.

The number of logistical issues will depend on whether the audit is internal or external, on-site or remote, the size of the organization, the size of the audit team, and the complexity of the area to be audited. Issues particular to on-site audits include but are not necessarily limited to:

- Meeting rooms for audit team use and for daily auditee briefings

- Office space for auditors to review past observations and prepare for the next interview

- Special safety, environmental, or security issues, as well as orientation and training programs

- Access to telephones or cell phones, high-speed internet, and other means to communicate with the auditee, audit team members, and audit program manager

- The distance between areas to be visited and logistical difficulties for bringing team members together

- Personnel facilities (rest rooms, lunchroom, break area, smoking area)

Issues for both on-site and remote audits or eAudits include:

- Access to necessary facilities and equipment required for verification activities

- Access to documents and records needed, such as manuals, procedures, process flowcharts, process maps, and PFDs

- Facilities or locations for the safe storage of proprietary and confidential information (this is especially important for remote audits or eAudits)

- Permission to use cell phones, cameras, or recording devices

- Permission for any out-of-the-ordinary event, such as a mandatory conference call from the main office, a personal call related to a family crisis that would require a change in the audit team, or a cancellation or rescheduling of the audit

- Availability of escorts or on-site guides

- Presentations and tours related to the area being audited

Most logistical items should be addressed before the data collection phase or performance phase activities, but no later than the close of the opening meeting if an on-site audit.

Escort

An auditee should provide an escort for each subgroup of the audit team. (An exception can be made for internal audits if the auditor is already familiar with the organization and activities being audited.) The escort accompanies the auditor on the entire data-gathering portion of the audit and serves as a liaison between the auditing organization and auditee management. The escort ensures that safety rules are followed, performs personnel introductions, and provides clarifying information as needed. For example, an escort can suggest a way of rephrasing a question, perhaps by substituting terminology more familiar to the person being interviewed. However, the escort should refrain from answering questions for the auditee unless asked to do so by the auditor.

Other duties of the escort include:

- Providing or requesting supplies and records required by the auditor

- Acting as an observer for management and providing an overview of the auditor's observations, findings, and conclusions to auditee management

- Acting as a guide for the auditor

- Confirming or denying that a discrepancy or nonconformity has been found before moving on to the next area to be audited

- Ensuring that auditors comply with company rules, including safety rules

- Ensuring communication equipment is functioning properly if a remote audit

If an escort suggests that the auditee may not understand the question, it may be possible that the escort or the interviewee is trying to dodge the question, or it may be that he or she doesn't understand the audit process terminology used by the auditor. In either case, the auditor should continue collecting the audit evidence necessary to verify conformity by the most effective means available.

Tours

A tour of the area to be audited is permissible and oftentimes highly desirable. An auditor may tour this area as part of a preaudit visit to review documents or before or after the opening meeting. Day-of-the-audit tours and presentations should be scheduled and are normally very brief (less than an hour). If tour activities start to take too much time, the lead auditor should politely curtail them so that the audit schedule remains on track.

In *Quality Audits for Improved Performance*, the author states, "Another way to understand the activity is to take a tour of the place. Watch the operations taking place and notice the location of major equipment. The tour is informal and short, generally without the rest of your team. What if you find something really bad? You have this natural desire to call home and report it. In doing so, you have started your audit—without a checklist, opening meeting, or even a team! You have totally destroyed the trust and respect building between auditors and auditees. Because of these dangers, think carefully before going on a pre-audit tour."[15]

In the book *The Process Auditing Techniques Guide*, the author explains, "For complex or external process audits, a post [opening] meeting tour is a good technique to become familiar with the layout, identify changes since the last audit, and align what you see with your expectations (the PFD). Tours should be brief. During the tour you should start recording numbers and observations. You should record part, batch, lot, traveler, routing card, form, room number, transaction, customer identification number, and order numbers. When doing a system audit or complex process audit, the auditor must have a means to connect the different processes. Knowing what is being processed, readied to ship, or what the new inputs are will be very useful."[16] However, auditors should not start their investigation at that time and should remember that they will have plenty of time during the interviews and data collection phase to get their questions answered.

5. AUDITING TOOLS AND WORKING PAPERS

Preparation of Audit Checklists, Guidelines, and Log Sheets

An audit checklist is the primary tool for bringing order to an audit. A well-planned and well-defined checklist helps ensure the audit will be comprehensive. Without a checklist, an auditor has a disjointed, disorganized activity and no place to record failed efforts. Before developing the checklists, an auditor must know what the governing requirement's documents say.

A completed checklist provides:

- Objective evidence that an audit was performed

- Order and organization

- A record that all applicable aspects of the program were examined

- Historical information on program, systems, or supplier problems

- The essence for the exit meeting and audit report

- An information base for planning future audits

- A vehicle for time management

- Sampling plans and strategies

The purpose of a checklist is to gather information during the course of an audit that the auditor will need in order to justify the audit findings and conclusion. The checklist guides each member of the audit team to ensure that the full scope of the audit is adequately covered. The checklist provides space for recording facts gathered during fieldwork, with places to answer questions and numerous areas for taking notes.

A *checklist* is a set of notes and instructions about specific areas, with specific questions to ask and specific techniques to use during an audit. Checklists or written procedures are used to ensure continuity and comprehensive coverage of the area of interest. They also provide evidence of the questions that were reviewed and a record of the review.[17]

A checklist may contain a standard set of information that every auditor looks for, such as the following:

- Does the person being audited have access to written procedures and applicable work instructions?

- Is the procedure up to date?

- Does the scope of this employee's training cover the observed activities?

- Is the organizational structure proper for what the employee is expected to do in the observed procedure?

- Are appropriate records being maintained?

The specific format and construction of a checklist may vary depending on what works best for the auditor. Some checklists are yes/no questions that reference a specified requirement, others are open-ended interview questions that test the limits of a procedure, and yet others are statements providing additional instructions for the auditor. Variations of checklist questions or statements may be: "Does the person being audited always have access to the latest version of the procedure?" "Verify—through observations, discussions, and review of documents—that individuals have access to written procedures and applicable work instructions that cover their activities."

In addition, many checklists contain a set of questions for each section of the requirement standard that is being audited against. This part of the checklist includes questions about management responsibilities, training, quality planning, and so on. These canned or generic checklist items should be supplemented with time- and circumstance-specific questions and observations that the auditor wants to make during the audit. Checklists should always be reviewed to make sure they are still current, since standards change.

Canned checklists with predetermined questions or statements from high-level documents such as ISO 9001 or ISO 14001 are very common. The use of canned checklists ensures all requirements are addressed, but they have limitations. In the book *The Internal Auditing Pocket Guide*, the author states that "canned checklists may not provide the flexibility that you may need for a specific audit. Canned checklists are good to use for comparison purposes, such as different suppliers, or comparing operating organizations."[18] Sole use of canned checklists can result in what is called a *checklist mentality*, with auditors asking only the questions on the checklist in audit after audit.

Deviations from the checklist may result from a change in the audit schedule or an observation that indicates a possible problem. A checklist can be expanded as necessary while still staying within the scope of the audit.[19]

An audit checklist is flexible; audit observations need not be restricted to what the auditor has planned. Also, it is permissible to abandon or make adjustments to the checklist items during daily meetings. A checklist is nonlimiting in that it does not restrict what an auditor needs to do, provided the auditor stays within the scope of the audit; it is simply a way to plan so that the auditor knows what to look for and observe in the given area.

The audit checklist may be forwarded to the auditee prior to the audit. This is a choice of the auditing organization. Normally, for first- and second-party audits, if the auditee requests a copy of the audit checklist, it is provided in the spirit of cooperation. Some audit organizations issue notifications when checklists are shared, to remind the auditee that the checklist is not the standard and that areas not on the checklist may be examined as long as they are within the purpose and scope of the audit.

It may benefit the auditor to review previous audits after the checklist is completed, to see if anything that was a concern in the past should be added. The reason for waiting to review previous audits is to avoid bias in audit preparation due to some historical event. If a previous audit had a corrective action that requires follow-up, this is the time to add it to the checklist. There may even have been some complaints that were not completely answered. These are important issues that cannot be ignored.

Guidelines are additional documented instructions that are considered good audit practice that may provide additional information for conducting the audit. Guidelines are not mandatory and are normally prepared in a statement format.

Log sheets are another kind of working paper prepared in advance of an audit. A log sheet contains auditor notes and becomes a record of activities performed during an audit—what the auditor observed and with whom the auditor talked.

> **Example Log Sheet**
>
> One example of a log sheet is a white ruled pad that chronologically details where the auditor went and who was interviewed.

Example Area Guidelines for an Auditor

- Make sure that posted instructions are approved (signed) and that any changes are also approved (signed).

- If cyclical reports are kept, be sure older ones are marked as historical or reference. This also applies to drawings or specifications.

- Everyone with a need to know should be able to use the intranet to view practices and specifications. Make sure all stations are capable.

- Changes (to routings, for example) must be approved (such as being initialed).

- All products should be identifiable (for example, routing, tag) and nonconforming material segregated in the Materials Review Board (MRB) area (quarantined) or status clearly marked.

- Housekeeping need not be what we do for VIPs, but there should be some orderliness, and debris should be removed.

- Any instruments used for pass/fail decisions or that potentially impact or measure product quality should be calibrated, and calibration checks should be up to date. Also check for dates that expire the following week.

- Personnel training records must be current and available.

Sampling Plan

A sampling plan must be developed for each audit. The audit program manager should determine the overall sampling policy and guidelines to avoid the personal bias and ensure consistency between audits. The type and extent of sampling for each individual audit are normally the responsibility of the auditor, based on the purpose and scope of the audit. Questions regarding the adequacy of the sampling plan should be addressed by the lead auditor.

The purpose of sampling is to gain information about an entire group of units, items, things, or people based on observing and/or inspecting a segment of the group. Sampling is a technique to gain the needed information at a reduced cost (compared to 100% inspection). To be valid, the segment or sample selected should be representative of the entire group. It is important that the sampled group be recorded. For example, an auditor may sample the shipping records for the current month or sample all corrective action records since the last audit. It is important that the auditor not let the auditee pick the samples. He or she may pick only favorable samples or pick the same ones from audit to audit. Samples include not only documents, records, and product but also areas or activities to observe and people to interview.

Sampling of information for an audit is not always statistically valid, however. The auditor normally does not have time to review a statistically valid sample from a large number of instruments that need calibration or a filing cabinet full of engineering records. In such cases, the auditor should quantify the number of instruments or records evaluated and identify the areas where they were obtained. Items from a population could be sampled several times; each time, the auditor will identify the number (quantity) and location. This sampling technique allows the client and the auditee to appreciate the significance of the results and better focus their corrective action activities. Reviewing instruments or documents from a variety of areas, although not statistically sound, will reveal if a problem is systemic or focused in certain areas.[20]

Statistically valid sampling plans are normally used for product, process, and compliance audits. It would be common for a product audit plan to require statistically valid sampling.

Working Papers

Working papers include the documents we have discussed in this section. Overall, working papers facilitate the auditor's investigation and are used to record and report results. Working papers are an aid to the auditor and should not restrict the scope of the audit activities or hinder the effectiveness of the investigation or report.

Audit Trail Documentation

Auditors require working papers to record audit results during fact-finding interviews. The following working papers may be used during audits:

- Related audit procedures/instructions/guidelines
- Sampling plans
- Pertinent audit standards (if any)
- Questionnaire (questions requiring evidence)
- Audit checklists (yes/no, sufficient/deficient, acceptable/not acceptable)
- Memory joggers
- Auditee feedback/evaluation forms
- Log sheets/forms
- Forms to record negative results that require corrective or preventive action
- Attendance record form

Audit checklists and questionnaires provide objective evidence of conformance as well as providing consistency between auditors. Forms and other papers may also be used to record objective evidence. Working papers provide a place to record not only observations during the audit but also historical evidence of the audit when the audit is complete. Because working papers are audit records, the lead auditor should approve all working papers used during the audit.

Record of Observations

Recorded observations provide the audit evidence for reporting the results of the investigation. It is imperative that auditors record their observations rather than relying on memory. Observations must be traceable back to where they were made to ensure credibility.

Auditors should obtain the auditee's acknowledgment (not agreement) of observations identified as noncompliance/nonconformance or negative findings. Auditee acknowledgment provides support for the auditor's work during the exit meeting. This acknowledgment also confirms the auditee's review and agreement that nonconformities were noted. Obtaining the auditee's acknowledgment of nonconformities prior to the exit meeting ensures a more productive exit meeting. If the auditor has effectively communicated with the auditee, there should be no surprises during the audit or during the exit meeting.

Observations can be positive or negative. Positive observations may be reported as a positive practice, a noteworthy achievement, or a positive finding. Negative observations may be reported as part of a noncompliance/nonconformity or finding.

6. AUDITING STRATEGIES

Regardless of whether the subject of the audit is a product, process, or system, the auditor should use a general auditing strategy, or audit path, so that data are collected in a logical and methodical manner. Effective audit planning ensures that an auditor will have the time and the means to conduct a thorough investigation of the audited organization that is consistent with its purpose and scope. It also enables the auditor to segment the audit by element or department, or to use the discovery method or tracing techniques to gather data. Adhering to such strategies helps an auditor gain insight into the actual practices employed throughout an organization and assists in the identification of problems.

Tracing

Tracing, or following the chronological progress of something as it is processed, is a common and effective means of collecting objective evidence during an audit. In forward tracing, an auditor starts at the beginning or middle of a manufacturing or service process, for example, and traces forward (downstream). In backward tracing, the auditor starts at the middle or end of a process and traces backward (upstream). Backward tracing can be more revealing than forward tracing because the auditor examines the process from the perspective of seeing the results (product or service) of the preceding activity.

The mechanics of tracing are relatively simple:

- Start at the beginning, middle, or end of the process.

- Choose an action, such as painting a wall.

- Gather information on the six process forces (methods, machinery, material, manpower, measurement, and environment) for that action. Be sure to record this information on your checklist. Write down what you see, the person you are talking to, where you are, when the action was done, why the action is accomplished, how it is accomplished, and how well the action was performed (results). These become your facts for later use.

- Follow the path of the transaction backward or forward through the process.[21]

Tracing may be used in process and system audits. The tracing method is useful when a procedure is unclear, when the audit evidence to verify conformity or nonconformity is elusive, and when evaluating performance issues. Tracing is also used as a strategy for process audits and auditing process-based management systems.

Part IIA

Process Method

The *process method* is an expansion of the tracing technique for use as an over-all audit strategy. The process method, or process technique, tests the sequential steps and interaction of activities and processes. The process method uses a flowchart, process map, or PFD as a guide during the audit. For a process audit, the scope may be a single process; for a system audit of a process-based management system, the scope may be the design function, purchasing, laboratory, document control, or operations. When auditing a process-based management system, the sequence and interaction of processes have already been defined. However, for an audit of a single activity or process, it is common for auditors to create their own flowchart.

The process method is effective for identifying weaknesses within the organization's management system, breakdowns in securing appropriate inputs, and achievement of output objectives. A disadvantage of the process method is a lack of linkage to requirements in external standards to ensure ongoing conformance/compliance. In the book *How to Audit a Process-Based QMS*, the authors recommend that organizations that have a process-based management system audit by function. If all the functions are audited against all the external standard requirements, there will be a high level of confidence that the organization conforms.

To conduct effective audits, auditors should:

- View the management system as a set of integrated processes (by understanding the interfaces and interactions)
- Adopt the process approach for audits
- Add value by looking at more than just conformity
- Evaluate the linked processes for their "effectiveness"
- Verify process controls and identify any process risks
- Determine opportunities for improvement[22]

An example of a process method audit is a subcategory called *product line audit*. This audit is used to follow an item that has undergone maintenance backward through the system to ensure all requirements—such as calibrated equipment, processes performed (including subcontractor qualification), personnel training, and all process certifications—are present and correct. See Appendix J, "Product Line Audit Flowchart."

Department Method

The *department method* is another way of dividing an auditing task that works especially well when accountability at the department or function level is important. The auditor focuses on the entire operation of one department or function rather than on segments of it by reviewing numerous elements within the department or function. This auditing strategy touches on almost everything in an audited facility. Here, the auditor's ability to identify applicable elements for that department is put to the test. While this is an excellent strategy when the audit team wishes "to slice the apple a different way," it should not be overused. Focusing too much on one small group of people (one department) may not accurately represent what is happening throughout an organization.

Element Method

The *element method* is a commonly employed auditing strategy that can refer to any element of any standard or the auditee's management system. Examples of elements are:

- 18 elements from 10 CFR 50, Appendix B

- 10 elements from 10 CFR 830, Subpart A (120–122)

- Categories from the Malcolm Baldrige National Quality Award

- Elements (clauses) from the ISO 9001 QMS standard

The auditor examines each element individually to see how it affects the entire system. This method is thorough and adequate in a single-system audit with a team of auditors. The advantage of the element method is that there is direct linkage between external requirements and verification of conformity/compliance.

In the book *The Internal Auditing Pocket Guide*, the author explains that the "element method is auditing horizontally across different departments or units. It is good for linkage to standards. The element method has been abused in the past, which has resulted in very narrowly defined audit scopes that do not include inputs, outputs, and other process linkages."[23]

Discovery Method

The *discovery method* is sometimes called random auditing. This method investigates what is currently taking place and therefore reflects prevailing work procedures. However, the discovery method offers no discernible pattern to an audit, and an auditor can become disoriented or spend too much time in the facility.[24]

In most situations, the discovery method should not have to be used if the audit has been adequately planned. However, this method can be effective if the auditor knows that a problem exists but has not yet located it. By going into the audit area and looking around, an auditor may be able to bring the problem to the surface. However, the auditee may perceive that the auditor is only interested in finding a nonconformity to report (sometimes called a witch hunt). The discovery method is not a substitute for adequate process audit preparation.

To compare auditing strategies, refer to Table 6.1.

Table 6.1 Summary of auditing strategies.

Strategy	Advantages	Disadvantages
Tracing	• Applied anytime during a system audit to follow sequential steps of a work instruction or procedure forward or backward • Able to identify inputs and outputs • Able to select different audit paths (forward, middle, or reverse) Note: Historically, tracing has been used during system audits as a tool to collect additional evidence when needed to verify conformity or nonconformity.	• Difficult to verify element requirements of a standard • Not able to assess overall system effectiveness
Process	• Applied to process audits for following sequential process steps from inputs to outputs • Verification and validation of procedures and work instructions • Investigate problems to identify root causes • Follow-up corrective actions • Identify opportunities for improvement at the process level Note: Process and tracing strategies are very similar except process strategies are normally applied to an entire process audit.	• Auditors need to be knowledgeable of the process being audited • Difficult to verify element requirements of a standard • Not able to assess overall system effectiveness
Process-based management system	• Apply to a management system by aligning requirements of a standard with the natural order of a process • Verify sequential steps as applied to the elements of the standard • Verify element requirements of a management system standard • Verify system effectiveness • Identify opportunities for improvement at the system level	• Takes longer than an element strategy • Limited to verification of controls required by a standard • Auditors may require training in the process-based auditing strategy
Department	• Audit focused on a particular department for a specific purpose such as performance and criticality of the function • Able to use any audit strategy • Can be used to verify multiple requirements for a single department	• Limited to the particular department and does not assess interaction with other functions

Table 6.1   Summary of auditing strategies. *(continued)*

Strategy	Advantages	Disadvantages
Element	• Verify organization conforms to each element requirement • Most efficient method to verify document or standard requirements are implemented • Good traceability between requirements and organization actions	• Interaction of system and processes not verified • A compliant system may not be an effective system
Discovery	• Requires the least amount of planning and preparation • Uncover problem areas not previously known	• Conclusions about the areas audited are limited or suspect

7. COMMUNICATION AND DISTRIBUTION OF THE AUDIT PLAN

An *audit plan* is the primary product and communication tool of the preparation phase of the audit process. An audit plan is not the same as an audit schedule. The audit plan tells us what will be covered in a particular system audit or sequence of process audits. The *audit schedule* tells us what audits will be performed within a certain block of time.[25] Figure 6.1 showed a sample audit plan.

Communication of an Audit Plan

Before issuing an audit plan, the lead auditor should contact the auditee to verify the proposed date of the audit. According to ISO 19011, clause 6.3.2, "The audit plan may be reviewed and accepted by the audit client, and should be presented to the auditee. Any objections by the auditee to the audit plan should be resolved between the audit team leader, the auditee and the audit client."

After an audit plan has been finalized, the date and logistics of the impending audit should be confirmed and recorded. For an internal audit, notification is done by memo or published schedule. For a second- or third-party audit, it is done by letter. The notification letter or memo should be addressed to the senior person in charge of the area to be audited or his or her designee, such as an auditee coordinator. For internal audits, this person is probably the department manager or area superintendent. For external audits, it is probably the plant manager, president, or head of quality. Figure 6.5 shows a sample audit notification letter.

Even if the lead auditor prepares the letter or memo, the client should sign it. This formal notice should be delivered before the visit. The timing of the notice should be consistent with organizational procedures and common courtesy, varying from one week to several months. An advance notice of 30 days is common but not required. For some compliance audits or those where there is suspicion of wrongdoing, there may be no notification.

February 23, 20XX

Mr. Dale Smith
1 ABC Blvd.
ABC Industries
ABC, FL XXXXX

Dear Dale,

The audit team will perform a quality system audit of the ABC facility to assess conformance to ISO 9001 standard requirements. The scope of the audit will be limited to the requirements stated in ISO 9001 and existing internal quality system policies and procedures. The audit process will be conducted according to recognized auditing conventions as defined for ASQ Certified Quality Auditors.

You should plan for the audit to require two days of on-site interviewing and verifying of requirements. A draft report will be left after the audit, and the final report will be forwarded within two business days. Jane Red and I will be the auditors.

The on-site audit is scheduled for March 23 through March 24. The audit team will need a room with a table, telephone, internet access, and electrical outlets for computers and printers. The audit plan is enclosed. As agreed, please forward the management system manual to my attention to arrive no later than two weeks before the scheduled audit.

Thank you for your cooperation in making the necessary arrangements for the planned audit. If you have any questions I can be reached at XXX-XXX-XXXX or John.Doe@anymail.com.

Sincerely,

John Doe
John Doe, ASQ CQA

Chip Jones
Chip Jones, Client

Copy: Jane Red
Enclosures: 1

Figure 6.5   Notification letter.

Distribution of an Audit Plan

Members of an audit team receive copies of the audit plan, as does the auditee. The auditee is responsible for distributing the audit plan within the organization to be audited.

Several parallel activities are involved in the preparation of an audit plan: scheduling the audit, notifying the auditee, and lining up audit resources. Once the audit plan is prepared, it is formally communicated to the auditee. The lead auditor should publish the audit plan, notify the client and the auditee of the impending audit, and confirm that any special needs or plans, such as travel requirements, communication devices, or equipment and security clearances, have been arranged. Once these steps have been completed, the performance stage of the audit may begin.

Problems Commonly Encountered during the Audit Planning Stage

Problems likely to be encountered during the planning stage of an audit include difficulties related to the availability of personnel and other audit resources and scheduling the audit.

Availability of Audit Team Personnel

A common detriment or hindrance to effective planning for an internal audit is the reluctance of some organizations to release their people to do effective audit planning. For many organizations, audit team members are not full-time members of a quality, environmental, or safety department staff or of an auditing organization. They are either volunteers or people drafted from other areas of the company, such as production, accounting, engineering, sales, and personnel. It is often difficult for them to find the time needed to effectively plan an audit—generally four to six hours per person.

Availability of Other Resources

The lack of availability of other resources, such as funding, can have an effect on audit planning. Another potential problem is that the auditee may fail to forward the necessary documents to the auditor in time to allow adequate preparation.

Scheduling Difficulties

Other events often take priority and make the audit difficult to schedule. Such events could include a major reorganization or a merger. Perhaps the auditee has just received a major contract, or the audit is scheduled at the same time a regulatory agency plans a visit. The audit is an important event, but sometimes other events take priority.

Auditee Availability

At times, in spite of all good intentions, some auditees cannot be available due to prior business commitments or personal emergencies. If the auditee shows reluctance or wants to postpone the audit because of problems with readiness or availability, it means that he or she is not ready to be audited for customer approval or certification. Therefore, the audit should be postponed or canceled.

Chapter 7
Audit Performance/Part IIB

The performance phase of an audit is often called the *fieldwork*. It is the data-gathering portion of the audit and covers the time period from arrival at the audit location up to the exit meeting. It consists of the following activities:

- On-site audit management

- Meeting with the auditee

- Understanding the process and system controls

- Verifying that these controls work

- Communicating among team members

- Communicating with the auditee[1]

1. ON-SITE AUDIT MANAGEMENT

The lead auditor is responsible for managing the audit process. The audit is a process with inputs and outputs. Prior to arriving at the audit location, the lead auditor should confirm that all other auditors are properly prepared and that they are aware of the location and starting time. The lead auditor is also responsible for managing any audit risk identified by the audit program manager or client as well as identifying any new risk to the audit objectives. The lead auditor is determined by the client or the audit program manager; this terminology should not be confused with national certification programs that classify auditors as an auditor or a lead auditor.

Audit Team Management

The lead auditor should convene the audit team in a quiet location in the facility or in a conference room at least once a day throughout an audit. Some teams prefer to hold daily meetings in the morning, while others prefer to hold them before lunch or at the end of the day. The timing of the meeting is less important than the topics discussed.

First, audit team members share the information they have gathered so far. Then team members propose conclusions or identify potential problem areas on the basis of the information gathered. If contradictory information has been gathered or if team members disagree about what has been observed, the team must

82

gather additional information. Finally, in an effort to keep the audit on schedule, the audit team discusses what areas may need more or less attention than originally thought. This discussion redirects or modifies the remaining audit schedule, which helps keep the audit on track and prevents the audit team from becoming distracted by minor issues.

Between meetings, the audit team members are on their own. If a team member runs into a problem during the audit and is uncertain about how to handle the situation, he or she should contact the lead auditor immediately.

The ISO 19011:2011, clause 6.4.4, Guidance, indicates the audit team should confer periodically to (a) exchange information, (b) assess audit progress and when needed, and (c) reassign work between audit team members. Clause 6.4.8, Guidance, indicates that audit teams should confer to (a) review the audit findings and any other appropriate information collected during the audit against the audit objectives, (b) agree on the audit conclusions, taking into account the uncertainty inherent in the audit process, (c) prepare recommendations, if specified by the audit objectives, and (d) discuss audit follow-up, if included in the audit plan.

In general, daily meetings help an audit team do the following: (1) discuss and confirm observations and potential findings, (2) determine whether they relate to other areas being audited, (3) plan for the next day, and (4) prepare for the daily meeting with the auditee. If there is only one auditor, the auditor should allow time to review the information collected and prepare for the next step. Daily meetings may not be appropriate for process audits with a limited scope and only one auditor.

Communication of Audit Status to Auditee

At the beginning or end of each day, the audit team should meet with the auditee to discuss what will be or has been done that day. This meeting gives the lead auditor an opportunity to explain what has been looked at, what will be observed next, and where problems may exist.

Communicating potential findings every day serves two purposes. First, the auditee can communicate potential findings up the chain of command so that auditee management is aware of problems before the exit meeting. Second, the auditee can either confirm or deny that a problem exists. An auditee who believes that a problem does not exist can offer more data in an attempt to demonstrate to the auditor that there is not a problem.

A daily meeting of the audit team and the auditee can help prevent difficult situations, such as auditee management's refusing to acknowledge the audit team's findings at the exit meeting. If an auditee will not agree to a daily meeting, the lead auditor must take responsibility for informing the escort and area supervisors of potential findings in an area. For internal audits, formal meetings may not be needed or desirable. However, the auditee should still be informed daily of progress and any significant nonconformities, whether by voice mail, e-mail, on-the-spot conversations, or other means.

Audit Plan Changes

The lead auditor ensures that any change in the audit plan or schedule is proactively discussed during the opening meeting and obtains consensus for changes. The lead auditor needs to be flexible enough to make changes in the audit plan and schedule at the auditee's request. This is critically important to ensure that the audit gets off to a good start. At the same time, the lead auditor must be understanding if the auditee refuses to make schedule changes at the request of the audit team.

The lead auditor ensures that all discussed and agreed-upon schedule changes are fully documented in a revised schedule and communicated to all involved parties or departments prior to the interview process. The auditors are responsible for ensuring that audit plan changes do not result in sacrificing the original time allocations established to effectively evaluate conformance to requirements.

The ISO 19011, clause 6.4.4, Communications during the audit, provides the following guidance:

> During the audit, the audit team leader should periodically communicate the status of the audit and any concerns to the auditee and audit client, as appropriate. Evidence collected during the audit that suggests an immediate and significant risk (e.g., safety, environmental, or quality) should be reported without delay to the auditee and, as appropriate, to the audit client. Any concern about an issue outside the audit scope should be noted and reported to the audit team leader, for possible communication to the audit client and auditee.
>
> Where the available audit evidence indicates that the audit objectives are unattainable, the audit team leader should report the reasons to the audit client and the auditee to determine the appropriate action. Such action can include reconfirmation or modification of the audit plan, changes to the audit objectives or audit scope, or termination of the audit.
>
> Any need for changes in the audit scope which can become apparent as on-site auditing activities progress should be reviewed with and approved by the audit client and, as appropriate, the auditee.

Discussion of Auditee Concerns

It is normal for an auditee to be concerned about an audit. He or she may be unfamiliar with the auditor's methods and demeanor. The auditee may become overly concerned about potential nonconformities due to personal or organization expectations or objectives. The opening meeting and daily briefings can serve to lessen auditee anxiety.

For third-party audits, the lead auditor addresses and obtains consensus for the following potential concerns of the auditee during the opening meeting:

- Audit plan or schedule changes

- Nonconformity or noncompliance reporting

- Process for providing additional evidence to address a potential nonconformance or finding

For second-party audits, the lead auditor addresses all clarifications related to the criteria or guidelines against which the audit will be performed and the usage of the audit results.

For first-party audits, the lead auditor addresses concerns related to the reflection of auditee job performance based on the audit results. Auditee difficulties with the implementation of a procedure or work instruction are the greatest concern during first-party audits. It may be helpful if the auditor emphasizes that the systems and processes are being audited and not the individual employees.

Final Team Meeting

The final audit team meeting is held after improvement areas have been identified and just prior to the exit meeting. The team collects all information and identifies significant areas to be mentioned at the exit meeting. The team:

- Decides on the content and emphasis of the report
- Summarizes all nonconformities/noncompliances and/or findings
- Finalizes a list of opportunities for improvement
- Decides on a list of positive practices or noteworthy achievements

The lead auditor prepares a preliminary draft of the audit report based on the conclusions formed at this meeting. The draft report can be handwritten or typed on a computer. Chapter 8 presents additional information about audit conclusions and reporting the results of the investigation.

2. OPENING MEETING

Introduction

Soon after the arrival of the audit team at the audit site, the audit team and the auditee gather for an opening meeting, sometimes called a preaudit conference or entrance meeting. This meeting starts the data-gathering phase of the audit. Both on-site and remote audits require an opening meeting.

The management systems auditing standard (ISO 19011) states that the purpose of the opening meeting is to:

- Confirm the agreement of all parties to the audit plan
- Introduce the audit team
- Ensure that all planned audit activities can be performed

Review of the Audit Plan and Audit Activities

The following action items may need to be included in the opening meeting:

- Introduce participants, including audit team members, guides, and observers, and outline their roles
- Establish communication links and the role of the escort
- Communicate the audit plan by:
  - Reviewing and confirming the scope and purpose of the audit
  - Reaffirming audit criteria and the reference standards being used
  - Describing the methods and procedures to be used during the audit, including evidence based on samples taken

- Inform the auditee how the results will be reported (nonconformities, noncompliances, findings, improvement points, or other) and the methods used to classify, grade, and/or rank (prioritize) results

- Confirm that the auditee will be kept informed of the audit progress

- Inform the auditee of the possible outcomes of the audit

- Confirm logistics such as hours, escorts, tentative schedules, needed facilities, and availability of resources

- Confirm time and date of exit meeting as well as interim auditee daily briefings

- Confirm health, safety, emergency, and security procedures

- Ensure that the audit team understands the confidentiality agreement

- Report identified audit risks to the auditee organization and how they will be monitored and/or treated. When appropriate, such as with internal audit team aspects, audit risks should be kept private and be addressed by the audit team and/or the auditing organization

Additionally, if applicable, the opening meeting may:

- Review the findings of previous audits

- Explain conditions that could result in terminating or canceling the audit

- Verify required security clearances

- Identify local language issues and concerns (different languages used in the workplace, slang, word-usage level)

- Identify work agreement requirements between management and labor that may affect the performance of the audit

- Review information about auditee feedback regarding auditee findings or audit process issues (normally done during the exit meeting)

- Discuss how to deal with potential findings during the audit

- Schedule training or a tutorial on navigation methods for electronic documentation software, if appropriate

The opening meeting establishes the best climate for developing rapport and sets the ground rules for conducting an audit. Before an audit starts, individuals should know the daily audit schedule and what to expect in the exit meeting, written report, corrective action requests, and possible follow-up. The structure of the opening meeting should be flexible, and the level of formality will depend on several factors, including the audit scope, the purpose, the size of the audit team, and whether the audit is internal or external.[2]

While an opening meeting should always take place, in the case of an internal audit, it is frequently short and informal. Often there is more interaction between the audit team and management in the preparation stage of internal audits. Since internal audits usually occur on a fairly regular basis, all parties normally understand what will be examined and the methods to be used before the audit takes place. Opening meetings for external audits are more formal than opening meetings for internal audits. In general, opening meetings for system audits are more formal than those for process or product audits.

For remote audits or eAudits, the opening meeting should include communication equipment and software issues as well as protocols for a microphone, a mouse, and desktop and keyboard controls. Use of a webcam or other means is recommended so that the participants can be viewed. There should be agreement on the scheduling methods and the collaborative meeting program.

Opening-Meeting Roles and Responsibilities

Roles and Responsibilities of an Auditor

The entire audit team should attend the opening meeting, which is conducted by the lead auditor or the audit team leader. The lead auditor prepares the meeting agenda and often hands out copies in advance. At the opening meeting, the lead auditor:

- Introduces audit team members and presents their credentials.

- Restates the purpose and scope of the audit in a clear and diplomatic fashion.

- May refer to previous audits of the facility and previously required corrective action.

- May ask specific questions as a result of the document review or other information provided to the audit team.

- Solicits areas of interest from the auditee or mentions areas of specific concern.

- May present the audit checklist to the auditee.

- Sets the detailed audit schedule (see Figure 7.1 for an example).

- Describes the documents used to develop the audit plan.

- Ensures meeting minutes and attendance are recorded. (These duties may be completed by the lead auditor, or the lead auditor may assign the duties to an audit team member.)

- Verifies that auditee's management has communicated to employees and other interested parties, such as a union, that the audit is being conducted.

The lead auditor should also describe the audit process and the anticipated benefits. The lead auditor should allow time in the schedule to answer any questions from auditee personnel.

Day one: March 23, 20XX

Item/Element	Area/Function	Contact	Auditor	Time
Opening meeting	Conference room	All	All	9–9:30 A.M.
Document control	Quality assurance	Ms. Apostrophe	Mr. Brackets	10–11 A.M.
Customer requirements	Marketing	Mr. Colon	Ms. Dash	10–11 A.M.
Design and development control	R&D	Ms. Parentheses	Mr. Brackets	11 A.M. — 12 P.M.

Figure 7.1 Detailed audit schedule.

Roles and Responsibilities of an Auditee

Auditors expect at least one representative of management to attend the opening meeting—for example, the person who coordinated the audit on behalf of the auditee organization. Other responsible and interested parties, such as the supervisors or managers of the areas to be audited, may attend. In some cases, the lead auditor may specifically request certain representatives or may suggest minimum attendance based on the auditor's judgment (for example, if the room is too small to hold many people, if the wrong people want to attend, or if there are culture issues). The auditee's senior management representative should be invited to introduce his or her attendees. For third-party audits, auditee management is expected to attend the opening meeting.

The auditee should be expected to achieve consensus with the auditor on the following:

- The individual who will represent the auditee on all matters during the audit

- Auditor access to areas and activities to be audited

- Facilities for the audit team's use

- Support personnel to be provided: escorts, specialists, line personnel, and so on

- Safety and regulatory requirements

- Protection of proprietary rights[3]

If members of an auditee's staff disagree with or need clarification on any of the lead auditor's statements, they should express an opinion or ask for clarification at this time. For example, if the stated scope of the audit does not match the auditee's expectations, the auditee must point this out at the opening meeting, rather than during or on completion of the audit.

Sometimes an auditee may wish to make a presentation to acquaint the auditor with the firm or give a plant tour to familiarize the auditor with the facility. Brief presentations or tours are permissible and at times highly desirable; but if too much time is spent on these activities, the lead auditor should politely halt the proceedings so that the audit schedule remains intact. The auditor should inquire in advance whether any safety, environmental, or health-risk presentations are required or suggested by the auditee so that they can be worked into the schedule.

> When an audit is not moving along as planned, the auditor can say:
>
> "I'm really enjoying this conversation, but all of us have a lot to do; so what do you say we get started?"
>
> "This tour has been very helpful, but I think it has accomplished what I needed; so let's start the audit interviews."
>
> "Since we have so many areas to cover today, can we speed things up so we don't have to stay after working hours to complete the audit?"
>
> "What's next on the schedule?" (The auditee notes the next step from the provided copy of the audit agenda.) "OK, let's move on so we don't affect the operation."

Schedule Daily Updates and Exit Meeting

Daily updates are scheduled during the opening meeting to keep the auditee regularly informed of the audit status. The auditee should be made aware that these meetings serve to:

- Ensure that the auditee is kept informed of the audit results

- Allow the auditee to provide additional information to the audit team

- Ensure that there are no surprises during the exit meeting

These daily updates are actually briefings (usually 15–30 minutes) on the issues and/or concerns the audit team has identified during the day. These meetings allow the auditee to provide additional information to the audit team and to confirm understanding of the day's results. The audit team can use the information to update the interview schedule or make minor adjustments to the audit plan, as appropriate, and to ensure that the audit objective is achieved.

The date and time of the exit meeting should also be confirmed to ensure that the appropriate people are available. Although the exit meeting is included in the audit plan, the date, time, and location should be confirmed during the opening meeting so that the audit team and the auditee have the opportunity to make any necessary adjustments.

3. AUDIT DATA COLLECTION AND ANALYSIS

An audit team may employ one auditing strategy or a combination of several auditing strategies during the data-gathering phase of an audit. As data are gathered, the audit team should reassemble periodically to sort the data and form tentative conclusions. If the data gathered are unclear or contradictory, the audit team should determine whether additional data are needed that can either confirm or deny tentative conclusions. The audit team is also responsible for ensuring that an auditee representative is made aware of potential problems as they surface.

Information gathering normally takes most of the time and effort in the performance phase of the audit process. The auditor's task is to collect factual audit evidence, analyze and evaluate it against the audit criteria (requirements), draw conclusions from this comparison, and report the results to management.[4]

When using a particular audit strategy (department, discovery, tracing, process, or element), the auditor must be aware of the interconnectedness of the departments and management system elements. If an auditor's focus is too narrow, the results of the investigation will not be comprehensive or reflect the actual situation. For example, an auditor conducting a system audit of the sales department should recognize the interconnection among the process of identifying customer requirements, activities related to design requirements, customer feedback activities, field failures and corrective action, credit approval guidelines, and so on. As another example, an auditor conducting a process audit of a gas chromatograph testing of an analysis must review the inputs and outputs (such as samples, containers, collections of samples, sample plans, output results, and the verification and use of outputs). It is important that auditors investigate sequential steps and the interconnectivity of the process with other processes.

In auditing, information or objective evidence can be gathered in several different ways. The auditor may examine documents and records; interview employees; physically examine samples of product, data analysis, performance reports, customer or user feedback, and websites; and observe work in progress. The auditor must sort the audit evidence (observations) gathered and then summarize it in a format that will be useful to the client and/or auditee.

Data Collection Plan

An auditor must develop a plan for collecting specific evidence needed to verify conformance to requirements. The collection plan provides the auditor with space for recording the results of examinations and identifying people who are interviewed. The auditor should ask open-ended questions that result in verifiable data. The questions asked may deal with causal groupings such as methods, materials, machinery, people, measurement, and environment, which may affect a specific action.

Information and data include any observation of facts and can be qualitative or quantitative. Sources of data could include records from the auditee as well as observations that an auditor makes during audit performance, such as counting the number of press cycle openings, noting the amount of liquid discharged, or observing an operator during a prescribed, defined operation.

Qualitative data indicate "yes, this was performed" or "this step was not conducted." Audit evidence must be available and reviewable for any data to be considered verifiable. Quantitative data are collected by measuring or counting, such as the number of defective pieces removed (inspected out) or the number of cycles of molding press observed during a period of time. The number of complaints that a complaint-handling system receives during a certain time period is another example of quantitative data.

An auditor, as part of the planning, will usually have access to work instructions or written procedures. If the management system is mature, the written procedures will describe what records need to be maintained, who maintains the records, who collects the data, and what kinds of data are collected. As a result of this preparation, an auditor should know what data sheets or records to expect when reaching the audit site.

An auditor should have a plan in mind for what needs to be examined, and it should be described on the audit checklist or noted on some type of process flowchart. For example, an internal auditor may be familiar with the inspection records on a production line and may decide to examine them. Next, the auditor may decide how many inspection records need to be examined. If conducting a process audit or an audit of a process-based management system, collection points and items are easily marked on a flowchart or PFD. Depending on the size of the auditee organization and the objective of the audit, a sampling plan may also need to be developed. (See Chapter 22 for more information on selecting samples.)

An auditor must be familiar with different data collection methods and their strengths and weaknesses. Proper training teaches auditors which methods can be used and which ones cannot be used for a specific task in particular situations. The audit program can dictate which data collection methods are for compliance and which ones can be used only for inference. Data collection plans may include interviewing, observing, reviewing records and documents, analyzing data, and performing statistical and nonstatistical sampling. An auditor needs to understand basic statistical methods and must be able to choose the one that gives the desired information.

Document Examination

An auditor must be well trained in methods for examining documents and records. A document specifies what should be done; a record specifies what has been done. *Documents* are written instructions or procedures that establish a practice or tell a person how to do a job. Examples of documents include written work instructions, guidelines, procedures, diagrams, drawings, and blank forms. In contrast, records result when a particular step or process is performed as directed in the documents. Technically, a *record* is a type of document whose purpose is to collect information about an output of a process. Some refer to a record as a special type of document that states results. Examples of records include meeting minutes, inspection results, completed check sheets, audit reports, printouts of data from equipment, and test data.

Records are evidence that practices outlined in documents have been performed. Thus, records verify that the actions specified in documents have indeed taken place as required.

Reasons for Examining Documents and Records

Documents and records must be examined for the following reasons:

- To ensure that documents adequately meet higher-tier requirements, such as policies, codes, and standards

- To ensure that records provide the objective evidence to demonstrate product acceptability and the appropriate implementation of system/process controls

- To provide the auditor with an understanding of the system/process/product under investigation

Document and record examination may reveal audit evidence regarding incomplete, conflicting, or incorrect documentation or implementation of the system by the auditee. The implementation (deployment) of documents (policy, procedure, plan, and so on) is normally verified through examination of records, interviewing, physical examination, and observing work.

Document and Record Considerations

Documents should be current and available to the people who need them. Sometimes the processes an auditor observes do not match the documentation, because the documentation has not been updated as practices have changed.

To ensure that documents and records reflect actual practice, the auditor should verify that they are secure, permanent, current, legible, and accurate. Records should not be accessible to unauthorized personnel. They should be backed up or stored in more than one location, such as another building. Written records should be permanent—written in ink, unless environmental circumstances do not allow recording data in ink. For example, some chemicals used in laboratories may cause reactions when they come into contact with ink, so an alternate means of recording data would be permissible. If written records must be changed, the changes should be dated and signed or initialed. The original information should be kept intact so that the new information and the reason for the change can be assessed. In many industries, erasures and the use of correction fluid are strictly forbidden on records.

Some documents and records reside in computer programs. Access and changes to documents, as well as changes to computer code, must be controlled. For records, controls should be in place to limit who can access records, enter data as a record control, record changes, and control code changes to the software. The integrity of the data must be maintained. The International Organization for Standardization (ISO) published *ISO 15489, Information and Documentation—Records Management* to provide guidance. Many national groups or government agencies have also issued guidance for control of electronic records.

Tracing is a common means of collecting objective evidence (facts) during an audit. An auditor may read a procedure or become familiar with a method and then observe others attempting to accomplish the procedure. If it cannot be done, the auditor needs to determine whether the procedure is inaccurate, which could indicate that the person who wrote the procedure did not understand the process or that the process was changed and the document was not updated. The alternative is that the process is being improperly performed, which could indicate that employees have not been adequately trained or may not be capable of performing the process.

An auditor may examine items to verify information. For example, if a record says, "This cabinet was painted blue," the auditor examines the item to see if it is indeed blue. If the record states, "There are 10 nonconforming items awaiting disposition," the auditor should go to the nonconforming hold area to count the number of items awaiting disposition.

Documents and records can be sampled to verify that they are accurate. Sampling is employed when 100% inspection is not practical. In the case of records, an auditor can sample portions of a record by verifying that the recorded result occurred. This verification can be done by talking to the person who recorded the information or by alternate means, such as cross-checking a log calculation.

Physical Examination

The types of physical examination tools used by auditors can vary widely depending on the industry. An auditor needs to be familiar with the tools and techniques applicable to the industry or company being audited. In addition to knowing which tool to use in what situation, the auditor should be aware of the problems that can arise if tools are used incorrectly or inconsistently. If the auditor has no experience with the necessary tools, a technical expert should be included as part of the audit team.

Physical examination tools are normally associated with product audits. In a heavy-manufacturing environment, an auditor may use calipers, steel rules, or micrometers, for example, to take measurements. An auditor may also observe others using these tools in order to verify that a product meets certain characteristics. In most circumstances, it is essential for tools to have been properly calibrated; however, exceptions do exist (for example, a volt meter may be used to determine whether power is turned on or off, not to measure voltage). If the auditor uses measuring devices that require periodic calibrating, the auditing organization should follow an accepted calibration program.

Beyond examination of finished product, all tangibles can be physically examined and characterized in some way. Tangible items that have physical properties may include markings on tags, types of packaging materials, condition of work area (housekeeping), or condition of equipment. Physical examination is one of the most reliable sources of objective evidence. Before taking an inspection tool in hand, however, the auditor should be aware of work rules and safety restrictions.

Observation of Work Activities

An auditor observes work in progress to see if it meets requirements. An auditor gains this knowledge by monitoring a process being performed to see how the work is done.

Observation means "to watch attentively" or "to watch or be present without participating actively." Auditors must be well trained in observation techniques so that they learn how to observe closely but not obtrusively. Because an auditor's presence may be distracting to people at work, the auditor needs to minimize any interference. An auditor should also realize that disrupting a worker may be unsafe. The risk of an auditor's presence interfering with normal operations should be managed.

An auditor should know the normal working hours of the auditee organization and should work the same hours. If the auditee starts work at 6 A.M., then the auditor should consider starting at 6 A.M. The same is true for quitting time.

An auditor needs to know when to observe work. For example, an auditor who wants to observe work being done by different shifts should be aware of when the shift changes take place. Auditors should avoid retaining people through shift changes or during their breaks. Besides the negative effect on relations with the auditee, it could result in overtime, scheduling issues, and even union grievances if the person being held over is not next on the overtime list.

Most importantly, auditors need to understand what to observe and what they have seen. For example:

- The auditor should establish whether the product is made according to the documented procedures by the individuals responsible for using the specified equipment. The auditor should record the results of the observations.

- When looking at equipment, the auditor should note the type, condition, use, and any identification tags or numbers. The auditor should also establish that the equipment has been properly maintained and calibrated, if applicable.

- The auditor should verify that employees are familiar with policies and procedures, that they know their responsibilities and roles, and that they have the necessary training, skills, experience, and authority to perform their jobs.

- When reviewing documents, an auditor should verify contents, type, scope, format, readability, and date. How the document has been filed and distributed and the method by which modifications have been made are also important.

- The auditor should look at the input and output of every process or activity to judge the effectiveness (results) of the process.

By listening and watching, an auditor should be able to ascertain whether what the worker is doing supports the procedures outlined in the system- or process-related documentation. It is usually best if an auditor observes people doing their actual work rather than creating work for them or conducting a simulation.

Data Patterns and Trends

At their final gathering before the exit meeting, audit team members evaluate the accumulated data. They sort the data, see what the data support, and look at the data away from the situation to see what they mean. Any finding should be clear to a reasonable person. The auditor has to look at the evidence found, its relation to the purpose of the audit, and its importance to the entire scope that has been audited.

The lead auditor must make every effort to resolve contradictory evidence or open issues prior to reporting the results of the audit. However, if contradictory evidence has been gathered and the audit team cannot obtain additional data, the contradiction should be included in the audit report as a finding or an observation, and clarification should be requested. A supplemental report can be generated if needed to clarify the original audit report.

Through analysis of audit data, the audit team can distinguish between systemic and isolated incidents. An auditor who detects a possible problem looks for a recurrence. If subsequent data show recurrence of the incident in several places, it is a systemic incident. Data that reveal a trend and pattern may also support a conclusion that an incident is systemic rather than isolated. For example, if one piece of equipment is overdue for calibration by about a month, but all other equipment is in calibration, the auditee may have a good calibration program and the one piece of equipment is an isolated case. However, if a high percentage of equipment has not been calibrated on schedule, the problem is systemic.

Thus, an auditor needs to look at data from a system standpoint and try to assess how the overall system is working. If after preliminary evaluation of data a problem appears to be systemic, the auditor may need to draw another sample. Once the problem has been identified as a systemic or isolated event, it can be classified for reporting purposes. Typically, when the auditee responds to the audit findings, an isolated occurrence is addressed by correcting the specific instance. An auditee responding to a systemic issue looks at what aspects of the system exist that permitted the problem to occur. For example, the auditee may need to perform an investigation to determine the root cause of the issue, optimize procedures and retrain personnel, and/or evaluate whether a process should be automated.

> The potential impact of an isolated occurrence should be considered when determining which findings to include in the audit report and how they should be rated. If an isolated occurrence of a nonconformance could result in poor quality or unsafe products that may harm the user, it should be included in the audit report and rated accordingly. For example, release of one batch of a drug product that did not meet specifications for potency may be an isolated occurrence, but it could cause patients to become more ill or to die. This nonconformance should be included in the audit report and be rated as critical or significant.

Interviews

Interviewing, the process of obtaining information from another person in response to questions, is an important and widely used form of data collection in auditing. Interviews are used in audits to gain insights, clarify information, confirm or deny suspicions, and elicit details that may not be brought out by other audit activities. The auditor may employ an interview format such as the six-step interview process developed by Frank X. Brown:[5]

1. Put the interviewee at ease

2. Explain your purpose

3. Find out what they are doing

4. Analyze what they are doing

5. Make a tentative conclusion

6. Explain your next step

When conducting an interview, the auditor should begin by providing a personal introduction and putting the interviewee at ease. The purpose of the interview should be explained, followed by general, open-ended questions that get an interviewee talking about the tasks he or she performs. An auditor may simply say, "What are you doing?" or "What tells you to do that?" If the interviewee's answers confirm the documentation, the information has been corroborated. If not, the auditor needs to probe by asking questions that are even more specific to ascertain whether a work problem does indeed exist, or whether the interview is being hampered by miscommunication. An auditor may not understand the process the interviewee describes, or the interviewee may misinterpret or fail to understand a question. An escort can often help clarify communication problems resulting from unfamiliar terminology by rephrasing a question. An escort should not be permitted to answer for an interviewee, however.

When auditors make a conclusion about whether necessary controls are in place, they must communicate the preliminary conclusions to the interviewee and/or escort. For example, an auditor could say, "That's good. It looks to me as though you have a thorough understanding of your job and are addressing all requirements." An auditor who suspects a potential finding could say, "It looks like we might have a problem in this area. I can't see where those controls are placed." Such comments give the interviewee an opportunity to offer more information. If the interviewee is able to allay the auditor's concerns, no problem exists. In general, people respond readily to inquiries and offer helpful suggestions for improvements if they feel that the audit team is sincere, appreciates their views, and has their needs and interests at heart.

The auditor usually takes notes during an interview and should take a few minutes at the end of each interview to ensure that the notes are complete and will be meaningful when reviewed later in the day. If the interviewee appears apprehensive, the auditor should explain that notes are taken to record information about the details of the interview. If extensive note taking is necessary, it may be best for the auditor to step out of the room or into a secluded location to record observations so that the interviewee will not become unnerved by the auditor's recording large amounts of information.

In all communications with the auditee, the auditor must focus on the situation, issues, documentation, activities, and/or behavior—not on the person. When communicating with auditee management, the auditor should avoid naming individuals whenever possible.

Interviews are an integral part of process and system audits. There may be no interviews during a product or service audit except to verify status. For product audits, the auditor simply verifies product or service characteristics. A product auditor may audit products to verify that inspection is effective or the reason for a returned or aged product. External audit interviews are more formal than internal audit interviews. Even if an external auditor has audited the same organization for a number of years, the auditor must not become too friendly or fraternize with the auditee personnel.

Also, it is useful to have interviewees agree with records or notations of their comments, and auditee personnel verify the accuracy of the auditor's observations of activities and status of items, when they are being recorded. This technique will help ensure that the auditee understands the results of the investigation.

Other interviewing techniques include (1) effective interviewing when no procedure exists, (2) what to do when supervisors are present, (3) handling hostile or difficult situations, (4) interviewing groups, (5) interpreting pauses, and (6) using a translator. Since interviewing is considered an important auditing skill, additional interviewing techniques can be found in Chapter 14, "Interviewing Techniques."

4. ESTABLISHMENT OF OBJECTIVE EVIDENCE

Characteristics

Evidence should be collected on any matter related to the audit objective and scope. Evidence can include procedures or work instructions and proof of their implementation, examination of personnel training and qualification records, examination of process controls and records, and reexamination of selected work. Evidence needed to support the auditor's findings may be physical, testimonial, documentary, or analytical. Objective evidence may be obtained internally from the organization under audit, externally from third parties, or by comparing evidence obtained from two or more sources. Evidence obtained from independent external sources is generally more reliable than information obtained from internal sources. Knowledge obtained through physical examination, observation, computation, and inspection is more reliable than interview comments. Evidence derived from records is likewise more reliable than oral evidence. Evidence must be sufficient, complete, and relevant to be useful as a sound basis for audit findings and recommendations. A rational relationship should exist between the cost of obtaining evidence and the usefulness of the evidence.[6] For example, the costs involved in shutting down a manufacturing plant to obtain data or in traveling to 100 service centers to verify that employees know the quality policy may not be justifiable.

ISO 19011 uses the term *audit evidence* instead of *objective evidence*. Any evidence collected during the audit should be objective and free from bias. Evidence should be recorded and verifiable. Evidence can be verified or confirmed by (1) records or documents, (2) verbal affirmations, (3) repeat observation, (4) measuring or testing, and (5) simulation. Audit evidence is based on the information gathered through sampling. Even though the sampling results are factual, there is an element of uncertainty regarding conclusions. The conclusions are only as good as the degree to which the samples represent the performance or actions of the area being audited.

Corroboration of Evidence

An auditee presents evidence to an auditor to prove that the audited process works as the auditee has explained it and that written documentation exists to support the process. If something cannot be observed, it must be verified with a record. Objective evidence may include minutes from a meeting or a check sheet that confirms a particular activity. If an auditor talks to a supervisor and gets one explanation and then talks to operators independently and hears the same explanation, the auditor has obtained corroboration of the evidence for the investigation.

Corroboration methods are used by the auditor to validate data that could be considered unreliable or questionable. Information from interviews must be corroborated by asking another person (in a different department or shift) or by checking records and documents to establish consistency or inconsistency.

Part IIB

There are three ways to corroborate the information received in an interview:

1. Another person says the same thing. Of course, he or she need not use the exact same words, but the message (information) is the same as that heard earlier. For maximum value, the auditor should try to choose someone from another group or management level to corroborate the first story.

2. Another member of the auditing team hears the same thing. The information can come from the same person spoken with earlier or another person. Regardless of the second source, another set of ears has received the same message, so the likelihood of a miscommunication is lower.

3. An item, document, or record verifies the action. For example, the auditor hears the explanation and then reads a procedure stating the action as explained. Or perhaps the auditor sees a completed form with the information just described.

None of these methods show that the action is correct, but they allow the auditor to place faith in the information just received. The methods described may be right or they may not be right, but they are now fact.[7]

5. ORGANIZATION OF OBJECTIVE EVIDENCE

Classification of Observations

An auditor uses several techniques to classify and prioritize observations before the exit meeting. In any audit, risk is associated with reporting a finding on the basis of available data. An auditor may fail to identify a significant problem or may identify a problem that is not significant. Evaluation is often based on a relatively small sample and, therefore, involves a high sampling risk. A problem area may be classified as a nonconformity, noncompliance, or finding. The auditor should also group like observations under similar findings or nonconformances.

The *risk-benefit ratio* is a method of analyzing the risk of reporting (based on the sample) or not reporting compared to the benefit to be gained by reporting or not reporting an area of concern. If there is significant opportunity for project failure or a safety concern, a critical activity or item should be reported after one occurrence, as opposed to multiple occurrences for an item of lesser importance. An observation of a critical step or activity may be an isolated event, yet important because of its nature. Other isolated observations, which represent low risk, are not considered significant.

In some cases, observations may be chronic or marked by long continuation or frequent recurrence. The chronic nature of an observation may mean risks are higher, and management may want to avoid the risk or treat it. Observations may also be systemic. Systemic observations relate to the system and will be repeated unless the system is changed. The need to change the system is based on the risk to the organization being audited. For example, finding a misspelled word in an organization's work instruction may be a systemic issue (likely to recur in other documents), but the risk to the organization is low and the cost of multiple editing and proofing is not justified. However, if your business is book publishing, it is important to determine whether the observation is systemic or an isolated incident associated with a special cause.

Additionally, observations may be classified as opportunities for improvement, improvement points, or positive practices (not a violation of a requirement). An observation of a highly effective process or system may warrant reporting the observation as a positive practice.

Depending on the client, the industry, and audit procedure requirements, auditors may define and report other classifications for observation. These include concern, issue, and continuous improvement. These are not violations of a requirement, but based on the auditor's experience, they are noteworthy and, in some cases, could develop into a problem if not corrected. All classifications of observations should be identified along with expected follow-up actions. For example, for third-party certification audits, organizations are not normally required to take action on improvement points; they are only required to address nonconformities.

Nonconformances and Their Classification

The terms *noncompliance* and *nonconformance* (see Appendix B, "Notes on Compliance, Conformance, and Conformity") are frequently used to report the results of the audit. In common practice, these terms are used interchangeably. Some reserve the use of *compliance* (when reporting the capability of the management system) for meeting statutory, regulatory, and contractual requirements. The most severe problems are often called major nonconformances. Reporting problems found during the audit as nonconformances is one of the most popular reporting techniques. A *nonconformity* is nonfulfillment of a requirement (ISO 9000:2005, 3.6.2) or, alternatively, failure to meet a requirement.

A nonconforming condition is adverse to the expected controls or interests of the organization. Some may characterize a nonconformance as a condition adverse to quality or safety or environmental controls and objectives.

An auditor must sort and classify facts based on the severity of the problem, the frequency of occurrence, and the risks associated with the problem. Most quality system certification/registrar auditors are trained to report nonconformances, and consequently, many auditors of registered organizations adopt the same method of reporting. A nonconformance or finding may be classified as systemic or isolated, major or minor, or it may be assigned a severity level or graded (such as A, B, or C), depending on its effect on the product, service, process, or system.

In the book *The Internal Auditing Pocket Guide*, the author states that data should be sorted based on importance (significance) and relevance.[8] Is the information relevant to the organization being audited? Has a requirement been broken (violated)? Importance can be judged based on:

1. Repeated occurrences

2. One-time occurrences that have high risk

Some audit organizations classify issues as nonconformities/noncompliances, and others report problems found during the audit as findings. In general, the reporting of findings is a technique in which the individual nonconformities are grouped to provide evidence supporting systemic issues or conclusions regarding processes or systems. The resulting findings statements are reported in a manner that clearly indicates the impact on the organization's performance.

In *Quality Audits for Improved Performance*, the author states that a finding is an audit conclusion that identifies a condition having a significant adverse effect on the quality of the activity under review. A finding has the following characteristics:

- It is negative. Something is amiss.

- It is a violation of a requirement. A promise was made and it was not kept.

- It is significant. It is a big deal. It relates to business values and is affecting those values in an adverse manner.[9]

Though many view an audit finding as negative, the ISO 19011 supports a definition that allows findings to be negative or positive when reporting the results of an investigation.

Audit findings can also be reported by risk. Evidence collected during the audit that suggests an immediate and significant risk (for example, safety, environmental, or quality) should be reported without delay to the auditee and the audit client. Besides immediate safety, health, or environmental risk, there is also risk to the organization. Risk is the possibility of loss, injury, disadvantage, or destruction. Risk is the combination of the probability of an event and its consequences. A finding may be systemic, but either the probability or the consequences may be insignificant. This is an important concept.

The ISO 19011 states that nonconformities may be graded. Prior national and international system auditing standards stated that auditors should report the importance or significance of what was found. The new international standard guidance reflects liability concerns regarding compliance to statutory, regulatory, and contractual requirements. For example, if a third-party auditor reports the little drip from a pipe as a minor nonconformity and later it is found to be a major source of pollution, the third-party audit organization may be liable for the leak not being fixed sooner. In this case the auditee is the best one to determine the significance of a nonconformity. The international auditing standard allows auditors to grade or not grade nonconformities depending on their situation.

Conclusions

According to ISO 19011:2011, clause 6.4.8, Preparing audit conclusions, the audit team should confer prior to the closing meeting in order to:

a. Review the audit findings, and any other appropriate information collected during the audit, against the audit objectives

b. Agree on the audit conclusions, taking into account the uncertainty inherent in the audit process

c. Prepare recommendations, if specified by the audit plan

d. Discuss audit follow-up, as applicable

For audits measuring conformance or fulfillment of requirements, the lead auditor should report the overall degree to which those requirements are being met. For audits measuring compliance, the lead auditor should report that the organization is compliant or noncompliant. The audit conclusion should match the audit purpose. For example, if the purpose of the audit is to determine whether the existing controls comply with international standards and are being maintained, then the audit conclusion should state the extent to which this has been accomplished.

The lead auditor's overall assessment of results plays a critical role in meaningful audits for improvement. The following items should be considered in the lead auditor's assessment:

- Management system maturity

- Overall system effectiveness, rather than segmental ineffectiveness

- Implementation of corrective and preventive actions and their effectiveness

- Internal audits and their effectiveness related to continual improvement mechanisms in place

- Organization performance compared to level of conformance

- Employee awareness, and dissemination of established quality, environmental, or safety policy

- Teamwork and employee involvement with management participation, and demonstrated resource commitment

- Auditee organization's business and strategic plans, culture, and values

- Severe system issues, rather than nitpicking trivialities

- Opportunities for improvements, without acting as a consultant

- Positives such as good practices and achievements since last audit

An auditor can get an indication of the effectiveness of controls by the nature and number of nonconformances observed and the achievement of organizational objectives for system and individual processes.

6. EXIT AND CLOSING MEETINGS

Purpose

The exit meeting—sometimes called a postaudit conference, closing meeting, or closure meeting—ends the performance stage of the audit process. At the exit meeting, the lead auditor presents a draft or preliminary audit report to the auditee.

Presentation of Audit Results

The *exit meeting* is a presentation of the audit results to the auditee organization and, in some cases, the client. The client may choose not to attend the exit meeting, in which case the auditor gives the auditee a preliminary view of the information that will be provided to the client. The purpose of the exit meeting is to present audit observations to top management to ensure that the audit results are

Part IIB

clearly understood. The exit meeting normally takes place after the conclusion of the interviews and the final team meeting.

The lead auditor should circulate an attendance roster for the exit meeting. Attendees should include the audit team, at least one auditee management representative, and other personnel deemed appropriate by auditee management. For example, the escort may be present to help explain the details of the findings. Usually, the same people who attended the opening meeting attend the exit meeting. Sometimes higher levels of management attend, since they want to be informed of the audit results. The lead auditor should do most of the talking, and a member of the audit team should keep minutes of the meeting. The minutes should include any agreed-on changes to the audit report.

The lead auditor may require individual auditors to present their own findings, or the lead auditor may present all findings and rely on the appropriate auditor to clarify and answer questions. Discussions should be kept brief and pertinent and should clarify the audit findings, not justify the audit method.[10] Finally, the lead auditor should present the audit team's conclusions about the management system's overall adherence to requirements and its effectiveness.

The primary duty of the lead auditor at the exit meeting is to be a clear communicator. To avoid misunderstandings, the lead auditor should provide written findings or nonconformances/noncompliances to the auditee organization at the exit meeting. Findings, nonconformances, and audit reports should be marked "draft" or "preliminary" since they have not been approved by the client and also may need to be edited for language and grammar. The audit team's written findings or nonconformances and the team's ability to explain the results at the exit meeting are important factors in ensuring that the auditee understands the results and will be able to identify necessary corrective actions.

Besides nonconformities, there may be recommendations or opportunities for improvement. Normally, recommendations or opportunities for improvement are not binding. Also, recommendations for improvement are not the same as recommending what corrective action should be taken to address audit findings or nonconformities. Auditors should not recommend the steps or actions an organization should take to address audit findings.

Presentation techniques employed by the auditor will vary depending on whether it is a first-, second-, or third-party audit and on what methods are considered most suitable for the situation (pass or fail). Exit meetings for first-party audits tend to be less formal than those for second- or third-party audits. One of the toughest challenges for the lead auditor is the delivery of bad news. The actual methods and equipment (flip chart, computer side show, digital camera link, or data projector) used will depend on the availability of resources and what best fits the situation (mature system, awarding a contract, small organization).

> In some cases, the lead auditor has the authority to issue the final report at the exit meeting. It could be considered the preliminary or conditional report, since the lead auditor would be willing to correct or clarify its contents and the report represents only a recommendation. This has the advantage of saving costs by avoiding the report as a work item later on and perhaps speeding up the corrective action process.

System, process, and product audits should have an exit meeting. In the book *The Process Auditing Techniques Guide*, the author states, "As required by good audit practices, there must be a closing meeting. The size, formality and length will vary depending on the purpose, scope and findings of the process audit. Most process audit closing meetings will be very short. The process owners and decision makers should be at the closing meeting because they control the resources needed to address the findings."[11]

Discussion of Follow-up Actions

The lead auditor is expected to clarify all follow-up actions with the auditee and the client and to arrive at a consensus. The lead auditor will have an open discussion with the auditee organization at the exit meeting to determine adequate time for corrective action plans and/or corrective action implementation. The following are some guidelines for discussion with the auditee:

- Clear definition of nonconformance/noncompliance/finding

- Process for effective corrective action determination/implementation

- Emphasis on timely corrective action plans with accurate root cause determination

- Follow-up audit dates or follow-up corrective action review

- Areas and departments to be audited in follow-up audit

The most serious problems need the auditee's urgent attention, while the less important ones are given an appropriate time frame and priority. If the auditee needs additional time to analyze the root cause of a serious problem, the auditor should consider allowing it based on the criticality of the problem. The timing of corrective action is dependent on its importance and complexity and the availability of resources.

Keeping a Record

Reporting what was observed is what the exit meeting is all about, but there are three housekeeping items that should not be overlooked: (1) an agenda for the exit meeting, (2) a record of who attended the meeting, and (3) minutes of any discussions or agreements made at the meeting. Record keeping does not need to be a big deal and can be handled nicely with a one-page form that includes logistical information, agenda, minutes, and attendance. For remote audits or eAudits the auditor can either record the exit meeting using video equipment or give participants keyboard and mouse controls to enter their name, and the auditor can use the same form to record the minutes of the meeting.[12]

The agenda should include items typically covered at every exit meeting, plus space for specific topics to be added. Prior to the exit meeting, the auditor can review with the auditee contact what will be discussed and add any items that the auditor and the auditee representative agree to. People can sign in by printing their name on the form as they arrive at the exit meeting, and then the same form can be used to record any important items discussed during the meeting. The objective is to get everything on one piece of paper that can be filed or scanned into the records database.[13]

Part IIB

The exit meeting agenda may include:

- Audit purpose (objectives) and scope
- Background information
- Categorization and prioritization of results
- Audit sample limitations
- Summary of overall effectiveness
- Detailed findings
- Expected follow-up actions
- Timing of final report

Expectations of Auditors, Auditees, and Client

Role of an Auditor

The exit meeting is conducted by the lead auditor, who should:

- Thank the auditee for their cooperation
- Present the summary
- Read the results of the audit without interruption from the auditee
- Discuss audit details
- Allow individual auditors to clarify statements or respond to specific questions about the areas they audited
- Allow auditee to clarify any misunderstandings that may change or remove a nonconformity
- Indicate how audit results are categorized or graded and prioritized
- Explain the required follow-up and expected corrective action response[14]
- Obtain acknowledgment from the auditee representative
- Ensure that minutes and an attendance record are kept
- Affirm confidentiality of the report

A big problem at exit meetings occurs when communication between an auditor and an auditee was not reported to the top of the chain of command before the meeting. The auditee, caught off guard, may become defensive. Daily meetings help prevent this problem. If an auditee does not want daily meetings, the auditor can prevent problems by promoting communication during the audit. An auditor who suspects that information is not getting to top management should casually, but deliberately, inform management of audit progress and potential findings.

It is the lead auditor's responsibility to safeguard all documents. The lead auditor should:

- Return or secure storage or destruction of all supporting or evidentiary materials belonging to the auditee, according to the arrangements and applicable statutes and regulations

- Secure storage or destruction of any created reports, computer files, graphics, and so on, according to the arrangements and applicable statutes and regulations

- Confirm confidentiality by reminding all parties—including other auditors and language, technical, and clerical support staff—that data collected, conclusions, and all other aspects of the audit are confidential and that any disclosure of information could result in undesired consequences for several parties, including them

Remote audits or eAudits have additional information and document control challenges. An individual auditor's computer may have limited security and be subject to hacking.[15] The auditee and the auditor should agree on how auditee information stored as electronic files should be handled.

The formal, official audit report should be issued to the auditee by the client (or lead auditor, if authorized to do so by the client) within the time period previously agreed to or specified by organizational procedure. Lastly, at the end of the exit meeting, all parties amicably bid farewell to one another.

Role of an Auditee

The lead auditor should present the audit results to the responsible managers of the auditee organization. Including several layers of management may lead to an argument. It is human nature to want to defend one's position in front of the boss, even if that position is known to be wrong. Thus, a supervisor is obligated to argue a finding in his or her area if the director is present. Also, if all the managers are at the exit meeting, they are probably away from more productive work. The lead auditor can limit this arguing and unproductive time by requesting attendance by only a few.[16]

At the exit meeting, auditee representatives have the responsibility to listen attentively. There should be no extensive discussions unless the auditee needs clarification on items in the audit report. If the auditee and the auditor disagree as to whether a finding exists or have different opinions on the degree of severity of a finding, the auditee can present his or her view of the situation as part of the response to the requests for corrective action.

Role of a Client

The auditor should invite the client to attend the exit meeting. If this proves impractical, the auditor should arrange to debrief the client. The auditor expects the client's support in resolving any findings or issues. In some cases, the client and the auditee are the same and must undertake both roles.

Problems Commonly Encountered during the Audit Performance Stage

The following are examples of the types of problems commonly encountered during the performance stage of an audit.

Losing Track of Time or Scope

Problems regarding a lack of time or loss of focus or scope are frequently encountered during audits. Daily meetings that assess the

(continued)

audit's progress should help prevent such problems. Also, properly prepared working papers can help eliminate problems related to time management or the focus of the audit. Valuable time can be lost if an auditee disappears to find a document or record. Auditors should go with the person in those situations to see how documents and records are managed, to select their own samples, and to ensure the auditee doesn't introduce delays.

Unreasonable Absence or Unavailability of Key Personnel

An auditor needs to be able to work around the absence of key personnel. However, if this situation happens regularly during an external audit, the auditor may need to call a meeting with management or stop the audit. If an obstruction exists and no mutual agreement can be reached at the meeting, the auditor should report to the client for advice on how or whether to continue the audit. Of course, unreasonable absence assumes reasonable notification by the auditor or audit organization of the impending audit. In an internal audit, people often take the availability of the audit team for granted. They may feel free to handle their own crises as they arise because they believe it should be easy for the audit team to reschedule.

Interference from Internal Problems

Employees sometimes wish to involve the audit team in internal problems. For example, if employees believe that their performance would improve with the addition of a certain piece of equipment, they may attempt to enlist the auditor in lobbying management for the purchase of such equipment. It may be necessary to state that auditors do not get involved in advising the auditee how to run his or her organization.

Extensive Discussions or Arguments

The auditee may attempt to prolong the exit meeting with extensive discussion or arguments. For example, an auditee may want to argue the interpretation of a requirement, debate the significance of the nonconformity, or make a plea that a specific nonconformity is a special case and should not require corrective action. The exit meeting is not a time for negotiation; the lead auditor should present the information from the audit, make sure that the auditee understands the results and what is expected in the way of a corrective action plan, and end the meeting.

Lack of Effective Communication

Communication barriers pose a threat to the successful completion of an audit. This is why training in interviewing techniques is so important. Unless auditors can word questions in an unbiased and concise manner, they may not receive accurate responses.

Chapter 8
Audit Reporting/Part IIC

The purpose of the audit report is to communicate the results of the investigation. The report should provide correct and clear data that will be effective as a management aid in addressing important organizational issues.[1] The audit process may end when the report is issued by the lead auditor or after follow-up actions are completed.

1. REPORT DEVELOPMENT AND CONTENT

Review and Finalize Audit Results

After the audit results have been reported at the exit meeting, the lead auditor formally communicates the audit results in a written audit report. The audit team may have prepared a handwritten or typed report to present to the auditee at the exit meeting. The exit meeting should include a discussion of all significant findings so that the auditee is not surprised by information in the final audit report. The final audit report formally communicates the audit results to the client and the auditee. The audit report is prepared, signed, and dated by the lead auditor. It should be reviewed and approved by the management of the auditing organization as well as by the client before it is sent to the auditee.

The final audit report, if not already delivered at the exit meeting, should be sent to the auditee in accordance with a mutually understood time frame. Short timelines between performing and reporting on the audit are highly desirable. When a significant amount of time passes between the end of an audit and the issuance of the audit report, the urgency of the corrective action is diminished, misunderstandings or miscommunications are more likely to occur, the auditee may be less motivated to resolve problems, and the audit program may be viewed as inefficient.

An audit report serves the following functions:

- It supplies information that verifies adherence to requirements or that initiates corrective action and system improvement

- It guides management in subsequent decisions and activities

- It establishes a record of the investigation and conclusions

A report should be sent even if there are no deficiencies. Organizations may compare the results from year to year to identify positive and negative trends. This same type of analysis is valuable to the auditor, the auditing organization, and the auditee (internal department, supplier, or customer).[2]

Audit Report Details

While the format of the written audit report can vary widely from company to company or industry to industry, certain information should be included. Most audit reports contain an introduction, a summary, a listing of the findings/nonconformities, and requests for corrective action.

An audit report should not name individual employees of the auditee in connection with specific findings, observations, or nonconformances; a report should refer to positions, titles, or systems when identifying problems. However, an auditor may encounter a situation where naming an individual is appropriate and essential for effective corrective action. For example, if the individual has special knowledge of a situation, product, or process, the individual's name may be used in the audit report.

There is no standard length for audit reports. However, reports should be concise and should contain prescribed information. The content may depend on the size and complexity of the auditee organization and the number of findings/nonconformances identified, as well as client or audit organization report procedures and guidelines. Content can vary between first-, second-, and third-party audits. Additionally, pre-contract or follow-up audits include different information than a routine audit.

Reports may or may not contain attachments. Attachments (exhibits or examples) may include minutes from the opening and exit meetings; attendance rosters for the opening and exit meetings; requests for corrective action issued at the exit meeting; nonconformance forms issued at the exit meeting; audit schedule with auditor assignments; and charts, pictures of observations, calculations, documents, records, or other material required by audit procedure or that add value to the report.

The audit report starts with an introduction or background. Much of the introductory material included in an audit report can be completed using the audit plan before the audit is performed. The audit report introduction:

- States the purpose and scope of the audit

- Identifies the auditee, client, and auditing organization

- Identifies the audit team members and the lead auditor and presents their qualifications

- Specifies the audit dates and locations

- Specifies the standards (manuals, procedures, international standards, and so on) used for the audit

- Qualifies the results due to the sample taken

- Addresses confidentiality issues

- May list auditee personnel involved in or contacted during the audit

- Lists report distribution

Normally, an audit report identifies an area of nonconformance in the auditee's system and does not contain detailed technical information about a proprietary process or material. Any confidential information that appears in an auditor's notes or in the completed checklist must either be protected to prevent disclosing a confidence or be destroyed. The official records may contain a copy of a blank checklist that does not contain proprietary information.

Additionally, the introduction may mention the auditee's audit history, discuss the methods used during the audit, and mention the records or documents that were examined as part of the audit. Each report should be uniquely identified by title, number, letters, or a combination so that the report can be properly referenced and retrieved.

There may be situations where multiple clients require individual or separate audit reports. For example, one master audit report that includes everything goes to the auditee, a second audit report that includes only subjects of interest to the state environmental department goes to that group, and a third audit report that includes only subjects of interest to the EPA goes to that group. This can represent a significant increase in the reporting time if multiple clients have different requirements for the content of the audit reports and for the supporting documents that are to be sent with the reports.

Conclusions to Be Reported

In many cases, the overall conclusions are reported in the summary section of the audit report. The *summary* or *abstract* is a synopsis of the audit results. It should include the following information:

- Statements pertaining to the observations of nonconformities and findings

- The audit team's judgment of the extent of the auditee's conformance/ compliance with the applicable standard

- The system's ability to achieve defined objectives

- The effectiveness and efficiency of the system and processes, if included as an audit objective or purpose

The team will be recognized as competent and unbiased if the summary presents a professional, honest, and straightforward picture.[3] The conclusions reached, based on objective evidence, may be positive, negative, or both. There may be strengths as well as weaknesses to report.

- For a third-party certification body/registrar audit, the conclusion may be to recommend certification/registration or not recommend certification/registration of the organization's management system

- For a second-party audit, the conclusion may be that the supplier meets organization requirements or does not meet requirements for a new or ongoing business relationship

- For a second-party audit, the conclusion may be that problems have been corrected

- For a first-party audit, the conclusion may be that the department functions well but falls short of organizational objectives

- For a first-party audit, the conclusion may be that, pending resolution of the audit findings, the department may continue to function provided that specified remedial actions or countermeasures are immediately implemented

- For a first-party audit, the conclusion may be that, due to the conditions observed, the interval for periodic audits of the area will be extended (or shortened)

Conformance/Compliance

The results of the audit may be indicated as findings, nonconformities, deficiencies, adverse conclusions, or significant observations and conclusions. The most common terms used to report the results of an audit are *nonconformity*, *noncompliance*, and *finding*. The terminology used should be defined to ensure that the auditee understands it. Observations made during the audit that violate a requirement should be reported and their importance should be taken into account. Within each category, further classifications of severity may exist, such as critical, major, minor, and incidental.

Each problem area should be listed in one to three sentences. The comments should include the issue and facts or examples that support or explain each finding or positive practice. In system audits, communication with auditee management may be improved by including the "so what?"—a statement explaining why this is important to the auditee organization. The results of the audit may be listed in order of importance, in sequence of the procedure or performance standard clauses, or in no particular order. Noteworthy accomplishments, positive practices, best practices, or processes that work exceptionally well may be included and can be listed at the front or back of the report, depending on the auditor's preference. The auditor should note that the findings are symptoms, the causes of which remain to be identified.

The results section of a formal report should include the following information:

- Audit findings/nonconformities and number

- Specific requirement

- Audit evidence of the nonconformity or finding

- Provisions for auditee's response

- Provisions for recording corrective action and follow-up activities

- Opportunities for improving the management system, such as the quality, environmental, and/or safety program

Note that many organizations keep the response and corrective action tracking separate from the report content due to internal or regulatory issues.

The audit report should explain how the results of the audit are classified and prioritized. For an example of an audit report format, see Figure 8.1.

To: Auditee responsible for reply

From: Lead auditor

Subject: Audit of (procedure, title, and number or subject)

Reference: List of procedures audited and to which reference is made in the list of findings—that is, quality manual dated XX-XX-XX, MIL-STD-XXXX, and so on.

I. **Present audit**
   A. General
   State the purpose and objectives of the audit, where and when it was performed, and what was included or excluded; be specific on quantities audited.
   B. Summary
   Provide a synopsis of the most significant audit findings.
   C. Findings
   For each discrepancy, state the requirement, document the observations, show the effect, and identify the responsible supervisor contacted relative to each finding.

II. **History**
   A. Audit history
   State previous audit results and corrective actions taken.
   B. Analysis and evaluation
   Provide auditor's analysis and conclusion, including an evaluation of corrective actions taken.

III. **Required action**
   A. Response
   The persons listed below are requested to review and respond to this audit within 15 working days from the date of this report. The response should include the following:
   1. Corrective action taken and reason finding existed.
   2. Action taken to correct the cause.
   3. Date by which the corrective action will be complete.

Example	
Action addressee:	Finding #
Director of engineering	I.C.1
Director of operations	I.C.2, 3, & 7
Director of quality assurance	I.C.4, 5, & 6

   B. Follow-up
   Reference material pertaining to this audit is available from (the auditor) at extension XXXX/XXXX. Replies will be followed up and corrective action will be confirmed.

   _____
   Lead auditor

Figure 8.1 Typical audit report format.

Source: ASQC Quality Audit Technical Committee, Charles B. Robinson, ed., *How to Plan an Audit* (Milwaukee, WI: ASQC Quality Press, 1987), pp. 38–39.

In the book *The Process Auditing Techniques Guide*, the author states that an internal process audit report of a work instruction can be one or two pages.[4] It can be in a memo format (To-From-Date-Subject-CC) with standard identifiers (number, dates, and area audited). The audit report and corrective action record can be combined such that all follow-up actions are recorded in one place. Forms can also be used that provide space for overall findings with expandable row sizes.

Part IIC

It is convenient to use electronic forms so that rows can be expanded to fit the information. A process audit report can be very simple and functional. Individual problems and nonconformities can be listed along with the traceable requirement (paragraph, document, objective, and so on).

The auditee may request recommendations from the audit team. Auditors should not recommend or specify how audit nonconformities or noncompliances are to be corrected. If an auditor recommends an action to be taken to address an audit finding, the auditor is no longer an independent agent but has assumed the role of consultant and created a conflict of interest for future audits of the same area.

Request for Corrective Action

The management of an audited organization should be asked to review and investigate the audit findings to determine what actions will be taken.

The auditee should be asked to include the following in the corrective action plan:

- The finding or a reference to it (a restatement of the problem if not the finding)

- Short-term (remedial/containment/correction) actions completed or planned, if appropriate

- The root cause of the problem

- Long-term corrective action planned to eliminate the root cause

- Time frame and responsibilities for these actions

- Metric(s) to be used by the auditee to determine the effectiveness of actions taken

To prevent a nonconformity or problem from recurring, an auditor will normally request that the auditee take action on certain items. Depending on the audit's purpose and scope and the delegated responsibility of the auditing organization, the client or audit program management may instead request corrective action.

For external product, process, or system audits, the authority to request corrective action may be mandated by the law of the land or signed agreements by officers of the organization. For internal product, process, or system audits, addressing adverse audit findings may be a procedural requirement approved by management. For compliance audits, the request for corrective action may be submitted by a separate organization responsible for the enforcement of regulatory requirements.

System Effectiveness

A *system* is a set of interrelated processes supported by an infrastructure to manage and coordinate its function.[5] Typical systems are document control systems and training systems. In a system, processes interact and work together to achieve a common goal or objective.

It has become increasingly popular to identify an audit as either a compliance/ conformance audit or a performance audit. Compliance/conformance audits determine whether there are rules and whether they are being followed, not the effectiveness or suitability of the rules. Performance audits seek to determine both conformance and the effectiveness of controls. Performance audits are also called management audits, continual improvement audits, performance improvement audits, risk-based audits, and value-added assessments. A product, process, or system audit can be either a performance audit or a conformance/compliance audit, depending on the wishes of the client.

The effectiveness of a process or system is determined by its ability to achieve its objectives or intended purpose. Assessment of effectiveness goes beyond determining the degree of conformance to requirements and maintenance of procedures. When discussing the effectiveness of corrective action, Russell and Regel state that system effectiveness has two components: whether it is achieving the desired result and whether the process is capable, efficient, and consistent with objectives.[6] One measurement of effectiveness is the degree to which objectives are achieved in an efficient and economical manner. The ISO 9000 vocabulary standard states that effectiveness is the extent to which planned activities are realized and planned results achieved.

Other auditors in the field use the words *effectiveness* and *suitability* or *effectiveness* and *efficiency* to describe the same type of assessment. A suitability audit might report that the sum of the processes is achieving the desired results or that even though the process is performing according to requirements, those requirements are deficient. For example, "Because there is no requirement to review the software load specifications on a monthly basis, incorrect loads are occurring because the platform is changing so rapidly," or "The document control system is unsuitable to meet organizational needs, even though it is fully compliant with ISO 9001 and implemented throughout the facility." This type of audit examines performance, not just conformance. Process audits can also examine suitability.

Whether the word *effectiveness* or *suitability* is used, what is important is that audits may be performed to assess processes and systems in order to verify that organizational objectives are being met. An audit that examines effectiveness does not substitute for management's responsibility to monitor performance. Rather, audits provide an additional source of information to assist management in its evaluation.[7]

As part of a training class on how to audit for effectiveness, an actual production area was audited. The receiving area had procedures for nonconforming product control, which were maintained. There was nonconforming material, but the nonconforming components were properly marked and stored. Everything was excellent. Then the students were asked to find out how long the nonconforming items had been in the hold area. Most of the items had been in the hold area for more than 30 days, with one for nine months. An objective of the organization was to reduce working capital cost, yet expensive components were being held without disposition for up to nine months. Everyone agreed that this was not meeting organizational goals and was an area for improvement.

Obtain Approvals

The audit report should be reviewed and approved in accordance with the audit organization's procedures and guidelines. Normally, the lead auditor prepares and signs approval of the audit report. The lead auditor approves any inputs to the audit report by audit team members. In many organizations the client and/or the audit program manager review and approve the audit report before final release. Procedures may require other approvers due to risk or communication issues within the organization. However, reviewers should not change the factual information contained in the report.

There is no limit to the number of people who can review the audit report. The lead auditor may ask audit team members, technical experts, and audit program managers to review the report. However, too many reviewers and approvers could create lengthy delays in issuing the final report.

> Upon reviewing the internal audit report, the management of an organization with significant regulatory issues and personnel changes required that the auditor change the content to be less negative. The site management wanted corporate management to believe that there were no issues. The same organization required managers to include goals of zero nonconformances from internal audits in their annual objectives. In addition to compromising the ethics and objectivity of the internal auditors, this created an environment where issues were hidden so that they would not be reported in an internal audit. The nonconformances found during audits were not being adequately addressed because they were being downgraded or eliminated from the audit report. The audit team should be independent and have the authority to report the facts as they are found so that issues can be brought to light and addressed to prevent larger problems from developing.

Distribute the Report

The distribution list for an audit report should be noted on the report. Distribution is at the discretion of the client unless this task has been delegated to the lead auditor or auditing organization. An internal audit report is normally distributed to the supervisor of the audited area as well as to someone in higher management. An external audit report typically goes to a division manager or CEO. A second-party external audit report may be distributed to a site production or quality manager. In addition, the auditing organization maintains a copy of the report in its official files, and each member of the audit team may retain a copy.

The lead auditor should not automatically send a report directly to the auditee unless approved to do so by the client. The client is given the option of receiving the audit report first and attaching a cover letter before the report is distributed to the auditee. This procedure promotes accountability of the auditing function.

Responses by the auditee to requests for corrective action should be sent to the same people.

Communication Technology

In *Quality Audits for Improved Performance*, the author states, "Audit report distribution was much easier before the days of the Internet, Intranets, wide area networks, virtual private networks and the like. We would give our original report to the audit boss. The report with finding sheets, the CAR sheets, and the cover letter were copied as a package and sent out. The process today is much different. The days of paper-only distribution are forever gone. We know that very little information is private once it is released to the network. An e-mail message, once sent, cannot be unsent. It is difficult, if not impossible, to destroy virtual data with today's technologies."[8]

With the communication technology we have today, audit reports can be distributed within 24 hours of the exit meeting. Electronic communication is fast and convenient. However, there are some issues beyond internet or intranet security that should be considered when using electronic distribution systems.[9] The audit program manager of the auditing organization must be mindful of these issues when distributing audit reports. Table 8.1 lists some issues and their concerns that may affect audit reports.

Table 8.1   Report issues and concerns.

Issue	Concern
Control of distribution	Once in electronic format and put on the network, reports can be sent to anyone.
Lack of correctness	Reports that are not proofread may contain grammar, spelling, and word usage errors.
Not concise	Reports can become lengthy when boilerplate information is copied and pasted into them.
Tampering with report content	Unless content is secured (via word processing software or PDF file options), report content can be modified and information integrity can be lost.
Recalling reports	Storage medium may become obsolete or systems may become corrupted and make the reports inaccessible or too expensive to access. For example, what would be required to recall reports on the 5.25 disks or optical disks of the mid-1990s? What if a host server fails because of a virus or mechanical failure?
Removing (destroying) reports	Once in electronic format, the report may be nearly impossible to destroy. It may always be on someone's system.

Source: QualityWBT Center for Education training materials, http://www.QualityWBT.com (accessed May 13, 2005).

2. EFFECTIVE REPORTS

In *After the Quality Audit*, the authors say that "reporting problems to the auditee and then putting them in writing is the most difficult part of an audit. It requires skill and patience, because if done wrong the report most certainly will not result in improvement. There are several options for phrasing what is being reported. The method chosen to report the results will depend on the organization being audited (what is most effective) and the purpose of the audit. The reporting of problems is both the product of the audit and the input to the improvement process."[10] The product of the audit process (the report) should be presented for maximum effectiveness.

The ISO 19011, clause 6.5.1, Preparing the audit report, lists some desirable attributes for audit reports. Other texts refer to the six Cs (complete, correct, concise, clear, categorized, and confirmable) when describing attributes. See Table 8.2 for report attributes.

The authors of *After the Quality Audit* suggest the following for improving the effectiveness of reports (see Table 8.3):[11]

- Use terminology that the user of the report will understand

- Avoid acronyms or follow proper conventions for using them

- Don't pad reports with fluff; get to the bottom line

- Use a standard report format

- Reference requirements or objectives not fulfilled

- Define unfamiliar terms in the report[12]

> **Example Reports**
>
> Appendix I contains examples of audit reports provided by reviewers of this handbook. The 04-04, 04-05, and 04-10 reports are examples of traditional auditing by element and use tracing/process techniques. Audit report examples use an A B C grading system to report the relative importance of the nonconformity. The audit reports are internal audits conducted by an external audit organization. For this company, internal audits are outsourced. The reports are real-life examples but are not endorsed by ASQ or the ASQ Audit Division.

The effectiveness of reports can also be improved with a cover letter or executive summary. A cover letter or executive summary should link organization objectives to audit results. For a first-party audit, a cover letter or executive summary could link the audit results to risk or financial performance. A second-party summary may link audit results to a supplier's share of current and future business. A third-party executive summary may state that the certificate or license has been renewed. After all, auditing is a management oversight tool, and management should link the results to the reason for the audit. The author of *Quality Audits for Improved Performance* recommends that there be an executive summary of any findings or positive practices and how they affect products or deliverables.[13]

Table 8.2   Report attributes.

ISO 19011 report attributes	6 C's report attributes
Complete	Complete (thorough)
Accurate	Correct (accurate)
Concise	Concise (brief)
Clear record	Clear (simply expressed)
	Categorized (severity level of nonconformities)
	Confirmable (traceable and verifiable nonconformities)

Source: ISO 19011, clause 6.6.1, Preparing the audit report; Larry Whittington, training materials, http://www.WhittingtonAssociates.com. Used with permission.

Table 8.3   Suggestions for improving reports.

Suggestion	Reason
Report the right fact.	Some facts are just symptoms and are not directly related to the finding. Reporting the wrong fact could result in the auditee attempting to fix a problem that does not exist.
Don't stop with the first defect.	When auditors stop at the first defect, it is difficult to determine whether the finding is isolated or systemic.
Report on-the-spot corrective actions. Know the situation—system maturity.	Not reporting on-the-spot remedial actions could result in systemic problems being hidden.
Present the information in an effective manner.	Use digital cameras, data projector presentations, and new technologies to present results. Use color, charts, animations, and so on, as appropriate.
Use simple analytical tools (count, ratios, comparisons, matrix, link-to-dollars).	Quantify data so that the auditee is better able to understand the significance of the findings.

Organizations such as the Institute of Internal Auditors (IIA) fit system and process auditing into what can be called nonfinancial monitoring. Even though system or process auditors may monitor management systems such as quality, environmental, or safety management systems, the scope of their audits does not normally include evaluating financial results such as in an income statement. An article in *Internal Auditor* magazine states that although the majority of executives surveyed (249 executives and board members around the globe) cite nonfinancial factors as being critical to corporate success, only about one-third are proficient at monitoring them. The article continued on to say that "executives expressed a need for more non-financial information on their companies' ability to satisfy customers, deliver quality products and services, operate efficiently and to develop new products and services."[14] Almost 75% of the executives said they were under increasing pressure to monitor nonfinancial performance.[15]

Executives want to know more about organization processes and systems and how they relate to organization objectives. Financial monitoring is critical to every organization, but it is reactive in nature, whereas system and process auditing can be proactive.

Based on ISO 19011:2011, clause 6.5.1, the audit report can also include or reference the following, as appropriate:

- The audit plan

- A summary of the audit process, including the uncertainty and/or any obstacles encountered that may decrease the reliability of the audit conclusions

- Confirmation that the audit objectives have been accomplished within the audit scope in accordance with the audit plan

- Any areas within the audit scope that were not covered

- A management summary covering the audit conclusions and the main audit findings that support them

- Any unresolved diverging opinions between the audit team and the auditee

- Opportunities for improvement, if specified in the audit objectives

- Strengths and best practices identified

- Agreed follow-up action plans, if any

- A statement of the confidential nature of the contents

- The distribution list for the audit report

3. FINAL AUDIT REPORT STEPS

Records and documents related to audits may include:

1. Records

    — Audit reports

    — Corrective action requests, if any

    — Responses to the audit reports and corrective action requests

    — Corrective action completion and follow-up records

2. Supplemental documents or data supporting audit records

    — Audit plan and audit schedule (including blank audit checklists)

    — Audit notification letter (or e-mail message)

    — Opening and exit meeting attendance and minutes

> — Completed checklists (working papers)
>
> — Forwarding letter of audit report
>
> — Documents and records obtained from the auditee
>
> — Final closeout note to the auditee
>
> — Additional correspondence

(Note: Auditor qualification records are not listed here, because they are not the audit records. They should be maintained in accordance with the procedure for qualification records.)

Audit records are maintained primarily as evidence that the management system has been evaluated and, secondarily, to show that the audits were planned, conducted, and reported in accordance with established procedures. Maintaining the audit records is important for the following reasons:

- For review of audit work

- For follow-up on continuing corrective action success

- For future audit planning to ensure adequacy of coverage

- For reference when developing future checklists

- For potential litigation purposes

The organization responsible for conducting and reporting audits should retain all audit documents and records as agreed among the client, the auditing organization, and the auditee, in accordance with any regulatory requirements.

Records are distributed as part of the audit reporting. Other records and documents may be retained by the parties involved in the audit, such as the auditor and auditee representative(s). All parties (client, auditors, audit program management, auditee management) should follow their respective retention guidelines. Besides the audit report records, the audit team members have supplemental records and documents such as working papers and copies of audit evidence. In general, auditors should either destroy or transfer supplemental records and documents to the auditing organization. An auditor who needs records of audits to maintain a certification may seek verification signatures on a log from either the auditee or audit program managers. For certification purposes, auditors may be asked to keep a record of the type of audit performed, their role, and the number of days to conduct the audit.

Audit records should be kept in a reasonably secure place to prevent inadvertent access by outside parties. All audit records should be considered confidential. There may be detailed procedures for securing or destroying audit records for high-risk areas. Auditing organizations should adopt reasonable procedures to ensure the safe custody and retention of records for a period of time defined by the organization's audit program, audit authority, or client that is sufficient to satisfy pertinent legal and administrative requirements. If no time period is specified, at least five years' retention is recommended. Some regulated industries, such as pharmaceuticals, aerospace, and nuclear power, might require an even longer time period. Some records are lifetime records that need to be retained for the life of the program, product, device, or facility; therefore, the auditor should check with legal staff or contract administrators.

The data supporting the audit records may be kept as needed by the audit program manager or auditors, at least until completion of the next formal audit, and can be destroyed anytime after that.

When a period of recertification, reregistration, or license renewal is involved, it is advisable to retain audit records until the next certification/registration/renewal period. This provides evidence that the findings of an earlier audit have been identified, corrected, and maintained.

Upon the expiration date of the record retention period, the record may be destroyed or dispositioned at the discretion of the person responsible for retention. With computers, however, many records and data are stored in electronic media. They may be put into electronic archives on a hard drive or removable disks or memory sticks instead of being destroyed.

Things have changed considerably in the transition to virtual records. Networking and computers allow users to keep nearly everything almost indefinitely. Destruction of electronic records is quite difficult to accomplish completely. On the other hand, they are easy to lose at the press of a button. Virtual records also have the potential to be altered or manipulated, either by accident or by malicious intent. Organizations should implement controls to minimize loss or modification of electronic audit records.

Chapter 9
Audit Follow-up and Closure/Part IID

"The audit is completed when all the planned audit activities have been carried out, or otherwise agreed with the audit client" (ISO 19011, clause 6.6). Clause 6.7 of ISO 19011 continues by stating that verification of follow-up actions may be part of a subsequent audit. Due to ISO 19011 users, various industry sectors (regulated and nonregulated), and different management systems, guidance is very limited beyond issuing the audit report. This is not so much a criticism as it is a recognition of the difficulty in achieving consensus from so many different users with different cultures and environments.

Requests for correcting nonconformities or findings are very common. *Corrective action* is action taken to eliminate the causes of an *existing* nonconformity, defect, or other undesirable situation in order to prevent recurrence (reactive). Corrective action is about eliminating the causes of problems and not just following a series of problem-solving steps. *Preventive action* is action taken to eliminate the causes of a *potential* nonconformity, defect, or other undesirable situation in order to prevent occurrence (proactive).

1. ELEMENTS OF THE CORRECTIVE ACTION PROCESS

The auditee is responsible for taking corrective action and keeping the client informed of its progress. Sometimes an auditee will look to the auditor for a solution or recommendation, but the auditor should proceed with caution. While not precluded from providing a solution, the auditor may not have the technical knowledge to address and solve the problem. In addition, an auditor who advances a solution takes ownership of solving the problem. An auditor who has studied a process may have an excellent understanding of it and may be able to offer assistance to an auditee who seems genuinely confused about what is expected in the way of corrective action. It is important, however, that the auditee take responsibility for the solution. An auditor who participates in implementing or modifying a management system compromises the objectivity of later audits of that area. For these reasons, many company auditors and most third-party auditors are prohibited from recommending corrective action.

Since corrective action is required by several management system standards, it is imperative that auditors understand what is expected.

> *Corrective action:* (1) Action taken to eliminate the causes of an *existing* nonconformity, defect, or other undesirable situation in order to prevent

recurrence (reactive). (2) Action taken to eliminate the cause of a detected nonconformity or other undesirable situation (ISO 9000). Corrective action is reacting to a problem and taking steps to eliminate the cause so the problem never recurs.

Both internal and external audit results are used as inputs to the corrective action process. Effective corrective action processes can result in significant benefits to an organization. The purpose of this part of the handbook is to make suggestions on how auditors can most effectively carry out their responsibilities relative to correcting deficiencies found during the audit. It is not a discussion about the organization's corrective action process.

Criteria for Acceptable Corrective Action Plans

The auditee's management is responsible for setting priorities on corrective action requests as a result of an audit. An auditee should draw conclusions in order to focus on those problems whose solutions will provide the greatest benefit for the least effort and expense. As the group responsible for developing the corrective action plan, auditee managers have to know what resources they have and what to fix first.

An auditee sets priorities by looking at the range of problems in relation to the entire system and noting where problems are clustering. Additionally, the auditee is responsible for recognizing the potential for similar conditions elsewhere in the organization or system and taking the necessary steps to rectify those problems. The system/process audit is not intended to identify each and every instance of a problem—it is not a 100% inspection activity. Rather, an audit may reveal trends that suggest a systemic problem.

After receiving the formal audit report, the auditee should prepare a corrective action plan and issue it to the auditor or auditing organization within a specified time. The first step in the development of a corrective action plan is to identify the problem and determine the root cause. After a problem has been identified, the auditee may sometimes take immediate or short-term corrective action (also correction). Such action, usually considered remedial or temporary, is a quick containment action and is not necessarily the action needed to solve the problem permanently. On the other hand, long-term corrective action is permanent and addresses the underlying cause. An auditee needs to implement a solution to ensure that the problem will not recur.

Once a deficiency and its root cause have been identified, the corrective action plan can be developed. The plan should cite action already taken to correct the deficiency and to preclude a similar occurrence. The plan should identify not only the action to be taken but also who is responsible for that action along with the proposed implementation date(s).

Overall, fundamental components of a corrective action plan should accomplish the following objectives:

- Identify the problem, nonconformity, or undesirable situation

- Identify immediate remedial or containment actions, if appropriate

- Identify the potential underlying cause(s) of the problem

- Identify the likelihood that the problem will recur or occur in other areas

- Evaluate the need for corrective action

- Use problem-solving techniques to verify underlying cause(s), determine a solution(s) to eliminate the cause(s), and develop an action plan

- Identify responsibilities of personnel for the corrective action plan

- Determine monitoring actions and measures of effectiveness

- Establish timelines and provide a schedule of the dates when action is to be initiated and completed

- Document the corrective action plan

In some cases, the audited organization will provide information as to why no corrective action is needed. Perhaps it is an isolated incident or the problem doesn't trigger the organization's preset corrective action threshold. In other cases, the auditee will acknowledge that the corrective action request has been received and that it is understood, but that more time is needed to work on it and a plan to address the problem will be prepared at a specified future date. The auditor must assess each case to approve (or not approve) a request for an extension. The use of extension requests, reviews, and subsequent grants should be formalized in the corrective action system.

2. REVIEW OF CORRECTIVE ACTION PLAN

The client (or another designated person) coordinates the review of the auditee's response to the corrective action request. The client or the audit program manager reviews the corrective action plan or assigns the review to others, such as the lead auditor or an audit team member. The reviewer must do one of the following: accept the corrective action plan, reject it, or ask for additional information for clarification purposes. Figure 9.1 is an example of one company's form for recording reviewer results.

Corrective action must be timely and effective, and it must prevent recurrence of the same problem. It is sometimes necessary to implement immediate remedial or containment actions. Such actions as recalling, replacing, or stopping product delivery will not prevent recurrence but may enable a process to continue pending the implementation of a long-term solution. For example, when an automatic measuring device on a production line is found to be out of calibration, immediate action could be taken to check the measured parameter with a hand-held calibrated instrument before releasing components for use and revising the procedure. A technical specialist may be utilized to assess the proposed corrective action plan if the auditor or client does not have the expertise to do so.

If the proposed corrective action plan seems feasible and reasonable, it should be accepted. When evaluating a proposed corrective action plan, the reviewer (auditor, client, audit program manager, or other person assigned) should make sure that the auditee is treating the underlying cause, not a symptom of the problem, thus verifying that a true root cause analysis was performed. The proposed

Request for Corrective Action			
C/A REQUEST NO:	❏ INTERNAL	❏ EXTERNAL	AUDIT/WN/PO:
ISSUED TO:			
REQUESTED BY:			PART NO.:
DATE:			
C/A REQUESTED FOR:			
C/A REQUIRED DATE:	RETURN TO ATTN: John Doe		
Corrective Action Response			
PROBABLE CAUSE:			
C/A TAKEN:			
EFFECTIVITY DATE:	SUBMITTED BY:		DATE:
REVIEW OF C/A:			
❏ SATISFACTORY	❏ UNSATISFACTORY	❏ C/A IMPLEMENTED & EFFECTIVE:	
COMMENTS:			
REVIEWED BY:		DATE:	

Figure 9.1 Sample request for corrective action form for first-party audits.

Source: Provided by Solar Turbines, 1998 Malcolm Baldrige National Quality Award Winner. Used with permission.

solution might address the issue on the surface but may not prevent the problem from recurring, so the reviewer should ask whether the corrective action plan is specific enough to ensure that changes will be permanent. The auditee must also ensure that the corrective action does not cause another problem.

Corrective action must be timely. It is permissible for an auditee to request reasonable extensions, since some problems take longer to solve. However, the auditee may be asked to provide periodic status reports with supporting evidence on the corrective action progress.

It is important for the auditee to understand that action taken to prevent the recurrence of a given problem is *not* preventive action. Preventive action is a discipline geared to preventing the occurrence of a potential problem.

The principle of corrective action is that conditions adverse to a management system must be identified and corrected. True corrective action is difficult to implement, since the real causes of problems are seldom easy to identify.

A five-step process is recommended to ensure the acceptability of the corrective action:

1. Determine the problem and implement immediate remedial or containment action.

2. Conduct an investigation to identify root causes.

3. Design and implement the corrective action and verify its effectiveness.

4. Ensure that the nonconformity is managed and controlled to avoid the potential of recurrence that causes a nonconformity elsewhere in the process.

5. Analyze the effects of the findings on the product or services being provided. For example, what, if anything, does the organization need to do (remedial/containment action) about products shipped or systems that were active while the product or service was in noncompliance?

Reviewers should avoid the temptation to accept human error as a cause. Ask why it is human error. Perhaps the error is due to a complex process, poor documentation, inadequate training, weak supervision, and so on.

Follow-up action may be accomplished through written or electronic communication, review of revised documents, reaudit after the reported implementation date, or other appropriate means. The auditee's corrective action should be accepted if it corrects the problem and prevents recurrence.

Negotiation of Corrective Action Plans

Some organizations want to involve audit team members in the corrective action process and others do not. The auditor who collected the evidence and found the problem could be a valuable resource for ensuring effective corrective action from audits. However, involvement of audit team members could create a conflict of interest for future audits or be an added liability for an external auditing organization. Because of the difficulties of being involved in a team approach for correcting findings from audits, some organizations do not allow auditors to be involved in the corrective action process. However, when the audit team members are involved, they should provide only factual data regarding audit investigation and explain their opinion of why the corrective action will be ineffective. Auditors must avoid providing solutions to process owners and taking ownership of the problem. Another option that may avoid conflict-of-interest issues is to assign an auditor different from the one who reported the issues needing improvement as a subject matter expert or team member.

The auditor should clearly state the findings, and the auditee should indicate that they are understood. A clear statement of nonconformance should include the stated requirements and then the gap between the requirement and the actual practice. However, the auditor and the auditee may not always agree on the proposed action plan or the timing of the corrective action. In most cases, additional explanation of the requirements and/or the conditions that led to the identification of the finding may be sufficient for the auditee to develop an effective corrective action plan. Some situations are complex and require more data and alternate evaluation methods by both the auditor and the auditee.

A difference of opinion should not lead the reviewer or auditor to automatically assume that the auditee is wrong. Forcing one's will on the auditee is unacceptable and may lead to disastrous results for the audit function. Instead, the reviewer or auditor should attempt to understand the auditee's interpretation of the requirement and the underlying reasoning for the proposed corrective action. In some cases the auditee's proposed action plan will address system issues that were not identified during the course of the audit. If the auditee's reasoning is valid, the proposed action plan should be accepted. On the other hand, if there are specific identified weaknesses in the action plan, these should be presented to the auditee so that they may be understood and addressed.

The review of the corrective action progress may indicate that the auditee is unresponsive or evasive or that the proposed action is inadequate. When a response is questionable or unacceptable, the reviewer (or other designated person) should contact the auditee to resolve the concern or perception. A simple telephone call by the reviewer or auditor could alleviate the concern. The reviewer or audit team members should take care not to become combative. If it is clear that discussions are not going to result in the successful resolution of the corrective action plan, the matter should be escalated up the management chain.

3. VERIFICATION OF CORRECTIVE ACTION

A review of the corrective action response and its timeliness is, in some instances, all the follow-up action required by the client or the organizational procedures. In most cases, auditors are directed to verify corrective actions. One method of verification is for an auditor to return to the work area, observe the new process, ensure that the paperwork has been done, and confirm that employees have been trained in the new method. Auditors may also use performance records to verify the effectiveness of the corrective action.

The auditor's evaluation should be documented to ensure that all findings on the corrective action request have been addressed. The auditor records actions taken in order to verify the corrective action and the results of that verification. The auditor may record the verification on a corrective action form, an audit report, or both. The auditee's actions must be traceable to facilitate verification.

All audit findings do not have to be closed at the same time; they may be closed out individually instead. Verification for such corrective actions need not be done immediately; rather, it may be combined with another visit, if possible, or another auditor may be asked to verify the corrective action and collect supporting information of the corrective action. A finding may be closed pending final verification.

Follow-up Audits

Follow-up audits may be required in some situations, but due to cost consider-ations, many organizations do not require them. Instead, follow-up activities are included with the next regularly scheduled audit. When follow-up audits are per-formed as a separate activity, the audit schedule is determined by the findings opened during the original audit. These audits can also provide independent veri-fication of corrective action effectiveness.

> A "for cause" audit was performed of raw material supplier XYZ because contaminated product was sent to customer ABC. The audit resulted in critical observations regarding lack of cleaning processes at XYZ. ABC halted orders of raw materials until corrective actions were implemented at XYZ and a follow-up audit could be performed to confirm their effectiveness.

ISO 19011, clause 6.7, states that the completion and effectiveness of corrective actions should be verified. This verification can be part of a subsequent audit.

For internal audits and some external audits, follow-up activities may be accom-plished in another way. The auditee may provide the auditor with periodic reports and records containing evidence that the corrective action plan has been imple-mented and is effective. In this way, the auditor may be able to verify that the action plan is effective, without the added expense of another audit. The auditor still has the option of verifying the effectiveness of these activities during subsequent visits.

When an auditor accepts an audit assignment, the scope may include verifi-cation of corrective actions from previous audits. In most cases, the verification activity can be easily integrated into the audit schedule by looking at the audi-tor assignments and areas visited during that audit. Sometimes, there may be too many corrective actions or they may be too complex to verify them in the amount of time allotted for the audit. If corrective action verification jeopardizes the objec-tives of the current audit process, the lead auditor should notify the audit program manager or client.

Remote audit techniques may be used to follow up corrective actions in a timely and economical manner.[1] There is no need to wait until the next scheduled audit to verify the corrective action. Perhaps the criticality of the corrective action implementation requires immediate verification. Subsequent on-site visits could be used to verify long-term effectiveness of corrective actions.

Verification of Corrective Action Completion

For effective implementation, the auditor should verify that people did what they said they were going to do and that everyone involved in the change is informed. People can be informed by means of a discussion, a training session, a memo-randum, or an e-mail or by another method. This is important for a new process, process changes, or personnel changes. The auditor should verify that records are retained to provide evidence that everyone involved is aware of the changes.

Verification is a logical close to the corrective action sequence of an audit. Consider the following flow of events:

1. Findings and nonconformities are identified by the auditor through corrective action requests

2. The auditee acknowledges the corrective action request and submits a plan to correct the deficiencies and prevent the occurrence of new problems

3. The client and/or the lead auditor (if assigned to do so) approve the plan of action

4. The auditee effectively implements the corrective action

5. Through verification activities, the client or the lead auditor confirms the effectiveness of the corrective action[2]

Effectiveness of Corrective Action

Management (or the auditor, if assigned to do so) must review the results of the corrective action plan to determine whether the actions implemented achieved the desired result. To demonstrate effectiveness, the auditee should determine the appropriate measures to be monitored. The reviewer will then be able to verify effectiveness of the corrective action by comparing the end result with the original conditions.

Effective implementation of a corrective action plan is not the same as an effective corrective action. The first indicates that the actions were implemented, while the second indicates that the actions worked. Two elements are involved in effective corrective action:

1. Achieving the desired result is proof that the process improved and the actions implemented are consistent with the organization's goals

2. The fact that the process is capable, efficient, and meets stated objectives requires evidence that it consistently achieves the desired results in a cost-effective manner

The auditor does not determine effectiveness by verifying that a change occurred. Effectiveness is verified when the auditor determines that a change has occurred and that the product and process achieved the desired result.

4. FOLLOW-UP ON INEFFECTIVE CORRECTIVE ACTION

Follow-up audit reports may indicate serious problems with claimed implementation and/or effectiveness. Auditors and/or clients must be objective when determining what strategy to employ when corrective action is not implemented or is not effective. Change may be required in both the audit function and the auditee's organization. Auditors will need to draw on their communication and negotiation skills to ensure that the appropriate actions are initiated. The auditor must evaluate each occurrence of lack of implementation or ineffective corrective action based on its own merits.

Rather than assume that the auditee is at fault, the auditor should reevaluate the corrective action and follow-up process with an open mind. Perhaps an incorrect conclusion was reached due to a lack of time to verify evidence. Available evidence may indicate an error in judgment on the part of the corrective action team, or there may be inadequate resources. The lack of resources may be due to a change in business conditions beyond the auditee's control. Lack of success when attempting to implement corrective action could indicate a lack of management support for the corrective action process.

When the corrective action is not implemented, the auditor should take time to evaluate the situation thoroughly before making any attempt at escalation (top management involvement). Prematurely jumping into the role of enforcer puts the auditor in a negative position. It is in the auditor's best interest to be viewed as one who is interested in helping the auditee achieve the desired results. As a last resort, the auditor may need to go up the chain of command to the next level of management. However, the process for involving the next management level should be formalized and documented.

When the corrective action is not effective, the auditor and/or the client should either recycle the finding or issue a new finding (referencing the original) to start the corrective action process again. Failure of the corrective action is serious and should be considered a form of rework. If this is a frequent occurrence, the corrective action process may be suspect and may indicate that true root cause analysis methods are not being utilized.

For third-party and some second-party audits, failure to implement a corrective action could result in suspension, being taken off the approved list, or loss of registration/certification.

5. AUDIT CLOSURE

After verifying corrective action implementation, the auditing organization may prepare a follow-up report and distribute it in a manner similar to the original audit report. Closure requires verification that corrective actions have been implemented as planned. The auditor notifies the auditee that the audit is closed. The auditor may then discard certain papers accumulated during the audit but is generally required to retain defined records for specific time periods.

Criteria for Closure

Written notification of closure, including an assessment of the auditee's corrective action plan implementation and effectiveness, should be submitted to the client and/or the auditee for their records.

When the client is not the auditee, communication between an auditor and an auditee will usually go through the client, since the client is the primary link with the audited organization. For an external audit, the contract may specify a contact person. Internally, closeout reports go to the original distribution of the audit report, such as the audit manager and the audited organization. A summary report of all audits performed and their closure status goes to upper-level managers.

Sometimes each corrective action request is individually tracked. Tracking each individual corrective action and closing out a portion of an audit are acceptable. Upon resolution of each finding, written notification should be sent to those who received a copy of the initial report. This written notification not only satisfies the auditing department's records but also lets the auditee know that the corrective actions have been accepted. If a satisfactory resolution cannot be reached with the auditee, the finding should be forwarded to upper management for resolution and then closed out, if so directed.

Timeliness

The primary concern with timeliness is the completion and verification of the effectiveness of the corrective action. An administrative concern may be the timely closure of a request for corrective action or the audit report once the corrective actions have been verified. The audit should be closed out as soon as the corrective action is verified and not carried as an open item or backlog activity.

Timeliness of corrective action does not mean that all corrective actions will be closed in 30 days or some other fixed time period. Timeliness with regard to corrective action is not compared against a fixed time period but rather an agreed-upon time period. The specified time should be based on the importance of the corrective action and the availability of resources. Some corrective actions may be completed in a few minutes, while others may take weeks or months. The auditor is limited to reaching agreement with the auditee on the date for completion of each corrective action plan. If these are completed on schedule, then corrective action is considered to be timely. There are times, however, when delays occur that are beyond the auditee's control. The auditor should accept these when there is sufficient evidence that the auditee has initiated actions and recorded the reasons for the delays in completing the action plan.

It is in the auditee's best interest to close out audit findings in a timely manner. Correcting nonconformities normally lessens risk to the organization. Less risk may reduce costs such as waste or reduce the potential of a major upset or injury.

Problems Commonly Encountered during the Audit Reporting and Closure Stage

The following are examples of the types of problems commonly encountered during the audit reporting and closure stage.

Lack of Response or Inadequate Response

Sometimes an auditee will fail to take the action specified in the corrective action plan. The auditee may fail to notify the auditing organization when action is taken, or the action taken may not be sufficient to warrant closing out the finding. The auditee may lose sight of the original intent of the corrective action request and address a different issue. At times, an auditee may not understand what a standard says or means and may argue the issue's importance or relevance. As a result, an auditee may try to fix a problem haphazardly without understanding the need for action or training. Sometimes the person involved in fixing a problem was not involved in the audit and may not have all the needed information. An auditee may try to pit one audit team against another and argue that the other audit team had no findings in a certain area.

On-the-Spot Corrective Actions

Some organizations may ask for a list of findings prior to the exit meeting so that corrective action can be implemented before the auditors leave the building. The immediate management response should be recognized by the audit team, but in most cases, the underlying cause of the problem is not eliminated. Auditors should use their best judgment, but true root cause analysis, leading to effective corrective actions, is difficult at best when the auditee proposes to solve a problem quickly.

Continual Requests for Extensions

Sometimes an auditor and an auditee may not agree on the significance of a problem. When vested interest is not the same, agreement on the importance or priority of solving a problem may be difficult to achieve. An auditee may request continual extensions for fixing the problem. Excuses can range from "We're working on a big order and don't have time to fix it right now" to "We forgot."

Part IID

Part III

Auditor Competencies

[25 of the CQA Exam Questions or 16.7 percent]

Auditors with only the knowledge of audit techniques may understand the technical requirements for an effective audit yet may not be effective auditors. They must not only present themselves professionally but also demonstrate the ability to apply their knowledge and skills effectively. This section addresses the competencies required of an auditor in order to be effective.

Chapter 10
Auditor Characteristics/Part IIIA

Auditor characteristics are those qualities that make auditors effective. They become integrated into the auditor's behavior so that they appear to be a natural pattern of conduct. Characteristics such as interpersonal skills, problem solving, and the ability to work independently as well as on a team are learned through study and practice. For that reason, most audit programs require knowledge and skill competencies gained through a combination of education, training, experience, and demonstration of personal traits.

Auditor competence is composed of several things, including:

- Education, training, and knowledge

- Work experience

- Audit skills

- Communication skills

- Personal traits

Auditors must understand how to conduct an effective audit in the auditee organization environment and be able to apply the audit criteria. Auditors must possess the personal attributes necessary for conducting an effective and efficient audit.

EDUCATION AND EXPERIENCE

Institutions providing auditor certification, such as ASQ, the IIA, and RABQSA International (formerly the Registrar Accreditation Board of the United States and the Sydney-based Quality Society of Australia), require knowledge and skill competencies as well as minimum levels of formal education. Neither ASQ nor RABQSA International requires an advanced degree, as the IIA does for the Certified Internal Auditor. The requirements for auditor certification are summarized in Table 10.1.

Once a candidate has completed the prerequisite education and experience, received the training (when required), and successfully completed the examination(s), the ongoing maintenance phase required for continued certification begins. Maintenance may include seminars, conferences, auditing, serving on professional committees, examinations, and so on. The RABQSA certification requires passing a knowledge examination, skills examination (witnessed audit), and the Personal Attribute Assessment examination (personal traits). A quality auditor must meet requirements to conduct quality audits; an environmental

Table 10.1 Auditor certification requirements.

	ASQ Certified Quality Auditor	IIA Certified Internal Auditor	RABQSA Quality Management System-Auditor
Years of experience required based on completed formal education:			
High school diploma	8 years	Ineligible	Ineligible
Technical/trade school diploma	7 years	Ineligible	2 years
Associate degree	6 years	Ineligible	2 years
Bachelor's degree (four-year postsecondary education)	4 years	2 years	2 years
Master's degree or doctorate	3 years	1 year	2 years
Training/Work experience:			
Audit experience	8 years less credit for advanced degree	2 years	2 years
Training	NR	NR	NR
Sponsor (verifying professionalism)	Yes	Yes	NR
Examination, knowledge	5 hours	4 parts at 3.5 hours	3 parts at TBD
Examination, skills	NR	NR	NR
Continuing professional development	18 RUs in 3 years	80 hours in 2 years	Examine in 4 years

Sources: ASQ Certification Department, CQA Brochure, Item B0020, revised December 2003, p. 10; IIA, Certified Internal Auditor Brochure, revised January 2004, pp. 1–3; IIA CIA, http://www.theiia.org/Certification/ (accessed July 2012); RABQSA International Criteria for Accredited QMS Auditor Certification, http://www.rabqsa.com/cb_qms.html (accessed July 2012).

Note: RU = recertification unit (generally 1 RU = 0.1 continuing education units)

auditor must meet environmental education and experience requirements to conduct environmental audits. The same is true for auditors in other sectors such as aerospace, medical, and automotive.

An auditor must be able to comprehend the materials presented during an audit. Some industries and market sectors have their own language and ways of conducting business. An auditor may gain this knowledge through a combination of work experience and training. For example, the knowledge and experience needed for auditing a medical facility may be very different from what is needed to audit an education facility or assembly plant.

Beyond the nominal education requirements, an auditor needs to understand improvement tools and techniques to be an effective auditor. Table 10.2 gives

Table 10.2 Tools and programs.

Data analysis tools	Improvement tools	Improvement programs
Pareto charts	Corrective action	ISO 9001
Cause-and-effect diagrams	Preventive action	Total quality management
Flowcharts	Root cause analysis	Six Sigma
Control charts	Plan-Do-Check-Act	Lean
Check sheets	Cost of quality	Statistical control
Scatter diagrams		
Histograms		
Descriptive statistics		
Matrix		
Sampling techniques		

example data analysis tools and improvement tools and programs. Part V of the handbook discusses the tools and techniques that a quality auditor should know. These same topics and tools (such as descriptive statistics, sampling, flowcharts, and diagrams) are relevant to many other types of auditing.

Environmental auditors need to know common environmental tools such as mass balance, risk assessment and probabilities, contingency planning, ecosystems, abatement, and so on.

Additional value-added training is discussed in Part IV, "Audit Program Management and Business Applications."

INTERPERSONAL SKILLS

Regardless of education or training, an auditor who lacks certain interpersonal skills (see those listed in Tables 10.3 and 10.4) will not be able to conduct an effective audit. Audit relationships are very important, especially in internal audits, and the auditor must be able to maintain healthy relationships even when critiquing another's work or questioning the validity of someone's actions.

An auditor must be able to understand the technical materials presented during an audit. Depending on the complexity of an audit, the auditor must be able to ask probing questions and get to the heart of the problem.

If an auditor is expected to conduct remote audits or eAudits, additional communication knowledge and skills will be needed.

ISO 19011:2011, clause 7.1, states:

> Confidence in the audit process and the ability to achieve its objectives depends on the competence of those individuals who are involved in planning and conducting audits, including auditors and audit team leaders. Competence should be evaluated through a process that considers personal behavior and the ability to apply the knowledge and skills gained through education, work experience, auditor training and audit experience. This process should take into consideration the needs of the audit program and its objectives. Some of the knowledge and skills described in this section are common to auditors of any management system discipline; others are specific to individual management system disciplines. It is not necessary for each auditor in the audit team to have the same competence; however, the

Table 10.3   Communication skills.

Listening	Being clear and concise
Questioning	Good writing skills
Probing	Good oral skills
Critiquing	Appropriate body language
Handling conflict	Tact

Table 10.4   Auditing skills.

Evaluating and judging	Drawing conclusions	Observing
Controlling an audit	Understanding technical	Identifying problem areas
Planning and preparing	material	Knowledge of audit
Maintaining confidentiality	Presenting (reports and at	principles and functions
Leading	meetings)	Applying knowledge
Supervising	Verifying evidence (no	Collecting data
Recording	assumptions)	Organizing
Administering	Discovering the truth (but	Time management
Decision making	not a witch hunt)	Reviewing
Analyzing evidence	Awareness of authority level	Sampling
	Business understanding	Assessing

overall competence of the audit team needs to be sufficient to achieve the audit objectives.

The evaluation of auditor competence should be planned, implemented, and documented in accordance with the audit program, including its procedures to provide an outcome that is objective, consistent, fair, and reliable. The evaluation process should include four main steps, as follows:

a. Determine the competence of audit personnel to fulfill the needs of the audit program

b. Establish the evaluation criteria

c. Select the appropriate evaluation method

d. Conduct the evaluation

The outcome of the evaluation process should provide a basis for the following:

• Selection of audit team members

• Determining the need for improved competence (e.g., additional training)

• Ongoing performance evaluation of auditors

Auditors should develop, maintain, and improve their competence through continual professional development and regular participation in audits.[1]

ISO 19011 does not list formal education, training, or experience competency needs. For example, instead of needed knowledge and skills such as basic reading, writing, and oral communication, auditors should be able to communicate effectively, orally and in writing (either personally or through the use of interpreters and translators).

Competencies for first-, second-, and third-party auditors may be different. Competencies will change for industry and system sectors. General auditor competencies may be based on job performance. Key auditing competencies include:

- Being able to implement an audit

- Maintaining communication

- Collecting and verifying audit evidence

- Composing findings and conclusions

For lead auditors, there is added emphasis on leadership, formal communication, and skills needed to manage the audit process.

PERSONAL TRAITS

To be effective, the auditor must have the traits listed in Table 10.5.

The emphasis on desirable personal traits may vary by type of audit. For example, versatility may be more important in second- and third-party audits than in first-party audits. The courage to point out problems may be more important for internal auditors who know and interact with the auditee.

Table 10.5 Auditor personal traits and attributes.

Personal traits for auditors	Personal attributes list in ISO 19011
1. Independent 2. Systematic 3. Trustworthy 4. Persistent 5. Positive 6. Curious 7. Open-minded 8. Mature 9. Tenacious 10. Patient 11. Adaptable 12. Unbiased 13. Has no hidden agenda 14. Courageous 15. Ethical 16. Diplomatic 17. Versatile	a) Ethical—fair, truthful, sincere, honest, and discreet b) Open-minded—willing to consider alternative ideas or points of view c) Diplomatic—tactful in dealing with people d) Observant—actively aware of physical surroundings and activities e) Perceptive—instinctively aware of and able to understand situations f) Versatile—adjusts readily to different situations g) Tenacious—persistent, focused on achieving objectives h) Decisive—reaches timely conclusions based on logical reasoning and analysis i) Self-reliant—acts and functions independently while interacting effectively with others j) Acting with fortitude—able to act responsibly and ethically, even though these actions may not always be popular and may sometimes result in disagreement or confrontation k) Open to improvement—willing to learn from situations, and striving for better audit results l) Culturally sensitive—observant and respectful of the culture of the auditee m) Collaborative—effectively interacting with others, including audit team members and the auditee's personnel

Chapter 11
On-Site Audit Resource Management/ Part IIIB

TIME-MANAGEMENT SKILLS

Proper preparation in the audit planning stage can eliminate many delays in the audit performance stage. To make the most efficient use of time, the auditor must plan an audit on several levels. First, the audit manager must schedule each individual audit in relation to other audits being performed so that the availability of auditors and other resources can be assessed. Next, the lead auditor must prepare the audit plan for the individual audit. The steps involved in this audit phase were discussed in the audit process section of this handbook. Once the lead auditor establishes the auditing strategy, a detailed schedule must be prepared that specifies which areas are to be visited at various times throughout the day. The detailed schedule may be constantly revised during the audit, but the lead auditor must inform auditee management about planned activities. An audit team member who makes no attempt to stick to the proposed schedule may antagonize members of the auditee organization who have made arrangements to be available as requested.

The lead auditor's notification letter to the auditee should specify special arrangements such as transportation from one audit site to another, the need for an escort, the use of special safety equipment, or the need for a conference room. At this time, the lead auditor should list required equipment or supplies, such as access to copy machines, printers, data or overhead projectors, and extension cords. By anticipating needs and making them known to the auditee in advance, the lead auditor communicates preparedness and a strong desire to focus on the important task of gathering information at the audit site.

To ensure the efficient use of time during the audit performance stage, the audit team should arrive promptly at the audit site at the agreed-upon time for the opening meeting. The lead auditor should retain control of the opening meeting and should not allow the auditee to take control with extended plant tours or lengthy presentations, unless such time has been scheduled into the audit.

Auditors should allow several minutes at the end of each interview to review notes, present conclusions, and reach a consensus with an auditee representative, such as the area supervisor or the escort. If data indicate that certain areas need additional attention, auditors' assignments may need to be changed. Findings that indicate severe ramifications for the program being audited should be thoroughly investigated and recorded as soon as possible after they are discovered.

Lead auditors often prefer that the audit team have a working lunch on-site instead of going off-site to a restaurant. Scheduling a small amount of time for an audit team meeting during the lunch break aids the auditors in gathering additional information and corroborating information with other audit team members. A poorly organized lunch can cost the audit team precious time and cause embarrassment if auditors are late for the next scheduled interview. If an off-site lunch is appropriate for communicating with auditee management or for team management purposes, adequate time should be scheduled. For remote audits, the lead auditor can set specific times for meals and breaks. There are no host or long lunch break issues.

The audit team should also meet each day to summarize its information, to review progress, and to ensure that the audit objective can be achieved. Usually, this meeting is held prior to the daily update with the auditee. If the lead auditor finds that another meeting is necessary, the team may meet again following the daily briefing with the auditee. These meetings not only help identify instances where additional information needs to be gathered but also facilitate the preparation for the exit meeting by ensuring that there is sufficient evidence to support the team's conclusions and that evidence is appropriately documented.

An audit team should schedule sufficient time to prepare for the exit meeting, especially when an audit lasts several days. The team summarizes the information gathered for presentation in the exit meeting. The team leader prepares a draft of the final report with the audit team's input and may assign portions of the presentation to specific team members.

Chapter 12
Conflict Resolution/Part IIIC

CAUSES OF CONFLICT

The most effective method of resolving conflict is to take steps to prevent conflict occurrence. Within the audit team, the team leader may establish ground rules for communication, interaction, and performance of team members prior to the audit. The audit team may reduce conflict during the audit by eliminating misunderstandings, remaining open-minded and flexible, and avoiding surprises during the audit process.

Misunderstandings are the most common cause of conflict during an audit. Sources of misunderstanding are poor communication, poor listening, and auditor or auditee bias. Auditors must always be on the lookout for signs of misunderstanding. Indicators include a less than cooperative attitude on the part of an interviewee, repeated questions about the audit scope and purpose, and the provision of inadequate or incorrect records for review. In these situations, the best course of action is for the auditor to repeat or clarify the information that was not fully understood before proceeding. Also, auditors must be active listeners, meaning they must not only hear what is being said but also recognize when the message is clouded by a possible contradictory meaning. Finally, the auditor should always assume that the auditee is acting in good faith. He or she must not assume that a misunderstanding is on the part of the auditee. Instead, the auditor should rephrase the question in a different way, being careful to avoid terminology that has confusing meanings. Auditors must not assume that the auditee is familiar with specific industry jargon. However, in some cases, the auditee may not act in good faith or may be uncooperative, and the auditor should watch for those situations.

During an audit, auditors must remain open-minded and flexible. Auditors must bear in mind that when they conduct an audit, for whatever reason or from whatever source of authority, they are disrupting the daily routine of the auditee. Auditors should also consider the effect of special requests on the audited organization and ensure that the audit takes into consideration the work norms and culture of the auditee.

Unnecessary and unreasonable demands are often a source of conflict during the audit. This becomes especially true when the auditee is intimidated by the audit team and, as a result, is unwilling to say anything ahead of time. These kinds of issues can manifest themselves later in the form of uncooperativeness, avoidance, belligerence, or even sabotage.

A sure way to create conflict during an audit is to withhold important information about the audit's status or results and surprise the auditee at or after the exit meeting. It is important, therefore, that auditors share information with the auditee on a regular basis. This is usually done during informal daily meetings or during actual audit performance. In addition, auditors have an obligation to inform auditee personnel of the nature of the information they are recording, how it will be used, and so on. Being up front with auditees not only helps address some of their concerns about the audit process but also puts them at ease, thus reducing the likelihood of conflict.

If conflict should develop during an audit, the best course of action is for the auditor to temporarily stop the audit and allow a cooldown period before proceeding. If auditors don't take this action, they run the risk of getting overly involved and losing control of the audit process. The ultimate result of losing control is the premature termination of the audit or the auditee not allowing the auditor to proceed. Neither of these situations is acceptable to the auditor's organization or the client. Once the conflict has been defused, the auditor can meet with the auditee to determine the source of the misunderstanding. Auditors must remain open to the possibility that they may be a direct cause of the conflict. To resolve the conflict and allow the audit to proceed, auditors must remain open-minded and listen to the auditee.

An auditor does not have the option of avoiding or trying to smooth over an issue with an auditee. Nor should an auditor attack individuals or attempt to use his or her position to overpower them. Forcing a conflict escalates it and increases the chance of recurrence later in the audit with the same person. Sometimes successful resolution of conflict is agreement that there is disagreement.

MANAGING DIFFICULT SITUATIONS

Challenging situations include antagonism, coercion, and even time-wasting techniques employed by the auditee to slow down or stop the audit process.

Difficult Situations May Arise

At times, an auditor may encounter difficult situations that are counterproductive to the auditing process. For example, an auditee may be antagonistic or coercive. Interviewing may be made ineffective by an interviewee who talks too much or not at all. An auditee may also use time-wasting tactics by deviating from the audit plan. In any difficult situation, the auditor should remain polite but firm, maintaining self-control and complete control of the audit.

Defusing Antagonistic Situations

Sometimes employees are openly hostile to an auditor for reasons unrelated to the audit, or the employees may be reacting to what they feel is a personal attack by the auditor on their abilities to do their work. An employee may have been part of the team that developed a process or a particular system, or he or she may have just gone through a six-month-long endeavor to improve something that the auditor is now picking apart. When auditees get defensive, the auditor should separate them or suggest a break to defuse the situation. The auditor should continue the conversation at a later time, when everyone is calm.

Combating Time-Wasting Techniques

An experienced auditor will immediately recognize most time-wasting tactics employed by an auditee. An auditor needs to lead an audit and not allow the auditee to take control. If an auditee attempts a lengthy presentation at the opening meeting or an extended plant tour, for example, the lead auditor should halt these activities or limit the time spent on them. Often, a lead auditor can eliminate wasted time by making specific requests during the audit planning stage. For example, many audit teams prefer an on-site lunch to going off-premises for several hours. Of course, auditee management and the client should be notified when an audit team repeatedly encounters delay tactics or if the audit schedule is severely compromised by such delays.

> Another subtle time-wasting technique is for the auditee to find a topic to engage the auditor. This may be about quality, environmental rules, politics, or a pet peeve. While the auditor is bloviating, he or she is not auditing. This plays on the auditor's ego. In classes, I have had auditors defend their actions, saying that if the auditee asks about their views on a topic relevant to the audit (such as the corrective action process), it is their duty to share their expertise (opinion) about the subject. As an auditee, I constantly explore topics until I find one the auditor wants to talk about. I may be sincerely interested in the topic, too, but the point is, the auditor is not auditing while he or she is expounding and explaining.

Figure 12.1 lists some common time-wasting ploys and suggests possible solutions that an auditor may use when faced with each problem. An auditor adjusting to specific situations could likely think of equally effective solutions.

The problem	One solution
Requested personnel are unavailable to the audit team.	Depending on the situation, the auditor may interview the backup or politely state that absence of key personnel may prolong the audit or that the audit's scope may have to be modified.
The escort is repeatedly late in the mornings.	The auditor could ask the escort for suggestions for starting the meeting on time and make the necessary changes to the schedule.
The auditee repeatedly makes the auditor wait for needed supplies or requested documents and records.	The auditor should request needed supplies during the audit planning stage and anticipate document and record needs in advance. The auditor could also travel with the auditee to select the documentation sample or supplies.
Constant distractions occur during interviews (area is noisy, constant phone ringing, or other interruptions).	The auditor could suggest that they move away from the area or close doors if possible; phones should be set to call forwarding or answered by someone else.
Interviewees state that they were not informed of the audit and are not prepared.	The auditor should confirm that employees are aware that an audit is taking place and ask auditee management about the state of readiness of the management system to be audited.

Figure 12.1 Common time-wasting ploys and possible solutions.

Part IIIC

TEAM CONFLICT

Conflict can also occur within the audit team. There can be differences of opinion about the interpretation of a requirement and the severity of the finding. How conflict affects the team depends on how members respond to it.

In assessing their response to conflict, auditors should ask themselves two questions. First, how important is the opinion, goal, or perspective under discussion? Second, how important is it to maintain good relationships with the people involved in the conflict?[1]

Conflict responses include the following guidelines:

- *Avoiding* an issue or a person is not an option if the conflict is relevant to the audit. If the conflict is a nonaudit issue, avoiding the conflict allows everyone to save face, but the conflict goes unresolved.

- *Smoothing over* may be an option if the issue is minor or irresolvable. Those in conflict should focus on what they agree on instead of what they disagree on. Trying to address the conflict may detract from the effectiveness of the audit team.

- *Forcing someone to accept an opinion* or overpowering him or her is not good practice unless it remains the only course of action to ensure a successful audit. In some situations, a quick decision is needed and there is no time for investigating and evaluating the issue. The "my way or the highway" approach can lead to resentment and detract from team effectiveness. The lead auditor should consider all inputs before making a final decision.

- *Compromising* assumes everyone can accept less than their original position. Compromise can result in no one getting what they wanted. A compromise may be to agree to cite both clause numbers in the nonconformity statement when the team cannot agree on which requirement is more applicable. A less desirable compromise may be to remove the nonconformity because the audit team could not agree on the best clause to cite in the nonconformity statement.

- *Collaboration or problem solving* seeks to find a mutually agreeable solution to the conflict. It is a win-win approach. Tactics include stating the problem, identifying core issues, and listening to each other. The basis is that given the same facts, two reasonable people will come to the same conclusion. Collaboration should be used when resolution of the conflict is very important and there is sufficient time to explore rational and alternate solutions.

Chapter 13
Communication and Presentation Techniques/Part IIID

BASIC RULES FOR EFFECTIVE COMMUNICATION

System and process auditing require effective communication with the auditee organization and the auditor's organization and within the audit team itself. This communication can take many forms, including written memos, automated notifications, e-mails, chats, and verbal conversations before and during an audit performance. Basic rules for effective communication include (1) ensuring that the message is clear, (2) verifying that the message is received and understood, and (3) using the appropriate medium for transmittal.

To ensure the message is clear, the auditor should:

- Use appropriate terminology and avoid terms that are hard to understand

- Avoid lengthy explanations that dilute the point of the message

- Ensure the accuracy of the information

- Adapt the level and approach of the communications to the audience (for example, the CEO, technicians, or engineers)

To verify that the message is received and understood, the auditor should:

- Verify that the auditee received all messages sent (for example, via telephone, fax, or e-mail)

- Look for signs of understanding, such as nods of the head and expressions like "I see"

- Seek feedback by asking clarifying questions and listening to the responses

- Determine when a written record of the communication is needed

To determine the appropriate medium for transmittal, the auditor should:

- Take into account the formality of the message

- Determine the technology in use by the receiver

- Use the appropriate format for transmission (for example, letter, memo, e-mail, or phone)

In initial meetings, the lead auditor has much work to do to establish effective communication. Communication techniques that may be used during the preaudit phase include:[1]

- Building rapport by exchanging small talk, perhaps over a cup of coffee.
- Establishing trust by ensuring confidentiality.
- Showing empathy for the disruptions that will be inevitable and assuring the auditee that distractions will be kept to a minimum.
- Demonstrating professionalism and working hard to be organized.
- Explaining the process by reviewing the audit plan and showing how the auditee will be kept informed.
- Ensuring that the auditee buys in. The auditor should ask: Does this seem reasonable? Do you recommend any changes to make the process run more smoothly?
- Maintaining flexibility by considering all options, yet never relinquishing authority to conduct the audit (be firm but flexible).

Effective communication during the performance phase of an audit involves a variety of factors, including:[2]

- Active listening
- Working with auditee escorts
- Facilitating audit teamwork
- Holding daily auditee briefings
- Accommodating auditee language requirements
- Incorporating technology that improves effectiveness
- Accommodating changes in the audit schedule, if appropriate

COMMUNICATION TECHNOLOGY

The popularity, advancement, and affordability of electronic devices have improved the effectiveness of audits. Auditors do not purchase every new gimmick, but they are constantly looking for value-added technology that will make audits more effective and efficient. Specifically, auditors should look for technology that will reduce audit cycle time, reduce paper, reduce travel costs, reduce physical collection of audit evidence, and improve the overall effectiveness of the audit. Here are a few.

Electronic Mail

Electronic mail allows auditors to communicate with everyone involved in an audit prior to and after the audit. It is excellent for one-way communication and is a move toward real-time reporting of deliverables (being more responsive). A person can send and receive messages from anyone around the globe. E-mail requires the user to check his or her mailbox periodically (at least every other day), and it can be used anytime since it is not limited to business hours. Some cell phones allow a person to access his or her e-mail account anywhere there is internet access. Some programs send a notification when a message has been received.

> Not all auditors have phones that allow them to access e-mail. Cell phones are a great addition to communication technology and a good auditor tool, but not all auditors use them. When auditors are traveling outside their home country, these tools may not function; in some countries, internet access is not available or is unreliable. Even in some U.S. hotels the internet connection can be spotty.

E-mail is a great time-saver and is useful for sending deliverables (audit plans, audit reports) to the auditee in a timely manner. When a message is received, a reply can be sent instantly (no need to make a note or start a to-do list) and a report can be sent—without printing, stuffing, stamping, and mailing.

It is also possible to attach files to the message. If the receiver of the message with an attached file has the same software or is able to convert the file, he or she will be able to read the report or letter in the original format. Anything can be attached—from an entire book to presentation slides. It is quick, easy (most of the time), and extremely useful when time and cost are factors. Electronic versions of audit reports should be protected from tampering by employing a password using the word processing software or by saving in an electronic format such as Adobe PDF with a no-changes security setting.

Internet access also allows auditors to participate in discussion groups and access websites. Discussion groups can keep auditors up to date on what is going on in the audit world. Auditors can also access the home pages of ASQ and other organizations and download or read online a wealth of information.

Fax Modem

Using a fax modem makes for nice-looking reports and letters because it will transmit whatever is on the computer directly to a fax machine. A letter or report file does not need to be converted to ASCII in order to be sent. The fax can be sent to one person or, by using address books or contact lists, to an entire group of people. The auditor can send the audit plan, audit report, and checklist instantly from his or her computer, and they will arrive in the correct format—a necessity for the auditor's deliverables to look their best.

Electronic Device Choices

People have more and more choices of electronic devices to best suit their needs. Net books are small computers the size of a book that have the computing power of a regular computer but without add-ons such as CD or DVD player-recorders. Tablets and iPads provide internet access and enhanced graphics as handheld devices. Cellular phones have advanced to "smartphones," which can access the internet, take pictures, record videos, and monitor e-mails. Functionality can be added to smartphones by adding custom software called apps (applications software).

Part IIID

Voice Mail

Voice mail, like e-mail, allows remote retrieval of messages, but it is limited to one-way voice communications. Some people prefer calling a voice mailbox and listening to messages over reading e-mail messages. Certainly, by listening to another person's voice, it is easier to detect the need to respond or the urgency of a certain matter than it is with e-mail. However, some people are wordy on voice mail and take up a lot of space (time), which is less likely to happen with e-mail. People who are not efficient keyboard users may prefer using voice mail. Voice mail utility has improved with being able to send voice message audio files to a person's e-mail. The person can open the e-mail message and play the recorded voice message.

Cellular Telephones

Cellular telephone technology allows a person to make or receive calls from almost anywhere. Cellular phones are useful in situations where an auditor needs to be able to contact the client or the audit coordinator quickly. They are also useful when the auditor is auditing a large or remote facility where phones are not easily accessible. Cellular phones can increase productivity for persons who experience a lot of waiting time (in airports, offices, or their vehicle). Some cell phones have voice recorders that can be used to record brief comments during an audit.

Audit Software

Auditors should view audit software as they would working papers. Working papers need to be flexible and should not, in any way, detract from the effectiveness of the audit. Software should have (1) checklist questions that can be changed or bypassed, (2) a scoring system that can be bypassed, and (3) reports that can be easily modified to ensure that they fit the auditor's style and are effective.

> Audit software makes the auditing process easier, as one reviewer of this handbook notes: "I have found a software program with all the line items of ISO 9001 preloaded and a great deal of flexibility in creating and modifying ISO checklists and reports. I can select whatever paragraphs of ISO I want to audit and then individually select line items from that paragraph to include on the final checklist. I have also created audit checklist categories for my other audit requirements such as 14CFR, Part 145; EASA Part 145; Calibration Lab Audit; Vendor Audit and Product Line Audit (although I prefer using a flowchart instead of the checklist). If the Corrective Action module is also purchased, the program will generate the corrective action(s) directly from any nonconformities (NCs) indicated on the audit checklist (the user has to enter the handwritten checklist data in the program). While this program is not perfect, it meets most of my evaluation criteria. It does take a little experience with the program to become familiar with its capabilities—like anything else."

Part IIID

Digital Cameras

Auditors can use digital cameras to take pictures of problems (a rusty container, a defect, damage, and so on) while they are auditing. The digital camera can be connected to a notebook computer or printer, and pictures taken with the camera can be shown on the computer screen or an image printer. The pictures can be shown at the exit meeting and/or included in the report. Bringing images of problems to management is very powerful. The use of digital cameras does much to improve the effectiveness of audits.[3] Auditors can also use cellular phones that have good-quality cameras. Cellular phones and small digital cameras are less intrusive than regular full-size cameras or single-lens reflex cameras. Small cameras and smartphones can be worn on the belt or clipped to clothing for easy access. Some organizations do not allow auditors to take pictures during audits. Before taking a picture, ensure that the organization permits this evidence-gathering method.

Video Conferencing

Video conferencing is routinely used by some auditing organizations. It is a valuable method for bringing groups of people face-to-face without incurring travel expenses. In the future, video conferencing may prove to be especially important in auditing by eliminating preaudit visits and even follow-up audits in some situations. Collaborative software includes video conferencing and many meeting function features that make virtual meetings more effective.

The use of electronic media requires that other issues be addressed, such as security, confidentiality (especially for networks), electronic interference, and document controls (viewing and changing documents, changing code, and backing up data).

Digital Voice Recorders

A digital voice recorder (DVR) allows authors to make verbal notes for themselves or record an interview or testimonial. Some DVR's are about the size of a flip chart marker and have several hours of recording capacity. However, if you record several hours of information, you will need to listen to several hours of information unless you use voice recognition software. Voice recognition software can convert your audio recording to a word processing document that can be edited and printed. Digital voice recorders are good for making notes and recording an interview or meeting that must be retained for legal or liability purposes. To avoid recording empty space, set the digital voice recorder to voice activated. Before using a voice recorder, make sure that the organization permits its use.

Remote (Computer) Access

Remote access allows an auditor to access the auditee organization information. This approach allows auditors to review electronic documentation in advance of the on-site audit, or even to begin the performance stage of the audit and reduce the number of on-site audit days. Some auditing organizations are currently investigating this new style of remote auditing. Current Microsoft operating systems already include remote desktop server software. Several software options are available with various capabilities such as viewing or exchanging files. Remote access has serious security issues that must be addressed.

PRESENTATION TECHNIQUES

Auditors must create a favorable impression for auditee management, in both appearance and ability. Auditors should dress appropriately for the opening meeting. The credentials of the audit team members may be presented at this time to instill confidence that the audit is being performed by competent, well-qualified individuals.

The lead auditor conducts the opening and exit meetings, as well as separate daily meetings with the auditee and the audit team members. By using appropriate aids and handouts, the lead auditor ensures that the auditee is in agreement with the details outlined in the audit plan and understands the auditing methods to be used. In addition, the auditor should ensure that the auditee is able to interpret data correctly, agrees with the audit evidence presented in the audit report, and agrees to address the needed corrective action.

The lead auditor is responsible for ensuring that a location has been set aside for presentations. The location may be a training room, a conference room, or even a break area. The lead auditor should ensure that there is adequate space for expected meeting attendees. This may include determination of seating arrangements, such as classroom style, at a conference table, or at a U-shaped table. The lead auditor must secure the equipment needed to make the presentation, such as flip charts, data projectors, pointers, and associated support equipment and supplies (electrical outlets, markers, extension cords). Finally, the lead auditor must ensure that visual-aid materials will be prepared and will be available at the meeting. Such materials may include copies of printed reports, copies of completed handwritten forms (for example, corrective action requests), slides, and prepared charts.

The lead auditor should be certain to communicate the data analysis to the auditee both orally and visually. Using simple statistical techniques to recognize patterns and trends and evaluate their significance enables an auditor to prepare an audit report. These results must be communicated to the auditee in a timely and effective manner, and the inclusion of simple charts, matrices, or graphs in the audit report, or their display on a data projector, can assist the auditee in gaining the necessary understanding of a problem.

Chapter 14
Interviewing Techniques/Part IIIE

The interview is the most challenging aspect of an audit for new auditors. Yet, the interview process may be the most important element of an audit. For that reason, auditors must be able to apply various techniques to gather information with minimum auditee stress and anxiety. One auditee may be familiar and comfortable with the audit process, while another may be nervous and apprehensive. Eliciting information from the former may be simple, but from the latter it may be difficult and time consuming. The manner in which an auditor initiates the interview process may well determine the success of the interview.

CONVERSATIONAL PROCESS

Interviews should be relaxed and conversational. Auditors should not simply dive into the checklist. Instead, they should take time for introductions by the guide before they ask about the interviewee's position, duties, and so on. After a short time, the interviewee should have mentioned a topic that is of interest to the auditor, who may ask for more information. From that point, the audit is under way, with the auditor linking questions to other topics of interest and documenting evidence, as appropriate.

When the auditor uses a conversational process to conduct the audit, the interviewee is the central figure rather than the checklist. The auditor's focus should be to understand the process and the person's role in that process. Once the focus shifts from the process to the checklist, the conversation and the information the auditor needs in order to verify effectiveness will lag.

The use of open-ended questions is necessary to gather information during the interview process. Auditors need to ask "who," "what," "when," "where," "how," and "why" questions, as these types of questions elicit information from the interviewee. Because these questions require the interviewee to provide an explanation of the process and related activities, the auditor will receive more information and be able to ask follow-up questions to ensure understanding. When the auditor relies only on questions beginning with phrases such as "Does the organization . . ." or "Is there a . . . ," the auditor will be talking more than the auditee and, as a result, will learn very little.

Checklist questions may be written as yes/no questions in order to facilitate note taking and link questions to requirements. Questions are constructed by converting a statement in a procedure, a standard, a work instruction, and so on, to a question. For example, a document may state, "Process settings must be recorded on the work order." An auditor will construct checklist questions from this document, such as, "Are process settings recorded on the work order?" yet the questions during the interview may be very different. An interview with an operator may go something like this:

    AUDITOR: How do you know what the process settings should be?

    OPERATOR: I look on the work order before I start the job.

    AUDITOR: Could I see the work order for the job you are working on?

    OPERATOR: Yes, here it is.

    AUDITOR: Thank you.

The auditor is able to verify that the operator has access to the work order and that the settings are recorded on the work order.

    AUDITOR: Could you show me where you make the setting adjustments?

Then the auditor verifies that the settings on the work order match the settings on the machine. Good follow-up questions for the auditor to ask may be:

    What do you do if the settings are not on the work order?

    What do you do if you think the settings are wrong?

    Do you ever change the settings?

AVOID ASKING LEADING QUESTIONS

Leading questions are questions that are asked with the expectation of a specific answer. An auditor should not lead an interviewee through the questions asked during the interview. Leading questions can be avoided if the auditor asks open-ended questions such as those listed in Figure 14.1. Additionally, if an

The auditor should say	Not
How (where, when, why) do you record the test results?	Do you record the test results in the lab logbook?
How do you know this value is right?	This instrument is calibrated, isn't it?
What is the first thing you do?	First you set up the equipment, right?
How do you know this is the current (correct) version of the drawing?	Is this drawing current (correct)?
How were you trained to perform this procedure?	Did you read the standard operating procedure (SOP) during training?
What are the reporting requirements for nonconformances?	Don't you have to notify your supervisor whenever a nonconformance occurs?
What is the standard procedure for responding to customer complaints?	When a customer calls, don't you have to record the details on Form X?
Is this equipment calibrated? How do you know?	Does this sticker indicate that the equipment is calibrated?
How do you know how to do this operation?	Do you follow the procedure for this operation?
What do you do with the finished product?	Do you place the finished product on the rack?

Figure 14.1 Open-ended questions contrasted with closed-ended questions.

auditor goes into an interview expecting to hear certain answers, the audit results will be biased.

INTERVIEWING A GROUP OF PEOPLE

Interviewing a group of people is not the preferred method of conducting an interview, and its use should be limited. Auditors should avoid this method of interviewing unless there is a very good reason for doing so. For example, an auditor may want to interview a project team to better understand the team dynamics or a group of sales representatives before they leave on an assignment. One of the difficulties is being able to read the body language of several people at the same time. When conducting an interview with one person, the auditor may easily recognize that a sensitive question has been asked. However, in a group interview, the auditor may have to watch each person's reaction to each question asked in order to ask the appropriate follow-up questions. An auditor should also look for informal hierarchical relationships such that group members seek one team member's approval through eye contact, nods, or gestures or by deferring the question.

When this method must be used, two auditors should be present and the group should be as small as possible, ideally no more than five people.

USING A TRANSLATOR

Audits should always be conducted in the language of the auditee. Unfortunately, this is not always possible and the services of a translator must be utilized. If at all possible, the translator should be independent of the operation being audited as well as the firm conducting the audit in order to ensure credibility of the audit.

The use of a translator requires much more time for conducting interviews, evaluating evidence, and summarizing audit results. Therefore, the audit team leader must adjust the time allotment for interviews requiring a translator. The auditor's questions must be short and to the point for the translator to convey the proper meaning. Otherwise, questions will have to be interrupted for the translator to communicate a portion of the question to the auditee, allow the auditor to complete the question, and then complete the translation of the question to the auditee. While simultaneous translation may be a little faster, the auditor will not be able to read body language as easily since the auditee will be attending to the translator's voice rather than the auditor's voice. Only appropriate planning with a skilled translator will result in an effective audit.

CORROBORATING INFORMATION

Each person in an organization has a unique perspective, as does each member of the audit team. One person can filter information differently than another, miss an angle, or stop short of getting the full story. For these reasons, facts stated and other data collected during an audit interview must be corroborated to ensure accuracy. Auditors may corroborate information by:

- Asking for information in a different way

- Asking for evidence demonstrating that an activity is performed as described

- Asking other people the same question

- Observing the activity in question being performed

- Reviewing the evidence of other audit team members

- Reviewing other evidence such as procedures, instructions, and records

POTENTIAL PROBLEMS

Communication problems are probably the principal difficulty that must be overcome during an audit. An auditor can minimize the effects of miscommunication by relying on the escort to correct misunderstandings and by corroborating all information through one of the methods already mentioned. Occasionally, an auditor who does not have a good grasp of the process being audited may not ask the right questions and may realize only after completing the interview that important issues were not addressed. To recover from such an oversight, after the interview the auditor may revisit the area or raise the issue at the daily meeting for necessary action. To ensure that the right questions are asked during the interview, an auditor could end the interview by asking if the person is responsible for any other activities or ask for his or her opinion on how well the process is performing.

Another problem that auditors should be able to recognize and overcome is delay tactics. Common time-wasting techniques employed by auditees and possible solutions by auditors are listed in Figure 12.1 in the conflict resolution section. Several types of problems may occur during interviews, and auditors should be trained in techniques that minimize such interference. When an auditee's repeated time wasting, or other tactics (such as the examples that follow), hinders the progress of an audit and threatens to severely compromise the audit schedule, the lead auditor is responsible for notifying auditee management and the client.

Steering the Auditor

An auditee may attempt to steer the auditor toward specific interviewees or areas. Auditees often prefer that auditors interview certain personnel and avoid certain others. However, this person's knowledge may not be typical of others in the organization. Therefore, the auditor should take charge of the selection process.

An auditor should approach a work area and determine the people performing different tasks. Candidates for interviews can be randomly chosen as long as it is safe to interrupt them in their jobs. The auditor should follow the interview protocol previously described.

If an auditee insists that a specific person is unavailable for interviewing, the auditor should be considerate but persistent if the interview is vital to the success of the audit. Without being threatening, the auditor can suggest that the person's unavailability may prolong the audit. A statement such as "I may have to stay over for another shift" may gain the auditor the desired cooperation.

Additionally, the auditor should guard against reacting improperly to employees who have hidden agendas or "axes to grind."

Answering for the Auditee

Another common problem occurs when an escort or area supervisor answers for or intimidates the interviewee. An escort generally stays within listening distance and takes notes, but should step back slightly. An ideal arrangement is for an auditor to sit or stand between the interviewee and the escort, facing the interviewee.

An escort is to be an observer only and should not be involved in the interview unless there are communication problems. An auditor can minimize an escort's participation in the interview by directing questions to and maintaining eye contact with the interviewee. For example, questions about machine setups and the measuring of parameters are normally beyond the knowledge of an escort. If an escort starts to answer for an auditee, the auditor needs to redirect the question to the interviewee, avoiding eye contact with the escort. If an escort continues to interfere, the auditor should say, "I prefer to get the information from the staff member."

The "Too Busy" Response

Whereas some interviewees are intimidated by the audit, other interviewees are unable to concentrate because they are distracted by the fact that their jobs are not getting done. People are afraid to say, "I am very busy. I need to complete this test. Can you come back in 10 minutes?" A good auditor will sense when an interviewee is preoccupied and will find other ways to keep the audit moving. Other times it is appropriate to go ahead and ask to see the interviewee perform the work if the auditor needs to observe it anyway. Completing the task may relax the auditee, making him or her able to concentrate on the auditor's additional questions.

Such problems may be avoided by stating in the opening meeting and subsequent interviews that the purpose of the audit is to evaluate the effectiveness of the system by focusing on the processes, not the people. The audit team leader may also state that the audit team will complete the audit within the allotted time but will remain on-site as long as necessary to complete the audit objective. However, the audit team leader and the audit team members should communicate any potential problems so that they may be resolved quickly and the audit team leader can avoid having to extend the audit.

Rambling or Introducing Irrelevant Information

Some auditees are not intimidated by the audit but introduce irrelevant information during the interview. They do so in a manner such that the information may be related but is not pertinent to the topic. However, the result is that the time allotted for the interview is wasted without providing the auditor with any relevant information. The auditor must bring the auditee back to the topic of interest without alienating the interviewee. This may be accomplished by politely interrupting the flow of conversation when there is a slight pause, reminding the auditee that there is a limited amount of time for the interview and that the audit plan may be adjusted if necessary. Other methods are to ask for specific evidence in the manner in which the process or operation is performed, or show the person the checklist question that you are seeking to verify.

Chapter 15
Team Dynamics/Part IIIF

1. TEAM BUILDING

Audit teams are ad-hoc teams formed to carry out the audit plan and achieve the audit objectives. Most audit teams are informal (no team-meeting agendas). Audit teams may or may not be cross-functional. The leader of the team is normally selected by the client or the audit program manager.

The audit team process is normally task-driven and established for only one audit. Task-driven process teams stay focused on team objectives such as the audit objectives. On occasion, audit team activities may include actions to preserve the team spirit and intrateam relationships.

There are seven primary elements of task-driven audit process teams:

1. Following the audit plan and considering modifications as necessary

2. Monitoring team progress and the audit schedule

3. Completing assigned tasks

4. Recording the results of the audit

5. Verifying audit objectives are being achieved

6. Making evidence-based decisions relative to the audit findings and audit progress

7. Identifying new action items, responsibilities, and timing issues

Managing audit teams involves working with different personalities and ensuring that the team is an effective, cohesive unit. The duration of most audit teams makes this a short-term issue. However, there are still some basic techniques for ensuring that the team works together in the most effective and efficient manner.

There is always a lead auditor. Even if there is only one auditor conducting the audit, that auditor is the lead auditor. For audits, the lead auditor should apply the following team management techniques:

1. Team member role: The lead auditor ensures that everyone understands his or her assignment before the audit starts.

Material taken from QualityWBT Center for Education training materials, http://www.QualityWBT. com (accessed May 15, 2005).

2. Team membership: The lead auditor ensures that all team members are aware of the other members, their assignments, and their contact information. Audit team members should be given time to get acquainted, such as at a preaudit meeting.

3. Methods and deliverables: The lead auditor should ensure that audit team members understand their deliverables (completed checklist, records of evidence, written nonconformities, and opportunities for improvement) and procedures they are to follow.

4. Resources: The lead auditor should provide the necessary resources for the team members, such as forms, examples, and working papers, and, if necessary, instruct team members on the use of working papers.

5. Leadership: The lead auditor should lead by example, show enthusiasm for other members, and support and congratulate members for a good job. The lead auditor should ensure that members know where to go when they need help. He or she should also make sure that assignments are equitable (treat everyone the same).

6. Work environment and personal needs: The lead auditor should ensure that the audit team member's work environment needs are met. If a team member has a personal emergency, the lead auditor must take action to support the team member. (Note: The lead auditor should have access to emergency contact information for each auditor.)

7. Good time management: The lead auditor should ensure that the audit starts and ends on time, that team members are on time for meetings, and that team member requests are responded to.

Team Member Roles

Audit teams have leaders (audit team leaders) and auditors (audit team members). Their roles are listed in Chapter 4.

Lead Auditor

The lead auditor is responsible for calling the meetings, making meeting arrangements, running the meetings, and reporting progress to the client and the auditee. The team leader should take ownership of the audit process. The lead auditor normally controls the team output or deliverables. Team leaders need to be able to guide the team and make decisions as needed to ensure that the team is effective. The lead auditor should be a qualified (competent) auditor.

Audit Team Member

Team members may include qualified auditors, auditors in training, and technical experts. Team members accept assignments and report progress to the team leader or the team as a whole. Team members may be given responsibilities such as keeping records or taking meeting minutes.

Facilitator/Coach

A team may have a facilitator to assist the team leader in organizing the team and making it more effective but not participate as a team member. In the cross-functional team for a specific purpose and the long-term project team, the facilitator (or coach) is included as needed. The facilitator's role is to help the team resolve issues and reach its purpose or achieve its goals effectively. For the audit team made up of qualified auditors with team experience, a facilitator is unnecessary. If the lead auditor needs help, he or she should appoint the coleader or one of the team members to act as the facilitator. Audit team facilitators should be knowledgeable of the audit process, team dynamics, and tools such as matrices, ranking or grading, sorting, and flowcharting.

2. TEAM FACILITATION

Facilitation techniques needed for the cross-functional team and the long-term project team normally include the following:

- Ensuring that necessary team-analyzing resources are available, such as flip charts, a data projector, and so on

- Recognizing and defusing clashes between members

- Ensuring that all team members have a voice and that the team is not controlled by domineering personality types

- Using diverse views to strengthen team deliverables

- Keeping the team focused on the audit objectives, evidence-based decision making, and the schedule

- Using organizational tools (outlines, plans, flowcharts, sorted information) as necessary to facilitate decisions

- Cultivating a professional, impartial, and objective environment (such as testing outputs to ensure that no bias could be perceived by the auditee)

- Identifying problems or potential problems that influence team effectiveness (such as a disgruntled auditee, known hostile or difficult situations, and potential conflicts of interest)

- Establishing team rules or agreements as necessary (for example, members must be on time to all scheduled meetings, members must be willing to listen to other members' views, and so on)

- Keeping communication lines open between members and the auditee

- Keeping everyone informed of team progress

- Presenting team views or issues for discussion and resolution

The need for facilitators and facilitation techniques decreases with team member training, experience, and successful team history. The better qualified the team members and the more they have worked together on other audits, the less active facilitation will be necessary.

Part IIIF

3. STAGES OF TEAM DEVELOPMENT

Teams are said to progress through a development cycle.[1] The development stages are identified as *forming, storming, norming,* and *performing.* The stages were developed for cross-functional teams with a specific purpose and the long-term project team, but they can also be used for the audit team, which is ad hoc. Figure 15.1 demonstrates the usual progression of a team developmental cycle.

1. *Forming:* The team is first organized and members are welcomed. There is a certain amount of distrust, and team members push their own ideas. This is the time the team gets organized (purpose, team member roles, objectives, and so on).

2. *Storming:* Storming is related to rushing around, attacking, and moving impetuously. Individual team members attempt to win over others to support their view or to test authority or the legitimacy of the team. As the team members start to interact and the responsibility they have been given sinks in, they may become testy to see if management is committed and if management supports the team and its objectives.

3. *Norming:* Although *norming* is not a word, the intent is that members start accepting the team rules and guidelines and start cooperating. *Accepting* would be a good word to replace *norming.*

4. *Performing:* The team is cohesive and has worked out team issues. The members trust each other and build on team member strengths. The team has matured, has worked through the individual and turf issues, and is able to achieve objectives.

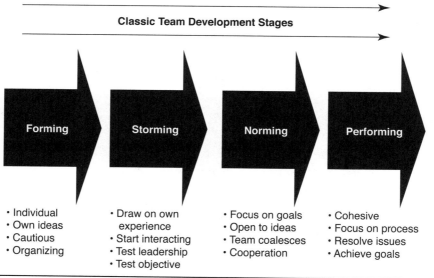

Figure 15.1   Team developmental stage progression.

If the basis for the team (goals, support, and purpose) changes, the team dynamics can slide back to forming or storming.

Most audit teams start at the performing stage. Part of the reason for training and providing competent auditors is that teams can be formed as needed to conduct an audit.

Auditors have been trained and understand the need to work together to achieve the audit objectives from the very beginning. Plus, auditors spend much of their time operating independently of the team, and the duration of audit team activities and interaction is short.

Part IV

Audit Program Management and Business Applications

[30 of the CQA Exam Questions or 20 percent]

Chapter 16   Audit Program Management/Part IVA
Chapter 17   Business and Financial Impact/Part IVB

T he purpose of this part of the Body of Knowledge (BoK) is to understand the management controls needed for an effective audit program. Auditors conduct audits under a prescribed set of rules that are controlled by management. Recognition of audit program management responsibilities will result in an effective auditor program that meets customer needs and requirements.

Chapter 16
Audit Program Management/Part IVA

uditing is an important program that must be well managed. Significant organization resources are used to conduct audits and to follow up on audit findings.

Audit program managers should be competent and maintain high levels of integrity.

1. SENIOR MANAGEMENT SUPPORT

Competent individuals who gather and handle all information pertaining to the audit program in an unbiased and ethical manner ensure a credible audit program. An audit group should be structured so that it does not report directly to the manager of the function being audited. For very small organizations, the audit program manager or auditor may report to the person he or she is expected to audit. The consequences of this type of conflict of interest should be discussed. For example, an auditor does not report a nonconformity that is related to his or her boss, but later a regulatory body or certification body reports the nonconformity or noncompliance, which results in economic consequences.

Management must use the audit results appropriately to establish and maintain the credibility of the program. The misuse of audit results or failure to initiate corrective actions will erode the credibility of the audit program, regardless of the performance of the auditors.

Management's Role

Support by top management helps the rest of the organization keep a positive attitude about the audit and its credibility. When management emphasizes the importance of the audit function and its usefulness to the organization, the attitude permeates the entire organization. If management fears or resents the intrusion of the auditing function, this attitude will likewise infiltrate the organization. An audit program set up to collect worthwhile information provides management with an oversight tool for:

- Verification of ongoing system compliance to requirements

- Identification of continual improvement opportunities within the organizations audited

- Verification and measurement of effectiveness and efficiency

Management's responses to audit results are also important. If data obtained improve the management system, the employees will see the benefits. This fact is especially true in an internal audit program, which helps a company identify its own weaknesses before customers or others do.

On the other hand, if an auditor or management focuses on the people being audited rather than on the processes or systems, the value of the audit program can rapidly decline. Rarely is it one individual's fault when there are many audit findings or when system implementation is poor. System structure and lack of management support are often the *causes* of such problems.

> While auditing a company I had visited many times in the past, I noticed coldness and an unwillingness to cooperate by many of the employees. I had found these same employees to be very friendly and cooperative during prior audits. Finally, someone confided to me that results from the previous audit I had performed provided a basis for employees' performance appraisals. Although I tried to discuss the situation with the manager of that area, he insisted that performance appraisal was a proper use of audit results.
>
> *Note:* One auditor's reaction to this dilemma was to state in the audit report that this was an inappropriate use of the audit results, and that corrective action eliminating the practice of using audit results in employee performance appraisals was required. In another case, the auditor declined future audit assignments in that particular department.

> I inform top management that audit results are not to be used for performance appraisals. It is a penalty-free period of time to correct problems and improve performance. However, if the audit alerts management to unknown problems and managers decide to monitor that area more closely, then any new incidents are fair game for performance evaluations (but without reference to the prior audit results). If audit results become part of performance appraisals, the audit program will suffer.

2. STAFFING AND RESOURCE MANAGEMENT

A group responsible for performing audits should have a documented, formalized program. The program that includes selecting and training auditors and monitoring their performance is robust.[1]

Some companies have a separate audit group to perform internal audits, reporting to either an audit manager or a functional manager responsible for quality, environmental, or safety programs. Other companies use part-time or subcontracted auditors. Sometimes an audit program coordinator or a functional manager recruits and trains individuals to perform audits part-time, in addition to their regular assignments. Either arrangement or a combination of both is workable as long as the auditors are well-qualified, technically competent people who know the audit system and can perform internal audits.

Similar principles apply when staffing a second-party (supplier) audit group. Sometimes part-time auditors are used, other times full-time auditors are used, and sometimes internal auditors perform supplier audits. Second-party auditors need to be able to accommodate different organizational cultures and be able to travel.

> An external auditor relayed the experience of one company that designated the tool-room attendant as the internal auditor. This person reported directly to the president of the company. The person was knowledgeable about the processes but had no direct influence on the quality of the process. All the plant personnel knew the tool-room attendant. The company president asked the attendant to observe operations, interview operations and support personnel, and write up findings based on the observations. These observations went directly to the president of the company. Personnel responded well to the situation.

> The justification for resources is based on the audit program schedule, which in turn should be based on internal organizational needs such as evaluating process changes and external requirements such as those established by contract or regulation. The audit program manager should ensure that sufficient resources are available to conduct the quantity and types of audits required. If there are objections to the amount of resources needed, management should reassess organizational needs and external requirements.

Auditor's Role

The use of unqualified auditors who possess little knowledge or who do not have the ability to assist management in making good decisions or improving a process can discredit the entire audit process.

An auditor aims to keep the credibility of the audit function on a high plane. The auditor does this by looking at information objectively and avoiding ethical conflicts. An auditee must trust that an auditor will not divulge proprietary information to competitors or other outsiders who can use it to their benefit. Even internally, auditors must be careful to maintain confidences. This is especially true when the locations or departments report to different management (see "5. Internal Audit Program Management").

3. AUDITOR TRAINING AND DEVELOPMENT

Training is one method of ensuring that auditors are competent. Auditors are trained either through the audit program directly or through a training organization. Once competency needs are determined, training may be employed to meet those needs. Training can be knowledge based or skills based. Likewise, auditor competencies can be divided into knowledge and skill requirements. For example, in knowledge-based training, the auditor may be trained in regard to a standard, along with the requirements and their interpretation. For skills-based training, an auditor may be trained in interview and presentation techniques.

An auditor must be knowledgeable in auditing skills, related standards and regulations, the general structure of management systems, auditing techniques, and other work-specific skills. Competence can be developed through the following methods:

- Orientation on related standards

- Implementation procedures

- Training programs on subjects related to auditing

- On-the-job training[2]

Auditors can maintain their technical competence through continuing education and current relevant auditing experience.

Companies can offer an organization-wide certification program for all auditors, which includes training. Recognition and certificates identify those auditors who are approved according to the company's standards. An auditor needs training in:

- The standards to be applied

- Evidence gathering

- Interpersonal relations

- Report writing

- Interview techniques

- The ASQ CQA BoK

- Improvement tools and techniques

- Auditing methodology

Auditors should be trained to use checklists for audit observations, to make notes that will be used by audit teams, and to gather evidence. At least one team member should be familiar with the department operation or the scope of audited activities.

A lead auditor usually has more experience, may be more highly trained in the applicable audit standards, and may have more training in conducting audits. Policies and procedures defining the qualifications for lead auditors often require a certain number of years of experience or performance of a specific number of audits before promotion to this level.

Auditors should be requalified at planned intervals. Continuing their training helps auditors maintain skills and knowledge. Training may include a refresher course periodically. The refresher course, coupled with experience in performing audits, is a reasonable expectation. Such requirements help auditors keep up with changes in standards and auditing techniques.

Ongoing Qualification—Continuing Education

The field of auditing changes as standards change and more effective auditing techniques surface. Auditors must strive to keep abreast of changes and trends, and they must embrace current technology to avoid becoming liabilities rather than assets. Committed professionals can increase their knowledge and improve their skills through continuing education. The following are continuing-education resources:

- Reading technical literature (auditing-related books, newsletters, and periodicals)

- Reading case studies

- Reading research papers

- Attending seminars and classes (or e-learning webinars and web-based training)

- Participating in professional organizations

- Consulting with peers[3]

- Attending professional conferences such as the ASQ Audit Division annual conference

More training organizations, colleges, and universities are providing network courses over the internet. This technology provides easy access to courses for individuals in remote locations. Near-real-time communications can be arranged.[4]

Many continuing-education opportunities are available through ASQ. The Audit Division offers annual tutorials to reflect current events and trends in auditing, and holds an audit conference to expand auditors' knowledge in auditing and related fields. Many other organizations offer correspondence courses in standards and management systems. Continuing education may consist of attending conferences or taking formal courses. Books and magazines are also available to expand an auditor's knowledge.

ASQ also offers e-learning classes, which do not require travel and being away from home. These classes are prescreened and approved. Before paying for an e-learning class, determine whether the class is simply taking online tests, which authority would be granting the continuing education units, and whether the class is asynchronous (online, 24 hours a day) or more like a correspondence course using e-mail technology. For some e-learning classes, students are given books to read and then asked to go online to take a test to determine their knowledge of the material. Other e-learning products consist of a series of lessons, illustrations, diagrams, interactive exercises, graded assignments and tests, quizzes, and a desk reference or book.

ASQ requires an auditor who has passed the CQA examination and has been certified by ASQ to recertify within three years. This can be accomplished by earning recertification units (points) or retaking and passing an examination. An auditor must collect a specified number of points in a three-year period to remain certified. Points accumulate by attending regular ASQ section meetings. Points are also awarded for:

- Completing additional course work

- Being employed in the field

- Writing about topics included in the BoK

- Attending or leading seminars or training sessions

- Teaching a class about topics included in the BoK

Recertification encourages auditors to remain in touch with the audit curriculum and maintain a professional level of expertise. Some companies have additional training and qualification requirements for members of their internal audit functions.

Auditors may benefit from staying abreast of technology outside the field of auditing, as specified in the CQA's BoK. For example, auditors may take courses in leadership, project management, or computer training. They may brush up on their facilitation and presentation skills, public-speaking techniques, and time-management techniques. All enhance an auditor's performance and professionalism.

An informal type of internal continuing education is forming discussion groups at meetings or training sessions. Another type of continuing education is to hold auditor debriefings after an audit to learn from what took place and to better prepare for the next assignment. Group interactions can play a vital role in ensuring that auditors follow unified policies and perform similarly. Auditor discussion groups can review unusual situations, findings, or problems encountered during an audit. Such discussion promotes:

- Team spirit within a department

- Open communication

- Uniformity of auditing practices

Any specific discussion about an auditee must be kept confidential. Release of confidential information without proper permission is unethical and compromises a department's integrity.

Auditing is not a stagnant process; it is a continuous learning experience. The auditor should aim to:

- Stay current with product and processes

- Conform to changes in general auditing standards

- Meet the ever-changing needs of management

International Auditing

As auditing has become increasingly global, many auditors are finding the ability to speak a second language essential. The auditor should be able to use tactics that ease cultural differences, such as:

- Employing an interpreter to facilitate an audit

- Familiarizing himself or herself with cultural differences that could affect relations with the auditee

- Preventing serious misunderstandings by becoming acquainted with local customs

These tactics avoid cultural differences that could interfere with the audit process.

Part IVA

Auditor Performance

The evaluation of auditors occurs at the following stages:

1. The initial evaluation of persons who wish to become auditors

2. The evaluation of the auditors as part of the audit team selection process

3. The continual evaluation of auditor performance to identify needs for maintenance and improvement of knowledge and skills

Three steps could be used for an effective performance evaluation:

Step 1: Communicate expectations. A meaningful performance evaluation is one that measures performance against clearly defined standards. Audit management must provide a consistent explanation of these standards during the initial training session. Proper training provides auditors with day-to-day performance expectations as well as insight into the basis for performance evaluation.

Step 2: Evaluate the auditor's performance. Performance evaluation should assess the competency of individual auditors, as well as the consistency between them, against established standards. As mentioned earlier, audit management measures performance by:

— Observing auditor performance during an audit

— Reviewing auditor evaluations completed by auditees (audit service customer)

— Reviewing audit deliverables

— Employing an independent auditor to evaluate auditor techniques

— Appraising general auditor credentials

Step 3: Communicate the auditor's performance. Audit management should report performance evaluation results to the auditor. To improve performance, an auditor must understand his or her strengths and weaknesses. Audit management should review evaluation results with the auditor so they can work together on a plan to improve performance.

This completes the evaluation loop. The performance evaluation provides a monitoring function for competency. The evaluation provides feedback for improving the auditor selection process.

4. AUDIT PROGRAM EVALUATION

Periodic evaluations of all audit programs and audit teams can uncover improvement opportunities. Audit programs are evaluated through periodic management reviews. Management can review records, analyze performance, or appoint an independent team or individual to review audit results. In the case of a company with multiple locations, auditors from another location can come in annually to audit the audit team. This evaluation could include:

- Observing audit teams perform an audit

- Examining auditor training records and audit schedules

- Looking at sample audit results, corrective actions, and follow-up activities to see if the program is working as intended

Additional data can be collected by asking an auditee to rate audit team members in the following areas:

- Interviewing skills

- Interaction with personnel

- Reporting results

Critical reviews by peers, subordinates, and superiors provide exceptional opportunity for growth and maturity. While the reviews may be slightly unpleasant to those being assessed, they also help keep things in perspective.

Management should treat the audit function the same as other organizational functions and departments.[5] Effective measures of an audit program include audit service performance, auditor performance, and value-added contributions (Figure 16.1).

Measures are effective only to the extent that they meet the audit program's needs. An audit program must select its measures based on documented standards and objectives. In addition, it must use data collected over time to accurately reflect ongoing program performance.

Audit Service Performance

Audit service performance determines whether the audit program meets audit service customer expectations. Sources of input data for managing the audit program may include:

- Performance evaluations from audit service customers

- Focus groups to gather direct audit service customer feedback

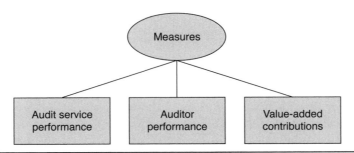

Figure 16.1   Audit program measures.

- Audit-related loss of customer time, resources, or both
- Contract term fulfillment
- Audit program deliverables, including audit reports
- An independent auditor to audit the audit program
- The number and severity of external audits performed on the audit organization[6]

Auditor Performance

Auditor performance assesses the competency of individual auditors as well as consistency among team members. To apply the measurement, management could:

- Observe auditor performance during an audit
- Review customer performance evaluations
- Review audit deliverables
- Appraise general auditor credentials

Performance Improvement Contributions

Performance improvement contributions looks at how the audit program improves the organization's business performance. To apply the measurement, management could:

- Compare planned completion of corrective action with actual completion
- Track the number and severity of noncompliances issued by external audits
- Plot the corrective action from the initial performance level through the stated performance goal
- Determine the degree to which planned corrective action is effective the first time
- Identify the number of "recycled" corrective actions that failed to address root causes the first time
- Identify the number of repeat problems due to the same cause
- Determine the benefit of corrective action
- Benchmark audit performance against other companies in the same industry
- Plot measures such as types of customer complaints, warranty costs, and scrap and rework costs, and compare trends with audit results
- Determine the opportunities for and effectiveness of preventive actions

Review of the Audit Program

In many organizations, the audit program is a key oversight tool for maintaining programs (safety, quality, environmental, improvement) and ensuring that the organization operates effectively and efficiently. In these organizations, management has a vested interest in the audit program's annual results.

How to Summarize Results

Audit program management should address three questions in its annual summary.[7] The first question is, How did the audit department contribute to the organization last year? Management wants to know what the audit program contributed to the organization's business performance during the previous period.

The audit program should not attempt to address this question directly before the review. It must compile and define program contributions throughout the review period. Figure 16.2 summarizes the actions described in each section.

The audit program direction comes from the analyses of the consolidated data. Typically, the significance and trends reflect areas of strength as well as points of vulnerability in the program. Therefore, the audit program's annual contribution to the organization is the result.

The second question is, What will the audit program contribute to the organization next year? The audit program can recommend future audit activity and define its intended benefit to the organization on the basis of historical trends.

The third question is, Is there anything management should know to avoid future risks to the organization's health? The audit program should identify potentially critical information, such as regulatory changes or defunct programs, and include them in the summary report.

Typically, the audit program's summary report is one of many that compete for management attention. It must be concise, accurate, and eye-catching. Accompanying graphs, matrices, and data summaries must capture and focus attention on the issues. Figure 16.3 provides two samples that can enhance the summary report. Graphs such as these allow management to appreciate the value of the audit program at a glance.

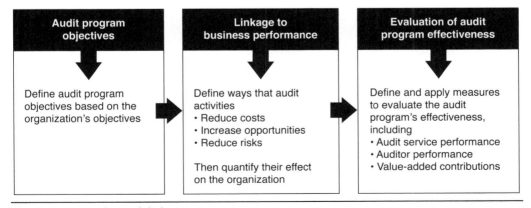

Figure 16.2 Audit result linkages.

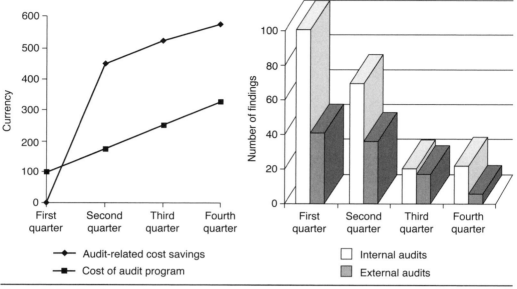

Figure 16.3   Charting results.

5. INTERNAL AUDIT PROGRAM MANAGEMENT

Regardless of the department in which it resides within the organization, the auditing function should be (1) independent of the audited areas, (2) supported by management, and (3) deployed positively. The degree of independence needs to be appropriate and practicable to the specific audit situation and circumstances. One common guideline is that auditors should not audit their own work.

Management of the audit function includes the following activities:

- Establishing a reporting relationship for the audit function
- Establishing audit authority, operational freedom, constraints, and boundaries
- Establishing and maintaining timely and effective communication with senior management
- Ensuring the availability of adequate resources for all audits
- Determining whether to use a single auditor or an audit team
- Staffing and training auditors
- Establishing procedures, processes, and criteria for an effective and efficient audit program
- Establishing methods for evaluating an audit program
- Establishing audit schedules
- Confirming audit dates and any requested changes of audit dates
- Setting priorities for audit subjects

- Promoting and rewarding ethical behavior within the audit function
- Reviewing audit function performance
- Providing periodic reports to management on the status of the audit program
- Identifying risks to be managed, monitored, and reported

The audit manager or audit coordinator is responsible for:

- Preparing an overall audit schedule
- Budgeting resources
- Assisting with or overseeing other administrative duties related to the auditing function

Additionally, the audit manager staffs and trains the audit department and monitors and evaluates auditors in the performance of their duties.

Objectives

An audit program is the organizational structure, commitment, and documented methods used to plan and perform audits. Operational effectiveness of the audit program depends on clearly defined objectives.

A well-managed audit program:

- Plans and performs the audit
- Strives to standardize and improve its performance
- Produces meaningful audit results
- Verifies compliance
- Promotes continual improvement within the organization

The first step in successfully implementing an audit program is to define its objectives. Some audit organizations may choose to limit the objective of their audit program to verification of compliance/conformance to standards, while others also evaluate management controls. While objectives vary from one organization to another, they often include the following statements:

- Perform and present audits meaningfully to those who receive the audit results and use or act on them
- Ensure regular performance of required audits, and ensure frequent audits of critical functions
- Ensure that audits are performed by persons who are appropriately trained and qualified and suitably independent
- Promote a strong alliance between the audit function and the auditee
- Standardize the auditing process and determine a basis against which to measure continuous improvement of the audit program
- Support the objectives, strategies, and goals of the organization

- Ensure product and operational safety and proper environmental stewardship

- Support management objectives for improving organization performance

Audits are valuable tools for evaluating a company's ongoing conformance and performance when they meet management's needs. Benefits realized from the performance of an audit are weighed against the cost of performing the audit. According to Allan J. Sayle, author of *Management Audits: The Assessment of Quality Management Systems*, such costs include:

- The auditor's time spent preparing, performing, following up and completing an audit

- The auditee's time spent participating in audit process

- Overhead costs associated with an audit[8]

- The lead auditor/audit manager's time spent analyzing the audit program and making improvements

Audit program objectives should address the questions "who," "what," "where," "when," "why," and "how"—for example:

- Who performs and who participates in the audits?

- What activity or system is being audited?

- Where are the audits performed?

- When are the audits performed?

- Why are the audits performed? What is the need for the audit?

- How is the audit performed?

Link Audit Function Goals to the Strategic Plan

Just as an audit program's mission should be linked to the organization's mission, the audit program's results should be linked to the organization's needs. Linking results to needs demonstrates that the audit program recognizes and is committed to the organization's success. It aligns itself with business purposes. One method of linking audit results to issues that affect the organization is to group benefits in terms of cost savings, risk reduction, and increased opportunity.[9]

Cost Savings

Audit-related corrective action may produce savings by:

- Lowering cost per unit, per service, or per entry variable costs

- Lowering daily expenses or fixed costs

- Reducing working capital requirements

- Lowering capital expenditures

- Identifying inefficiencies, redundancies, and waste

- Identifying ineffective processes, systems, and corrective or preventive actions

- Avoiding penalties and lost business

Such organizational savings offset some of the cost of supporting the audit program. The total savings, then, are the net of the savings produced less the cost of the audit program.

Figure 16.4 illustrates the program cost and savings accrued from audit activities. This is an illustrative sample only. Details regarding particular savings vary from company to company and industry to industry. The sample shows that the audit program saved the organization $236,000 over the cost of the audit program's expenses. Distilling the savings further, some internal audit programs may subtract costs incurred by the auditee, such as preparation time, lost productivity, and corrective action initiation. It all depends on what numbers best measure audit program progress or contribution.

Increased Opportunity

Identification of opportunities is of significant interest to management and a potential audit-related contribution. The results of the audit and subsequent follow-up actions may increase the organization's opportunity to develop new products, open new markets, add new services, lower prices, continually improve effectiveness, and increase services or production capacity.

Audit program expense	Yearly cost ($)*	Audit-related cost savings ($)*				Net
		First quarter	Second quarter	Third quarter	Fourth quarter	
Salaries	57		(60)			(3)
Indirect	96		(233)	(56)	(24)	(21)
Overtime	25			(20)		5
Fringes	61		(102)	(26)	(8)	(75)
Subtotal	239		(395)	(102)	(32)	(290)
Outside services	50		(23)			27
Maintenance supplies	7					7
General supplies	13					13
Travel	2					2
Office supplies	3					3
Subtotal	75		(23)			52
Depreciation	4		(7)			(3)
Rent	5					5
Subtotal	9		(7)			2
Gross operating expenses	323		(425)	(102)	(32)	(236)

*In thousands of dollars.

Figure 16.4 Sample audit program contributions.

Part IVA

Long-Term Audit Planning

Long-term audit planning completes the loop in audit administration. The process begins with defining a mission statement and establishing objectives. From the mission and objectives flow the audit program and its boundaries (scope), policies, and high-level procedures. These documents guide daily activity. The process ends with long-term planning. The program patrols the boundaries and ensures that the policies and procedures still make sense before the process proceeds.

The Malcolm Baldrige National Quality Award Criteria support the idea that long-term or strategic planning should align the work processes with the organization's strategic direction. There are three steps in strategic planning that are especially important for the audit program:

Step 1: Identify information that might affect the program's future opportunities and directions. Attempt to take as long a view as is practicable. This first step provides the realistic content for strategy development. Figure 16.5 provides a focus list of open-ended questions to help with the identification process.

Step 2: Define a strategic direction. With the information gathered in step 1, the audit program devises a long-term strategy to guide ongoing decision making, resource allocation, and program management.

Step 3: Put the strategy into operation. The audit program develops and deploys an action plan to make the strategy operational. This process includes:

— Defining new processes to accommodate strategic change

— Defining key measures, indicators, or both to track progress

— Communicating a new strategic direction and new processes to the audit team and the organization

— Providing resources to support the new strategic direction, including procedures, training, and incentives

Customer-related
- Who are our customers?
- What do they need and want?
- How are we doing in their eyes?

Auditor-related
- What are the auditor's needs and concerns?
- What new tools and techniques are available to help auditors be more effective?
- What do they need to do a great job?
- How are we doing in their eyes?
- Who is making a real effort?
- How do we say thank you?

Organization-related
- How does the organization's structure support what we are trying to do?
- What organizational issues will ultimately affect us (for example, new product lines, new business risks, new management structure)?
- How can we make better use of management experience and support?
- How can we help management improve?

Figure 16.5 Open-ended questions.

Audit Program Administration

Development and Implementation of Audit Program Procedures

Documented procedures are critical to the success of an auditee's management system. A procedure answers the reporter's questions of who, what, where, when, why, and how. Documentation of procedures is objective evidence that:

- A process is defined

- The procedures are approved

- The procedures are under change control

Procedures also allow for distribution control, ensuring that those who need information have access to it.

The same ideas apply to the audit program. Procedures are critical to the program's success, and they promote constancy within the audit execution. Procedures also provide a means to define and enforce intangible standards and expectations, such as ethical behavior.

Procedure Development

Three areas typically require procedures, as shown in Figure 16.6.
Procedures for audit programming should include:

- Guiding principles for developing audit schedules

- Focus areas for auditing based on the relevant requirements or standards

- A process for creating an overall periodic audit schedule

Procedures for auditor qualification should include:

- General auditor qualifications

- Standards for ethical conduct

- A process for selecting and approving new auditors

- A process for training new and existing auditors

- A process for assessing auditor performance

- A process for refreshing and replenishing the auditor pool

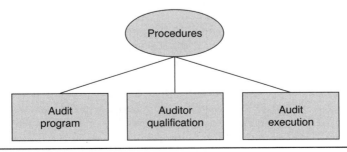

Figure 16.6 Areas requiring procedures.

Procedures for audit execution should include:

- A process for planning audits
- A process for conducting audits, to include
  - — Creating and maintaining forms used in the audit process
  - — Recording and reporting audit results
  - — Providing corrective action follow-up
  - — Interacting with the auditee throughout the audit
  - — Method to appeal audit findings
- A process for retaining and handling audit records
- A process for billing audit customers, such as
  - — Invoicing and collecting payment from third-party audit customers
  - — Conducting internal money transfers for first- and second-party audit customers

Audit procedure development is a collaborative effort. Audit program managers should be experienced in and cognizant of these processes and procedures, and should develop functional, streamlined procedures using their strategic perspective. If individual auditors have any comments after following the prescribed audit process, they should propose improvements to the audit program manager.

Procedure Implementation

For successful procedure implementation, the audit program must communicate with the auditors and the organization. Each auditor must understand the importance and proper use of procedures. Members of the organization should also have a general understanding of audit procedures in order to avoid confusion.

Forms Control/Working Papers

Both internal and external auditors use many forms. Forms are used to ensure consistency and an effective audit. The organization may provide forms for the audit plan, interview schedule, agenda, report, nonconformities, improvement points, and so on. Example third-party audit organization forms are in Appendix H.

Development and Implementation of Audit Program Schedule

When scheduling an audit, an audit program manager typically identifies the client and the client's requirements and obtains initial information about the auditee. The audit program manager may also select the audit team (often with recommendations from the lead auditor) and identify other resources needed, such as a technical specialist, expert, or consultant. Audit program management should issue an audit program schedule and update the schedule as changes occur. Many audit organizations issue schedules annually, semiannually, or quarterly. The auditee facility should have a copy of the plan in advance, showing the time period (week or month) that an audit will occur at the site.

Some audit program managers develop schedules using a horizontal or vertical audit strategy. A *horizontal audit* is an audit of one process, such as training or corrective action, across several departments. A *vertical audit* is an audit of several processes, such as testing, test equipment, test status, and nonconformances, within one department.

To develop a schedule, the audit program follows three process steps. The first step is to identify the needs of the auditee and the client. With limited resources, the audit program must determine which areas warrant scheduled audits. Some areas may need an audit each year. Others may require an audit to maintain certification/registration or satisfy a regulatory requirement. Still others may need an audit to monitor new products or processes. There should be some type of defined rationale for developing audit schedules or audit program plans.[10] The rationale may include factors such as routine check, regulatory or registrar requirements, changes to processes, new product or service introductions, previous audit results, high-risk processes, or reported problem areas. Another rationale for adjusting the audit schedule could be management requests. The auditor will know the internal audit program is successful when management requests additional audits beyond those planned (because it has experienced the value).

The second step is to assign available resources. The audit program must assign available resources, particularly a team of auditors, to execute required audits.

The third step is to schedule individual audits. The audit program has to organize the required information to schedule activity for the upcoming year. Appendix G shows an example audit program schedule.

The audit program manager has several types of audit services that can be scheduled to meet organization needs. There are product, process, and system audits. Audits can be face-to-face on-site audits, eAudits, or a combination of both. Audits can include inspections, risk-based audits, follow-up audits, capabilities assessment, pre-award surveys, compliance, project, performance, and so on. The different types of audits have different objectives and benefits to the organization. We have discussed the various types of audits throughout the handbook.

To implement an audit schedule, the audit program should notify auditees and auditors of the upcoming schedule and update and redistribute the schedule as changes occur.

6. EXTERNAL AUDIT PROGRAM MANAGEMENT (SUPPLIER AUDITS)[11]

Many of the program requirements for internal and external audits are the same. However, external audits are different due to the relationship between customer and supplier.

Organizations continue to focus on core competencies resulting in greater dependence on high-quality materials and services from suppliers. Now more than ever, supply chain management is important to ensure that organizations can compete in the global market and network community. The audit program is a key player in monitoring the external supply chain. Supply chain management is an enterprise within an enterprise.

Audit program managers will need to interface with procurement to ensure that contracts contain access clauses and to understand procurement needs to schedule audits or other oversight services of the global supply chain. Oversight may be needed for first-, second-, and perhaps third-tier suppliers depending on organization objectives, customer requirements, and risk. A *first-tier supplier* is an organization that is a direct supplier. A *second-tier supplier* is an organization that provides a critical component to the first-tier supplier that is used by the customer. Interruption of supply of critical components for second- and third-tier suppliers could have a significant impact on the customer's operations.

The supply chain enterprise may include:

- Procurement

- Requirements flow down

- Logistics network

- Manufacturing and technology, obsolescence management

- Demand forecasting

- Customer service relationship

- Risk management

- Performance management

The external audit program will most likely be involved with the procurement, performance management, and risk management aspects of the supply chain.

Procurement

In many cases the procurement department is the client that needs services of the audit program. Procurement personnel may be called procurement specialists, buyers, and purchasing agents as well as purchasing managers and supervisors. Depending on its needs, the organization may employ procurement and auditing personnel with international experience.

Procurement duties and responsibilities that may involve the auditing function are the following:

- Creating and implementing performance metrics (key performance indicators [KPIs]).

- Monitoring and reporting trends in the supplier and contract base that could affect supply. Establishing and promoting relationships with suppliers and customers: The organization may need to develop close relationships with suppliers of critical material and services. In some cases partnerships will need to be established.

- Following up on and monitoring supplier performance to ensure corrective action is taken on identified issues.

- Verifying special programs as needed, such as vendor projects, changes, buy-resale, private label, and so on.

The audit program management and auditors are usually not involved in establishing supplier requirements but are likely to be involved in their oversight. Requirements may be technical, supplier process related, logistical, administrative, or legal. Technical requirements typically come from the process designer or process owner; quality (improvement) function; or technical, procurement, or legal department.

Example technical requirements include:

- Physical characteristics such as weight or dimensions

- Chemical composition

- Physical properties such as hardness, smoothness, and finish

- Performance results

Example supplier process requirements include:

- Process variation monitoring

- Certificate of compliance

- First article inspection or other test requirements

- ISO 9001 plus or minus requirements

Example logistical requirements include:

- Identification such as bar code, name, serial number, or color code

- Packaging such as padding, box, pallet, spacing, and so on

- Instructions

- Packing list

- Special storage conditions listed on package

- Storage service requirements (operate, change fluids, exercise, rotate, and so on)

Example administrative and legal requirements include:

- Hazardous response instructions and markings

- First aid instructions

- Purchase order number or contract number

- Disaster recovery plans (such as natural disaster, cyber attack, material outage)

There may be other requirements depending on the risks involved, for example, source inspection for expensive and/or large equipment. Inspection type, sample size, and rejection criteria may be part of the product or service requirements.

The expansion of the supplier base for many organizations has spawned the evolution of logistics management. The globalization and outsourcing of products and services has led to increasingly complex supply chains with longer lead times, more pipeline inventory, and the need to control downstream and upstream logistics.

Establishing a supply chain network may include supplier selection and movement of goods and services to their final destination. Audit programs may not develop the supply chain network, but they may need to verify and monitor activities to ensure requirements are met. External audits may need different capabilities in order to be effective.

Movement of goods and services may include:

- Modes of travel such as train, air, roadway, and sea

- Distribution and storage services

- Storage conditions

- Technical service

- Expedited services

- Controlling storage costs and expenses such as detention and demurrage fines

Supplier selection may include:

- Initial evaluation

- Maturity model results

- Assessment of capabilities

The supply chain may stretch across the globe, but in all cases deadlines must be met and the customer must be satisfied. Language and cultural barriers may need to be overcome. Effective communication is an important factor for success. Conducting eAudits may be an important audit program strategy to ensure proper oversight and control of risks.

Risk Management—Supply Chain

Management is always concerned about risk. MBAs are taught about business risk and the risk of failure. Management has been taught to avoid unnecessary risk. The ISO standards themselves represent strategies to reduce risk for selected areas such as product liability, environmental controls, and occupational safety and health. Increasing the supply chain may or may not increase organization risk. However, since fewer business processes are being controlled internally, there is a greater need to manage the supply chain risk. Increasing dependence on supplier organizations increases a customer's business risk.

The risk management scope should include controls throughout a product's life cycle, across all company processes and its external supply chain. The scope of the program could be limited by product or may include select enterprise processes. The purpose of the program should be to ensure that customer requirements are being met and to prevent external product failures and nonconformities. An effective risk management program will reduce the chances of undesirable and harmful consequences to the organization.

The absence of a risk management program exposes the organization to unknown problems in a reactionary mode. A risk management program allows the organization to be proactive by eliminating problems before they occur.

The benefits of proper verification and monitoring of the supply chain include:

- Reduced probability of delivering nonconforming products and services

- Increased probability of achieving organizational objectives

- Reduced probability of delivering product or services behind schedule

- Increased probability of compliance to quality, environmental, and safety regulations and the avoidance of undesirable consequences

If there are specific identified risks and risk treatments, the audit function may be asked to verify that they are being controlled and properly treated. Auditor and audit program managers are usually not asked to assess identified risks unless they are specifically assigned to the team for such purposes.

During any visit or interface with a supplier, an auditor has a duty to report any potentially significant risk to the audit program manager and the client.

Performance Management

Supplier monitoring may include many activities depending on the risk and criticality of the product and/or service. Monitoring and reporting needs will continue to change due to organizational needs, changes, and relationships with suppliers.

Monitoring and verification may include:

- Assessment of capabilities

- Source inspection

- Ongoing inspection (100% inspection, acceptance, and skip lot inspection)

- Certification of conformance

- Surveys

- Conformity audit

- Contract audit

- Risk-based audit

- Verification of corrective actions

In many cases, suppliers are asked to conform to a management system standard such as ISO 9001. If a supplier is asked to comply with a management system standard such as ISO 9001 plus specific additional requirements that may be found in another standard, such as ISO 13485 (medical devices) or ISO/TS 16949 (automotive), it may be called an ISO 9001 plus audit. Audits of very small supplier organizations that are asked to implement only certain parts of a management standard such as ISO 9001 are called ISO 9001 minus audits.

External auditors may need additional training in working with different cultures. A misunderstanding can delay an audit or damage a business relationship. External auditors may need to have appropriate technical knowledge about the part and the processes that yield the product being supplied.

Audit results are one input in maintaining a supplier report. The results may be the basis for increasing or decreasing oversight of the supplier organization. Some organizations have supplier levels that affect not only oversight but also the share of the business and have monetary consequences. The higher the supplier level, the less oversight needed.

Part IVA

7. BEST PRACTICES

The identification of best practices and actions to implement them are as important as addressing nonconformities. Best practices are known ways to operate a process that is effective and efficient. Every manager should want to implement best practices. However, best practices may be more difficult to implement than corrective actions.

Some managers have issues with the term *best practice* and expect a best practice to be the best in the world or among their competitors. Effective and efficient practices identified by auditors may not be industry best-in-class benchmarks, yet they are still valuable to the organization. Hence, some organizations call them good practices or noteworthy achievements to avoid discussions regarding the credibility of the improvement.

Many managers are more willing to correct a problem or nonconformity than implement an improvement suggested by another party. There may be cultural issues or individual competitive concerns, or it may be the "not invented here" syndrome. Organizations must give priority to improving processes over fixing problems. Organizations should also be on the lookout for opportunities for improvement (OFIs) reported by auditors. OFIs may not be a best practice but may make a process more effective or efficient (type of incremental improvement).

Best practices may be identified by auditors through an analysis of area measures or metrics or by observation during the audit. When preparing for the audit, an auditor reviewing area performance measures may observe something that appears to be noteworthy, such as no finishing defects for the last six months or some other measure indicating a process is operating at a very effective and efficient level. During the audit the auditor can verify what he or she identified during preparation and/or identify other best practices.

Best Practices Checklist or Form[12]

The top section of the Best Practices Checklist (Figure 16.7) is used to gather key information for establishing a process as a best practice. It focuses on the metrics, trends, and other indicators such as awards, customer recognition, and auditee feedback that can establish the practice as truly superior. The bottom section of the checklist is used to help analyze the processes to the extent practicable. It gathers information on the key benefits, performance measures, before-and-after conditions, potential enablers, and contact information. This section can be used by potential adopters of the best practice to better evaluate whether they can adapt the best practice to their processes. By keeping the information on the checklist short and to the point, the evaluation of the best practice should not interfere with the primary goal of the audit, to identify the systemic weaknesses in the management system.

Communicating Best Practices[13]

Simply identifying and documenting best practices in an audit report is not sufficient. There must also be a systematic means of communicating best practices throughout the organization. A database should be developed to facilitate this

Ask the following questions once a best practice has been identified to better define the best practice and to identify the process enablers.	**Process:** _____
	Description of best practices:
In what ways has this practice benefited the organization?	
Quality benefits ❏	**Quality metric:** _____
Cost benefits ❏	Performance:_____ Trend: _____
	Was:
Efficiency/time savings ❏	**Cost metric:** _____
Productivity improvements ❏	Performance:_____ Trend: _____
	Was:
Other (morale, cohesion, etc.) ❏	**Efficiency metric:**_____
Summarize key metrics and performance levels in the column to the right. Summarize previous performance (before the best practice), if possible, below the metric.	Performance:_____ Trend: _____
	Was:
	Productivity metric:_____
	Performance:_____ Trend: _____
	Was:
	Other indicators:
Was/is any special training required? ❏ Yes ❏ No	**Enablers:**
If yes, describe:	1._____
	2._____
How experienced or skilled are the people who perform the practice (the level of experience or skill is often one of the key enablers)?	3._____
	Contact information:
❏ Low ❏ Moderate ❏ High ❏ Very high	
Is any unique equipment, software, or information needed to perform the practice? ❏	
Is there anything else that is critical to being able to perform this practice or to do it this well (research key inputs and resources)? ❏	

Figure 16.7 Best Practices Checklist.

Part IVA

communication. The database must allow searching by fields and keywords. At a minimum, include in the database the following information:

- Functional area or activity
- Summary description of the best practice
- Performance metrics that support the best practice
- Key enablers (process owner, those with authority to authorize change, etc.)
- Contact information
- Keywords to allow retrieval

Implementation

When good practices have been identified and need to be implemented system wide, they should be assigned to appropriate process owners or enablers for implementation. The assignment and follow-up may be similar to the assignment of nonconformities and their corrective action.

Nonconformities may exist because persons performing an activity discover an easier or quicker way to accomplish requirements but do not receive authorization for changing the method. Also, workers may discover a quicker, easier method but do not want their workload reevaluated. A new way of doing things could be a good practice or a misguided attempt to circumvent the required procedure.

Identification of OFIs or best practices must be included in the purpose/objectives if they are to be included in the audit report. In certain industry cultures (regulated and nonregulated), change, even for improvement, is extremely difficult and even undesirable.

8. ORGANIZATIONAL RISK MANAGEMENT[14]

All organizations exist in an environment of uncertainty. The source for this uncertainty can be either external or internal to the organization. Management may develop objectives, goals, strategies, budgets, and plans based on certain data and assumptions, but changes both within the organization and outside the organization may affect previous decisions and assumptions.

Management must deal with and anticipate these uncertainties, whether economic, competitive, technological, environmental, political, or legal. It does this by allowing for and managing risk through what can be termed *risk management*. This can be seen in:

- The purchase of insurance for specific or general risks
- Contingency funds allocated in budgeting for unforeseen or larger-than-expected expenses
- Hedging in commodities, other investments, or currencies to lessen losses from a particular purchase of materials or changes in exchange rates
- Alternate or fallback provisions in product or business plans

- Consideration of plans to ensure business continuity in the event of disaster or economic adversity

What is new is the more conscious consideration of risks, their management, and the broader application of these approaches. This is driven by:

- A more unstable world situation

- Increased reliance on computer systems and electronic records storage

- Increased concerns about international and domestic uncertainty

- The globalization of markets and competition

- A more complex regulatory environment affecting many aspects of the organization, its operations, and its administration

- The litigious nature of our society

- A heightened awareness and appreciation of uncertainties and tenuousness of our business and personal lives

What constitutes risk and appropriate or typical actions taken as part of risk management varies from organization to organization. Some focus on the possible outcomes or foreseen consequences, either real or imagined, regardless of their feasibility or likelihood. Others focus on the probability or likelihood alone but do not involve the evaluation of the consequences or the ability to detect or prevent the outcome. Some risk estimates are mathematical in nature; others are fairly descriptive.

Audit programs should avoid equating their value with only the costs saved. In some cases, cost savings are irrelevant because the organization seeks to reduce risk, such as the risk of noncompliance to a law, a regulation, a standard, or contractual requirements. For instance, noncompliance could result in loss of a license or operating permits, which may impact revenues.

Risk reduction in terms of safety, health, and environmental concerns is another way that audit programs contribute to organization performance. Audit results may reveal risks to the organization's wealth or well-being. Auditing may reveal situations that could result in fines, legal violations, negative publicity, or customer loss. In some cases, auditing is needed to provide positive demonstration of due diligence within the framework of legal relations.

Organization Risk Management scope may include how audits lower risk, risks associated with auditing, verifying risk treatments, or reporting risks observed while conducting an audit.

Risk Management versus Monitoring and Reporting

The topic of risk can be confusing. One reason is that people tend to intermingle the need to manage risk with the need to monitor and report risks. ISO 31000[15] states that the risk management process involves:

1. Establishing context (scope and objectives)

2. Identifying risk

3. Analyzing risk

4. Evaluating risk

5. Treating risk

If you are asked to manage risk, you need to follow the risk management process steps or similar model. If you are asked to monitor and report risk, you need to be able to recognize it or know it when you see it. Another excellent guidance standard concerning risk is ISO 14971, Application of risk management to medical devices, that establishes requirements for risk management to determine the safety of medical devices by the manufacturer during the product life cycle.

In many cases auditors and others are asked to monitor or report what they observe relative to risk treatments or the context of risky processes (criticality) or activities. The reporting may be based on intuitive assessment such as a finding that could result in loss of license, certification, or a customer order. Auditors may also be directed to report that risk treatments are implemented and effective.

Audit (Service) Risk (Conducting the Audit, Performance)

An audit is a service performed by auditors that may be internal or external to the organization being audited.

ISO 19011:2011 specifically lists audit performance risks that should be addressed. The first risk to address is in preparing the audit plan (clause 6.3.2.1), the audit team leader should be aware of the risks to the auditee organization created by the audit. For example, the presence of audit team members could influence health, safety, environmental, or quality controls. Someone could be sick, get injured, cause pollution, or interfere with an inspection. There may not be a specific audit objective that auditors should avoid injury but it is a risk that should be considered depending on the auditee site and requirements. Here you are being asked to analyze and evaluate risks associated with the audit. To manage the risk you may want to consider the aspects related to the product or services as well as the causal factors such as people, equipment, environment, materials, methods, and measures. For example: auditors could contaminate a clean room, ruin a circuit board with a static spark, void a calibration due to equipment damage, and so on. To identify potential risks, first consider the aspects that can create risks relative to the environment (nature of the organization).

Any methods that will be used to mitigate or treat risks should be discussed in the opening meeting and included in the audit plan. You can include managed risks in the audit plan under managed risks or another suitable title. Many auditors have done this in the past but they may have used titles such as special requirements or special topics or issues.

One of the biggest risks in conducting an audit is the risk associated with sampling. Samples may not be representative of the population from which they are selected and any conclusions based on the sample would be wrong. Auditors conducting external audits are more likely to experience sampling error than internal auditors. You should always be a vigilant and attentive listener to monitor any indication that the sample may be skewed. Perhaps the auditee changed processes 45 days ago, or the form you selected is just for special orders, or the records selected are for a service that is no longer provided.

As part of the performance of the audit, any evidence collected during the audit that suggests an immediate and significant risk (*effect of uncertainty on objectives*) to the auditee should be reported without delay to the auditee and, as appropriate, to the audit client.[16] Reporting something that suggests an immediate and significant risk is subjective, but in auditing, auditors must use their judgment. If the risk does not have a significant impact, the auditee will let you know. This type of activity isn't managing risk; it's reporting risk.

Audit results may be classified by level of risk. This may be as simple as reporting results as major or minor, on a scale of 1–10 or relative to the business bottom line or budget. Here auditors are being asked to assess their observations and report audit findings based on relative risk.

There are many risks to the audit process and they vary from audit to audit and organization. For each audit, risks should be managed and risks with a significant impact should be treated, such as changing the likelihood, changing the consequences, avoidance, removal, or other means. In general, the overall management of audit process and audit program risks should be the responsibility of audit program management personnel.

Auditing for Risk (a Deliverable, a Process Output)

Some audit programs or objectives include risk. Organizations may conduct risk audits while they conduct compliance audits. At other times, the identification of risky processes or activities beyond conformity or compliance to requirements is added to the purpose of the audit.

Conducting a risk audit may be collecting evidence to verify known risks are being controlled and that risk treatment plans are effective. The objective or purpose of the audit would be to start with a list of identified and treated risks and then verify they are effective. This process is very similar to an auditor verifying corrective actions have been implemented and are effective. Risk treatments need to be verified both short and long term and when there are changes to processes related or linked to identified risks. Some standards such as food safety ISO 22000 have plans to treat/mitigate significant hazards and risks.

Process audits would be a good approach for identification of new risks. Auditors conducting process audits are more familiar with the process being audited and would be able to spot and identify activities or events that could be a significant risk to the organization. However, system and product audits are not excluded from auditor identifying activities or events that could be a significant risk. The auditor is not charged with conducting a formal risk management analysis; they are only making observations that might be an aspect of risk that needs formal evaluation. Later an auditor may be assigned to a team that conducts a formal risk management analysis.

For example, an auditor may observe that the ink on a product label with return instructions is smearing. This may be a performance issue of the product not being returned in an efficient manner or it could be a potential risk to the organization if product is put in a landfill in lieu of proper instructions.

Audit Program Risk Management (Evaluate, Monitor and Report)

Audit program managers have always dealt with risk in some manner. Now it is becoming a formal part of the duties of an audit program manager. Managers are required to analyze and evaluate risk as well as monitor and report it.

Part IVA

Job responsibilities regarding risk may be sorted in terms of monitoring and reporting or analyzing and evaluating. The two are different cognitive levels requiring different knowledge and skills. See Figures 16.8 and 16.9 as example job duties regarding the management of risk are sorted between monitoring and analyzing.

The audit program should be evaluated relative to its performance regarding risk to the organization. For example, has the audit program contributed to lowering and/or maintaining its risk? Does the audit program help ensure risk treatments are effective and that management controls are maintained to avoid unnecessary risks? The audit organization should determine metrics for monitoring and reporting their performance relative to risk.

Organizations should analyze how the audit program affects an organization's risk level and how the risk level may influence the scheduling of audits. If the organization has identified risks, there would be levels of risk. Risk levels may be described in financial and nonfinancial terms. One of the most obvious risks is that the organization could lose its certification or license. Loss of license or certification could result in loss of revenue or shutting down operations. Riskier operations may be audited more frequently than less risky operations. Riskier operations may be more likely to be dangerous, hazardous, unsafe, costly, or noncompliant.

ISO 19011, clause 5.1 states that priority should be given to allocating the audit program resources to audit those matters of significance within the management system. Matters of significance would be high-level risks that need to be treated (monitored, mitigated, avoided, etc.) such as known hazards or costly consequences. This could be a type of risk-based auditing.

An audit organization needs to establish audit program objectives or goals. The person or person(s) managing the audit program should identify and evaluate

Monitor and report	Analyze and evaluate
• Know risk management tools and report observations • Report sampling risks • Report (potential) immediate and significant risks • Report audit results by risk level • Verify risk treatments and effectiveness	• Identify individual audit risks • Identify auditee risks created by the audit (the audit plan) • Assess and classify audit results by risk level

Figure 16.8 Auditor or lead auditor risk management duties.

Monitor and report	Analyze and evaluate
• Consider risks when allocating and managing resources • Establish procedures for monitoring and reviewing risk • Establish procedures that include risk factors when scheduling audits • Review effectiveness of risk measures • Keep records	• Identify and assess risks to audit program objectives • Analyze how risk levels may influence scheduling of audits • Identify risks to the audit process (conducting) • Evaluate audit program performance regarding risk to the organization (higher or lower?)

Figure 16.9 Audit manager risk management duties.

the risks for the audit program. ISO 19011 standard, clause 5.3.4 has identified specific risks that need to be managed. The risk aspects are:

- Failing to set relevant audit program objectives and determining the extent of the audit program (planning);

- Allowing insufficient time for developing the audit program or conducting an audit (resources);

- The selected team does not have the collective competence to conduct audits effectively (selection of the audit team);

- Ineffective communication of the audit program (implementation);

- Failing to adequately protect audit records to demonstrate audit program effectiveness (records and their controls);

- Ineffective monitoring of audit program outcomes (monitoring, reviewing, and improving the audit program)

The audit program manager should analyze and evaluate risk. Managers need to follow the risk management process steps (described in ISO 31000) or similar model.

The audit program schedule procedure should include considerations for risks when planning and scheduling audits for the organization. There are many risks that should be considered based on the type of audit, audit history, and nature of the organization to be audited. Some audit process aspects are (1) criticality of the processes to be audited, (2) past audit performance, (3) changes in the processes or personnel, and (4) maturity of the system.

ISO 19011 also requires that procedures include monitoring and reviewing audit program risks. The ISO 19011 definition is that risk is the *effect of uncertainty on objectives*.[17] The audit program has objectives; any risks to the objectives should be identified. Significant risks should be treated or avoided. Monitoring might include risk-based audits or periodic reassessments.

Managing the audit program resources should include consideration for audit program risks. The aspects of the audit program that represent a significant risk should be considered when budgeting resources. For example, if you need to audit critical processes that are remote, you will need a travel budget. If an audit objective is to initiate remote or eAudits, capital equipment may be needed and IT expertise needs to be available.

ISO 19011 (clause 5.4.5, Assigning responsibility for an individual audit to the audit team leader) states that when an audit team leader is assigned to an individual audit, he or she should be given information needed for evaluating and addressing identified risks to the achievement of the audit objectives or purpose. There are many risks, mostly minor, that could influence the achievement of the individual audit objective. What is important is to know the activities that could have a significant impact on the achievement of the audit objectives. This could be done intuitively or by using a matrix listing the aspects and potential impacts and their estimated probabilities. Risks might include getting a sufficient sample, completing the audit within a specified timeframe, availability of competent auditors, and so on. Here the audit team leader is expected to manage risk by analyzing and evaluating the impact of risks on the audit process.

Part IVA

Conclusion

In lieu of a standard or procedure requiring management of certain risks, the key to a risk management program is identification and assessment of risks. Risk management tools can be used to monitor and report risk as well as to identify and assess risks. There are many aspects of a process or organization that represent a risk. The organization personnel must determine which aspects are significant and must be treated. The decision to treat or mitigate risk aspects depends on the level of risk the organization is willing to accept.

Where there is a risk management program, auditors may be asked to verify that risk treatments are maintained and effective. Also, when part of the purpose of an audit, auditors may identify potential risks that need to be assessed.

Risk management is a proactive approach to avoid surprises to the organization that could affect its sustainability and survival.

9. MANAGEMENT REVIEW INPUT

Senior management establishes the aim (mission, objectives) of the overall system and defines how each component of the system contributes to the aim. This guides the auditing function as to how to define the audit program in terms of:

- Whether it is process or organizational-element oriented

- What is important

- How and with whom to schedule the audits

- How to look at individual activities and their effectiveness or performance

- How to report the results to management to stimulate action

Auditing then shifts toward looking at the points in a process where various components or elements of the system or organization interact, looking for miscommunication, misunderstandings, conflicts of aims, pursuit of short-term goals or advantages, and so forth. An example could be a purchasing organization that pursues reductions in piece cost without looking at total costs or the overall impact on the organization, such as delivery performance, supplied product quality, or engineering or technological advantage.

Managers need to have information that is properly gathered, analyzed, and presented. Accordingly, management relies on the various operating units and functions within the organization, as well as its suppliers and customers, to provide information regarding the operation of the organization and its products.

Management can obtain unbiased information on the status of its activities and opportunities for intervention and continual improvement through audit programs of suppliers or internal operations and processes. For the audit program to be meaningful, management must:

- Properly structure and coordinate the various audit processes within the organization and align them with the goals, objectives, strategies, and initiatives of the organization

- Supply the audit programs with sufficient resources, including trained personnel and time to accomplish the task intended

- Most importantly, give the results and findings of the audit function due consideration and take appropriate action involving a process of management review, deliberation, and follow-through

All of this gives the process transparency, promotes a sense of openness, and shows evidence of due care. Management, in its review process, may make assignments and allocate resources to take action on the system, or for business (financial) reasons, it may choose to let the system remain unchanged.

MANAGEMENT REVIEW

The issue of management taking the results of the audits seriously—giving them attention, consideration, and judgment through a process of review—and following through on the results of the audits for remediation or continual improvement is the key role of management with regard to the audit function. Regardless of the kind of audit (quality, operations, safety, environmental, or financial), if auditors are properly trained and qualified; are provided resources, access, and support; are capable of rendering fair, unbiased, and disinterested findings; are able to make judgments, evaluate and follow through, and demonstrate due care, then management must give them sufficient credibility and value their reports and act on their findings.

Management should review individual audit program performance and how the program has benefited the organization. Some topics to review are:

- Audit program objectives and their achievement

- Results of audits and impact of risks

- Status of corrective and preventive actions and their contribution

- Organizational risks and control measures such as risk-based audits

- Recommendations for improvement

System, process, and product audits are management tools for oversight of organizational controls. Audits should be used to ensure conformance to requirements, ongoing maintenance of controls, achievement of objectives, and continual improvement.

Part IVA

Chapter 17
Business and Financial Impact/Part IVB

1. AUDITING AS A MANAGEMENT TOOL

The history of auditing and early public exposure have created a rather restricted, negative stereotypic image of the term *audit*. Widespread use of audits in the quality field increased after World War II with compliance audits in the defense industry. Usually they emphasized corrective actions of "doing it by the book," rather than examining the plan or procedure for potential change to "the book." In their earliest form, compliance audits did not even check the effectiveness of procedures, just whether the procedure existed and was under document control. Aggravating this situation was the fairly common practice of assigning personnel with low potential or competence to the audit function due to the perception that audits did not accomplish anything positive. The history of auditing has been a barrier to using system and process audits as a management oversight tool for sustaining and improving organizations. Management must view system/process auditing as a process for collecting factual data, providing management oversight, and creating knowledge—not as it was viewed and practiced by previous generations. In today's world, audit program objectives must go beyond compliance monitoring and enforcement.

Since system and process auditing are processes for collecting and transforming data into factual information about the organization (specifically, the activities defined by the audit's scope and purpose), they can be useful management tools. Audit services can range from simple verification of compliance audits that maintain a system at its design potential operation level to determination of effectiveness and efficiency to promote continual improvement of the organization. Management must first decide the strategies for the organization and then use audit-generated factual information to support those strategies. In essence, auditing can provide information upon which strategic decisions are based, or it can be a tactical tool for driving different initiatives, including continual improvement.

Management can benefit from the use of process auditing techniques because it requires the evaluation of interactions and relationships of activities that compose the system. Unfortunately, many organizations have no knowledge of overall systemic interactions and relationships between departments and activities, other than the auditor's working papers. Management knows what happens next in the flow of a product or paperwork, but may not know the interactions or relationships beyond the next phase or department. Without this knowledge of the organization's systems, redundant, counterproductive, and unneeded actions not only may exist but may even be included in policies and procedures and be perpetuated by conformity auditing.

Management can address this quagmire by implementing contemporary process-based audit practices that focus on the system, by reading the audit reports in their entirety, and by using this information to allocate resources to implement changes for improvement.

Linkage to Continuous Improvement

In the 1970s, the principal focus of audits was to attain compliance. Today, companies are shifting their focus from compliance to customer satisfaction and improvement and controlling risk. Many firms see this as an operational imperative. Fewer and fewer organizations feel completely at ease with their current customer relationships. Listening to the voice of the customer and acting on that intelligence to develop new products become a necessary marketing strategy.[1]

Definition of Continuous Improvement

Continuous improvement is a philosophy that assumes that organizations can always make improvements. ASQ has provided a couple of definitions:[2]

Continuous improvement (CI): Sometimes called continual improvement. The ongoing improvement of products, services, or processes through incremental and breakthrough improvements.

Continuous quality improvement (CQI): A philosophy and attitude for analyzing capabilities and processes and improving them repeatedly to achieve the objective of customer satisfaction.

The marketplace is constantly shifting. Continuous improvement allows organizations to meet customer needs and remain competitive.

Continuous Improvement in the Audit Program

By looking at the data collected in audits, management can begin to analyze the data and act on the conclusions. This analysis of causes, corrective actions, and preventive actions provides direction for audit program improvements. Techniques to integrate continuous/continual improvement into the audit process include:

- Establishing teams to implement opportunities for improved audit service performance

- Providing training and resources to assist introduction and implement indicated changes

- Developing an audit program structure that supports future anticipated demands from the customer, market, or regulatory agency, and other external and internal requirements

Continuous improvement is an ongoing process. The audit program never finishes making improvements. The successful implementation of one improvement simply flows into the next investigation.

Part IVB

Within the audit organization, the audit program provides the seeds for change and the continuous improvement process. The audit program serves as a primary source of corrective action input. When the audit program becomes trusted and credible, employees may share information with auditors that they would not typically share with management. Employees' candid suggestions, ideas, complaints, and observations are invaluable to continuous improvement.

> In a small manufacturing firm, the general manager coached the truck drivers on observation techniques. The transportation supervisor debriefed the drivers after every delivery. He asked for observations that supported other marketing information and potential opportunities for improvement. The delivery routine was one more source being cultivated for information on competitive advances. This same company actively encouraged all employees to forward observations on improvement opportunities, and it listened to and acknowledged each observation. Management exhibited a uniform posture about external and internal observations made by its employees.

The audit also provides an improvement support network. An organization may welcome corrective action and fully intend to complete it, but it may fail to implement the action. By providing support throughout the corrective action process, the audit program can promote process completion while gaining insight into how corrective action helps or hinders the organization.

> In a service organization, day-to-day firefighting left little time for focusing on corrective action. After experiencing significant numbers of nonconformances, management started to see a pattern of common cause and directed that a root cause analysis be used. The actions determined and implemented significantly reduced customer complaints. After the actions were complete, several managers commented, "We should have done this years ago."

Risk Management

Whether they perform financial, internal control, environmental, process, health and safety, or quality audits, auditors are key players in the management of risks for the organization. In many cases, they are the ones most familiar with the legislation, regulations, and technical subject matter that form the basis of certain types of risk. In addition, they are often the ones who are most familiar with the operations and conditions present within the organization. They can also have the dispassionate perspective to identify and describe situations that expose the organization to various risks, and the mind-set and tenacity to ensure effective follow-up and implementation of measures to address risk situations.

For some time, international environmental and quality management system standards have addressed risk to the effect of stating that the internal audit programs take into consideration the status and importance of the processes and other areas audited. The results of these audits, in turn, typically are addressed during management reviews. By identifying and evaluating the risks posed in all the areas mentioned earlier, top management can come up with a coherent, consistent set of risk assessments that can be used to develop the various types of audit plans and, where possible, integrate or harmonize them. This would ensure that audit resources supplement or reinforce each other and that they are focused on what really matters to the organization. The audit plans and audit program documentation would be linked to the risk assessments and would provide management with a measure of actions taken and provisions implemented, and their effectiveness. Corrective and preventive actions as well as management reviews would be documented. All of this establishes a continuous thread from the risk assessment through the management review, which reinforces due care.

Conclusion

Using auditing as a management tool can be summed up by the statement "Results come from checking, not expecting."[3] This statement means that managers and leaders must hold people accountable for the programs, goals, and objectives assigned to them. Even the captain of a ship must check on progress from time to time to ensure that the course has been maintained and that conditions have not changed to warrant a course change. For an organization, auditing is a management tool for checking results so that management can hold people accountable for their actions.[4]

While many state that auditors don't add value, others state that management needs auditors (or similar function) to effectively manage the organization. Whether the audit program is a necessary evil or an important member of the management team may depend on attitudes and perceptions—is the glass half full or half empty?

Tenets for Audits That Add Value[5]

Audits add value when:

- Auditors demonstrate professionalism, integrity, confidentiality, and discretion

- Audits are conducted by competent auditors

- Auditors learn and practice their skills

- Organizational risks are identified, managed, monitored, and reported

- Findings (reports) result in corrective action and continual improvement

- The audit function is part of the management team and strategic planning

2. INTERRELATIONSHIPS OF BUSINESS PROCESSES

In 1950, while on a U.S. government–sponsored mission to Japan, W. Edwards Deming sketched out a graphic to develop the idea of a system among the attendees. While simplistic to some, it is quite profound in its starkness (see Figure 17.1).

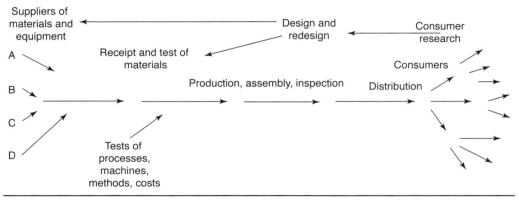

Figure 17.1 Production viewed as a system.

Source: Derived from W. Edwards Deming, *Out of the Crisis* (Cambridge, MA: MIT Press, 1986), p. 4.

On the right side of Figure 17.1, the focus is on the customer and includes the distribution network necessary to deliver the product (or service) to the customer. The left side of the figure includes other organizations and the suppliers of goods and services to the system. In between are all other operations that transform the inputs to achieve the objectives of the organization. The system has feedback from the customers that goes into design (engineering), which in turn feeds back to the suppliers, to production, and to other activities in the organization. Also evident are the interrelationships among the components or activities within the system that work together and depend on one another.

This concept of interdependence is important for auditors and managers to understand. It is critical that goals or objectives for each individual component or activity be meshed so that one component does not thrive at the expense of the others. If this occurs, the net effect will be the suboptimization of the performance of the system as a whole. In the past, the danger in compliance-focused auditing was the driving of activities or elements of an organization to suboptimize, without looking at the broader picture.

Recent developments in quality thinking focus not on organizational elements but on processes that would tend to cross organizational boundaries.

Conducting process audits, which look more closely at the interrelationships and interdependence among process and organizational elements, blurs the functional, smokestack-type view and leads to an increased "systems centric" approach.

Key to the understanding of a system is that a system must be managed and that management of the system requires an awareness of its components, the interrelationships among them, and the people who work in them.[6]

3. COST OF QUALITY (COQ) PRINCIPLES[7]

Cost of quality is a method used by organizations to show the financial impact of quality activities. Attaching a dollar amount to quality-related activities clarifies where there may be significant opportunities for quality improvement. Once recognized, process improvement efforts can be focused on those with the higher potential payoff.

In the 1950s, Armand Feigenbaum saw value in a management reporting system focusing on quality costs, their causes, and their effects. During this time, it was recognized that costs buried in standards and buried in overhead rates were not addressed. During the same period, Joseph Juran wrote of the importance of measuring quality in terms best understood by upper management: dollars. These concepts were the basis of what has evolved into cost of quality programs. No one method exists for collecting and reporting an entity's quality cost drivers because each company's accounting system collects and reports costs differently. By applying the concept of cost of quality, however, any accounting or quality manager can design a meaningful measurement tool that can be used to report on and highlight quality issues and that will help the company undertake meaningful quality improvement activities.

By the 1980s, the costs of quality were categorized: failure costs, internal and external; prevention costs; and appraisal costs. In the efforts to learn more about and attempt to control the true costs of quality, certain facts became evident:

- Most quality costs are not identified in the financial records and statements of the organization

- Most organizations were not aware of the cost to produce nonquality

- Increasing sales does not decrease the cost of nonquality

- The focus should really be on cost of poor quality and its impact on the organization (financial, competitiveness, customer retention and satisfaction, employee motivation)

Because it is measuring dollars, cost-of-quality reporting is one of the best tools available to raise an organization's awareness of quality issues. Some basic education on the concept and methods of cost of quality must be done, with an initial focus on top management. The educational process might also be deployed to other levels, however, as workers who understand how costs are collected and reported are more likely to understand how their work influences the company's performance.

Part IVB

Categorizing Quality Costs

There are three major categories of quality costs: *appraisal*, *prevention*, and *failure*. In his book *Quality Is Free*, Phil Crosby asserts that quality does not cost money; rather, it is the absence of quality (the nonconformances and failures) that increases total costs. Crosby popularized the terms *cost of poor quality* or cost of nonquality, emphasizing that to avoid these bad costs money would have to be spent up front on prevention and appraisal.

When designing a cost-of-quality program and setting up accounts to track the elements, attention must be given to the four categories of quality costs typically used: prevention, appraisal, internal failure, and external failure. Because the total cost of quality can often be 20 percent to 30 percent of sales, these dollars must be traced to their sources to understand their cause-and-effect relationships.

- *Internal failure costs* occur before the product is delivered to the customer. Examples are costs of rework and repair, reinspecting and retesting of product, material downgrading, inventory shrinkage, unscheduled downtime, and internal miscommunications that result in delays.

- *External failure costs* occur after the delivery of product or while furnishing a service to the customer. Examples include the costs of processing customer complaints, field service, customer returns, warranty claims, product recalls, and product liability lawsuits.

- *Appraisal costs* are costs associated with measuring, evaluating, or auditing products or services to ensure conformance to quality standards and performance requirements. They include the costs of incoming and source inspection/test of purchased materials; validation, verification, and checking activities; in-process and final inspection/ test; product, service, or process audits; and calibration of measuring and testing equipment, including associated supplies, materials, and external services.

- *Prevention costs* are costs incurred in minimizing failure and appraisal costs throughout the entire organization's processes. Examples include new-product design reviews, quality planning, supplier quality surveys, process capability evaluations, quality improvement team meetings, and quality education and training.

- *Total cost of quality* is the sum of all failure costs + appraisal costs + prevention costs.

For example: The total cost of quality, before improvement, was 30 percent of sales, broken down into internal failures at 45 percent, external failures at 30 percent, appraisal costs at 20 percent, and prevention costs at 5 percent. Once known, these were unacceptable. The organization's objective is to reduce the total costs by decreasing failure costs, minimizing appraisal costs, and increasing prevention costs only to the extent necessary to achieve the failure and appraisal cost decreases.

The objectives for a cost-of-quality improvement initiative were: total costs of 3 percent of sales, broken down into internal failures at 20 percent, external failures at 5 percent, appraisal costs at 25 percent, and prevention costs at 50 percent.

Quality costs apply to all departments and should not be confined to those associated with production. Often the costs generated within support functions represent a significant portion of total quality costs and may be hidden within standard costs. In addition, labor expenses might be reported with an overhead allocation that includes benefits and other indirect expenses. These issues require care in properly determining true and comparable costs.

The cost-of-quality categories also apply equally well to nonmanufacturing situations. Consider the training conducted in a restaurant to help ensure that food and service quality is maintained (prevention), as well as the sampling done by the cook and customer feedback cards used to measure quality (appraisal). Internal failure costs are incurred if food must be returned to the kitchen due to inadequate preparation or if the customer refuses to tip based on poor service. In this case, as is true with many service processes, direct external failure costs are absorbed by the customer who ends up with indigestion or food poisoning, but the loss of future business (and perhaps litigation) is incurred by the restaurant. Other service examples include:

- *Prevention costs*—time and expenses related to an accounting firm learning about changes in tax laws

- *Appraisal costs*—screening of baggage by an airline

- *Internal failure costs*—incurred when a technician in a hospital must repeat a chest X-ray because the first one was not clear

- *External failure costs*—correction of an error found by a customer in his or her banking statement

Initiating a Cost-of-Quality Program

For an organization that has not used cost-of-quality measurement before, education of senior management in the methods for and benefits of such a program must first be done. Once management has agreed to implement cost of quality, a pilot program can then be used to help demonstrate the process and benefits without fully involving the entire organization and extensive resources. For example, a product line where there are obvious opportunities for improvement, but where the improvements are not expected to be overly complex to attack, might be a good place to start.

Key management/supervisory personnel from the pilot area should be involved in estimating the cost of quality, working with accounting and quality personnel. A rough estimate may be all that is required to show the opportunities, which can then be addressed through either a process improvement team or other organized method for improvement.

Establishing and Tracking Measurements

Once the organization is convinced and committed to using cost of quality, a more detailed cost-of-quality baseline should be established that allows the organization to know where it is and will allow tracking of overall improvement. In developing the details of the quality cost system, there are two important criteria to follow: (1) recognize that quality cost is a tool to justify improvement actions and measure their effectiveness, and (2) realize that including insignificant activities is not essential.

Several methods are available for measuring cost of quality. One method often used in manufacturing organizations is to analyze the company's chart of financial accounts. If the accounting manager and quality manager were to review the accounts on the expense side, they would quickly find that some contain expenses obviously related to quality (for example, salary of the quality manager and metrology technicians, scrap of nonconforming material, travel expenses to visit customers when problems occur), while others have no or very little quality-related expenses (for example, tooling and accountant's salary).

The accounts that do contain quality expenses can then be pulled out separately and categorized as to whether they contain prevention, appraisal, internal failure, or external failure costs. The proportion of each account that should be allocated to each cost-of-quality category can then be estimated, and a rough estimate of cost of quality can be obtained by totaling the actual expenses for the last year as indicated by the allocations. The total then needs to be normalized to adjust for changes in volume of business. Reporting cost of quality as a percentage of sales is typical.

Another method is simply to do an activity assessment of the organization. By listing the activities that fit into the cost-of-quality categories and estimating the amount of time invested in each activity, a rough calculation of cost of quality can be obtained. This process could be used more accurately at the department level, although it must be understood that failures may be created in one part of the organization, but found in another.

Some organizations also elect to measure only failure costs. Depending on where they are in their quality journey this may be sufficient to provide the incentive to move forward with continual improvement and to see the results. For organizations that are using activity-based costing/management (ABC/M), quality cost dollars are more easily obtained. Activity-based costing allocates overhead expenses to the activities based on the proportion of use, rather than proportion of costs.

Institutionalizing Cost of Quality

Once an organization is comfortable with the concept and usefulness of cost of quality, a formal reporting process needs to be developed. Quality costs should be a performance measure used for decision making for continuous improvement and strategic planning. Responsibilities for and the format for collecting and reporting the information must be defined, as well as the frequency and agenda where it will be used for decision making.

Education of the workforce, either on an ad hoc basis (for example, just before beginning a cost-of-quality driven improvement project in a particular area) or overall (everyone learns about cost of quality), can then help the company to make a permanent connection between quality performance and cost performance.

Activity-Based Costing

The objective of activity-based costing (ABC) is to improve the organization's effectiveness through the identification of quality costs associated with specific activities, analyze those costs, and implement means to lower total costs. Under the ABC approach, costs of resources used are allocated in proportion to the use of the resource for given activities.

This method contrasts with traditional cost accounting whereby costs were allocated based on some arbitrary percentage of direct labor. With direct labor becoming a smaller portion of the cost of producing a specific product or service, this approach is no longer viable for many organizations.

Employing ABC, some organizations have indicated that they have discontinued producing unprofitable products. They hadn't realized the extent to which such products were eating their profits.

Although cost of quality is not in the scope of the auditor's responsibilities, the auditor should know the concept of quality costs and be able to assess its use.

4. EMERGING ROLES OF THE AUDITOR

No one knows for certain what changes will occur in the auditing field in the next decade. Trends suggest that assessment will continue to be an important management oversight tool. Changes in the formation of audit groups, through joint audits or round-robin consortiums, will ensure greater auditor independence and result in a cross-fertilization of ideas among industries. Standards, such as AS9100 and ISO 19011, have been created and old ones revised to address societal and global needs. Advances in communications technology and the increase in the internationalization of businesses will lead to many ongoing changes.

In the 1970s, the primary purpose of auditing was compliance. Auditing in certain highly regulated fields, such as the nuclear industry, is likely to remain compliance oriented. The current direction of the international standards groups is to make all management system standards more compatible. Some standards, such as ISO 9001, have de-emphasized required procedures and refocused on continual improvement and customer satisfaction. Combining the management system audit guidelines (ISO 19011) has emphasized conformance-oriented auditing.

Internal process auditing and system auditing are expected to focus more on effectiveness and improvement as they become more performance based. Rather than focusing just on adherence or compliance to a certain standard, companies are assessing their operations against those of world leaders by using benchmarking or by comparison with criteria such as those for the Malcolm Baldrige National Quality Award or ISO 9004. As there is a shift from compliance to performance, organizations will see the viability of using process and system audits as a management oversight tool to monitor, promote, and sustain continual improvement.

As companies try to achieve continual improvement and reach world-class levels, they not only focus on complying with a particular standard but also ask, How far can we reach, what are our goals to get there, and how do we go about that process? As a result, a large percentage of the applications handed out for the Malcolm Baldrige National Quality Award every year are used for self-assessments within a company and are never used to apply for the award. The comprehensive criteria are based on how a system needs to be structured to attain total customer satisfaction. *Benchmarking*, one of the tools used during that process, can be defined as the process of identifying, understanding, and adapting best (outstanding) practices to help an organization improve its performance. Winners of the Malcolm Baldrige National Quality Award are required to share with other companies what they learn from the process, resulting in an open invitation for others to learn from them.

The emerging role of the auditor may be tied to the emerging role of auditing. Is auditing the cost of appraisal or cost of prevention? In a culture of pass-fail compliance audits, auditing may be considered the cost of appraisal. In a culture of audits that gather factual data, audits may be considered the cost of prevention.

The emerging role of auditing may be to use auditing to ensure the organization stays on course.

Part V
Quality Tools and Techniques

[26 of the CQA Exam Questions or 17.3 percent]

Auditors use many types of tools to plan and perform an audit, as well as to analyze and report audit results. An understanding of these tools and their application is essential for the performance of an effective audit since both auditors and auditees use various tools and techniques to define processes, identify and characterize problems, and report results. An auditor must have sufficient knowledge of these tools in order to determine whether the auditee is using them correctly and effectively. This section provides basic information on some of the most common tools, their use, and their limitations. For more in-depth information on the application of tools, readers should consult an appropriate textbook.

Part V

Chapter 18
Basic Quality and Problem-Solving Tools/ Part VA

PARETO CHARTS

Pareto charts, also called Pareto diagrams or Pareto analysis, are based on the Pareto principle, which suggests that most effects come from relatively few causes. As shown in Figure 18.1, a Pareto chart consists of a series of bars in descending order. The bars with the highest incidence of failure, costs, or other occurrences are on the left side. The miscellaneous category, an exception, always appears at the far right, regardless of size.

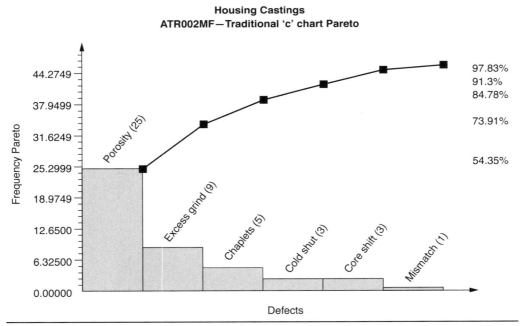

Figure 18.1 SQM software example of a frequency Pareto analysis.

Source: Courtesy of CIM Vision International.

Pareto charts display, in order of importance, the contribution of each item to the total effect and the relative rank of the items.

Pareto charts can be used to prioritize problems and to check performance of implemented solutions to problems. The Pareto chart can be a powerful management tool for focusing effort on the problems and solutions that have the greatest payback.[1] Some organizations construct year-end Pareto diagrams and form corporate improvement teams in the areas determined to be in need of the greatest attention.

CAUSE-AND-EFFECT DIAGRAMS

The *cause-and-effect diagram* (C-E diagram) is a visual method for analyzing causal factors for a given effect in order to determine their relationship. The C-E diagram, one of the most widely used quality tools, is also called an Ishikawa diagram (after its inventor) or a fishbone diagram (because of its shape).

Basic characteristics of the C-E diagram include the following:

- It represents the factors that might contribute to an observed condition or effect
- It clearly shows interrelationships among possible causal factors
- The interrelationships shown are usually based on known data

C-E diagrams are an effective way to generate and organize the causes of observed events or conditions since they display causal information in a structured way.

C-E diagrams consist of a description of the effect written in the head of the fish and the causes of the effect identified in the major bones of the body. These main branches typically include four or more of the following six influences but may be specifically tailored as needed:

1. People (worker)
2. Equipment (machine)
3. Method
4. Material
5. Environment
6. Measurement

Figure 18.2 is a C-E diagram that identifies all the program elements that should be in place to prevent design output errors.[2]

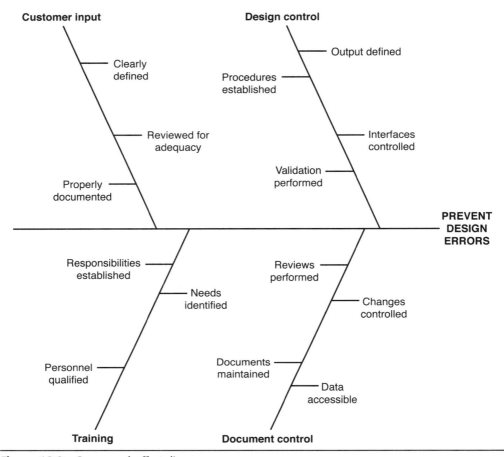

Figure 18.2 Cause-and-effect diagram.

Source: Rudolph C. Hirzel, "A Systems Approach to Auditing Systems" (presented at ASQ Quality Day, Motorola University, April 10, 1997).

FLOWCHARTS AND PROCESS MAPPING

Process maps and flowcharts are used to depict the steps or activities in a process or system that produces some output. *Flowcharts* are specific tools for depicting sequential activities and typically use standard symbols in their creation. Flowcharts and process maps are effective means for understanding procedures and overall processes and are used by auditees to help define how work is performed. Flowcharts are especially helpful in understanding processes that are complicated or that appear to be in a state of disorder. Auditors may also use flowcharts to help understand both production and service processes during audit preparation.

A flowchart may be used to describe an existing system or process or to design a new one. It can be used to:

- Develop a common understanding of an overall process, system, and sequence of operations

- Identify inspection and checkpoints that result in a decision

- Identify personnel (by job title) performing specific steps
- Identify potential problem areas, bottlenecks, unnecessary steps or loops, and rework loops
- Discover opportunities for changes and improvements
- Guide activities for identifying problems, theorizing about root causes, developing potential corrective actions and solutions, and achieving continuous improvement

Flowcharting usually follows a sequence from top to bottom and left to right, with arrowheads used to indicate the direction of the activity sequence. Common symbols often used for quality applications are shown in Figure 18.3. However, there are many other types of symbols used in flowcharting, such as ANSI Y15.3, Operation and Flow Process Charts (see Figures 18.4–18.8). Templates and computer

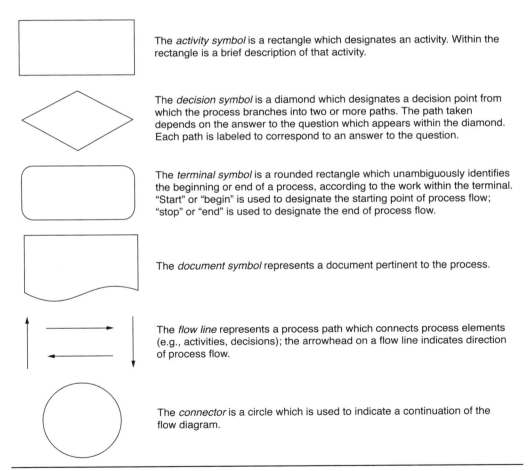

The *activity symbol* is a rectangle which designates an activity. Within the rectangle is a brief description of that activity.

The *decision symbol* is a diamond which designates a decision point from which the process branches into two or more paths. The path taken depends on the answer to the question which appears within the diamond. Each path is labeled to correspond to an answer to the question.

The *terminal symbol* is a rounded rectangle which unambiguously identifies the beginning or end of a process, according to the work within the terminal. "Start" or "begin" is used to designate the starting point of process flow; "stop" or "end" is used to designate the end of process flow.

The *document symbol* represents a document pertinent to the process.

The *flow line* represents a process path which connects process elements (e.g., activities, decisions); the arrowhead on a flow line indicates direction of process flow.

The *connector* is a circle which is used to indicate a continuation of the flow diagram.

Figure 18.3 Common flowchart symbols.

Source: J. M. Juran, ed., *Juran's Quality Control Handbook*, 4th ed. (New York: McGraw-Hill, 1988), p. 67. Reproduced with permission of the McGraw-Hill Companies.

Part VA

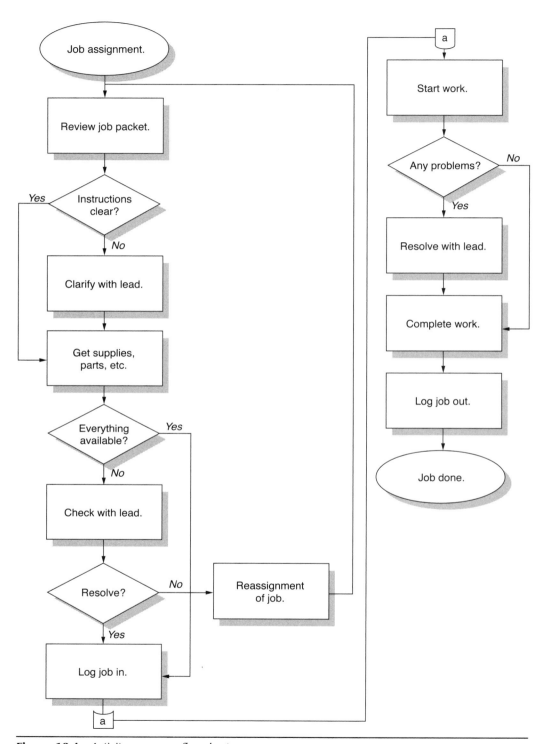

Figure 18.4 Activity sequence flowchart.

Source: From Rudolph C. Hirzel, "A Systems Approach to Auditing Systems Workshop" (presented at 28th annual EED conference, October 1998).

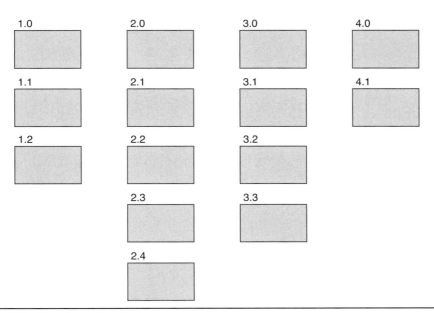

Figure 18.5 Top-down flowchart.

Source: Dan Entner, "Basic Tools for Process Improvement," Delaware Community College. Used with permission.

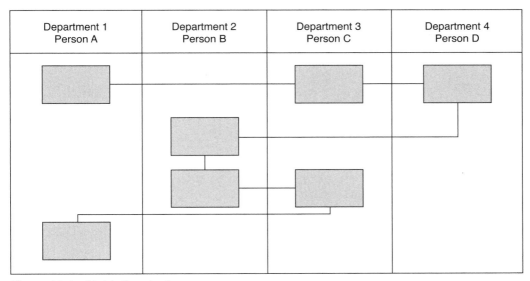

Figure 18.6 Matrix flowchart.

Source: Dan Entner, "Basic Tools for Process Improvement," Delaware Community College. Used with permission.

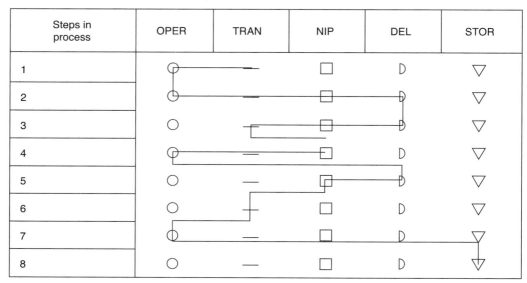

Figure 18.7 Flow process worksheet.

Source: Dan Entner, "Basic Tools for Process Improvement," Delaware Community College. Used with permission.

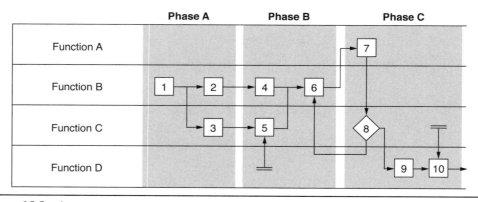

Figure 18.8 A process map.

Source: Jack B. Revelle, *Quality Essentials* (Milwaukee, WI: ASQ Quality Press, 2004), p. 211.

software, both of which are easy to use and fairly inexpensive, are available for making flowcharts.

The implementation of a process-based QMS (such as ISO 9001:2008) and the use of process auditing techniques have made charting an important auditing tool. In the book *How to Audit the Process-Based QMS*, the authors state, "Many auditors find it useful to draw a flowchart of the operations about to be audited. What processes are performed and what are the linkages? This also helps to define the interfaces where information and other resources come into and flow out of the audited area." They continue by stating, "To make maximum use of the process approach to auditing, the work papers should reflect the flow of activities to be audited."[3]

In the book *The Process Auditing Techniques Guide*, the author explains, "The primary tool of process auditing is creating a process flow diagram [PFD] or flowchart. Charting the process steps [sequential activities] is an effective method for describing the process. For auditing purposes, process flow diagrams should be used to identify sequential process steps [activities] and kept as simple or as reasonable as possible."[4]

Another variation of a flowchart is a process map. *Process maps* are very good tools that show inputs, outputs, and area or department responsibilities along a timeline. The complexity of process maps can vary, but for auditing, simplicity is the key.

STATISTICAL PROCESS CONTROL (SPC) CHARTS

Many companies use statistical process control (SPC) techniques as part of a continuing improvement effort. Auditors need to be knowledgeable about the methods and application of control charts in order to determine the adequacy of their use and evaluate the results achieved. Auditors need this knowledge for observation purposes, but they are not required to plot control charts as part of the audit process. *Control charts*, also called process control charts or run charts, are tools used in SPC.

SPC recognizes that some random variation always exists in a process and that the goal is to control distribution rather than individual dimensions. Operators and quality control technicians use SPC to determine when to adjust a process and when to leave it alone. The ability to operate to a tight tolerance without producing defects can be a major business advantage. Control charts can tell an organization when a process is good enough so that resources can be directed to more pressing needs.[5]

A control chart, such as the one shown in Figure 18.9, is used to distinguish variations in a process over time. Variations can be attributed to either special or common causes. *Common-cause variations* repeat randomly within predictable limits and can include chance causes, random causes, system causes, and inherent causes. *Special-cause variations* indicate that some factors affecting the process need to be identified, investigated, and brought under control. Such causes include assignable causes, local causes, and specific causes. Control charts use operating

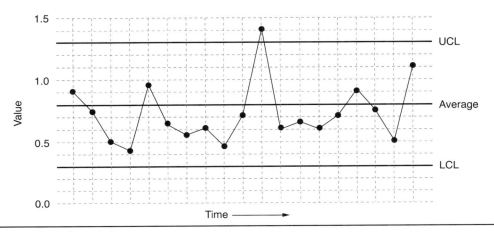

Figure 18.9   Control chart.

Source: Nancy R. Tague, *The Quality Toolbox* (Milwaukee, WI: ASQC Quality Press, 1995), p. 86. Used with permission.

Part VA

data to establish limits within which future observations are expected to remain if the process remains unaffected by special causes.

Control charts can monitor the aim and variability, and thereby continually check the stability of a process. This check of stability in turn ensures that the statistical distribution of the product characteristic is consistent with quality requirements.[6]

Control charts are commonly used to:

1. Attain a state of statistical control

2. Monitor a process

3. Determine process capability[7]

The type of control chart used in a specific situation depends on the type of data being measured or counted.

Variable data, also called continuous data or measurement data, are collected from measurements of the items being evaluated. For example, the measurement of physical characteristics such as time, length, weight, pressure, or volume through inspection, testing, or measuring equipment constitutes variable data collection. Variable data can be measured and plotted on a continuous scale and are often expressed as fractions or decimals.

The $\overline{X}$ (average) chart and the R (range) chart are the most common types of control charts for variable data. The $\overline{X}$ chart illustrates the average measurement of samples taken over time. The R chart illustrates the range of the measurements of the samples taken. For these charts to be accurate, it is critical that individual items composing the sample are pulled from the same basic production process. That is, the samples should be drawn around the same time, from the same machine, from the same raw material source, and so on.[8] These charts are often used in conjunction with one another to jointly record the mean and range of samples taken from the process at fairly regular intervals. Figure 18.10 shows an $\overline{X}$ and R chart.

Attribute data, also referred to as discrete data or counted data, provide information on number and frequency of occurrences. By counting and plotting discrete events—the number of defects or percentage of failures, for example—in integer values (1, 2, 3), an auditor is able to look at previously defined criteria and rate the product or system as pass/fail, acceptable/unacceptable, or go/no-go. Several basic types of control charts can be used for charting attribute data. Attribute data can be either a fraction nonconforming or number of defects or nonconformities observed in the sample. To chart the fraction of units defective, the p chart is used. The units are classified into one of two states: go/no-go, acceptable/unacceptable, conforming/nonconforming, yes/no, and so on. The sample size may be fixed or variable, which makes the technique very effective for statistically monitoring nontraditional processes such as percentage of on-time delivery. However, if the sample size is variable, control limits must be calculated for each sample taken.

The np chart uses the number of nonconforming units in a sample. This chart is sometimes easier for personnel who are not trained in SPC. It is easier to understand this chart when the sample size is constant, but it can be variable like the p chart.

The c chart plots the number of nonconformities per some unit of measure. For example, the total number of nonconformities could be counted at final inspection

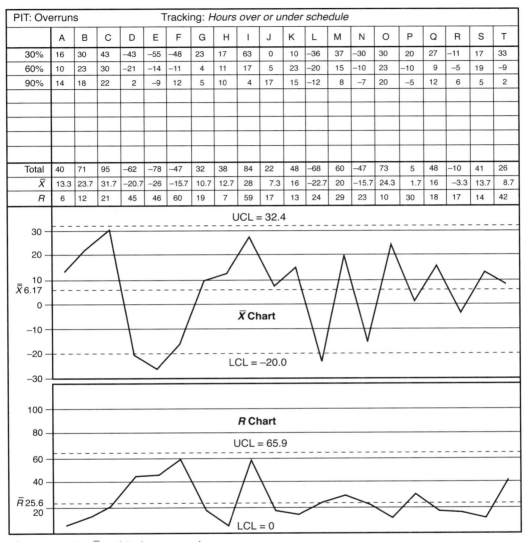

PIT: Overruns						Tracking: *Hours over or under schedule*													
	A	B	C	D	E	F	G	H	I	J	K	L	M	N	O	P	Q	R	S	T
30%	16	30	43	−43	−55	−48	23	17	63	0	10	−36	37	−30	30	20	27	−11	17	33
60%	10	23	30	−21	−14	−11	4	11	17	5	23	−20	15	−10	23	−10	9	−5	19	−9
90%	14	18	22	2	−9	12	5	10	4	17	15	−12	8	−7	20	−5	12	6	5	2
Total	40	71	95	−62	−78	−47	32	38	84	22	48	−68	60	−47	73	5	48	−10	41	26
$\bar{X}$	13.3	23.7	31.7	−20.7	−26	−15.7	10.7	12.7	28	7.3	16	−22.7	20	−15.7	24.3	1.7	16	−3.3	13.7	8.7
R	6	12	21	45	46	60	19	7	59	17	13	24	29	23	10	30	18	17	14	42

UCL = 32.4

$\bar{\bar{X}}$ 6.17

$\bar{X}$ Chart

LCL = −20.0

R Chart

UCL = 65.9

$\bar{R}$ 25.6

LCL = 0

Figure 18.10 $\bar{X}$ and R chart example.

Source: Clive Shearer, *Practical Continuous Improvement for Professional Services* (Milwaukee, WI: ASQC Quality Press, 1994), p. 241. Used with permission.

of a product and charted on a *c* chart. The number of nonconformities may be made up of several distinct defects, which might then be analyzed for improvement of the process. For this chart, the sample size must be constant from unit to unit.

The *u* chart is used for the average number of nonconformities per some unit of measure. Sample size can be either variable or constant since it is charting an average. A classic example is the number of nonconformities in a square yard of fabric in the textile industry. Bolts of cloth may vary in size, but an average can be calculated. Figure 18.11 is an example of plotting attribute data using a *u* chart.

Part VA

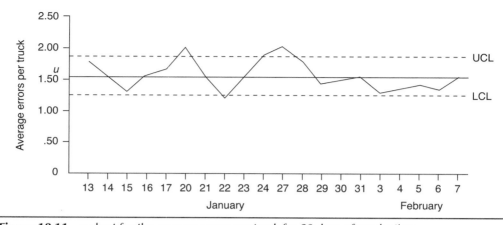

Figure 18.11 *u* chart for the average errors per truck for 20 days of production.

Source: John T. Burr, *SPC Tools for Everyone* (Milwaukee, WI: ASQC Quality Press, 1993), p. 58. Used with permission.

SPC Chart Interpretations

An SPC chart is essentially a set of statistical control limits applied to a set of sequential data from samples chosen from a process. The data composing each of the plotted points are a location statistic such as an individual, an average, a median, a proportion, and so on. If the control chart is one to monitor variable data, then an additional associated chart for the process variation statistic can be utilized. Examples of variation statistics are the range, standard deviation, and moving range.[9]

By their design, control charts utilize unique and statistically rare patterns that can be associated with process changes. These relatively rare or unnatural patterns are usually assumed to be caused by disturbances or influences that interfere with the ordinary behavior of the process. These causes that disturb or alter the output of a process are called *assignable causes*. They can be caused by:

1. Equipment

2. Personnel

3. Materials[10]

If the process is out of control, the process engineer looks for an assignable cause by following the out-of-control action plan (OCAP) associated with the control chart. *Out of control* refers to rejecting the assumption that the current data are from the same population as the data used to create the initial control chart limits.[11]

For classical Shewhart charts, a set of rules called the Western Electric Rules (WECO Rules) and a set of trend rules often are used to determine out of control (see Figure 18.12).

The WECO rules are based on probability. We know that, for a normal distribution, the probability of encountering a point outside $\pm 3\sigma$ is 0.3%. This is a rare event. Therefore, if we observe a point outside the control limits, we conclude the process has shifted and is unstable. Similarly, we can identify other events that are equally rare and use them as flags for instability. The probability of observing two points out of three in a row between 2σ and 3σ and the probability of observing four points out of five in a row between 1σ and 2σ are also about 0.3%. Figure 18.13 is an example

Any point above +3 sigma ---------- +3σ limit

Two out of the last three points above +2 sigma ---------- +2σ limit

Four out of the last five points above +1 sigma ---------- +1σ limit

Eight consecutive points on this side of control line ——— **Center line**

Eight consecutive points on this side of control line ---------- −1σ limit

Four out of the last five points below −1 sigma ---------- −2σ limit

Two out of the last three points below −2 sigma ---------- −3σ limit

Any point below −3 sigma

Trend rules: 6 in a row trending up or down, 14 in a row alternating up and down.

Figure 18.12   WECO rules for signaling "out of control."

Source: Adapted from http://www.itl.nist.gov/div898/handbook/pmc/section3/pmc32.htm#WECO%20rules.

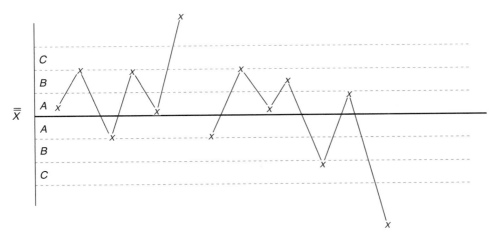

Note: The example control chart diagram has the following defined areas:
Zone A: The area defined by the average ±1S
Zone B: The area defined by the limits of $\bar{X} − 1S$ to $\bar{X} − 2S$ and $\bar{X} + 1S$ to $\bar{X} + 2S$
Zone C: The area defined by the limits of $\bar{X} −2S$ to $\bar{X} −3S$ and $\bar{X} + 2S$ to $\bar{X} + 3S$

Figure 18.13   Any point above +3 sigma control limit (a point above 3 sigma, C line).

Source: Mark L. Crossley, *The Desk Reference of Statistical Quality Methods* (Milwaukee, WI: ASQ Quality Press, 2000).

of any point above +3 sigma in Figure 18.12. Figure 18.14 is an example of eight consecutive points on this side of the control line in Figure 18.12.

While the WECO rules increase a Shewhart chart's sensitivity to trends or drifts in the mean, there is a severe downside to adding the WECO rules to an ordinary Shewhart control chart that the user should understand. When following the standard Shewhart "out-of-control" rule (i.e., signal if and only if you see a point beyond the ± 3σ control limits) you will have "false alarms" every 371 points on the average. Adding the WECO rules increases the frequency of false alarms to about once in every 91.75 points, on the average.[12] The user has to

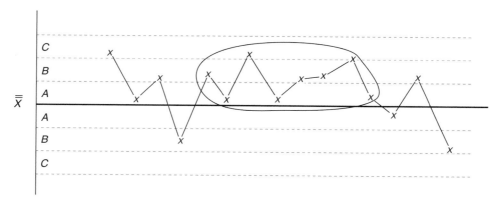

Note: The example control chart diagram has the following defined areas:
Zone A: The area defined by the average ±1S
Zone B: The area defined by the limits of $\bar{X}$ – 1S to $\bar{X}$ – 2S and $\bar{X}$ + 1S to $\bar{X}$ + 2S
Zone C: The area defined by the limits of $\bar{X}$ –2S to $\bar{X}$ –3S and $\bar{X}$ + 2S to $\bar{X}$ + 3S

Figure 18.14 Consecutive points above the average (trend: 8 points in a row but within 3 sigma, C line).
Source: Mark L. Crossley, *The Desk Reference of Statistical Quality Methods* (Milwaukee, WI: ASQ Quality Press, 2000).

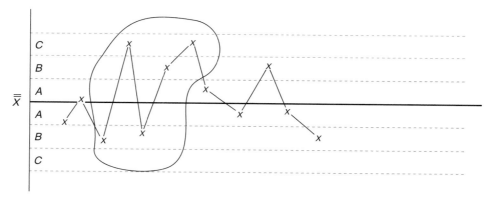

Note: The example control chart diagram has the following defined areas:
Zone A: The area defined by the average ±1S
Zone B: The area defined by the limits of $\bar{X}$ – 1S to $\bar{X}$ – 2S and $\bar{X}$ + 1S to $\bar{X}$ + 2S
Zone C: The area defined by the limits of $\bar{X}$ –2S to $\bar{X}$ –3S and $\bar{X}$ + 2S to $\bar{X}$ + 3S

Figure 18.15 Four out of the last five points above +1 sigma.

decide whether this price is worth paying (some users add the WECO rules, but take them "less seriously" in terms of the effort put into troubleshooting activities when out-of-control signals occur). Figure 18.15 is an example of four out of the last five points above +1 sigma in Figure 18.12.

CHECKLISTS, CHECK SHEETS, GUIDELINES, AND LOG SHEETS

Four basic tools are used by auditors in the performance of audits, to ensure consistency and effectiveness of the audit. Although each may be used independently of one another, they may be used together to document audit evidence. Also see "5. Auditing Tools and Working Papers" in Part II for more information about checklists, check sheets, guidelines, and log sheets.

Checklists

Checklists are the most common tools used to collect data during an audit. They provide an organized form for identifying information to be collected and a means for recording information once it is collected. In addition, the checklist serves as a tool to help guide the audit team during audit performance. A checklist usually contains a listing of required items where audit evidence is needed, places for recording acceptable responses, and places for taking notes. An auditor's checklist is either a list of questions to answer or statements to verify.

Figures 18.16–18.18 provide samples of checklists.

ISO 9001:2008 Checklist			
Ref.	**Question/Criteria**	**Yes/No**	**Comments/Data collection plan**
8.2.2	**Internal auditing**		
8.2.2-1	Are internal audits conducted at planned intervals?		
8.2.2-2	Are audits carried out to determine conformance of the QMS to planned arrangements, the organization's QMS requirements, this International Standard, and that the QMS has been effectively implemented and maintained?		
8.2.2-3	Does the audit program plan consider status and importance of the activities and areas to be audited and results of previous audits?		
8.2.2-4	Are audit criteria, scope, frequency, and methods defined?		
8.2.2-5	Are auditors selected and audits conducted to ensure objectivity and impartiality of the audit process? Are auditors prevented from auditing their own work?		
8.2.2-6	Are there documented procedures? Do the procedures cover responsibilities, requirements for planning and conducting, and recording and reporting results? [4.2.4]		
8.2.2-7	Is action taken by management responsible for the area to eliminate nonconformities and their causes? Is this done without undue delay?		
8.2.2-8	Are follow-up activities carried out to verify the implementation of the action? Are the verification results reported? [8.5.2]		

Figure 18.16   Sample checklist, ISO 9001, clause 8.2.2, Internal auditing.

Source: J. P. Russell & Assoc., ISO 9001-2008 Checklist, 2008.

A. Review of customer requirements
 1. Is there a quality review of purchase orders to identify special or unusual requirements?
 2. Are requirements for special controls, facilities, equipment, and skills preplanned to ensure they will be in place when needed?
 3. Have exceptions to customer requirements been taken?
 4. Are customer requirements available to personnel involved in the manufacture, control, and inspection of the product?
 5. Are supplier and subtier sketches, drawings, and specifications compatible with the customer's requirements?

B. Supplier control practices
 6. Is there a system for identifying qualified sources, and is this system adhered to by the purchasing function?
 7. Are initial audits of major suppliers conducted?
 8. Does the system ensure that technical data (drawings, specifications, and so on) are included in purchase orders?
 9. Is the number and frequency of inspections and tests adjusted based on supplier performance?

C. Nonconforming material
 10. Are nonconformances identified and documented?
 11. Are nonconformances physically segregated from conforming material where practical?
 12. Is further processing of nonconforming items restricted until an authorized disposition is received?
 13. Do suppliers know how to handle nonconformances?
 14. Are process capability studies used as a part of the nonconforming material control and process planning?

D. Design and process change control routines
 15. Are changes initiated by customers incorporated as specified?
 16. Are internally initiated changes in processing reviewed to see if they require customer approval?
 17. Is the introduction date of changes documented?
 18. Is there a method of notifying subtier suppliers of applicable changes?

E. Process and product audits
 19. Are process audits conducted?
 20. Are product audits used independent of normal product acceptance plans?
 21. Do the audits cover all operations, shifts, and products?
 22. Do audit results receive management review?
 23. Is the audit frequency adjusted based on observed trends?

Figure 18.17 Sample quality system checklist.

Source: Charles B. Robinson, ed., *How to Plan an Audit* (Milwaukee, WI: ASQC Quality Press, 1987), pp. 26–30.

Lab/Appraisal # _____ Date: _____ Page 1 of ____

Reference	Criteria	Results		Comments
		Sat	Unsat	
NL-QAM	1. Is monitoring and data collection equipment calibrated?			
NL-QAM	2. Is equipment calibration traceable to nationally recognized standards?			
NL-QAP-5.1	3. Is equipment calibration performed using approved instructions?			
NL-QAP-5.1	4. Are calibration records maintained for each piece of equipment?			
NL-QAP-5.1	5. Is a use log maintained?			

Figure 18.18 Calibration area checklist.

Source: Rudolph C. Hirzel, "Tools for Improving Audit Processes and Performance" (QAD conference presentation, Kansas City, MO, February 22–23, 1996).

Check Sheets

Of the many tools available to auditors, a *check sheet* is the simplest and easiest to construct and use because there is no set form or content. The user may structure the check sheet to meet the needs of the situation under review. Figure 18.19 shows an example of a check sheet used in an audit of QMS documentation.

The advantage of using a check sheet in this manner is the ability to demonstrate the magnitude of the impact of the issues identified in relation to the total population of the documents in the system. Rather than focusing on a single document, the auditor can easily demonstrate the impact on the process control (or process documentation) to the auditee. However, additional information will need to be provided to the auditee from the auditor's notes, such as:

- The document number, title, and so on

- A description of each nonconforming item

- The reason the item is nonconforming

For this reason, check sheets are often used with a log sheet or checklist to record the details of the issues found during the audit.

Using check sheets in this manner is advantageous for the auditor because the auditee may use this information to easily construct a Pareto chart for corrective action. By doing so, the corrective action team's efforts will not only be more focused, but also the team has baseline data from which improvement may be demonstrated.

Guidelines

Audit *guidelines* are used to help focus audit activities. Typically, these consist of written attribute statements that are used to evaluate products, processes, or systems. Audit guidelines are usually not prepared by the auditor but rather by the auditor's organization, client, or by a regulatory authority. They are often used to ensure that specific items are evaluated during each audit when audit programs cover several locations, departments, or organizations. The primary

Documentation check sheet				
Type	**Conforming**	**Nonconforming**	**Total**	**% NC**
Procedures	///// ////	/	10	10.0
Records	///// ///// ///// ///// ///// ///// ///// ///// /	///// ////	50	18.0
Forms	///// ///// ///// ///// /////	///// //	32	21.9
Labels	///// ///// ///// ///// ///	//	25	8.0
Tags	///// ///// ///// ///// ///// //	///// /	33	18.2
Summary	125	25	150	16.7

Figure 18.19 Check sheet for documentation.

Part VA

differences between checklists and guidelines are that audit guideline items are usually written in statement form rather than as questions, and guidelines don't include provisions for recording audit results. To provide for the latter, log sheets are often used.

Log Sheets

Log sheets are simply blank columnar forms for recording information during an audit. Often, a log sheet is a simple ruled piece of paper on which the auditor records information reviewed (such as the procedures, records, processes, and so on) or evidence examined during the audit. Used in conjunction with audit guidelines, check sheets, or to augment checklists, they help ensure that objective evidence collected during an audit is properly recorded.

SCATTER DIAGRAMS

Scatter diagrams (correlation charts) identify the relationship between two variables. They can also be applied to identify the relationship of some variable with the potential root cause. Scatter diagrams plot relationships between two different variables—independent variables on the x axis and dependent variables on the y axis. This tool can also be used by the auditor for analysis of audit observation results.[13] Typical patterns for scatter diagram analysis (as shown in Figure 18.20) include positive correlation, negative correlation, curvilinear correlation, and no correlation.

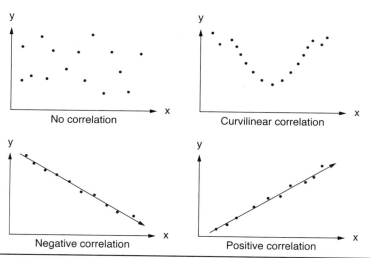

Figure 18.20 Data correlation patterns for scatter analysis.

Source: Jack B. Revelle, *Quality Essentials* (Milwaukee, WI: ASQ Quality Press, 2004), p. 167.

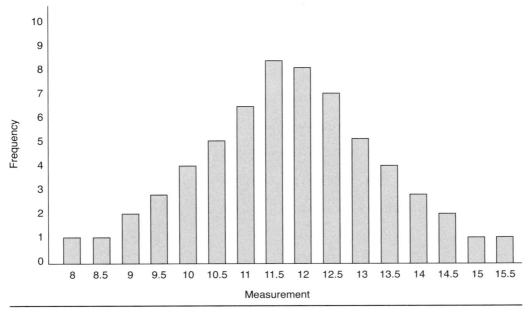

Figure 18.21 Histogram with normal distribution.

HISTOGRAMS

A *histogram* is a graphic summary of variation in a set of data. Histograms, such as the one shown in Figure 18.21, give a clearer and more complete picture of the data than would a table of numbers, since patterns may be difficult to discern in a table. Patterns of variation in data are called *distributions*. Often, identifiable patterns exist in the variation, and the correct interpretation of these patterns can help identify the cause of a problem.

A histogram is one of the simplest tools for organizing and summarizing data. It is essentially a vertical bar chart of a frequency distribution that is used to show the number of times a given discrete piece of information occurs. The histogram's simplicity of construction and interpretation makes it an effective tool in the auditor's elementary analysis of collected data.

Histograms should indicate sample size to communicate the degree of confidence in the conclusions. Once a histogram has been completed, it should be analyzed by identifying and classifying the pattern of variation, and developing a plausible and relevant explanation for the pattern. For a normal distribution, the following identifiable patterns, shown in Figure 18.22, are commonly observed in histograms.

   a. Bell-shaped: A symmetrical shape with a peak in the middle of the range of data. This is the normal and natural distribution of data. Deviations from the bell shape might indicate the presence of complicating factors or outside influences. While deviations from a bell shape should be investigated, such deviations are not necessarily bad.

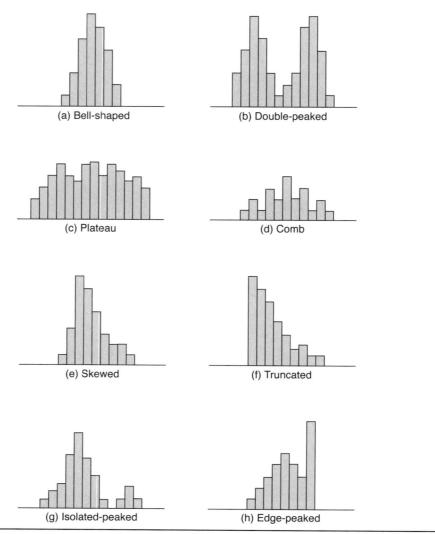

Figure 18.22 Common histogram patterns.

Source: Juran Institute, "The Tools of Quality, Part IV: Histograms," ASQC *Quality Progress*, September 1990, p. 76. Adapted from the Juran Institute's publication, *Quality Improvement Tools.*

b. Double-peaked (bimodal): A distinct valley in the middle of the range of the data with peaks on either side. Usually a combination of two bell-shaped distributions, this pattern indicates that two distinct processes are causing this distribution.

c. Plateau: A flat top with no distinct peak and slight tails on either side. This pattern is likely to be the result of many different bell-shaped distributions with centers spread evenly throughout the range of data.

d. Comb: High and low values alternating in a regular fashion. This pattern typically indicates measurement error, errors in the way data were grouped to construct the histogram, or a systematic bias in the way data were rounded off. A less likely alternative is that this is a type of plateau distribution.

e. Skewed: An asymmetrical shape in which the peak is off-center in the range of data and the distribution tails off sharply on one side and gently on the other. If the long tail extends rightward, toward increasing values, the distribution is positively skewed; a negatively skewed distribution exists when the long tail extends leftward, toward decreasing values. The skewed pattern typically occurs when a practical limit, or a specification limit, exists on one side and is relatively close to the nominal value. In this case, there are not as many values available on the one side as on the other.

f. Truncated: An asymmetrical shape in which the peak is at or near the edge of the range of the data, and the distribution ends very abruptly on one side and tails off gently on the other. Truncated distributions are often smooth bell-shaped distributions with a part of the distribution removed, or truncated, by some external force.

g. Isolated-peaked: A small, separate group of data in addition to the larger distribution. This pattern is similar to the double-peaked distribution; however, the short bell shape indicates something that doesn't happen very often.

h. Edge-peaked: A large peak is appended to an otherwise smooth distribution. It is similar to the comb distribution in that an error was probably made in the data. All readings past a certain point may have been grouped into one value.[14]

No rules exist to explain pattern variation in every situation. The three most important characteristics are centering (central tendency), width (spread, variation, scatter, dispersion), and shape (pattern). If no discernible pattern appears to exist, the distribution may not be normal, and the data may actually be distributed according to some other distribution, such as exponential, gamma, or uniform. Analysis of distributions of these types is beyond the scope of this text, and further information should be sought from specialized statistics texts.

All the topics in the remainder of this chapter are normally addressed by the auditee, but the auditor should have the knowledge to evaluate the auditee's improvement programs. Effective implementation and maintenance of improvement programs is critical to the ongoing success of the organization.

ROOT CAUSE ANALYSIS[15]

Although an effort to solve a problem may utilize many of the tools, involve the appropriate people, and result in changes to the process, if the order in which the problem-solving actions occur isn't logically organized and methodical, much of the effort is likely to be wasted. In order to ensure that efforts are properly guided, many organizations create or adopt one or more models—a series of steps to be followed—for all such projects.

Part VA

Seven-Step Problem-Solving Model

Problem solving is about identifying root causes that have caused the problem to occur and taking actions to alleviate those causes. Following is a typical problem-solving process model and some possible activities and rationale for each step:

1. *Identify the problem.* This step involves making sure that everyone is focused on the same issue. It may involve analysis of data to determine which problem should be worked on and writing a problem statement that clearly defines the exact problem to be addressed and where and when it occurred. A flowchart might be used to ensure that everyone understands the process in which the problem occurs.

2. *List possible root causes.* Before jumping to conclusions about what to do about the problem, it is useful to look at the wide range of possibilities. Brainstorming and cause-and-effect analysis are often used.

3. *Search out the most likely root cause.* This stage of the process requires looking for patterns in failure of the process. Check sheets might be used to record each failure and supporting information, or control charts may be used to monitor the process in order to detect trends or special causes.

4. *Identify potential solutions.* Once it is fairly certain that the particular root cause has been found, a list of possible actions to remedy it should be developed. This is a creative part of the problem-solving process and may rely on brainstorming as well as input from specialists who may have a more complete understanding of the technology involved.

5. *Select and implement a solution.* After identifying several possible solutions, each should be evaluated as to its potential for success, cost and timing to implement, and other important criteria. Simple processes such as ranking or multivoting, or more scientific analysis using a matrix, are likely to be used in the selection process.

6. *Follow up to evaluate the effect.* All too often problem-solving efforts stop after remedial action has been taken. As with any good corrective action process, however, it is necessary that the process be monitored after the solution has been implemented. Control charts or Pareto diagrams are tools used to determine whether the problem has been solved. Possible findings might be that there was no effect (which may mean the solution wasn't properly implemented, the solution isn't appropriate for the root cause, or the real root cause wasn't found), a partial effect, or full resolution of the problem. If there was no effect, then the actions taken during the previous steps of the problem-solving model need to be reviewed in order to see where an error may have occurred.

7. *Standardize the process.* Even if the problem has been resolved, there is one final step that needs to occur. The solution needs to be built into the process (for example, poka-yoke, training for new employees, updating procedures) so that it will continue to work once focused attention on the problem is gone. A review to see what was learned from the project is also sometimes useful.

Five Whys

Throughout most problem solving there is usually a significant amount of effort expended in trying to understand why things happen the way they do. Root cause analysis requires understanding how a system or process works, and the many complex contributors, both technical and human.

One method for getting to root causes is to repeatedly ask "why?" For example, if a car doesn't start when the key is turned, ask "why?" Is it because the engine doesn't turn over or because when it does turn over, it doesn't begin running on its own? If it doesn't turn over, ask "why?" Is it because the battery is too weak or because the starter is seized up? If it's because the battery is too weak, ask "why?" Is it because the temperature outside is extremely cold, that the battery cables are loose, or because an internal light was left on the previous evening and drained the battery? Although this is a simple example, it demonstrates the process of asking *why* until the actual root cause is found. It is called the five whys since it will often require asking *why* five times or more before the actual root cause is identified. The use of data or trials can help determine answers at each level. Figure 18.23 is adapted from a healthcare facility application.

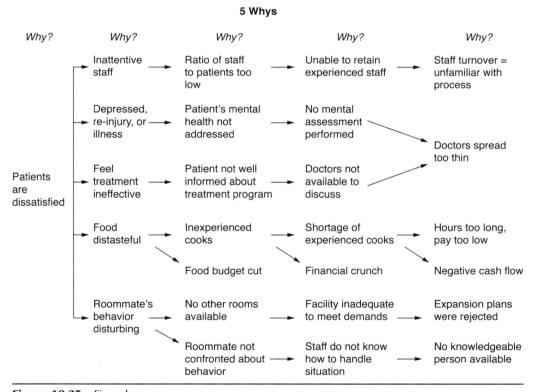

Figure 18.23 Five whys.

PLAN-DO-CHECK-ACT (PDCA/PDSA) CYCLE[16]

The seven-step problem-solving model presented earlier is actually nothing more than a more detailed version of a general process improvement model originally developed by Walter Shewhart. The plan–do–check–act (PDCA) cycle was adapted by W. Edwards Deming as the plan–do–study–act (PDSA) cycle, emphasizing the role of learning in improvement. In both cases, action is initiated by developing a plan for improvement, followed by putting the plan into action.

In the next stage, the results of the action are examined critically. Did the action produce the desired results? Were any new problems created? Was the action worthwhile in terms of cost and other impacts? The knowledge gained in the third step is acted on. Possible actions include changing the plan, adopting the procedure, abandoning the idea, modifying the process, amplifying or reducing the scope, and then beginning the cycle all over again. Shown in Figure 18.24, the PDCA/PDSA cycle captures the core philosophy of continual improvement.

SIPOC Analysis

Problem-solving efforts are often focused on remedying a situation that has developed in which a process is not operating at its normal level. Much of continual improvement, however, involves improving a process that may be performing as expected, but where a higher level of performance is desired. A fundamental step in improving a process is to understand how it functions from a process management perspective. This can be seen through an analysis of the process to identify the supplier–input–process–output–customer (SIPOC) linkages (see Figure 18.25).

SIPOC analysis begins with defining the process of interest and listing on the right side the outputs that the process creates for customers, who are also listed. Suppliers and the inputs they provide to enable the process are similarly shown on

4. Act:
  a. If it worked, institutionalize/standardize the change.
  b. If it didn't, try something else.
  c. Continue the cycle.

3. Check:
  a. Determine whether the plan worked.
  b. Study the results.

1. Plan:
  a. Study the situation.
  b. Determine what needs to be done.
  c. Develop a plan and measurement process for what needs to be done.

2. Do:
  Implement the plan.

Figure 18.24   PDCA/PDSA cycle.

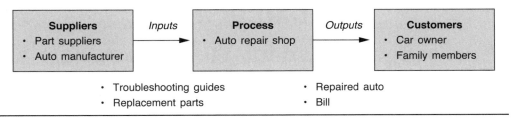

Figure 18.25 SIPOC diagram.

the left side. Once this fundamental process diagram is developed, two additional items can be discussed—measures that can be used to evaluate performance of the inputs and outputs, and the information and methods necessary to control the process.

Chapter 19
Process Improvement Techniques/Part VB

1. SIX SIGMA AND THE DMAIC MODEL

Statistically speaking, *sigma* is a term indicating to what extent a process varies from perfection. The quantity of units processed divided into the number of defects actually occurring, multiplied by one million results in defects per million. Adding a 1.5 sigma shift in the mean results in the following defects per million:

1 sigma = 690,000 defects per million

2 sigma = 308,000 defects per million

3 sigma = 66,800 defects per million

4 sigma = 6,210 defects per million

5 sigma = 230 defects per million

6 sigma = 3.4 defects per million

While much of the literature refers to defects relative to manufactured products, Six Sigma may be used to measure material, forms, a time frame, distance, computer program coding, and so on. For example: if the cost of poor quality, at a four sigma level, represented 15 percent to 20 percent of sales revenue, an organization should be concerned.

Six Sigma, as a philosophy, translates to the organizational belief that it is possible to produce totally defect-free products or services—albeit more a dream than a reality for most organizations. With most organizations operating at about three sigma or below, getting to perfection leaves much work to be done.

Motorola initiated the Six Sigma methodology in the 1980s. General Electric's CEO directed their Six Sigma initiative in 1995. Six Sigma constitutes an evolving set of principles, fundamental practices, and tools—a breakthrough strategy.

The evolving Six Sigma principles are:

1. Committed and strong leadership is absolutely essential—it's a major cultural change.

2. Six Sigma initiatives and other existing initiatives, strategies, measures, and practices must be integrated—Six Sigma must be an integral part of how the organization conducts its business.

Taken from Russell T. Westcott, *The Certified Manager of Quality/Organizational Excellence Handbook* (Milwaukee, WI: ASQ Quality Press, 2006), pp. 348–350 and 389–402.

3. Quantitative analysis and statistical thinking are key concepts—it's data-based managing.

4. Constant effort must be applied to learning everything possible about customers and the marketplace—intelligence gathering and analysis is critical.

5. The Six Sigma approach must produce a significant payoff in a reasonable time period—real validated dollar savings is required.

6. A hierarchy of highly trained individuals with verified successes to their credit, often referred to as Master Black Belts, Black Belts, and Green Belts, are needed to extend the leadership to all organizational levels.

7. Performance tracking, measuring, and reporting systems are needed to monitor progress, allow for course corrections as needed, and link the Six Sigma approach to the organizational goals, objectives, and plans. Very often, existing performance tracking, measuring, and reporting systems fail to address the level where they are meaningful to the people involved.

8. The organization's reward and recognition systems must support continuous reinforcement of the people, at every level, who make the Six Sigma approach viable and successful. Compensation systems especially need to be reengineered.

9. The successful organization should internally celebrate successes frequently—success breeds success.

10. To further enhance its image, and the self-esteem of its people, the successful organization should widely publicize its Six Sigma accomplishments and, to the extent feasible, share its principles and practices with other organizations—be a member of a world-class group of organizations who have committed their efforts to achieving perfection.

The following list contains fundamental Six Sigma practices and some of the applicable tools, commonly known by the mnemonic DMAIC, which stands for:

Define the customer and organizational requirements. Management prepares a team charter that includes the problem statement, scope, goals and objectives, milestones, roles and responsibilities, resources, and project timelines. In this phase, the customer, core business processes, and issues critical to quality (CTQ) are identified:

- Data collection tools: check sheets, brainstorming, flowcharts

- Data analysis tools: cause-and-effect diagrams, affinity diagrams, tree diagrams, root cause analysis

- Customer data collection and analysis: QFD (quality function deployment), surveys

Measure what is critical to quality, map the process, establish measurement system, and determine what is unacceptable (defects). The team gathers data from

Part VB

the targeted process to establish baseline performance, then benchmarks similar processes or operations in order to define a strategy for achieving objectives:

- Process control tools: control charts

- Process improvement tools: process mapping, Pareto charts, process benchmarking, TOC (theory of constraints), risk assessment, FMEA, design of experiments, cost of quality, lean thinking techniques

Analyze to develop a baseline (process capability). The data collected and process map are used to determine root causes of defects and opportunities for improvement. A number of statistical tools are used in this phase to ensure that the underlying issues affecting performance are understood and that the capability can be improved. The information collected is utilized to determine root causes and to identify opportunities for improvement:

- Identify root causes of defects

- Pinpoint opportunities and set objectives

Improve the process. This phase identifies solutions to problems through the application of advanced statistical tools and design of experiments. The solutions include performance measurements to ensure that the improvements are long term:

- Project planning and management

- Training

Control the system through an established process. Having improved and stabilized the process, the resulting capability is determined. The goal in this phase is to ensure that the process controls are in place to maintain the improvements attained. This includes updating process and system documentation as well as establishing ongoing performance measures so that performance gains are not lost.

The DMAIC phases are normally applied to a project. Individuals select or are assigned process improvement teams (PITs) and apply the Six Sigma approach. Six Sigma program/projects may contribute to corrective action, preventive action, or innovative actions. Auditors can verify benefits claimed, ensure that the program is sustained, and provide input for additional improvements using continual improvement assessment techniques.[1]

2. LEAN

Lean is a strategy for achieving the shortest possible cycle time. Based on the Toyota Production System, lean manufacturing aims to increase value-added work by eliminating waste and unnecessary process steps, reducing inventory, reducing product development time, and increasing customer responsiveness while providing high-quality products as economically and efficiently as possible. The techniques employed are focused on reducing the time from the receipt of a customer's order to its shipment. The goal is to improve customer satisfaction, throughput time, employee morale, and profitability.

Cycle-Time Reduction

Cycle time is the total amount of time required to complete a process, from the first step to the last. Today's methods for cycle-time reduction came about through Henry Ford's early focus on minimizing waste, traditional industrial engineering techniques (for example, time and motion studies), and the Japanese adaptation of these methods (often called the Toyota Production System [TPS]) to smaller production run applications.

Although cycle-time reduction is best known for application to production operations, it is equally useful in nonmanufacturing environments, where person-to-person handoffs, queues of jobs, and facility layout affect productivity of knowledge workers.

To be able to select where best to implement cycle-time reduction requires a high-level system analysis of the organization to determine where current performance deficits or bottlenecks are located. The organization's overall system has a critical path (the series of steps that must occur in sequence and take the longest time to complete). Clearly, improving a process that is not on the critical path will have no real impact on cycle time.

Typical actions to shorten the cycle time of processes include:

1. Removing non-value-adding steps.

2. Speeding up value-adding steps.

3. Integrating several steps of the process into a single step; this often requires expanding the skill level of employees responsible for the new process and/or providing technical support such as a computer database.

4. Breaking the process into several smaller processes that focus on a narrower or special product. This work cell or small business unit concept allows employees to develop customer-product-focused skills and usually requires collocating equipment and personnel responsible for the cell.

5. Shifting responsibility to suppliers or customers, or taking back some of the responsibility currently being performed by suppliers or customers. The practice of modular assembly is a typical example of this process.

6. Standardizing the product/service process as much as possible, then creating variations when orders are received; this allows the product to be partially processed, requiring only completion before shipment (for example, the practice of producing only white sweaters, then dyeing them just prior to shipment).

Other ways of improving cycle times include improving equipment reliability (thereby reducing non-value-added maintenance downtime), reducing defects (that use up valuable resource time), and reducing unnecessary inventory. Another fundamental process for improving cycle time is that of simply better organizing the workplace. (See "Five S" section.)

Reducing cycle time can reduce work-in-process and finished goods inventories, allow smaller production lot sizes, decrease lead times for production, and increase throughput (decrease overall time from start to finish). Also, when process steps are eliminated or streamlined, overall quality tends to improve. Because many opportunities might be identified when beginning the effort to reduce cycle time, a Pareto analysis (discussed in Chapter 18) can be performed to decide which factors demand immediate attention. Some problems might be fixed in minutes, whereas others might require the establishment of a process improvement team and take months to complete.

Although lean production is based on basic industrial engineering concepts, it has been primarily visible to U.S. companies as the Toyota Production System. The basic premise is that only what is needed should be produced, and it should only be produced when it is actually needed. Due to the amount of time, energy, and other resources wasted by how processes and organizations are designed, however, organizations tend to produce what they think they might need (for example, based on forecasts) rather than what they actually need (for example, based on customer orders).

Value Stream Mapping

Value stream mapping (VSM) is charting the sequence of movements of information, materials, and production activities in the value stream (all activities involving the designing, ordering, producing, and delivering of products and services to the organization's customers). An advantage to this is that a "before action is taken" value stream map depicts the current state of the organization and enables identification of how value is created and where waste occurs. Plus employees see the whole value stream rather than just the one part in which they are involved. This improves understanding and communications, and facilitates waste elimination.

A VSM is used to identify areas for improvement. At the macro level, a VSM identifies waste along the value stream and helps strengthen supplier and customer partnerships and alliances.

At the micro level, a VSM identifies waste—non-value-added activities—and identifies opportunities that can be addressed with a *kaizen blitz.*

Figures 19.1 and 19.2 are sample value stream maps (macro level and micro level).

Five S

The Japanese use the term *Five S* for five practices for maintaining a clean and efficient workplace:

1. *Seiri.* Separate needed tools, parts, and instructions from unneeded materials; remove latter.

2. *Seiton.* Neatly arrange and identify parts and tools for ease of use.

3. *Seiso.* Conduct a cleanup campaign.

4. *Seiketsu.* As a habit, beginning with self, then the workplace, be clean and tidy.

5. *Shitsuke.* Apply discipline in following procedures.

Note: The typical English words for Five S are Sort, Set, Shine, Standardize, Sustain.

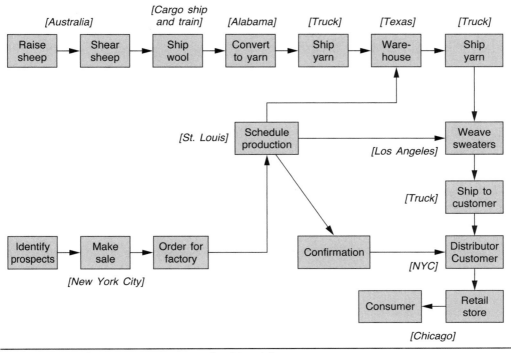

Figure 19.1   Value stream map—macro level (partial).

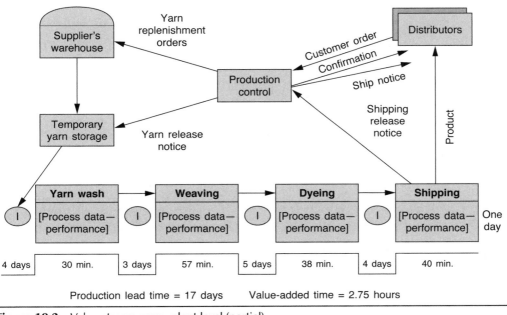

Figure 19.2   Value stream map—plant level (partial).

Far more than the good things they do, the Five Ss can:

- Build awareness of the concept and principles of improvement
- Set the stage to begin serious waste reduction initiatives
- Break down barriers to improvement, at low cost
- Empower the workers to control their work environment

Visual Management

This method is used to arrange the workplace, all tools, parts, and material, and the production process itself, so that the status of the process can be understood at a glance by everyone. Further, the intent is to furnish visual clues to aid the performer in correctly processing a step or series of steps, reduce cycle time, cut costs, smooth work flow, and improve quality. By seeing the status of the process, both the performer and management have an up-to-the-second picture of what has happened, what's presently happening, and what's to be done. Advantages of visual management are:

- Catches errors and defects before they can occur
- Quick detection enables rapid correction
- Identifies and removes safety hazards
- Improves communications
- Improves workplace efficiency
- Cuts costs

Examples of visual management are:

- Color-coded sectors on meter faces to indicate reading acceptance range, low and high unacceptable readings
- Electronic counters mounted over work area to indicate rate of accepted finished product
- Work orders printed on colored paper where the color denotes the grade and type of metal to be used
- Lights atop enclosed equipment indicating status of product being processed
- Slots at dispatch station for pending work orders, indicating work to be scheduled (and backlog) and when the work unit(s) will become idle
- Painted floor and/or wall space with shadow images of the tool, die, or pallet that usually occupies the space when not in use

Waste Reduction

Lean production focuses on reducing waste and goes against traditional mass production thinking by defining waste as anything that does not add value.

Waste is frequently a result of how the system is designed. The Japanese word for waste is *muda.*

Examples of seven types of waste are:

1. Overproduction

   — Enlarging number of requirements beyond customers' needs

   — Including too much detail or too many options in designs

   — Specifying materials that require sole-source procurement or that call for seeking economy-of-scale–oriented procurement

   — Requiring batch processing, lengthy and costly setups, or low yield processes

2. Delays, waiting

   — Holdups due to people, information, tools, and equipment not being ready

   — Delays waiting for test results to know if a part is made correctly

   — Unrealistic schedules resulting in backups in manufacturing flow

   — Part improperly designed for manufacture, design changes

3. Transportation

   — Non-value-added transport of work in process

   — Inefficient layout of plant causing multiple transports

   — Specifying materials from suppliers geographically located a great distance from manufacturing facility, resulting in higher shipping costs

4. Processing

   — Non-value-added effort expended

   — Designers failed to consider production process capabilities (constraints, plant capacities, tolerances that can be attained, process yield rate, setup time and complexity, worker skills and knowledge, storage constraints, material handling constraints)

   — Designs too complex

   — Pulse (takt time) of production flow too high or too low in relation to customer demand

5. Excess inventory

   — Stockpiling more materials than are needed to fulfill customer orders

   — Material handling to store, retrieve, store . . . as part proceeds in the process

   — Unreliable production equipment so safety stock is desired

6. Wasted motion

— Non-value-added movements, such as reaching, walking, bending, searching, sorting

— Product designs that are not manufacturing-friendly

— Requirements for lifting cumbersome and/or heavy parts

— Manufacturing steps that require many positioning-type moves

7. Defective parts

— Corrective actions, looking for root cause

— Scrap

— Downgrading defectives (reducing price, seeking a buyer) in order to recover some of the cost of manufacture

— Faulty design causing defects

— Excessive tolerances creating more defectives

Inventories (buffer stock and batch and queue processing) can be a huge waste. Consider this example. The objective is to complete 200 pieces. The process consists of three operations of 10 seconds each. If the 200 pieces are processed as a batch, the total cycle time is 6000 seconds (200 × 30 seconds). In a single-piece flow mode, there is no accumulation of material between steps. Cycle time is 30 seconds for a single piece (approximately 2000 seconds total). The reduction in total cycle time is 67 percent. Work in process has also been reduced from 600 pieces to 3 pieces.

Analyses of processes for waste usually involve diagrams that show the flow of materials and people and document how much time is spent on value-added versus non-value-added activity. Cycle time is affected by both visible and invisible waste.

Examples of visible waste are:

- Out-of-spec incoming material. For example, an invoice from a supplier has incorrect pricing or aluminum sheets are the wrong size.

- Scrap. For example, holes are drilled in the wrong place or shoe soles are improperly attached.

- Downtime. For example, school bus is not operable or process 4 cannot begin because of backlog at 3.

- Product rework. For example, failed electrical continuity test or customer number is not coded on invoice.

Examples of invisible waste are:

- Inefficient setups. For example, jig requires frequent retightening or incoming orders not sorted correctly for data entry.

- Queue times of work in process. For example, an assembly line is not balanced to eliminate bottlenecks (constraints) or an inefficient loading zone protocol slows school bus unloading, causing late classes.

- Unnecessary motion. For example, materials for assembly are located out of easy reach or workers need to bring each completed order to dispatch desk.

- Wait time of people and machines. For example, utility crew (three workers and truck) waiting until a parked auto can be removed from work area or planes are late in arriving due to inadequate scheduling of available terminal gates.

- Inventory. For example, obsolete material returned from distributor's annual clean-out is placed in inventory anticipating possibility of a future sale or, to take advantage of quantity discounts, a year's supply of paper bags is ordered and stored.

- Movement of material, work in progress (WIP), and finished goods. For example, in a function-oriented plant layout, WIP has to be moved from 15 to 950 feet to next operation or stacks of files are constantly being moved about to gain access to filing cabinets and machines.

- Overproduction. For example, because customers usually order the same item again, an overrun is produced to place in inventory just in case or extras are made at earlier operations in case they are needed in subsequent operations.

- Engineering changes. For example, problems in production necessitate engineering changes or failure to clearly review customer requirements causes changes.

- Unneeded reports. For example, a report initiated five years ago is still produced each week even though the need was eliminated four years ago or a hard copy report duplicates the same information available on a computer screen.

- Meetings that add no value. For example, a morning production meeting is held each day whether or not there is a need (coffee and danish is served) or 15 people attend a staff meeting each week where one of the two hours is used to solve a problem usually involving less than one-fifth of the attendees.

- Management processes that take too long or have no value. For example, all requisitions (even for paper clips) must be signed by a manager or a memo to file must be prepared for every decision made between one department and another.

Mistake-Proofing

Mistake-proofing originated in Japan as an approach applied to factory processes. It was perfected by Shigeo Shingo as *poka-yoke*. It is also applicable to virtually any process in any context. For example, the use of a spellchecker in composing text on a computer is an attempt to prevent the writer from making spelling errors (although we have all realized it isn't foolproof).

This analytical approach involves probing a process to determine where human errors could occur. Then each potential error is traced back to its source.

From these data, consider ways to prevent the potential error. Eliminating the step is the preferred alternative. If a way to prevent the error cannot be identified, then look for ways to lessen the potential for error. Finally, choose the best approach possible, test it, make any needed modifications, and fully implement the approach.

Mistakes may be classified into four categories:

- Information errors
  - Information is ambiguous
  - Information is incorrect
  - Information is misread, misinterpreted, or mismeasured
  - Information is omitted
  - There's inadequate warning
- Misalignment
  - Parts are misaligned
  - A part is misadjusted
  - A machine or process is mistimed or rushed
- Omission or commission
  - Material or part is added
  - Prohibited and/or harmful action is performed
  - Operation is omitted
  - Parts are omitted, so there's a counting error
- Selection errors
  - A wrong part is used
  - There is a wrong destination or location
  - There's a wrong operation
  - There's a wrong orientation

Mistake-proofing actions are intended to:

- Eliminate the opportunity for error
- Detect potential for error
- Prevent an error

Let's look at some examples. In the first situation, a patient is required to fill out forms at various stages of diagnosis and treatment (the ubiquitous clipboard treatment). The patient is prone to making errors due to the frustration and added anxiety of filling out subsequent forms.

After analyzing the situation, the solution is to enter initial patient data into a computer at first point of patient's arrival. Add to the computer record as the patient passes through the different stages with different doctors and services. When referrals are made to doctors outside the initial facility, send an electronic copy of the patient's record (e-mail) to the referred doctor. Except to correct a previous entry, the intent is to never require the patient to furnish the same data more than once.

Considering the four types of mistakes, we can see that information was omitted or incorrectly entered at subsequent steps. The solution eliminates resubmitting redundant data.

In the second example, a low-cost, but critical part is stored in an open bin for access by any operator in the work unit. While there is a minimum on-hand quantity posted and a reorder card is kept in the bin, the bin frequently is empty before anyone takes notice. The mistake is that there's inadequate warning in receiving vital information.

The solution is to design and install a spring-loaded bin bottom that is calibrated to trigger an alarm buzzer and flashing light when the minimum stock level is reached. The alarm and light will correct the mistake.

In the last example, there is a potential to incur injury from the rotating blades when operators of small tractor-mowers dismount from a running tractor. The solution is to install a spring-actuated tractor seat that shuts off the tractor motor as soon as weight is removed. Using this tractor seat will prevent a harmful action.

Careful elimination, detection, and prevention actions can result in near 100 percent quality. Unintended use, ignorance, or willful misuse or neglect by humans may still circumvent safeguards, however. For example, until operating a motor vehicle is prevented until all seatbelts are securely fastened, the warning lights and strict law enforcement alone won't achieve 100 percent effectiveness. Continually improve processes and mistake-proofing efforts to strive for 100 percent.

Setup/Changeover Time Reduction

The long time required to change a die in a stamping operation meant that a longer production run would be required to absorb the downtime caused by the changeover. To address this, the Japanese created a method for reducing setup times called single minute exchange of die (SMED), also referred to as rapid exchange of tooling and dies (RETAD). Times required for a die change were dramatically reduced, often reducing changeover time from several hours to minutes.

To improve setup/changeover times, initiate a plan–do–check–act approach:

1. Map the processes to be addressed. (Videotaping the setup/changeover process is a useful means for identifying areas for improvement.)

2. Collect setup data times for each process.

3. Establish setup time reduction objectives.

4. Identify which process is the primary overall constraint (bottleneck). Prioritize remaining processes by magnitude of setup times, and target next process by longest time.

5. Remove non-value-adding activities from the targeted process (for example, looking for tools required for the changeover). Trischler lists dozens of non-value-added activities, most of which are applicable in a variety of industries and processes.[2] Note that there are some steps that fit the non-value-added category that cannot actually be removed, but can be speeded up.

Part VB

6. Identify setup steps that are internal (steps the machine operator must perform when the machine is idle) versus steps that are external (steps that can be performed while the machine is still running the previous part; for example, removing the fixture or materials for the next part from storage and locating them near the machine).

7. Focus on moving internal steps to external steps where possible.

8. Identify setup activities that can be done simultaneously while the machine is down (the concept of an auto racing pit crew).

9. Speed up required activities.

10. Standardize changeover parts (for example, all dies have a standard height, all fasteners require the same size wrench to tighten).

11. Store setup parts (dies and jigs) on portable carts in a position and at the height where they can be readily wheeled into place at the machine and the switchover accomplished with minimum movement and effort.

12. Store all setup tools to be used in a designated place within easy reach (for example, visual shadow areas on a portable tool cart).

13. Error-proof the setup process.

14. Evaluate the setup/changeover process and make any modifications needed.

15. Return to step 4 and repeat sequence until all setup times have been improved.

16. Fully implement setup/changeover procedures.

17. Evaluate effectiveness of setup/changeover time reduction efforts against objectives set in step 3.

18. Collect setup time data periodically and initiate improvement effort again; return to step 1.

Total Productive Maintenance

Maintenance typically may follow one of the following scenarios:

- Equipment is repaired when it routinely produces defectives. Maintenance is left to the maintenance crew's discretion. (Fix it when it breaks.)

- Equipment fails and maintenance is performed while the equipment is down for repairs. (Maintenance if and when the opportunity presents itself.)

- Equipment maintenance is on a predetermined schedule based on equipment manufacturer's recommendations or all maintenance is scheduled to be done during the annual plant shutdown (preventive maintenance).

- Operators are trained to recognize signs of deterioration (wear, loose fixtures and fasteners, missing bolts and nuts, accumulated shavings from the process, accumulated dirt and dust, over or under lubrication, excessive operating noise, excess vibration, spilled coolants, leaks, clogged drains, valves and switches not working correctly, tooling showing signs of excessive wear, increasing difficulty in maintaining tolerances) and act to eliminate or reduce the conditions (autonomous maintenance).

- Statistical analysis is used to determine the optimum time between failures. The equipment is scheduled for maintenance at a reasonable interval before failure is likely to occur (predictive maintenance).

- Maintenance is eliminated or substantially reduced by improving and redesigning the equipment to require low or no maintenance (maintenance prevention).

Total productive maintenance (TPM) is an organization-wide effort aimed at reducing loss due to equipment failure, slowing speed, and defects. TPM is critical to a lean operation in that there is minimum to no buffer stock to counter the effect of equipment malfunctions and downtime. The purposes of TPM are to:

- Achieve the maximum effectiveness of equipment

- Involve all equipment operators in developing maintenance skills

- Improve the reliability of equipment

- Reduce the size and cost of a maintenance staff

- Avoid unplanned equipment downtime and its associated costs

- Achieve an economic balance between prevention costs and total costs while reducing failure costs

Management's role in TPM is to:

- Enthusiastically sponsor and visibly support the TPM initiative

- Provide for documented work instructions to guide operators' TPM activities

- Provide for the training operators need to perform maintenance and minor repairs of the equipment assigned to them

- Provide for the resources operators need (special tools, cleaning supplies)

- Provide for the operators' time to perform TPM activities

- Adjust the compensation system as necessary to reinforce operators' TPM performance

- Provide for establishing the metrics that are used to monitor and continually improve TPM, including developing the economic case for TPM

- Provide for appropriate and timely operator performance feedback and recognition for work done well relative to TPM activities

Kaizen Blitz/Event

Kaizen is a Japanese word (*kai* means change or school, *zen* means good or wisdom). It has come to mean a continual and incremental improvement (as opposed to reengineering, which is a breakthrough, quantum-leap approach). A kaizen blitz or kaizen event is an intense process often lasting three to five consecutive days. It introduces rapid change into an organization by using the ideas and motivation of the people who do the work. It has also been called zero investment improvement.

In a kaizen event, a cross-functional team focuses on a target process, studies it, collects and analyzes data, discusses improvement alternatives, and implements changes. The emphasis is on making the process better, not necessarily perfect. Subprocesses that impact cycle time are a prime target on which to put the synergy of a kaizen team to work.

The typical stages of a kaizen event are:

- Week before blitz

  — *Wednesday.* Train three or four facilitators in kaizen blitz techniques and tools, as well as enhance their facilitation skill level.

  — *Thursday.* Target the process to be addressed.

  — *Friday.* Gather initial data on the present targeted process.

- Blitz week

  — *Monday.* Train the participants in kaizen blitz techniques and tools.

  — *Tuesday.* Training (AM), process mapping present state (PM).

  — *Wednesday.* Process mapping future state. Eliminating non-value-added steps and other waste. Eliminating bottlenecks. Designing new process flow.

  — *Thursday.* Test changes, modify as needed.

  — *Friday.* Implement the new work flow, tweak the process, document the changes, and be ready for full-scale production on Monday. Prepare follow-up plan.

- Post blitz

  — Conduct follow-up evaluation of change (at an appropriate interval).

  — Plan the next blitz.

Kanban

This method is used in a process to signal an upstream supplier (internal or external) that more material or product is needed downstream. Originally it was just a manual card system, but has evolved to more sophisticated signaling methods for some organizations. It is referred to as a pull system because it serves to pull material or product from a supplier rather than relying on a scheduling system to push the material or product forward at predetermined intervals. It is said that the kanban method was inspired by Toyota's Taiichi Ohno's visit to a U.S. supermarket.

Just-in-Time

Just-in-time (JIT) is a material requirements planning system that provides for the delivery of material or product at the exact time and place where the material or product will be used. Highly coordinated delivery and production systems are required to match delivery to use times. The aim is to eliminate or reduce on-hand inventory (buffer stock) and deliver material or product that requires no or little incoming inspection.

Takt Time

Takt time is the total work time available (per day or per shift) divided by the demand requirements (per day or per shift) of customers. Takt time establishes the production pace relative to the demand. For example, let's say customer orders (demand) average 240 units per day. The production line runs on one shift (480 minutes) per day; so takt time is two minutes. To meet demand one unit must be completed every two minutes.

Figure 19.3 shows an analysis of actual time versus takt time for a process consisting of four operations.

Line Balancing

Line balancing is the method of proportionately distributing workloads within the value stream to meet takt time. The analysis begins with the current state. A balance chart of work steps, time requirements, and operators for each workstation is developed. It shows improvement opportunities by comparing the time of

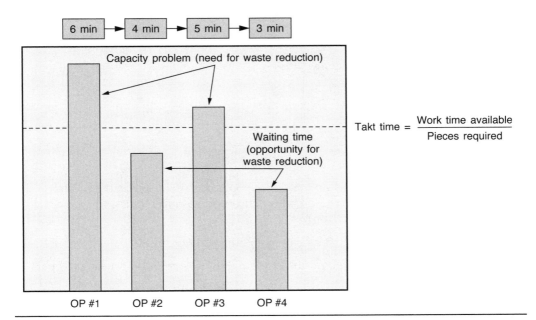

Figure 19.3   Takt time analysis.

each operation to takt time and total cycle time. Formulae are used to establish a proposed-state balanced line.

Standardized Work

Standardized work consists of agreed-to work instructions that utilize the best known methods and sequence for each manufacturing or assembly process. Establishing standardized work supports productivity improvement, high quality, and safety of workers.

Single-Piece Flow

One-piece flow is a product moving through the process one unit at a time. This approach differs from batch processing that produces batches of the same item at a time, moving the product through the process batch by batch. Advantages of single-piece flow are:

- It cuts the elapsed time between the customer's order and shipment of the order

- It reduces or eliminates wait time delays between processing of batches

- It reduces inventory, labor, energy, and space required by batch-and-queue processing

- It reduces product damage caused by handling and temporary storing of batches

- It enables the detection of quality problems early in the process

- It allows for flexibility in meeting customer demands

- It enables identification of non-value-added steps, thereby eliminating waste

Cellular Operations

A work cell is a self-contained unit dedicated to performing all the operations to complete a product or a major portion of a production run. Equipment is configured to accomplish:

- Sequential processing

- Counterclockwise flow to enable operators to optimize use of their right hands as operators move through the cell (moving the part to each subsequent operation)

- Shorter movements by close proximity of machines

- Position the last operation close to the first operation for the next part

- Adaptability of cell to accommodate customers' varying demands

The most prevalent layout is a U shape (see Figure 19.4), although L, S, and V shapes have been used. Product demand, product mix, and constraints are all considerations in designing a work cell.

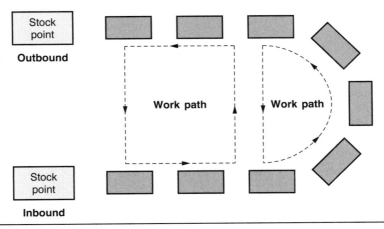

Figure 19.4   Typical U–shape cell layout.

Chapter 20
Basic Statistics/Part VC

Descriptive statistics furnish a simple method of extracting information from what often seems at first glance to be a mass of random numbers. These characteristics of the data may relate to:

1. Typical, or central, value (mean, median, mode)

2. A measure of how much variability is present (variance, standard deviation)

3. A measure of frequency (percentiles)[1]

Statistics is concerned with scientific methods for collecting, organizing, summarizing, presenting, and analyzing data, as well as drawing valid conclusions and making reasonable decisions on the basis of such analysis. In a narrower sense, the term *statistics* is used to denote the data themselves or numbers derived from the data, such as averages.

An auditor must look at how an auditee defines the process and necessary controls, and must establish some type of measurement system to ensure that the measurements or the process was properly defined. The auditor looks at the results of what other people have done, and if they used statistical tools, the auditor must be knowledgeable enough to decide whether the information being gathered from the data is valid. The phase of statistics that seeks only to describe and analyze a given group (sample) without drawing any conclusions or inferences about a larger group (population) is referred to as *deductive* or *descriptive statistics*. Measures of central tendency and dispersion are the two most fundamental concepts in statistical analysis.

1. MEASURES OF CENTRAL TENDENCY

"Most frequency distributions exhibit a 'central tendency,' i.e., a shape such that the bulk of the observations pile up in the area between the two extremes. Central tendency is one of the most fundamental concepts in all statistical analysis. There are three principal measures of central tendency: mean, median, and mode."[2]

Mean

The *mean, arithmetic mean,* or *mean value* is the sum total of all data values divided by the number of data values. It is the average of the total of the sample values.

Mean is the most commonly used measure of central tendency and is the only such measure that includes every value in the data set. The arithmetic mean is used for symmetrical or near-symmetrical distributions, or for distributions that lack a single, clearly dominant peak.

Median

The *median* is the middle value (midpoint) of a data set arranged in either ascending or descending numerical order. The median is used for reducing the effects of extreme values or for data that can be ranked but are not economically measurable, such as shades of colors, odors, or appearances.

Mode

The *mode* is the value or number that occurs most frequently in a data set. If all the values are different, no mode exists. If two values have the highest and same frequency of occurrence, then the data set or distribution has two modes and is referred to as bimodal. The mode is used for severely skewed distributions, for describing an irregular situation when two peaks are found, or for eliminating the observed effects of extreme values.

2. MEASURES OF DISPERSION

Dispersion is the variation in the spread of data about the mean. Dispersion is also referred to as variation, spread, and scatter. A measure of dispersion is the second of the two most fundamental measures of all statistical analyses. The dispersion within a central tendency is normally measured by one or more of several measuring principles.

Data are always scattered around the zone of central tendency, and the extent of this scatter is called dispersion or variation. There are several measures of dispersion: range, standard deviation, and coefficient of variation.

Range

The *range* is the simplest measure of dispersion. It is the difference between the maximum and minimum values in an observed data set. Since it is based on only two values from a data set, the measurement of range is most useful when the number of observations or values is small (10 or fewer).

Standard Deviation

Standard deviation, the most important measure of variation, measures the extent of dispersion around the zone of central tendency. For samples from a normal distribution, it is defined as the resulting value of the square root of the sum of the squares of the observed values, minus the arithmetic mean (numerator), divided by the total number of observations, minus one (denominator). The standard deviation of a sample of data is given as:

$$s = \sqrt{\frac{\sum (X - \overline{X})^2}{n-1}}$$

s = standard deviation

n = number of samples (observations or data points)

X = value measured

$\overline{X}$ = average value measured

Coefficient of Variation

The final measure of dispersion, *coefficient of variation* is the standard deviation divided by the mean. *Variance* is the guaranteed existence of a difference between any two items or observations. The concept of variation states that no two observed items will ever be identical.

Frequency Distributions

A *frequency distribution* is a tool for presenting data in a form that clearly demonstrates the relative frequency of the occurrence of values as well as the central tendency and dispersion of the data. Raw data are divided into classes to determine the number of values in a class or class frequency. The data are arranged by classes, with the corresponding frequencies in a table called a frequency distribution. When organized in this manner, the data are referred to as grouped data, as in Table 20.1.

The data in this table appear to be normally distributed. Even without constructing a histogram or calculating the average, the values appear to be centered around the value 18. In fact, the arithmetic average of these values is 18.02.

The histogram in Figure 20.1 provides a graphic illustration of the dispersion of the data. This histogram may be used to compare the distribution of the data

Table 20.1   Frequency distribution.

Class boundaries	Midpoint	Frequency	Cumulative frequency
14.5–15.4	15	2	2
15.5–16.4	16	9	11
16.5–17.4	17	24	35
17.5–18.4	18	29	64
18.5–19.4	19	25	89
19.5–20.4	20	8	97
20.5–21.4	21	3	100

Part VC

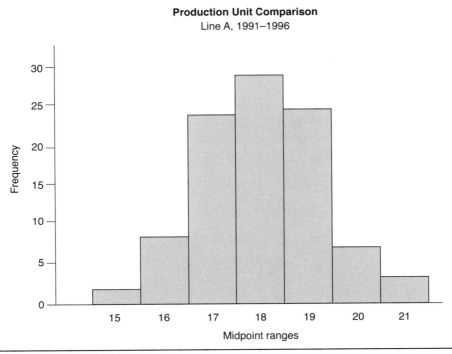

Figure 20.1 Histogram data dispersion.

with specification limits in order to determine where the process is centered in relation to the specification tolerances.

Frequency distributions are useful to auditors for evaluating process performance and presenting the evidence of their analysis. Not only is a histogram a simple tool to use, it is also an effective method of illustrating process results.

3. QUALITATIVE AND QUANTITATIVE ANALYSIS

Types of Data

During an audit, an auditor must analyze many different types of information to determine its acceptability with the overall audit scope and the characteristics, goals, and objectives of the product, process, or system being evaluated. This information may be documented or undocumented and includes procedures, drawings, work instructions, manuals, training records, electronic data on a computer disk, observation, and interview results. The auditor must determine if the information is relevant to the audit purpose and scope.

Quantitative data means either that measurements were taken or that a count was made, such as counting the number of defective pieces removed (inspected out), the number of customer complaints, or the number of cycles of a molding press observed during a time period. In short, the data are expressed as a measurement or an amount. IIA's *Internal Auditing: Principles and Techniques* suggests that there are many sources of quantitative data, such as:

- Test reports
- Product scrap rates
- Trend analyses
- Histograms
- Regression analyses
- Ratio analyses
- Lost-time accidents
- Frequency distributions
- Chi square tests
- Risk analyses
- Variance analyses
- Budget comparisons
- Mean, mode, median
- Profitability
- Cost/benefit studies[3]

In contrast, *qualitative data* refers to the nature, kind, or attribute of an observation. Qualitative data may include single observations or data points, such as in the following examples: last month's withholding tax deposit was three days late; the paycheck amount was wrong; the injection needle was contaminated; the wrong reference standard was used; the purchase order specification gave the wrong activity level; computer equipment was missing from the clerk's office; or a regulatory violation was reported. Whether the evidence is qualitative or quantitative, it should be objective, unbiased, and proven true.

The auditor must analyze the data to determine relevancy. Some data are important and should be reported due to frequency or level. Other data are important due to the nature or kind of information even though an event occurred only once.

With quantitative information, the determination of acceptability is fairly straightforward for two reasons. First, a direct comparison can be made between the information and the requirements or criteria for the audit. For instance, suppose the measure of system effectiveness used in an audit is found to have less than a predetermined number of customer complaints about product quality in a three-month period. Analysis would consist of comparing customer complaint records against the criteria to determine whether the system is effective. Second, most quantitative information is considered reliable because by nature it should be free of emotion and bias.

Qualitative data must be unbiased and traceable, just like any observation that is used as objective evidence by the auditor. Additionally, the auditor should determine the usefulness or relevance of the information. For instance, the auditor may be informed that one customer complaint turned into a $10 million lawsuit. In this case, the data must be verified, and the auditor will seek to determine whether the data have any bearing on the management system. Once the information has been determined to have a real effect on the system, the auditor may use the data to draw conclusions about system effectiveness. Or the auditor may determine that the data represented a once-in-a-lifetime event and are not relevant to current operations.

PATTERNS AND TRENDS

Pattern analysis involves the collection of data in a way that readily reveals any kind of clustering that may occur. This technique is of major value in internal audits, since it is so effective in making use of data from repetitive audits. It can be both location- and time-sensitive. Pattern analysis is of limited value in external audits owing to the lack of repetition in such audits.[4]

While no one specific tool exists to determine patterns and trends, the following tools, matrices, and data systems are among the many tools that can help make such determinations. Patterns and trends can often indicate the severity of a problem and can be used to help determine whether a problem is a systemic issue.

Line/Trend graphs connect points that represent pairs of numeric data, to show how one variable of the pair is a function of the other. As a matter of convention, independent variables are plotted on the horizontal axis, and dependent variables are plotted on the vertical axis. Line graphs are used to show changes in data over time (see Figure 20.2).

A trend is indicated when a series of points increases or decreases. Nonrandom patterns indicate a trend or tendency. (Experience is required for proper interpretation.) Pareto charts and scatter diagrams are used as necessary.[5]

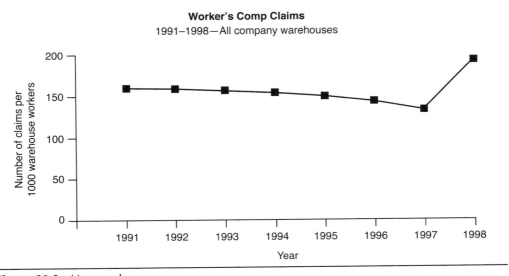

Figure 20.2 Line graph.

Part VC

Following are characteristics of trend analysis:

- Allows us to describe the historical pattern in the data

- Permits us to project the past patterns and/or trends in the future

- Helps us understand the long-term variation of the time series

Bar graphs also portray the relationship or comparison between pairs of variables, but one of the variables need not be numeric. Each bar in a bar graph represents a separate, or discrete, value. Bar graphs can be used to identify differences between sets of data (see Figure 20.3).

Pie charts are used to depict proportions of data or information in order to understand how they make up the whole. The entire circle, or "pie," represents 100% of the data. The circle is divided into "slices," with each segment proportional to the numeric quantity in each class or category (see Figure 20.4).

Matrices are two-dimensional tables showing the relationship between two sets of information. They can be used to show the logical connecting points between performance criteria and implementing actions, or between required actions and personnel responsible for those actions. In this way, matrices can determine what actions and/or personnel have the greatest impact on an organization's mission. Auditors can use matrices as a way to focus auditing time and to organize the audit.

In Table 20.2, the matrix helps the auditor by identifying organizational responsibilities for the different audit areas. This particular matrix is used to maximize use of time during the site visit.

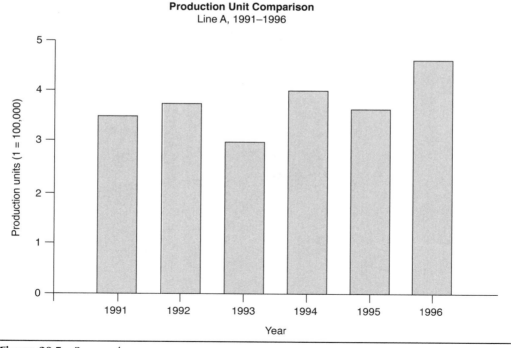

Figure 20.3   Bar graph.

Source: Jerry Nation, Nation Quality Associates, Inc.

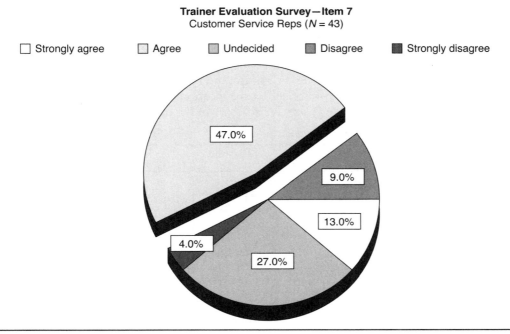

Figure 20.4 Pie chart.

Source: Jerry Nation, Nation Quality Associates, Inc.

Table 20.2 Area of responsibilities matrix.

	Program development	Deficiency tracking	Training	Work control	Document and records retention	Assessment
Director		X				X
Ops office			X	X	X	
Ops support	X	X	X			
Tech support		X	X	X		X
Admin.			X		X	

Source: Rudolph C. Hirzel, "Audits Making a Difference" (presented at the ASQC Fifth Annual Quality Audit Conference, Kansas City, MO, February 22–23, 1996).

Table 20.3, a much broader matrix, allows the auditor to do the long-range planning necessary for ensuring proper application of the audit program. In this example, the various audited areas (y axis) are applied against the different organizations to be audited.

Data systems exist in a wide range of forms and formats. They may include the weekly and monthly reports of laboratory or organizational performance that are used to alert the auditing organization of potential audit areas, or computerized databases that link performance to specific performance objectives or track actions to resolve programmatic weaknesses. In any case, data systems are important tools that provide the auditor with the data needed to focus on audit activities.

In Table 20.4 information on lost-time injuries is displayed in tabular form; the same information is displayed as a graph in Figure 20.5. This information can be used to focus the assessment on either the location of the injuries or the work procedures involved to identify any weaknesses in the accident prevention program.

Table 20.3 Audit planning matrix.

	Administration	Chemistry	Biology	Materials	Building services	Engineering
Industrial hygiene		A		A	A	A
Radiation protection	B		B	B		
Fire protection			C	C	C	C
Industrial safety	A	A			A	
Environmental	C	C	C			C
Personnel training	B	A		B		C
Conduct of operations			C	C	C	
Quality assurance		A	C		A	C

A = First assessment   B = Second assessment   C = Third assessment

Source: Rudolph C. Hirzel, "Audits Making a Difference" (presented at the ASQC Fifth Annual Quality Audit Conference, Kansas City, MO, February 22–23, 1996).

Table 20.4 Lost–time accident monthly summary.

Date	Type	Area	Work procedure	Work crew	Days lost
5/3	Sprain	Bldg 12	CAP-101	Mech	4
5/5	Sprain	Bldg 5	MAP-2-12	Elec	5
5/12	Burn	Area 8	PMP-1-4	Mech	2
5/15	Abrasion	Area 10	PMP-3-7	Grnds	3
5/23	Burn	Bldg 12	CAP-103	Elec	1
5/25	Sprain	Admin bldg	N/A	N/A	1
5/29	Cut	Bldg 5	MAP-2-17	Elec	1

Source: Rudolph C. Hirzel, "Audits Making a Difference" (presented at the ASQC Fifth Annual Quality Audit Conference, Kansas City, MO, February 22–23, 1996).

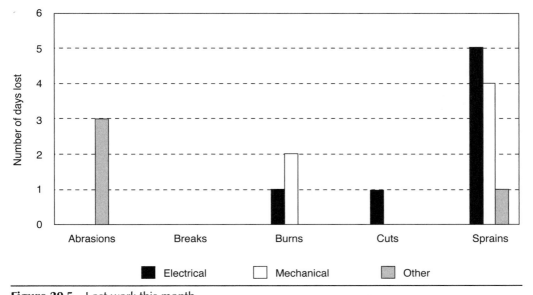

Figure 20.5   Lost work this month.

Source: Rudolph C. Hirzel, "Audits Making a Difference" (presented at the ASQC Fifth Annual Quality Audit Conference, Kansas City, MO, February 22–23, 1996).

Chapter 21
Process Variation/Part VD

1. COMMON AND SPECIAL CAUSES (THEORY OF VARIATION)

Variation is inherent; it exists in all things. No two entities in the world have exactly the same measurable characteristics. The variation might be small and unnoticeable without the aid of precise and discriminative measuring instruments, or it might be quite large and easily noticeable. Two entities might appear to have the same measurement because of the limitations of the measuring device.

Factors Affecting Variation

Everything is the result of some process, so the chance for some variation in output is built into every process. Because material inputs are the outputs of some prior process, they are subject to variation, and that variation is transferred to the outputs. Variation will exist even in apparently identical processes using seemingly identical resources. Even though a task is defined and performed in the same manner repeatedly, different operators performing the same task and the same operator performing the same task repeatedly introduce variation. Precision and resolution of the measuring devices, and techniques used to collect data also introduce variation into the output data.

Variation can result from changes in various factors, normally classified as follows:

1. People (worker) influences
2. Machinery influences
3. Environmental factors
4. Material influences
5. Measurement influences
6. Method influences

The resulting total variation present in any product is a result of the variations from these six main sources. Because the ramifications of variation in quality are

Taken from Russell T. Westcott, ed., *The Certified Manager of Quality/Organizational Excellence Handbook* (Milwaukee, WI: ASQ Quality Press, 2006), pp. 436–440.

enormous for managers, knowing a process's capabilities prior to production provides for better utilization of resources. Operating costs are reduced when inspection, rework, safety stock storage, and troubleshooting are eliminated. Proper management requires a deep appreciation of the existence of variation as well as an understanding of its causes and how they can be corrected.

Types of Variation

Walter Shewhart, the father of modern quality control, was concerned with the low-cost reduction of variation. Shewhart distinguished two kinds of processes: (1) a stable process with "inevitable chance variation" and (2) an unstable process with "assignable cause variation." If the limits of process variation are well within the band of customer tolerance (specification), then the product can be made and shipped with reasonable assurance that the customer will be satisfied. If the limits of process variation just match the band of customer tolerance, then the process should be monitored closely and adjusted when necessary to maximize the amount of satisfactory output. If the limits of process variation extend beyond the band of customer tolerance, output should be inspected to determine whether it meets customer requirements.

When the amount of variation can be predicted with confidence, the process is said to be in a state of statistical control (stable). Although a singular value cannot be predicted exactly, it can be anticipated to fall within certain limits. Similarly, the long-term average value can be predicted.

In an unstable process every batch of product is a source of excitement! It is impossible to predict how much, if any, of the product will fall within the band of customer tolerance. The costs necessary to produce satisfactory product are unknown because the organization is forced to carry large quantities of safety stock, and bids for new work must include a safety factor.

Shewhart developed simple statistical and graphical tools to inform operators and managers about their processes and to detect promptly when a stable process becomes unstable and vice versa. These tools, called *control charts*, come in various forms to accommodate whether measures are attributes or variables, whether samples are of constant size or not. Deming also recognized Shewhart's two sources of variation, calling them *common causes* and *special causes*. He also distinguished between the duties of those who work in the process and the managers who work on the process.

Common Causes

Variation that is always present or inherent in a process is called *common cause variation*. It occurs when one or more of the six previously mentioned factors fluctuate within the normal or expected manner and can be improved only by changing a factor. Common causes of variation occur continually and result in controlled variation. They ensue, for example, from the choice of supplier, quality of inputs, worker hiring and training practices, equipment selection, machinery maintenance, and working conditions. If the process variation is excessive, then the process must be changed.

Eradicating these stable and predictable causes of variation is the responsibility of the managers of the process. Common causes are beyond the control of workers, as was demonstrated by Deming's famous red bead experiment.[1] In that experiment, volunteers were told to produce only white beads from a bowl containing a mixture of white and red beads. Monitoring or criticizing worker performance had no effect on the output. No matter what the workers did, they got red beads—sometimes more, sometimes less, but always some—because the red beads were in the system.

Deming estimated that common causes account for 80 percent to 95 percent of workforce variation. This is not the fault of the workers, who normally do their best even in less-than-ideal circumstances. Rather, this is the responsibility of the managers, who work on, not in, the process.

Management decides how much money and time is to be spent on designing processes, which impacts the resources and methods that can be used. It is the design of the process that impacts the amount of common cause variation.

Special Causes (also called assignable causes)

When variation from one or more factors is abnormal or unexpected, the resultant variation is known as special cause variation. This unexpected level of variation that is observed in an unstable process is due to special causes that are not inherent in the process. Special causes of variation are usually local in time and space, for example, specific to a change in a particular machine or a difference in shift, operator, or weather condition. They appear in a detectable pattern and cause uncontrolled variation. Special causes of variation often result in sudden and extreme departures from the normal, but can also occur in the form of gradual shifts (or drifts) in a characteristic of a process. When a control chart shows a lack of control, skilled investigation should reveal what special causes affect the output. The workers in the process often have the detailed knowledge necessary to guide this investigation.

Structural Variation

Structural variation is inherent in the process;[2] however, when plotted on a control chart, structural variation appears like a special cause (blip), even though it is predictable. For example, a restaurant experiences a high number of errors in diners' orders taken on Saturday nights. The number of diners increases by 50 percent or more on every Saturday night, served by the same number of waitpersons and chefs as on other nights.

Achieving Breakthrough Improvement

Building on Shewhart's notions to develop a systematic method for improvement, Juran distinguished between sporadic and chronic problems for quality improvement projects (QIPs). Starting from a state of chaos, a QIP should first seek to control variation by eliminating sporadic problems. When a state of controlled variation is reached, the QIP should then break through to higher levels of quality by eliminating chronic problems, thereby reducing the controlled variation. The notions of control and breakthrough are critical to Juran's thinking.

The following scenario demonstrates this concept: A dart player throws darts at two different targets. The darts on the first target are all fairly close to the bull's-eye, but the darts are scattered all over the target. It is difficult for the player to determine whether changing stance (or any other variable) will result in an improved score. The darts thrown at the second target are well off target from the bull's-eye, but the location of the darts is clustered and therefore predictable. When the player determines what variable is causing the darts to miss the bull's-eye, immediate and obvious improvement should result.

The impetus behind Juran's work is to achieve repeatable and predictable results. Until that happens, it will be almost impossible to determine whether a quality improvement effort has had any effect. Once a process is in control, breakthroughs are possible because they are detectable.

The following points are essential to an understanding of variation:

- Everything is the result or outcome of some process.

- Variation always exists, although it is sometimes too small to notice.

- Variation can be controlled if its causes are known. The causes should be determined through the practical experience of workers in the process as well as by the expertise of managers.

- Variation can result from special causes, common causes, or structural variation. Corrective action cannot be taken unless the variation has been assigned to the proper type of cause. For example, in Deming's bead experiment (white beads = good product, red beads = bad product) the workers who deliver the red beads should not be blamed; the problem is the fault of the system that contains the red beads.

- Tampering by taking actions to compensate for variation within the control limits of a stable process increases rather than decreases variation.

- Practical tools exist to detect variation and to distinguish controlled from uncontrolled variation.

Variation exists everywhere (even the earth wobbles a bit in its journey around the sun). So, too, variation exists at an organizational level—within management's sphere of influence. The organization as a system is subject to common cause variation and special cause variation. Unfortunately, members of management in many organizations do not know about or understand the theory of variation. As a result of this, management tends to treat all anomalies as special causes and therefore treats actual common causes with continual tampering. Three examples follow:

- A donut shop, among its variety of products, produces jelly donuts. The fruit mix used to fill the jelly donuts is purchased from a long-time, reliable supplier. From time to time, a consumer complains about the tartness of the donut filling (nature produces berries of varying degrees of sweetness). The shop owner complains to the jelly supplier who adds more sugar to the next batch (tampering). Several consumers complain about the overly sweet donut filling. The shop owner complains to the supplier who reduces the amount of sugar in the next batch (tampering). Some consumers complain about tartness, and so it goes.

- Susan, a normally average salesperson, produces 10 percent fewer sales (number of sales, not dollar value) this month. The sales manager criticizes Susan for low sales production and threatens her with compensation loss. Susan responds by an extra effort to sell to anyone who will buy the service, regardless of the dollar volume of the sale (tampering). The sales manager criticizes Susan again, pointing out that dollar volume is more important than number of sales made. Susan concentrates on large-dollar buyers, which take several months to bring to fruition. Susan's monthly figures show a drastic drop and she is severely criticized for lack of productivity. Susan leaves the company and takes the large-dollar prospects with her to a competitor. The system failed due to tampering, but the worker was blamed.

- A VP of finance of a widely known charity continually tinkers with the organization's portfolio of investments, selling or buying whenever a slight deviation is noted, resulting in suboptimal yield from the portfolio.

An organization must focus its attempts at reducing variation. Variation does not need to be eliminated from everything; rather, the organization should focus on reducing variation in those areas most critical to meeting customers' requirements.

2. PROCESS PERFORMANCE METRICS

Process capability is the range within which a process is normally able to operate given the inherent variation due to design and selection of materials, equipment, people, and process steps. Knowing the capability of a process means knowing whether a particular specification can be held if the process is in control.

If a process is in control, one can then calculate the process capability index. Several formulae are used to describe the capability of a process, comparing it to the specification limits; the two most popular indexes are C_p and C_{pk}. C_p indicates how the width of the process compares to the width of the specification range, while C_{pk} looks at whether the process is sufficiently centered in order to keep both tails from falling outside specifications. Following are the formulae:

$$C_p = \frac{\text{Specification range}}{\text{Process range}} = \frac{\text{Upper spec} - \text{Lower spec}}{6\sigma}$$

$$C_{pk} = \frac{|\text{Upper spec} - \text{Lower spec}|}{3\sigma} \ (or) \frac{|\text{Lower spec} - \text{Average}|}{3\sigma}, \text{whichever is smaller}$$

Note that the σ used for this calculation is not the standard deviation of a sample. It is the process sigma based on time-ordered data, such as given by the formula $R\text{-bar}/d_2$.

Following are the rules often used to determine whether a process is considered capable:

$C_{pk} > 1.33$ (capable)

$C_{pk} = 1.00 - 1.33$ (capable with tight control)

$C_{pk} < 1.00$ (not capable)

Initial process capability studies are often performed as part of the process valida-tion stage of a new product launch. Since this is usually a run of only a few hundred parts, it does not include the normal variability that will be seen in full production, such as small differences from batch to batch of raw material. In this case the study is called potential process capability, with the symbol P_{pk} used instead of C_{pk}. To compensate for the reduced variability the decision points are typically set at:

$P_{pk} > 1.67$ (capable)

$P_{pk} = 1.33 - 1.67$ (capable with tight control)

$P_{pk} < 1.33$ (not capable)

Capability is then studied soon after production release and on an as-needed basis during normal production. Changes to the process due to engineering changes or as part of continuous improvement should also be evaluated for their impact on process capability.

If process capability is found to be unsatisfactory, the following may be considered:

- Ensure that the process is centered

- Initiate process improvement projects to decrease variation

- Determine if the specifications can be changed

- Do nothing, but realize that a percentage of output will be outside acceptable variation

When using statistical software programs to evaluate process capability, it is important that the user understand the specific terminology used by the program-mers. Although the same concepts may be used, different symbols or formulae may be used.

3. OUTLIERS

The dictionary defines outlier as a statistical observation not homogeneous in value with others of a sample. An outlier is a special case of a special cause. An outlier is a data point that deviates markedly from the other data points collected or in the sample. An outlier is a result of a special cause such as using the wrong test equipment or pulling the sample from the wrong bin. A data point identi-fied as an outlier is abnormal and if not removed from the data base will result in skewed, misleading, or false conclusions.

Outliers are the most extreme observations and are either the sample maxi-mum or sample minimum. However, sample maximums and minimums are not normally outliers. Outliers are data points so extreme, they do not appear to belong to the same data base.

Deletion of outlier data may be the correct thing to do but it is a subjective judg-ment. The practice of deleting outliers is frowned upon by many scientists due to the potential of researchers manipulating statistical data for their own self-interest. If the cause of the outlier data point is known, it should be verified before removal from the data base. When data points are excluded from data analysis, the ratio-nale should be clearly stated in any subsequent report.

Chapter 22
Sampling Methods/Part VE

T he auditor should follow the sampling plan required by audit program management. Normally, statistical sampling plans are not required for process or system audits. However, knowledge of sampling methods and techniques may be needed to evaluate auditee sampling processes. Also, auditors need to know the limitations and biases created by taking samples.

Sampling is the practice of taking selected items or units from a total population of items or units. The method and reason for taking certain samples or a certain number of samples from a population should be based on sampling theory and procedures. Samples may be taken from the total population or universe, or the population may be separated into subgroups called *strata*. Inferences drawn from the sampling of a stratum, however, may not be valid for the total population.

To infer statistical significance from any sample, two conditions must be met: The population under consideration must be homogeneous, and the sample must be random. *Homogeneous* means that the population must be uniform throughout—the bad parts should not be hidden on the bottom of one load—or it could refer to the similarities that should exist when one load is checked against others from a different production setup. *Random* means that every item in the population has an equal chance of being checked. To ensure this, samples can be pulled by a random number generator or other unbiased method.

The preferred practice is for the auditor to go to the location of the sample and select the sample for the audit. However, there are situations (long distances, convenience, files off-site, and so on) in which the auditee may be permitted to provide the sample population, such as in a file, folder, or logbook to the auditor, who may then select the sample. When sampling, auditors should record the identity of samples selected, the number in the population from which the samples were taken (if possible), and the number of samples selected for examination.

The goal is to provide management with supportable information about the company, with the expectation that management will take action based on the results presented. An auditor must be able to qualify the sampling methods used to management as either statistical or nonstatistical, but factual based.

TYPES OF SAMPLING

Haphazard sampling is used by auditors to try to gather information from a representative sample of a population. Items are selected without intentional bias and with the goal of representing the population as a whole. The auditor might ask to

266

see the deficiency reports on the coordinator's desk. These reports might be rationalized as being random and as representing the population as a whole. The auditor might ask for 10 deficiency reports, two from each line, and will ask to be the one who picks them. This might be rationalized as removing the bias from having the coordinator select the sample. The pro side of haphazard sampling is that it is easy to select the sample, so the audit can be completed more quickly. There is less preparation time, making it possible to do more audits.

The con side of haphazard sampling may outweigh its advantages. If the coordinator is reviewing the deficiency reports for a specific department at the time the auditor walks in, the results of the audit will show that this department has a disproportionate number of deficiencies when compared with the other departments in the sample. The auditor might pick deficiency reports that catch his or her eye for some unknown reason, thus introducing an unknown bias. Haphazard sampling is the easy approach to sampling, but the results may not reflect all departments, lines, items, people, problems, or a myriad of other considerations. The results are not statistically valid, and generalizations about the total population should be made with extreme caution. The results of haphazard sampling are difficult to defend objectively. Of all the nonstatistical audit sampling methods, haphazard is arguably the worst.

Block sampling or *cluster sampling* can be used by auditors to gain a pretty good picture of the population, if the blocks are chosen in a statistical manner. This requires that numerous blocks be chosen before an accurate representation of the total population is obtained, and often more items are examined than if a statistical sample was selected in the beginning. Normally, auditors don't use block sampling during audits but do use it extensively after a problem has been identified. Auditors and others use block sampling when trying to determine when or how a previously identified problem began, ended, or both. For example, if a problem began in May, the auditor might examine all items made or processed in May to try to determine when the problem began and whether it is still occurring. If a problem with calibration of balances was identified, every balance could be examined to determine when the problem began and whether it affected only those in one building or in one department. Some may recognize these activities as investigative actions taken subsequent to identification of a problem. Block sampling is also used in investigative actions.

The pro side of block sampling is that it allows statistically valid judgments about the block examined. With a sufficiently large number of blocks selected randomly using the same selection criteria, statistically valid judgments about the total population can be made. Single blocks allow the auditor to narrow down the root cause of a previously identified problem by focusing the investigation in the area of concern. Single blocks also allow the auditor to recognize a possible problem with a single machine or a specific process.

The con side of block sampling is that it requires sampling a large number of items—even more than statistically selected samples—before judgments about the total population can be made. Auditors often want more than just information on a particular block of time, products, or locations. Auditors want to be able to provide management with supportable statements about the entire population. For this reason, block sampling is normally not used during the audit to identify problems.

Judgmental sampling can be used by auditors to get a pretty good idea of what is happening, although the results are not statistically valid. In the first approach, the auditor selects samples based on his or her best judgment of what is believed to give a representative picture of the population. These samples are chosen based

Part VE

on the auditor's past experience. Often these samples are taken from areas that expose the company to the greatest risk, such as high-dollar orders, special orders, or critical application orders. The auditor may already know from past history (past audits) that problems have existed in department A, activity C, and with this knowledge, the auditor examines that area in an audit. In judgmental sampling, the auditor may also decide to look at all orders over $2 million or all orders destined for installation in the military aircraft. If a problem is found, the auditor examines additional samples to determine the extent of the immediate problem.

In the second approach (that is, looking at all orders over $2 million), the process or system has reached maturity, and very few problems are identified in a general audit using random sample techniques. The company may then decide to audit all areas in which problems were identified, with the intention of determining whether the activity can be improved beyond its current level. The nuclear industry and several other industries have reached this point and have begun to rely on judgmental sampling to identify areas for improvement.

The pro side of judgmental sampling is extensive. The auditor focuses on areas where previous problems were found and corrected. High-risk areas and activities historically have received the most attention from management. By doing judgmental sampling, the auditor will be providing information on areas known to be of interest to management. Judgmental sampling allows companies to focus their efforts on specific improvements rather than general assessment. It allows the auditor to more effectively use his or her time during the audit. And finally, selection of the audit sample is relatively simple, which leaves more time to prepare for and perform the audit.

The con side of judgmental sampling is that the results are not statistically valid or objectively defensible. Judgmental sampling is open to abuse through retaliation (selecting a group for a detailed audit because of some previous action). Judgmental sampling causes auditors to continue to focus on areas where problems were found previously. It is a fact that an auditor focusing on an area will probably find problems that get recorded and reported. An unwritten law of auditing is that "if we look for it, we will find it." If auditors continue to focus only on areas where problems are found, logic would take them to the extreme where they always audit the same thing over and over. Thus, certain areas would be seen as pristine, while others would be seen as consistently incompetent. Statistical sampling is needed to provide a baseline from which further auditing using judgmental sampling may proceed.

Haphazard sampling should be avoided if at all possible. Block sampling is effective in pinpointing problems, and statistically valid conclusions can be made about the block evaluated; but conclusions about the total population require more work. Judgmental sampling is effective in focusing the auditor's efforts and in identifying areas of improvement in a relatively mature program. The job of the auditor is to know which method is best for obtaining the information needed.

STATISTICAL SAMPLING (RANDOM AND SYSTEMATIC)

For a sampling approach to be considered statistical, the method must have random selection of items to be evaluated and use probability theory to quantitatively evaluate the results. Statistically valid sampling is necessary to quantify problems resulting from an administrative process or production line. Statistically valid sampling allows the auditor to state in the audit report that "we are 95 percent confident that the actual population deviation rate lies between 1.2 percent and 5 percent. Since this is less than the tolerable deviation rate of 6 percent, the control procedure appears to be functioning as prescribed." With a slightly different sampling technique, the auditor would be able to state, "We are 95 percent confident that the true population deviation rate is less than 4.8 percent, which is less than the tolerable deviation rate of 6 percent." These numbers and confidence levels mean more to upper management than, say, "We think there is a problem in document control."

There are two widely used methods of statistical sampling: simple random sampling and systematic sampling. *Simple random sampling* ensures that each item in the population has an equal chance of being selected. Random number tables and computer programs can help make the sample selections. *Systematic sampling* also ensures that each item in the population has an equal chance of being selected. The difference here is that after the sample size is determined, it is divided into the total population size to determine the sampling interval (for example, every third item). The starting point is determined using a random number table. Several computer programs are available to help determine the sample size, the sampling interval, the starting point, and the actual samples to be evaluated.

It's not difficult to plug numbers into a formula and calculate the results. Management likes to work with numbers that have meaning and that put boundaries around a question or an error rate. This is where statistical sampling comes in. With statistical sampling, auditors can state in the audit reports that "we have 95 percent confidence that the purchase orders are being correctly processed." Sample size depends on confidence level and what the auditor wants to determine.

Naturally, the larger the sample size, the more accurate the estimate. For small populations, the sample size is corrected. Auditing by statistical sampling is best suited to single-attribute auditing. However, once the item to be audited has been selected, many attributes can be checked during the audit. A purchase order has many attributes that can be checked simultaneously. In this way, one calculation for sample size can be used to report on many attributes.

Standards (discussed in the next section) or statistical formulas should be used to determine the appropriate sample size given a required confidence level, such as 95% or 99%. For more information concerning statistical sampling, Dodge-Romig or Bayesian sampling plans, and binominal distributions, consult a comprehensive statistical textbook.

SAMPLING STANDARDS (ACCEPTANCE SAMPLING)

In this section, three sampling procedures are discussed for application to auditing:

ANSI/ASQ Z1.4-2008: Sampling Procedures and Tables for Inspection by Attributes

ANSI/ASQ Z1.9-2008: Sampling Procedures and Tables for Inspection by Variables for Percent Nonconforming

ASQC Q3-1998: Sampling Procedures and Tables for Inspection of Isolated Lots by Attributes

Application

We are interested in determining conformance with procedures, instructions, and other program documentation. Audits for adequacy require a point-by-point comparison of the lower-tier document, such as a procedure, with the upper-tier document, such as a standard. This is a 100% check. Thus, statistical sampling does not apply. Effectiveness and performance audits require the judgment skills of the auditor, as applied to the results of the program. Again, statistical sampling does not apply.

Conformance is determining whether an activity or a document is satisfactory or unsatisfactory. This, then, is attribute sampling, rather than variable sampling. In addition, we are dealing with whole numbers (1, 2, 3), so we need to deal with discrete probability distributions. The most common of these are hypergeometric, binomial, and Poisson. For general discussion, we need to assume a large population, N. This condition is met if N is greater than or equal to $10n$, where n is the sample size. This condition is not required when the standards are used, as the sample size is corrected for small population (lot size). But what are the characteristics of the lot that we will examine during the audit?

The Moving Lot

Most audits are a snapshot covering a specific time period. Our snapshot is of a lot from a continuous production line. As part of the scope of the audit, we might have to examine the deficiency reports (DRs) for the last quarter. Obviously there were DRs written before our time period, and there will be DRs written after we are gone. This might look like:

The population (lot size) consists of the number of DRs written during the selected time period. During a subsequent audit, the lot might be completely separate from the lot selected during this audit, or it might overlap.

Thus, the lot moves for each audit performed, depending on the goals set for the audit. The process being examined can be said to have an acceptable quality level (AQL) set by the people doing the work. This is the work standard they are attempting to achieve. Now that we understand the nature of our lot, we are ready to use the standards.

Z1.9 Applicability

Z1.9 has been eliminated from consideration because it is variable sampling, and auditors need to concern themselves with attribute sampling. This leaves Z1.4 and ASQC Q3-1998 for possible use by auditors. We will consider them in turn.

ANSI/ASQ Z1.4-2008 Applicability and Use

ANSI/ASQC Z1.4-2008 is the revised and updated version of the old MIL-STD-105. This standard assumes that isolated lots are drawn from a process and sampled separately. The process AQL is a factor in determining the sample size in this case. In auditing, we want to know the maximum error rate, which translates into a limiting quality level (LQL) for the standards. Tables VI-A and VII-A of ANSI/ASQ Z1.4-2008 provide LQLs as a percent nonconforming with a probability of acceptance P_a = 10% and 5%, respectively. P_a = 10% means that there is only a 10% chance that we will accept a lot with a percent nonconforming greater than our specified LQL.

As an example, let's assume that we want a 10% LQL for our lot with P_a = 10% or less, and an AQL of 1.5% for a series of lots. Enter the ANSI/ASQ Z1.4-2008 sample size of 50, and we can accept the lot with two problems noted but must reject the lot if three problems are noted. The sample size of 50 implies that our population is approximately 500 (N is greater than or equal to $10n$). If the population is much less than 500, we need to use the calculations presented in "Proportional Stratified Sampling" in this chapter.

Continuing with the example, we need to choose a random sample of 50 items. Computer random number generator programs or random number tables provide the selection method for our sample. When completed, assuming the results are acceptable, we will be able to say that there is a 90% probability that the audited attribute has a percent defective less than 10%. When working to very exact requirements, such as low AQL and low LQL, we need to use the operating characteristic curves to determine the discrimination desired. The operating characteristic curves are imprecise when working in this area. This brings up the second standard applicable to auditing, ASQC Q3-1998.

ASQC Q3-1998 Applicability and Use

ASQC Q3-1998 is designed for isolated lots and uses the hypergeometric probability function. This applies even more directly to audits than ANSI/ASQC Z1.4-1993. ASQC Q3-1998 also uses the customer's specified limiting quality (LQ) as the basis for sample sizes. The goal is to have a very low probability of accepting (P_a) a lot that has a percent nonconforming equal to or worse than the LQ. ASQC Q3-1998 ties back to ANSI/ASQ Z1.4-2008 for AQLs to provide a commonality or cross-reference.

Because we will be pulling isolated lots from a continuous process, we will be working with Table B of the ASQC Q3-1998 standard. There are cases when we will work with truly isolated lots, in which case Table A would be used, but this is the exception.

ASQC Q3-1998 is fairly simple to understand. Let's assume that from the DR log, we counted 239 DRs written during the period being audited. Our client isn't overly concerned with detailed compliance with the procedures, but does want each deficiency corrected. For compliance, we select an LQ of 12.5%, which is fairly loose. Table B8 shows our sample size to be 32. For deficiency correction, we select an LQ of 2%, which is fairly tight. Table B4 shows our sample size to be 200. Please note that this is almost a 100% sample because our population is low. From Table C3, we find that in both cases we accept the lot if we find one or zero problems in our sample.

We approach this by selecting a random sample of 200 for auditing deficiency correction. Next, we divide 200 by the 32 samples needed for the compliance portion of the audit, to get a frequency of 6. Thus for the compliance portion, we will use every sixth item from our deficiency correction sample as one of our compliance samples, beginning with item 4 (chosen because it is less than 6). The sequence looks like this:

Deficiency correction	1 2 3 4 5 6 7 8 9 10 ... 190 191 192 193 194 195 196 197 198 199 200
Compliance	1 2 32 33

Note that because the division does not yield an even number, we end up with 33 total samples for compliance, rather than the 32 from the table. Use the extra sample as part of the audit.

We then perform the audit, and if one or zero problems is noted for each sample (200 and 32), we can be 90% confident that the DRs meet the LQ specified for the attribute being checked (12.5% for compliance and 2% for deficiency correction).

Summary

Two of the most familiar sampling plans, ANSI/ASQ Z1.4-2008 and ASQC Q3-1998, are readily applied to and used during audits. These allow the auditor to speak with authority to management about the results of the audit. There is a lot to learn about applying the standards to audits, but many people who have previously applied the standards to product acceptance will be able to apply the standards to their auditing. Consider using some of these sampling methods the next time you audit a large population to improve the audit credibility.

PROPORTIONAL STRATIFIED SAMPLING

Proportional stratified sampling can be used to gain an understanding of each stratum within a population, but it cannot be used to make statistical inferences for each stratum. The sample size is determined by any one of the statistical methods/standards. Then the sample size is divided and applied in proportion to the population of each stratum in the total population. If the sample is not statistically determined, the statistical validity is compromised, and no statistically valid conclusions can be drawn.

For example, the population is 1000 purchase orders over the past year. Eight hundred of these are for amounts of $500 or less; 150 are for amounts of $501–$1000, and 50 are for amounts over $1000. We chose an LQ of 5% and used ASQC Q3-1998, Table B6, to learn that the sample size is 80.

To apportion the sample to the stratum, simply set up a proportion for each:

$$\text{Under } \$500: \frac{800}{1000} = \frac{X_{500}}{80}$$

Then we solve for X_{500} ($500 or less):

$$X_{500} = 64$$

Similar proportions give us ($501–$1000):

$$X_{1000} = 12$$

and ($1000 or greater):

$$X_{1000+} = 4$$

The samples are chosen from each stratum using the random sampling technique. If the samples are not chosen using a random sampling technique, the results will not be statistically valid.

With this knowledge, we can accept the total population with one or zero deficiencies and reject the total population with two or more deficiencies. Although we cannot make statistical inferences on each stratum, we gain some information that we can use to further investigate the stratum. If all the deficiencies are found in a particular stratum, the auditor can revise the focus of the audit to further investigate that particular stratum, and the auditee could justifiably focus corrective action on that stratum.

This method places emphasis on the population of the strata within a population. This may not be desirable to management. For example, management may want the auditor to focus on the high-cost items, which is where the greatest risk lies.

Proportional stratified sampling is deceptive in that the auditor and the auditee could be misled into drawing conclusions about each stratum instead of the total population. The method, sample size, and results allow the auditor to draw conclusions about the total population only. The auditor can use the results to determine where to focus further investigation, and the auditee can use the results as a guide to determine where to focus corrective actions.

RISKS IN SAMPLING[1]

Hypothesis Testing is creating two hypotheses to arrive at a decision based on sampling. Sampling is used to make business decisions regarding the marketability of a product or quality control decisions regarding the acceptance of a batch, lot, or process. A hypothesis may be: *if the lot achieves a certain acceptable quality level (AQL), it will be approved.* Or a decision rule may be: *if X number of parts is found to be defective, the lot will be rejected.* Consumer and producer risk are the chances of making decision errors based on the sample taken.

Producer Risk, or Type I Error, is the probability that good quality product is rejected or the probability that a product survey would indicate that a product is not marketable, when it actually is. The producer suffers when this occurs because good product (or marketable product or service) is rejected. The math symbol used to represent producer risk is alpha (α risk). See Figure 22.1.

Consumer Risk, or Type II Error, is the probability that bad quality product is accepted or the probability that a product survey would indicate that a product is marketable, when it actually is not. The consumer suffers when this occurs because bad product is accepted (released). The math symbol used to represent consumer risk is beta (β risk). For example: A product recall may be the result of a Type II error. See Figure 22.2.

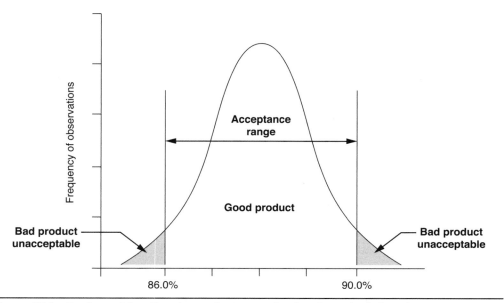

Figure 22.1   Producer risk or Type I error (note: sample taken from shaded area).

Source: Adapted from QualityWBT Center for Education training materials, *Quality Tools and Techniques,* Lesson 3 (2012).

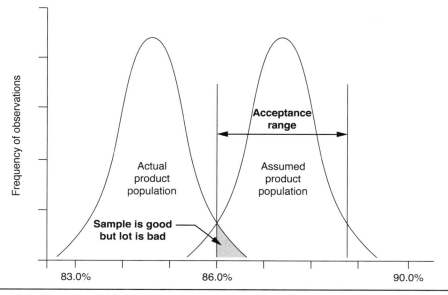

Figure 22.2   Consumer risk or Type II error (note: sample taken from shaded area).

Source: Adapted from QualityWBT Center for Education training materials, *Quality Tools and Techniques,* Lesson 3 (2012).

Sufficient samples of the population must be taken to achieve a certain confidence that Type I and Type II errors will be avoided. Statistically, we can define a sampling plan as one that will give us confidence in the results. Typical confidence levels are 95% or 99%. There is a trade-off between the confidence level you want to achieve versus the cost of sampling.

SAMPLING SUMMARY

This chapter has discussed methods of sampling that are commonly encountered in the performance of product, process, and system audits. Table 22.1 summarizes the methods, their advantages and disadvantages, and their applicability.

Statistically, random sampling must ensure that each item in the population has an equal chance of being selected. A sampling scheme is developed for selection of the samples. This scheme can use a strictly random selection based on random number tables or computerized random number generators, or a systematic sampling scheme based on the number of samples selected and the total population.

Nonstatistical sampling, although very easy and quick to perform, has many disadvantages, which include potential bias in the sample, inability to make generalizations about the total population, and indefensibility as objective sampling.

Statistically valid auditing must have random selection of items to be evaluated and use probability theory to quantitatively evaluate the results. Two methods can be applied to auditing to provide the ability to make statistically valid conclusions for use by management: statistical sampling for attributes and sampling with standards. These methods allow confidence levels and error estimation based on the results of the evaluation of the samples.

Auditors are encouraged to begin using statistically valid sampling when it adds value and improves the effectiveness of the audit report. When using statistical sampling techniques for the first time, the auditor may use one method during an audit and try a different one for the next to learn the various methods. This has the additional advantage of allowing the auditor to educate management on statistical methods and the accurate results that can be obtained. Often managers have not had extensive training in statistical methods (other than as applied to business applications and budget), so it may be the auditor's job to help familiarize management with the value of statistical methods. After the auditor and management become familiar with the methods, a complete audit using statistical methods should be performed and the results reported to management.

Part VE

Table 22.1 Sampling methods summary.

Method	Description	Advantages	Disadvantages	Application
Statistically random sampling methods				
Random sampling	Uses a random number table or generator and a sampling scheme	Ensures that each item in the population has an equal chance of being selected	Requires some time to develop scheme and select samples	Use when conclusions about a population are required
Systematic sampling	Equally spaced samples based on the sample size	Ensures that each item in the population has an equal chance of being selected; random sample table not required	Requires some time to develop scheme and select samples	Use when conclusions about a population are required
Nonstatistical sampling methods				
Haphazard selection	Auditor chooses sample using own selection method	Selection is easy, quick, and requires little planning	Cannot make generalizations about the total population	Use for system believed to have few errors; use when planning time is short
Block selection (also called cluster sampling)	Auditor chooses all items within a specified time period, over a specified dollar amount, and so on	Selection is easy; can make statistically valid comments about the block evaluated	Cannot make generalizations about the total population	Use when searching for the root cause or isolating a possible problem
Judgmental selection	Auditor chooses samples based on past knowledge or experience; focus on known problem areas and areas of high risk	Selection is easy, quick, and requires little planning	Selection may take time, if past performance and experience are reviewed; possible bias in the sample; cannot make generalizations about the total population; not defensible as objective	Use for mature system believed to have few errors

Table 22.1 Sampling methods summary. *(continued)*

Method	Description	Advantages	Disadvantages	Application
Statistically valid sampling methods				
Statistical sampling for attributes	Calculate sample size using formulas; use random or systematic sampling for selection	Can make generalizations about the total population	Requires some time to determine sample size and to develop scheme and select samples	Use when conclusions about a population are required
Sampling with standards	Use ANSI/ASQC Z1.4 and ANSI/ASQC Q3; use random or systematic sampling for selection	Sample size easily determined; can make generalizations about the total population	Requires knowledge of the use of standards; requires some time to develop scheme and select samples	Use when conclusions about a population are required
Proportional stratified sampling	Apportion a statistically valid sample among strata within a population	Ensures each stratum is examined	Deceptive in that the auditor and the auditee could be misled into drawing conclusions about each stratum instead of about the total population	Use when there are clear strata within a total population and when the auditor is trying to narrow the focus of further investigation

Part VE

Chapter 23
Change Control and Configuration Management/Part VF

S ince the advent of the industrial age, organizations have recognized the need to control products and the documents that describe those products to ensure that the latest models and their descriptions match. Historically, this involved blueprints and specification sheets that were updated and noted by date of revision or a revision of model code or letter. Over time, there has been a continual evolution in the means and techniques involved in managing change. However, change must be controlled so that unnecessary risks are avoided.

Before an organization offers a product or service for sale, it must figure out how to provide it. The established way for providing a product or service is to demonstrate how it is configured. A collection of documents such as procedures, specifications, or drawings defines the product or service configuration. Controlling the configuration is called *configuration management*. Configuration management can include planning, identification and tracking, change control, history, archiving, and auditing. Some companies call this management change control. If there is a change in the management system, it should be controlled relative to the risks to the organization.

One aspect of change control is the control of documents. Document control is not new and is a well-established management system control.

DOCUMENT CONTROL

All organizations have documents either internally or externally generated that need to be identified and controlled so that correct, complete, current, and consistent information is distributed among those who need it in order to do their jobs effectively and to meet customer and stakeholder requirements. These documents could be federal or other governmental registers or regulations, employment regulations, industry-specific material and product specifications, maintenance manuals, customer-supplied designs and specifications, standards, organization policies and procedures, price lists, contracts, other purchasing-related documents, business and project plans, and so on.

Which documents need to be controlled? Much depends on the nature of the organization's business and the types of products and services produced, the regulatory climate, federal and state law, industry practices, and organization experience. There are references available that provide guidance. Some of the standards have wording to the effect that documents required by the management systems for environmental concerns, quality, or whatever must be controlled.

Technology

Technology is a consideration in document management and change control. Many aspects of change control, such as revision levels, revision dates, signatures, distribution copies, distribution lists, distribution verifications, master lists, and so forth, are holdovers in the development of systems to control what could be termed hard-copy documents. In the past, there were master and derivative blue (or sepia) prints, carbon or mimeographed copies of procedures, and other documents, and the management, distribution, and updating of controlled documents often required a full-time position for one or more persons, depending on the size of the organization.

With the advent of word processing, distributed computing, shared drives, and designated or limited file access, the task of keeping documents current and ensuring appropriate distribution became somewhat easier. Many organizations evolved to the state where all of their controlled documents had only one controlled copy, and that copy was on a shared drive or in a certain computer or server. Hard copies were time and date stamped and considered to be uncontrolled; some were considered to be obsolete the day after they were printed, or as indicated by the time/date stamp. Even then, hard copies of references, industry specifications, customer documents, and the like still existed, requiring mixed systems of hard-copy and electronic documents.

With the advent of web-based technology, the internet, and company intranets, the evolution of document control has continued. Access and distribution are through web-page-access technology. One copy is maintained online by a designated individual/owner, who has electronic review and approval. However, when one abstracts the content from the technology, the elements of effective document control are still evident.

> Computer technology has helped with the mechanics of document generation, maintenance, and referencing. However, the discipline to follow the system as defined is still essential. Auditors can often find copies of documents that had been downloaded to personal files or directories, obsolete versions being used rather than referencing the current version, and unauthorized changes being made to documents. The problem is not the system, it is with the people using it and their human nature.

CONFIGURATION MANAGEMENT CONTROL

Configuration management is a management oversight activity for monitoring and controlling changes to configured products, services, and systems. Configuration management ensures that existing product, service, or system configuration is documented, traceable, and current (accurate) during its life cycle (series of stages or phases from beginning to end).

Configuration management includes planning, identification and tracking, change control, history, archiving, and auditing. Configuration management audits include auditing the configured documents to ensure they meet requirements and auditing the configuration management process/system to ensure it conforms and is effective.

Part VF

A configuration management program includes a plan, procedures, identification, change control, records, and audit processes, as described in the following list:

1. Plan: A configuration plan should include activities to be implemented and goals to be achieved—such as XYZ product line will be put under configuration management control, configuration management control process will be expanded, suppliers will be provided training, or there will be change control training for all administrative assistants, and so on.

2. Procedures and guidelines: An organization may need guidelines for the selection of items to be configured, review frequency, distribution, and contents and control of configuration reports. Guidelines may be needed for establishing the baseline configuration to be controlled (what is needed to define the product, service, or system).

3. Identification process: Items to be under configuration management control should be identified, such as drawings, specifications, control plans, and procedures. Conventions for marking and numbering should be established.

4. Change-control process: There should be a change-control procedure before and after the configuration baseline is established.

5. Records status process: There should be an established method for collecting, recording, processing, maintaining, archiving, and destroying configuration data.

6. Audit process: Process or product audits may be used to audit the configured items and the configuration management process.

Audits can be used to verify that the configured product/service conforms to specified characteristics (product/service audit) and that the product/service can perform its intended function.

Additionally, a process audit may be conducted on the configuration process itself. A configuration process audit should verify that the process is adequate, implemented, and maintained.

Within configuration management control, organizations should conduct audits of the document control system as they have done in the past. An auditor should verify the effectiveness of the document and record control system by verifying all aspects of the procedures, policies, and practices.

CONCLUSION

Change control includes product design (including hardware, software, and service), process design, project (including schedule), and the management system. The key principles of change control are what was done, why, when, where, by whom, and how, and the result, including the impact of changes to other processes.

Configuration management is a key factor of change control because any change could affect various processes and subprocesses and because it is necessary to have a good grasp of which process or part relates to which other process or part. Configuration management is the basis for good process management.

Chapter 24
Verification and Validation/Part VG

An audit is a systematic, independent, and documented process for obtaining audit evidence and evaluating it objectively to determine the extent to which audit criteria are fulfilled (ISO 19011:2011).

Auditors collect evidence to ensure that requirements are being met. Auditors may verify and/or validate that requirements (audit criteria) are being met. In general, verification is checking or testing, and validation is the actual performance of its intended use. The dictionary does not support the distinction normally associated between *verification* and *validation* in the management systems and system-process audit fields. However, definitions of these terms were used by the FDA in its GMP starting in the 1980s and were later incorporated into ISO 9000 series standards. Now we can reference the definitions of verification and validation provided in ISO 9000:2005 and the design and development model outlined in ISO 9001:2008, clause 7.3.

Verification should be performed to ensure that the system-process outputs have met the system-process requirements (audit criteria). Verification is the authentication of truth or accuracy by such means as facts, statements, citations, measurements, and confirmation by evidence. An element of verification is that it is independent or separate from the normal operation of a process. The act of an auditor checking that the process or product conforms to requirement is verification (as opposed to inspection checks). For example, ISO 9000:2005, clause 3.8.4 notes that verification activities include performing alternative calculations, comparing a new design specification to a similar proven design specification, undertaking tests and demonstrations, and reviewing documents prior to issue. The most common method of verification is the examination of documents and records. Records verify that a process or activity is being performed and the results recorded. Interviewing is another method of verifying that processes meet requirements through affirmation by the interviewee.

TECHNIQUES

- Verify by examination of records, documents, or interviewing
- Validate by observing or using the product or process

Portions taken from QualityWBT Center for Education training materials, http://www.QualityWBT.com (accessed May 17, 2005).

Part VG

Validation should be performed to ensure that the system-process outputs are meeting the requirements for the specified application or intended use. Validation is the demonstration of the ability of the system-processes under investigation to achieve planned results. According to ISO 9000:2005, clause 3.8.5, validation is confirmation, through the provision of objective evidence, that the requirements for a specific intended use or application have been fulfilled. Sometimes an activity cannot be verified by records or interviews, and the actual process must be observed as intended to be operated. The observation can be the real process or a simulated one.

Some activities can only be verified; for example, it would be too costly or impractical to validate a process such as a plant shutdown or start-up or the use of emergency procedures. Sometimes products or activities are only verified because the product would be destroyed or the process ruined by validating it (such as checking the seal on a container).

For example, an auditor may assume there is a requirement to post revision dates on revised documents. At the audit, he or she asks about this and is told the computer does it automatically. The auditor may want to validate this process by asking the document coordinator to make a change to a document and then see if the software program automatically posts today's date.

PROCESS AUDITING AND TECHNIQUES

One of the advantages of process-based management systems and using process auditing techniques is that the auditor follows along the process steps. In many cases an auditor is able to validate the audit criteria as opposed to just verifying them.

Chapter 25
Risk Management Tools/Part VH

R isk has four main components: probability, hazard, exposure, and consequences. Ropeik and Gray define risk using these components as "the probability that exposure to a hazard will lead to a negative consequence."[1] Other definitions look at risk as the combination of these components in some fashion or another, such as the mathematical, statistical expected value or a mathematical expression attempting to capture the essence of some, if not all, of the components. An example of the latter is the calculation of risk numbers or risk priority numbers in Design/Process Failure Mode (and Criticality) Analyses (DFMEAs, PFMEAs, DFMECAs). These analysis methods also expand on the hazard component by introducing an evaluation of how easily the failure mode can be detected or prevented—the idea being that something that cannot be easily prevented or detected will pose a higher level of risk than something that is more readily apparent.

QUANTIFICATION OF RISK

Assessment scales that assign numbers or weights in order to rank or prioritize components of risk are subjective and may cause confusion and false conclusions. A simple quantification approach is classification of the elements of risk by category, such as "high," "medium," or "low," and "red," "yellow," or "green." This may apply to risk assessments for disaster and recovery planning, financial plans, product development strategies, product and process design evaluations, product liability exposure, internal controls, environmental assessments, and production and quality systems. Evidence of such assessments can be used to demonstrate prudence and due care by establishing what risks were evaluated, how they were classified, and what was done to address or mitigate the effects. In general, elements of risk can be (1) designed out of a product or a process, (2) detected or the effects minimized, or if neither of these is feasible, then (3) warned against.[2]

A small company hired an outside firm to assist in a comprehensive assessment of regulatory, environmental, business, operational, and financial risks. The tools and techniques employed were way over the heads of the people involved, and the results were not actionable. In frustration, they turned to a local consultant, who sat the principals and outside counsel around a table and quickly had them list concerns, issues, and the like on a whiteboard. He then distilled these down and put them into general classifications. Next, he had the group rate them in terms of "high," "medium," or "low." After that, they developed short, doable action plans, taking each group in order. Within a couple of sessions they had a real plan with assignments, dates, and review points. This was then shared with investors, insurance providers, local officials, and other parties. When later issues arose, the existence of the plan was used as evidence that the company was diligent and using due care.

The following are methods to identify, assess, and treat risks. Though the techniques were originally designed for specific purposes, they can all be used as a tool to manage risks. FMEA was designed to assess product risk, HACCP (hazard analysis and critical control point) was developed to manage food safety hazards, and so on.

FAILURE MODE AND EFFECTS ANALYSIS[3]

Failure mode and effects analysis (FMEA) has been in use for many years and is used extensively in the automotive industry. FMEA is used for analyzing designs or processes for potential failure. Its aim is to reduce risk of failure. Therefore, there are two types in general use: the DFMEA for analyzing potential design failures and the PFMEA for analyzing potential process failures.

For example, a small organization engaged in bidding for military contracts for high-tech devices successfully used an FMEA to identify and assess risks for a product never made before. The FMEA aided in evaluating design inputs, assured that potential failure modes were identified and addressed, provided for the identification of the failure modes' root cause(s), determined the actions necessary to eliminate or reduce the potential failure mode, and added a high degree of objectivity to the design review process. The FMEA also directed attention to design features that required additional testing or development, documented risk reduction efforts, provided lessons-learned documentation to aid future FMEAs, and assured that the design was performed with a customer focus.

The FMEA methodology is:

1. Define the device design inputs or process functions and requirements

2. Identify a failure mode (what could go wrong) and the potential effects of the failure

3. Rank the severity of the effects (using a 1–10 scale, where 1 is minor and 10 is major and without warning)

4. Establish what the root cause(s) could be

5. Rate the likelihood of occurrence for the failure using a 1–10 scale

6. Document the present design or present process controls regarding prevention and detection

7. Rate the likelihood of these controls—detecting the failure using a 1–10 scale

8. Compute the risk priority number
   (RPN = severity × occurrence × detection)

9. Recommend preventive/corrective action (what action, who will do it, when)—note that preventive action is listed first when dealing with the design stage and corrective action first if analyzing potential process failures

10. Return to number 2 if other potential failures exist

11. Build and test a prototype

12. Redo the FMEA after test results are obtained and any necessary or desired changes are made

13. Retest and, if acceptable, place in production

14. Document the FMEA process for the knowledge base

The collaboration with employees who have been involved in design, development, production, and customer service activities is critical because their knowledge, ideas, and questions about a new product design will be based on their experience at different stages of product realization. Furthermore, if your employees are also some of your customers (end users), obtaining and documenting the employees' experience is most useful. This experiential input, along with examinations of similar designs (and their FMEAs, nonconforming product and corrective action records, and customer feedback reports), is often the best source for analysis input. Figure 25.1 shows a sample PFMEA.

CRITICAL TO QUALITY[4]

In the realm of Six Sigma methodology, there is a tool for displaying the causal relationship among the key business indicators (labeled as Y), the critical-to-quality (CTQ) process outputs (labeled y) that directly affect the Ys, and the causal factors that affect the process outputs (labeled as x). For example: One key business indicator (an outcome, a dependent variable) is customer retention (Y). CTQ outputs are services delivered on time (y), services delivered correctly (y), and customer satisfied (y). Factors affecting outputs (independent variables) are scheduling/ dispatch system (x); training of service personnel (x); supplies, vehicles, tools, and equipment (x); and time to complete service properly (x). See the relationship of x to y and y to Y in Figure 25.2.

Part VH

Item/Change Level __EVN-7823/C__ Process Responsibility __Housing Assembly__

Team Members __J. White, S. Burns, C. Smith__

FMEA No. __10554__

Page __1__ of __1__

Prepared by __J. White__

Date __4/3/05__

Operation No. Process function and/or requirements	Potential Failure Mode	Potential Effect(s) of Failure	Severity	Class	Potential Cause(s) of Failure	Occurrence	Current Controls Prevention	Current Controls Detection	Detection	RPN	Recommended Actions	Responsible and Target Completion Date	Action Results				
													Actions Taken	S	O	D	R P N
40 Press bearing into housing	Bearing not fully seated	Insufficient support for outer race, noisy gear	7		Improper setup of press	5	First-piece approval Machine setup training	Depth check by operator	7	2 4 5	Add auto depth check to force electronics	J. White 5/10/05		7	5	2	70
	Assemble wrong bearing	Bearing moves up when nut on mating shaft is torqued, bearing failure	9	X	Operator loaded wrong bearing to chute	8	Push-in force measurement	Daily inventory balance of bill of materials	2	1 0 8	None						

Figure 25.1 Consumer risk or Type II error.

Source: Used with permission of APLOMET.

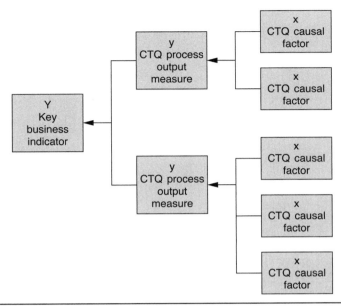

Figure 25.2 Causal relationship in developing key process measurements.

The selecting of the key metrics to be included in the balanced scorecard is illustrative of how key indicators are established. The top-level metrics of the scorecard (typically four) are the ones executives use to make their decisions. Each of these top-level metrics (dependent variables) is backed up by metrics on independent variables, usually available through computer access. Thus if the marketing vice president wants to know the cause for a negative trend in the customer metric of the scorecard, the vice president can drill down to the variable affecting the negative trend.

HACCP

Hazard analysis and critical control point (HACCP) is an effective tool to prevent food from being contaminated. HACCP is not a new concept. The Pillsbury Co. developed it for NASA in the late 1950s to prevent food safety incidents on manned space flights. The technique identifies hazards, assesses their significance, and develops control measures (treats the risk).

Seven Principles

1. Conduct a hazard analysis
2. Determine the critical control points (CCPs)
3. Establish critical limits (CLs)
4. Establish monitoring procedures
5. Establish corrective action

6. Establish verification plan

7. Establish records and documented procedures

12 HACCP Application Steps

1. Assemble the HACCP team

2. Describe the product

3. Identify the intended use

4. Construct flow diagram

5. On-site confirmation of flow diagram

6. List all potential hazards

   — Conduct hazard analysis

   — Consider control measures

7. Determine the CCPs

8. Establish critical limits for each CCP

9. Establish a monitoring system for each CCP

10. Establish corrective actions

11. Establish verification procedures

12. Establish documentation and recordkeeping

HHA[5]

The purpose of Health Hazard Assessment (HHA) is to identify health hazards, evaluate proposed hazardous materials, and propose protective measures to reduce the associated risk to an acceptable level.

The first step of the HHA is to identify and determine quantities of potentially hazardous materials or physical agents (noise, radiation, heat stress, cold stress) involved with the system and its logistical support. The next step is to analyze how these materials or physical agents are used in the system and for its logistical support. Based on the use, quantity, and type of substance/agent, estimate where and how personnel exposures may occur and if possible the degree or frequency of exposure. The final step includes incorporation into the design of the system and its logistical support equipment/facilities, cost-effective controls to reduce exposures to acceptable levels. The life-cycle costs of required controls could be high, and consideration of alternative systems may be appropriate.

An HHA evaluates the hazards and costs due to system component materials, evaluates alternative materials, and recommends materials that reduce the associated risks and life-cycle costs. Materials are evaluated if (because of their physical, chemical, or biological characteristics; quantity; or concentrations) they cause or contribute to adverse effects in organisms or offspring, pose a substantial present or future danger to the environment, or result in damage to or loss of equipment or property during the system's life cycle.

An HHA should include the evaluation of the following:

- Chemical hazards—Hazardous materials that are flammable, corrosive, toxic, carcinogens or suspected carcinogens, systemic poisons, asphyxiants, or respiratory irritants

- Physical hazards (e.g., noise, heat, cold, ionizing and non-ionizing radiation)

- Biological hazards (e.g., bacteria, fungi)

- Ergonomic hazards (e.g., lifting, task saturation)

- Other hazardous materials that may be introduced by the system during manufacture, operation, or maintenance

The evaluation is performed in the context of the following:

- System, facility, and personal protective equipment requirements (e.g., ventilation, noise attenuation, radiation barriers) to allow safe operation and maintenance. When feasible engineering designs are not available to reduce hazards to acceptable levels, alternative protective measures must be specified (e.g., protective clothing, operation or maintenance procedures to reduce risk to an acceptable level).

- Potential material substitutions and projected disposal issues. The HHA discusses long-term effects such as the cost of using alternative materials over the life cycle or the capability and cost of disposing of a substance.

- Hazardous material data. The HHA describes the means for identifying and tracking information for each hazardous material. Specific categories of health hazards and impacts that may be considered are acute health, chronic health, cancer, contact, flammability, reactivity, and environment.

The HHA's hazardous materials evaluation must include the following:

- Identification of the hazardous materials by name(s) and stock numbers (or CAS numbers); the affected system components and processes; the quantities, characteristics, and concentrations of the materials in the system; and source documents relating to the materials.

- Determination of the conditions under which the hazardous materials can release or emit components in a form that may be inhaled, ingested, absorbed by living beings, or leached into the environment.

- Characterization of material hazards and determination of reference quantities and hazard ratings for system materials in question.

- Estimation of the expected usage rate of each hazardous material for each process or component for the system and program-wide impact.

- Recommendations for the disposition of each hazardous material identified. If a reference quantity is exceeded by the estimated usage rate, material substitution or altered processes may be considered to reduce risks associated with the material hazards while evaluating the impact on program costs.

For each proposed and alternative material, the assessment must provide the following data for management review:

- Material identification. Includes material identity, common or trade names, chemical name, chemical abstract service (CAS) number, national stock number (NSN), local stock number, physical state, and manufacturers and suppliers.

- Material use and quantity. Includes component name, description, operations details, total system and life cycle quantities to be used, and concentrations of any mixtures.

- Hazard identification. Identifies the adverse effects of the material on personnel, the system, environment, or facilities.

- Toxicity assessment. Describes expected frequency, duration, and amount of exposure. References for the assessment must be provided.

- Risk calculations. Includes classification of severity and probability of occurrence, acceptable levels of risk, any missing information, and discussions of uncertainties in the data or calculations.

For work performed under contract, details to be specified in the SOW (statement of work) include:

- Minimum risk severity and probability reporting thresholds

- Any selected hazards, hazardous areas, hazardous materials or other specific items to be examined or excluded

- Specification of desired analysis techniques and/or report formats

Appendix A
ASQ Code of Ethics

Fundamental Principles

ASQ requires its members and certification holders to conduct themselves ethically by:

    I. Being honest and impartial in serving the public, their employers, customers, and clients.

    II. Striving to increase the competence and prestige of the quality profession, and

    III. Using their knowledge and skill for the enhancement of human welfare.

Members and certification holders are required to observe the tenets set forth below:

Relations with the Public

Article 1—Hold paramount the safety, health, and welfare of the public in the performance of their professional duties.

Relations with Employers, Customers, and Clients

Article 2—Perform services only in their areas of competence.

Article 3—Continue their professional development throughout their careers and provide opportunities for the professional and ethical development of others.

Article 4—Act in a professional manner in dealings with ASQ staff and each employer, customer or client.

Article 5—Act as faithful agents or trustees and avoid conflict of interest and the appearance of conflicts of interest.

Relations with Peers

Article 6—Build their professional reputation on the merit of their services and not compete unfairly with others.

Article 7—Assure that credit for the work of others is given to those to whom it is due.

Appendix B
Notes on Compliance, Conformance, and Conformity

Provided by handbook reviewer Akio Miura.

COMPLIANCE

An affirmative indication or judgment that **the supplier** of a product or service has met the requirements of a relevant specification, contract or regulation; also the state of meeting the requirements. (ANSI/ASQC A3-1978 and 1987)

The state of **an organization** that meets prescribed specifications, contract terms, regulations or standards. (ASQ Web Glossary, http://www.asq.org; search for Glossary)

Compliance refers to the delivery of contract items.

CONFORMANCE

An affirmative indication or judgment that **a product or service** has met the requirements of a relevant specification, contract or regulation; also the state of meeting the requirements. (ANSI/ASQC A3-1978 and 1987)

An affirmative indication or judgment that **a product or service** has met the requirements of a relevant specification, contract or regulation. (ASQ Web Glossary, http://www.asq.org; search for Glossary)

Conformance customarily refers to an assessment not dependent on the passage of time in product use, as contrasted to *reliability* which has a time connotation. (ANSI/ASQC A3-1978 and 1987)

CONFORMITY

The fulfilling by an item or service of specification requirements (may refer to a single quality characteristic in control or appraisal phases or to the entire set of specification requirements). (ANSI/ASQC A3-1978 and 1987)

Definitions of *conformity* and *nonconformity* are found in ISO 9000:2005, clauses 3.6.1 and 3.6.2 as: fulfillment of a requirement and non-fulfillment of a requirement respectively. The ISO 9000:2005 vocabulary standard specifies the terminology of quality management systems. The set of quality management system standards include: ISO 9000:2005, ISO 9001:2005, ISO 9004:2000, and ISO 19011:2002. The ISO definitions may not be appropriate for all industry sections.

Appendix C
Example Guide for Technical Specialists (or Subject Matter Experts)

Provided by handbook reviewer Norman Frank.

INTRODUCTION

As a technical specialist, you are responsible for using your technical expertise and experience to investigate, examine, and evaluate technical processes and end-product adequacy in the audit area where you have been assigned. You are also responsible for evaluating the effectiveness of the processes and implementation. You will be required to document the results of your efforts.

As the technical specialist, you are to evaluate the methodology and steps of the technical processes that have been developed. Whether or not the approach is the way you would do it, your job is to evaluate the adequacy and effectiveness of the approach that was actually used.

CONTACT

The team leader is your key contact for all audit activities and the one to whom you will report. When you are in direct contact with personnel from the auditee organization (the organization or area being audited), you will be accompanied by an audit team qualified auditor.

JOB DESCRIPTION

Prior to the audit:

- Identify the technical processes you need to review for adequacy during the audit.

- Determine and secure the information needed to conduct a thorough investigation, examination, and evaluation of the technical processes used.

- Indicate potential sources of the information (requirements, standards, specifications, operation manuals, test and evaluation methods, and so on) needed to evaluate process performance.

- Develop checklists covering the activities you will be monitoring.

Next you will need to prepare a checklist to guide your efforts. Some typical types of checklist questions include:

- Are technical requirements appropriately identified? Are they adequately implemented for the current process? Can they be traced to their source?

- Do technical documents show a clear flow of requirements from higher levels (policy and operation manuals) to lower levels (detailed work instructions and procedures)? Are the origins/sources of the requirements appropriately identified?

- Are the methods and techniques used to perform technical tasks effective? Do they meet the established criteria (for example, good practices, certification requirements, and so on)? Are they traceable to their source?

- Are applications of computer software appropriately documented? Are the codes adequately verified and validated?

- Are assumptions used in the performance of scientific and engineering work clearly identified and verified or identified for verification at a future time?

- Are the methods used to control identified errors, omissions, and deficiencies in technical work formalized in approved implementing documents? Are the methods effective in making corrections and adjustments? When appropriate, are corrective actions taken to prevent recurrence of errors, omissions, and deficiencies?

During the audit, as well as when documenting your results on the checklist, you should include:

- Identification number, title, and revision of any documents reviewed

- The results of the evaluation of objective evidence reviewed

- Name, title, and phone number of those individuals in the organization with whom you come in contact

Prior to the postaudit (exit) meeting, you must provide the team leader with a paragraph stating what you looked at and the final results, a statement evaluating the effectiveness of the processes in achieving the intended goals, and your completed checklists.

THE REPORT

The team leader may need your assistance following the audit to provide additional input or clarifications for the final report or to develop corrective action reports.

Appendix D
The Institute of Internal Auditors Code of Ethics

INTRODUCTION

The purpose of The Institute's Code of Ethics is to promote an ethical culture in the profession of internal auditing.

Internal auditing is an independent, objective assurance and consulting activity designed to add value and improve an organization's operations. It helps an organization accomplish its objectives by bringing a systematic, disciplined approach to evaluate and improve the effectiveness of risk management, control, and governance processes.

A code of ethics is necessary and appropriate for the profession of internal auditing, founded as it is on the trust placed in its objective assurance about risk management, control, and governance. The Institute's Code of Ethics extends beyond the definition of internal auditing to include two essential components:

1. Principles that are relevant to the profession and practice of internal auditing;

2. Rules of Conduct that describe behavior norms expected of internal auditors. These rules are an aid to interpreting the Principles into practical applications and are intended to guide the ethical conduct of internal auditors.

The Code of Ethics together with The Institute's *Professional Practices Framework* and other relevant Institute pronouncements provide guidance to internal auditors serving others. "Internal auditors" refers to Institute members, recipients of or candidates for IIA professional certifications, and those who provide internal auditing services within the definition of internal auditing.

APPLICABILITY AND ENFORCEMENT

This Code of Ethics applies to both individuals and entities that provide internal auditing services.

Adopted by The IIA Board of Directors, June 17, 2000

For Institute members and recipients of or candidates for IIA professional certifications, breaches of the Code of Ethics will be evaluated and administered according to The Institute's Bylaws and Administrative Guidelines. The fact that a particular conduct is not mentioned in the Rules of Conduct does not prevent it from being unacceptable or discreditable, and therefore, the member, certification holder, or candidate can be liable for disciplinary action.

PRINCIPLES

Internal auditors are expected to apply and uphold the following principles:

Integrity

The integrity of internal auditors establishes trust and thus provides the basis for reliance on their judgment.

Objectivity

Internal auditors exhibit the highest level of professional objectivity in gathering, evaluating, and communicating information about the activity or process being examined. Internal auditors make a balanced assessment of all the relevant circumstances and are not unduly influenced by their own interests or by others in forming judgments.

Confidentiality

Internal auditors respect the value and ownership of information they receive and do not disclose information without appropriate authority unless there is a legal or professional obligation to do so.

Competency

Internal auditors apply the knowledge, skills, and experience needed in the performance of internal auditing services.

RULES OF CONDUCT

1. Integrity

Internal auditors:

1.1. Shall perform their work with honesty, diligence, and responsibility.

1.2. Shall observe the law and make disclosures expected by the law and the profession.

1.3. Shall not knowingly be a party to any illegal activity, or engage in acts that are discreditable to the profession of internal auditing or to the organization.

1.4. Shall respect and contribute to the legitimate and ethical objectives of the organization.

2. Objectivity

Internal auditors:

2.1. Shall not participate in any activity or relationship that may impair or be presumed to impair their unbiased assessment. This participation includes those activities or relationships that may be in conflict with the interests of the organization.

2.2. Shall not accept anything that may impair or be presumed to impair their professional judgment.

2.3. Shall disclose all material facts known to them that, if not disclosed, may distort the reporting of activities under review.

3. Confidentiality

Internal auditors:

3.1. Shall be prudent in the use and protection of information acquired in the course of their duties.

3.2. Shall not use information for any personal gain or in any manner that would be contrary to the law or detrimental to the legitimate and ethical objectives of the organization.

4. Competency

Internal auditors:

4.1. Shall engage only in those services for which they have the necessary knowledge, skills, and experience.

4.2. Shall perform internal auditing services in accordance with the *International Standards for the Professional Practice of Internal Auditing*.

4.3. Shall continually improve their proficiency and the effectiveness and quality of their services.

Appendix E
History of Quality Assurance and Auditing

QUALITY ASSURANCE AND AUDIT FUNCTIONS

Quality has been defined as fitness for use, conformance to requirements, and the pursuit of excellence. Even though the concept of quality has existed from early times, the study and definition of quality have been given prominence only in the last century. Following the Industrial Revolution and the rise of mass production, it became important in the 1920s to better define and control the quality of products. Originally, the goal of quality was to ensure that engineering requirements were met in final products. Later, as manufacturing processes became more complex, quality developed into a discipline for controlling process variation as a means of producing quality products.

In the 1950s, the quality profession expanded to include the quality assurance and quality audit functions. The drivers of independent verification of quality were primarily industries in which public health and safety were paramount. In the 1980s, businesses realized that quality wasn't just the domain of products and manufacturing processes. Total quality management (TQM) principles were developed to include all processes in a company, including management functions and service sectors.

Over the past several years, there have been many interpretations of what quality is, beyond the dictionary definition of "general goodness." Other terms describing quality include *reduction of variation*, *value-added*, and *conformance to specifications*. ISO 9000:2005 defines quality as the degree to which a set of inherent characteristics fulfills requirements.[1] Simply stated, quality is meeting customer requirements. Others prefer to describe quality in terms of achieving customer satisfaction. Another description of quality that takes into account the customer and the provider of the product or service is "Quality for the customer is getting what you were expecting and quality for the provider (supplier) is getting it right the first time."[2]

A system of quality management includes all activities of the overall management function that determine the quality policy, objectives, and responsibilities and their implementation. A management system provides the means of establishing a policy and objectives and the means to achieve those objectives.[3]

Quality assurance and quality control are two aspects of quality management. *Quality assurance* consists of that "part of quality management focused on providing confidence that quality requirements will be fulfilled."[4] The confidence provided by quality assurance is twofold—internally to management and externally to customers, government agencies, regulators, certifiers, and third parties. While some quality assurance and quality control activities are interrelated, *quality control* is defined as that "part of quality management focused on fulfilling quality requirements."[5] While quality assurance relates to how a process is performed or how a product is made, quality control is more the inspection aspect of quality management. *Inspection* is the process of measuring, examining, and testing to gauge one or more characteristics of a product or service and the comparison of these with specified requirements to determine conformity. Products, processes, and various other results can be inspected to make sure that the object coming off a production line, or the service being provided, is correct and meets specifications.

Over the last several years, the concepts of quality have expanded from manufacturing to other sectors such as service. For some service organizations, the concept of quality control is foreign because there is no tangible product to inspect and control. The quality assurance function in a service organization may not include quality control of the service but may include quality control of any products involved in providing the service. A service may include products that are documents (such as a report, contract, or design) or tangible products such as a rental car or units of blood. It may be necessary to control product quality in a service organization to ensure that the service meets customer requirements.

Auditing is part of the quality assurance function. It is important to ensure quality because it is used to compare actual conditions with requirements and to report those results to management. "An audit is not an alternative to an inspection operation. . . . The auditor may use inspection techniques as an evaluation tool, but the audit should not be involved in carrying out any verification activities leading to the actual acceptance or rejection of a product or service. An audit should be involved with the evaluation of the process and controls covering the production and verification activities."[6] Auditors make observations and report their findings. During an audit or investigation, an *observation* could be information that may be evidence to support audit conclusions. A *finding* is a conclusion of importance based on observation. (Refer to ISO 9000:2005, pp. 7–18, and ISO 19011S:2004, pp. 2–3, for additional terms and definitions.)

Formal management systems have evolved to direct and control organizations. There are quality management systems (QMSs) as well as environmental or other management systems. There are standards such as ISO 9001 that list requirements for a QMS. Industry sectors such as automotive, aerospace, government, and telecommunications have their own versions of QMS requirements. Now, organizations may have several different management systems (such as quality, environmental, safety, and health), and each of these systems may be audited. An audit of a QMS is called a *quality system audit*. An audit of an environmental management system (EMS) is an *environmental system audit*.

Some standards require continual improvement, which is an integral part of many management systems. There are many improvement programs that claim to improve quality to reduce costs and increase customer satisfaction. In the 1980s, TQM programs were established. Most recently, programs such as Six Sigma and lean practices have renewed interest in the application of quality tools to reduce waste.

THEORIES AND PRACTICES IN AUDITING

Audits are fact-finding exercises that provide information to management. This information identifies opportunities and reduces the risk of decisions made by management. It is management's responsibility to take appropriate action based on the audit information provided.

The audit is a long-established and well-respected activity in the accounting profession. Because of the similarities in the activities of financial auditing and nonfinancial auditing, process and system audit professionals have adopted the same word, *audit,* complete with some of the same modifiers.

Audits emerged shortly after World War II and gained momentum when the military began issuing standards and specifications for products and the federal government issued safety regulations for food and worker safety. Auditing originally resembled an inspection activity and was developed primarily in large manufacturing industries (such as electronics) and in high-risk fields (such as the nuclear, food, pharmaceutical, and aerospace industries).

Audits are planned, objective, and independent investigations of products, processes, or systems. By examining documentation, implementation, and effectiveness, auditing is used to evaluate, confirm, or verify activities related to the audit criteria (such as standards, procedures, or customer requirements). "The audit may be a single occurrence or a repetitive activity, depending on the purpose and the results of both the audit and the product/service, process, or management system concerned."[7] A properly conducted audit is a positive and constructive process. It helps prevent problems through the identification of activities likely to create problems. Problems generally arise from the inefficiency or inadequacy of the concerned activity.

> All companies and enterprises, regardless of size, can benefit by examining their activities and management systems. This applies no less to local government, civil service, commerce and the service industries than it does to the manufacturing industry.[8]

The principles of auditing apply to any type of management assessment. No valid reason exists for separating management auditing into subcomponents. Management controls the resources. "The goals of quality, safety, environmental stewardship, and efficiency are all driven by the same set of rules: define requirements, produce to those requirements, monitor achievement of those requirements, and continuously improve on the requirements."[9]

In 1994 countries gave up their individual quality audit standards (in the United States it was ANSI/ASQC Q1-1986, Generic Guidelines for Auditing of Quality Systems) in favor of an international consensus auditing standard called ISO 10011:1994, Guidelines for Auditing Quality Systems. In 2002, a new standard (ISO 19011, Guidelines for Quality and/or Environmental Management System

Auditing) was issued that combines quality and environmental audit guidelines. Since auditing techniques can be applied to any system or process, the continued combining and evolution of good audit practices is to be expected.

What Audits Measure

Audits examine products, processes, and systems with respect to predetermined standards. Within this context, audits evaluate one or more of the following: the adequacy of the documentation, adherence to the documented and undocumented procedures, implementation and maintenance of the procedures, and the effectiveness of the procedures as implemented to accomplish intended objectives.

Adequacy is defined as "the state of being sufficient for a specified requirement." An audit evaluation for adequacy usually consists of reviews to verify the sufficiency of documentation for defining work and of records as evidence of satisfactory work completion. This typically includes a review to see if the document is legible, understandable, and can be reasonably implemented. Adequacy alone, however, does not verify whether work was performed correctly unless it is evaluated in conjunction with compliance/conformance or the implementation and maintenance of the documented system.

Compliance refers to the affirmative indication or judgment that the supplier of products or services has met the requirements of the relevant specifications, contract, or regulation. In auditing, the terms *conformity* and *compliance* may be used interchangeably to report the results. However, regulated industries tend to favor the use of the terms *compliance* and *noncompliance*. In the international conformity assessment program, the terms *conformity* and *nonconformity* are normally used. The term *compliance audit* is also used to indicate that the purpose of an audit is to determine the degree of compliance to rules and regulations.

> The idea of conformity assessment started in the 1970s as international trade increased under the General Agreements on Tariffs and Trade (GATT), now the World Trade Organization (WTO). It was, and continues to be, principally associated with the inspection of commodities such as grain, cement, and light bulbs. Sellers and buyers needed testing of shipped products, but they didn't trust each other's laboratories. So they agreed to use a trusted, third-party lab approved by the government or other neutral authority. As the first edition of the ISO 9001 QMS standard was published in 1987, the idea arose to apply this commodity testing approach to management systems. Whether it is a product or system, the name for all this is "conformity assessment."

Compliance looks for strict adherence to a set of rules, which may include requirements and standards. The compliance audit is not the arena for questioning these rules; they are set and identified for the audit. Examples of audits involving compliance include regulatory and high-risk processes or products (see Appendix B, "Notes on Compliance, Conformance, and Conformity").

Regulatory audits are used in cases where activities are regulated by the government. Among these regulated activities are production of energy, stewardship of the environment, production of food, protection of workers, and use of medical products. Auditors verify that the applicable laws and regulations in these areas are being implemented to ensure the health and safety of consumers.

High-risk audits are used when the consequences of failure are unacceptable, such as in the launching of airplanes, submarines, and rockets. A complete and thorough audit of the finished product is necessary before it is activated or placed into service. The audit checks inspection records, craft qualification records, design review records, and other forms of proof.[10]

A management system audit assesses conformity and whether procedures and instructions (and the implementation of those procedures and instructions) meet preestablished goals and objectives. The goals verified as part of effectiveness are usually related to overall objectives or ongoing improvement of the organization.

> There has been more than a decade of disagreement regarding whether compliance and conformance are the same thing. The Internal Organization for Standardization (ISO series standards) technical committees are making the case that there is a difference. They are promoting the idea that a noncompliance occurs when there is violation of a law, a regulation, a code, or a contract (if legally enforced), while a nonconformity occurs when there is a difference between actual performance and requirements. Further, the quality and environmental technical committees prefer to use the term *conformity* instead of *conformance*. ISO 9000:2005, clause 3.6.1 states that although *conformance* is synonymous with *conformity*, it is deprecated (out of favor). Even though it is not apparent that this tenet improves the effectiveness of audits or fixes any problems, it does highlight the need for compliance audits and helps stress the difference between compliance and other types of audits.

How Audits Measure Results

Auditing is an information-intensive activity. Therefore, auditors need clear, useful information to make effective auditing judgments and decisions. Information must be based on data, but merely obtaining data does not guarantee that the information will be useful. For successful data collection, an auditor must know what questions to ask in order to collect, process, analyze, and then present the specific results. In addition, auditors must ensure that the data they collect represent objective evidence and support the existence or the verification of something.[11] Objective evidence may be obtained through observation, measurement, testing, and other means.

Data must be precise and accurate so that an auditor can form reliable conclusions. When using measurement and test devices, the auditor needs to verify that data-generating equipment has been properly maintained and calibrated. If an auditor is relying on the auditee's data, the auditor needs to ensure that the audited company has an effective calibration system for maintaining the measuring and testing equipment. The objective of the system is to ensure that measuring and testing equipment is adjusted, replaced, or repaired before it becomes inaccurate.

The system should consist of:

- Labels, tags, color codes, engraved identification serial numbers, or other means of tracing the measurement device to the individual calibration record

- A requirement for calibration practices

- Certified primary company or reference standards traceable to industry, national, or international standards, such as the National Institute of Standards and Technology (NIST)

- Listings by department of calibration status and delinquents (instruments that are out of calibration cannot be used to certify product and must be removed from service until calibrated)

- All personally owned tools used to make pass-fail and go/no-go decisions should be in the system and calibrated

- Inspection checks of calibration should be made by inspection department personnel before items are signed off[12]

In addition to defining the accuracy of inspection equipment, an auditee's calibration procedures must address the issue of remedial action or correction if equipment is found to be out of calibration. In other words, how did the out-of-calibration equipment affect the products manufactured or tested with that piece of equipment? If necessary, production should be halted or a product recall issued.

ENVIRONMENTAL, SAFETY, AND HEALTH PROGRAMS AND AUDIT FUNCTIONS

Many special-needs programs have evolved during the twentieth century. These programs have been mandated by law to protect the public. Environmental, safety, energy, aerospace, and health laws and regulations have been passed, and organizations have established departments and functions to ensure compliance. Internal audit programs were established with the purpose of ensuring that procedures and activities conform to regulatory requirements. An audit department may be titled the Regulatory Compliance Audit Department. Internal compliance audits help organizations prepare for unannounced governmental audits. Failure to comply could result in fines or closure of an operation.

Similar to quality, management system standards are available for many special-interest programs. Based on the management system requirements, audits are conducted on environmental, safety, energy, health, aerospace, and laboratory programs. The purpose of the audit is to go beyond compliance. There are management systems that support compliance and self-evaluation to ensure adequate and effectively implemented programs.

Environmental auditing began in the United States in the 1970s as a way for organizations to ensure that they were complying with any number of federal and state rules and regulations developed to protect the environment. Today, in addition to judging legal compliance, environmental auditing is used by many organizations to help prevent and eliminate waste, minimize environmental impact, improve environmental management practices, and, in the long run, save money.

Like environmental auditing, information-systems auditing began as a complement to financial auditing, a tool to ensure that errors were not made and data were complete. With the technological advancements of the last few years, most organizations now consider their information technology (IT) to be one of their most valued assets. IT is widely used, from basic functions (such as producing payroll checks) to advanced functions (such as management decision making). Therefore, it is necessary to evaluate not only the accuracy of data but the controls (the process) that govern the origination of data, the access to data, the use of data, and the training that must accompany all these aspects.

Since the requirements of the Sarbanes-Oxley Act of 2002 have been instituted, some organizations are now faced with an even greater IT challenge. Computers are now entity-wide and are not just confined to the mainframe. The challenge is to develop plans that enable the achievement of entity-wide controls, such as identifying, assessing, and responding to IT risks. Since one of the objectives of auditing is to identify and mitigate risks, a well-planned and well-executed internal IT audit program is a valuable asset to an organization faced with this situation.

Although many companies continue to focus on compliance auditing for safety issues, forward-thinking companies are moving toward auditing the management process regarding safety, as an opportunity to look for areas of continual improvement. In order to audit effectively in this manner, management commitment and responsibility become a major area of the audit. An effectively implemented audit can reveal whether management understands why it is important to provide a safe environment for employees and the consequences of not doing so (such as financial loss due to fines and loss of reputation). The audit can also judge the effectiveness of the processes that have been put into place (process audit) to ensure a safe environment. The auditor needs to identify the inputs to this process—such as regulations, training, personal protective equipment, and the process itself—and the outputs (which hopefully are safe, protected, and happy employees).

Auditing is the final step in the successful implementation of an occupational safety and health (OSH) program. It verifies that the planning, organization, and design of an OSH program have been implemented effectively and are working. Audits can also provide valuable information to individuals in management who wish to continually improve their processes. Audits are a way of identifying improvement opportunities without waiting for an accident to happen. These audits differ from safety inspection–type audits. They not only verify the effective implementation of an OSH program but also identify the strengths and weaknesses of a program and determine the extent of compliance to federal and state rules and regulations. Auditing steps used for any type of audit—such as planning, preparation, documentation review, personnel interviews, observing work activities, preparation of an audit report resulting in corrective actions, and an exit meeting apprising management of the results and any opportunities for improvement—are also used in an OSH audit. The most important part of an OSH audit is the audit report. The audit report serves as a valuable management tool informing management of the areas that are working well and those that need attention.

Appendix F
Certified Quality Auditor Body of Knowledge

The topics in this Body of Knowledge (BOK) include additional detail in the form of subtext explanations and cognitive level. These details will be used by the Exam Development Committee as guidelines for writing test questions, and are designed to help candidates prepare for the exam by identifying specific content within each topic that may be tested. The subtext is not intended to limit the subject matter or be all-inclusive of what might be covered in an exam but is intended to clarify how the topics relate to a Quality Auditor's role. The descriptor in parentheses at the end of each entry refers to the maximum cognitive level at which the topic will be tested. A more comprehensive description of cognitive levels is provided at the end of this document.

The CQA examinations will continue to present a number of case studies. Each case study will include a brief scenario outlining critical details about an audit situation. In addition, each case study will be supported by related audit documents. The documents will be contained in a separate booklet "Confidential Audit Documents—CQA Case Studies" that will be part of the test materials distributed at the examination. Approximately 15–20% (25–30 questions) of the test will be devoted to these case studies. Although the questions related to these cases will use the same four-choice answer format as the rest of the test, the use of scenario details and sample documents will allow the candidates to apply their critical thinking skills in evaluating realistic situations and accompanying documents, memos, etc.

   I. Auditing Fundamentals (27 Questions)

      A. Types of quality audits

         1. Method

            Define, differentiate, and analyze various audit types by method: product, process, desk, department, function, element, system, management. (Analyze)

         2. Auditor-auditee relationship

            Define, differentiate, and analyze various audit types by auditor-auditee relationship: first-party, second-party, third-party, internal and external. (Analyze)

3. Purpose

Define, differentiate, and analyze various audit types by purpose: verification of corrective action (follow-up) audits, risk audits, accreditation (registration) and compliance audits, surveillance and for-cause audits. (Analyze)

4. Common elements with other audits

Identify elements such as audit purpose, data gathering techniques, tracing, etc., that quality audits have in common with environmental, safety, financial, and other types of audits. (Apply)

B. Purpose and scope of audits

1. Elements of purpose and scope

Describe and determine how the purpose of an audit can affect its scope. (Apply)

2. Benefits of audits

Analyze how audits can be used to provide an independent assessment of system effectiveness and efficiency, risks to the bottom line, and other organizational measures. (Analyze)

C. Criteria to audit against

Define and distinguish between various audit criteria, such as external (industry, national, international) standards, contracts, specifications, quality awards, policies, internal quality management system (QMS), sustainability, social responsibility, etc. (Analyze)

D. Roles and responsibilities of audit participants

Define and describe the functions and responsibilities of various audit participants, including audit team members, lead auditor, client, auditee, etc. (Apply)

E. Professional conduct and consequences for auditors

1. Professional conduct and responsibilities

Define and apply the ASQ Code of Conduct, concepts of due diligence and due care with respect to confidentiality and conflict of interest, and appropriate actions in response to the discovery of illegal activities or unsafe conditions. (Apply)

2. Legal consequences

Identify potential legal and financial ramifications of improper auditor actions (carelessness, negligence, etc.) in various situations, and anticipate the effect that certain audit results can have on an auditee's liability. (Apply)

3. Audit credibility

Identify and apply various factors that influence audit credibility, such as auditor independence, objectivity, and qualifications. (Apply)

II. Audit Process (42 Questions)

A. Audit preparation and planning

1. Elements of the audit planning process

Evaluate and implement the basic steps in audit preparation and planning: verify audit authority; determine the purpose, scope, and type of audit; identify the requirements to audit against and the resources necessary, including the size and number of audit teams. (Evaluate)

2. Auditor selection

Identify and examine various auditor selection criteria, such as education, experience, industry background, and subject-matter or technical expertise. (Analyze)

3. Audit-related documentation

Identify the sources of pre-audit information and examine audit-related documentation, such as audit criteria references and results from prior audits. (Analyze)

4. Logistics

Identify and organize audit-related logistics, including travel, safety and security considerations, the need for escorts, translators, confidentiality agreements, clear right of access, etc. (Analyze)

5. Auditing tools and working papers

Identify the sampling plan or method and procedural guidelines to be used for the specific audit. Select and prepare working papers (checklists, log sheets, etc.) to document the audit. (Create)

6. Auditing strategies

Identify and use various tactical methods for conducting an audit, such as forward and backward tracing, discovery, etc. (Apply)

B. Audit performance

1. On-site audit management

Interpret situations throughout the performance of the audit to determine whether time is being managed well and when changes need to be made, such as revising planned audit team activities, reallocating resources, adjusting the audit plan, etc., and communicate with the auditee about any changes or other events related to the audit. (Analyze)

2. Opening meeting

Manage the opening meeting of an audit by identifying the audit's purpose and scope, describing any scoring or rating criteria that will be used during the audit, creating a record of the attendees, reviewing the audit schedule, and answering questions as needed. (Apply)

3. Audit data collection and analysis

Use various data collection methods to capture information: conducting interviews, observing work activities, taking physical measurements, examining documents, etc. Evaluate the results to determine their importance for providing audit evidence. (Evaluate)

4. Establishment of objective evidence

Identify and differentiate characteristics of objective evidence, such as observed, measured, confirmed or corroborated, and documented. (Analyze)

5. Organization of objective evidence

Classify evidence in terms of significance, severity, frequency, and level of risk. Evaluate the evidence for its potential impact on product, process, system, cost of quality, etc., and determine whether additional investigation is required to meet the scope of the audit. (Evaluate)

6. Exit and closing meetings

Formally manage these meetings: reiterate the audit's purpose, scope, and scoring or rating criteria, and create a record of the attendees. Present the audit results and obtain concurrence on evidence that could lead to an adverse conclusion. Discuss the next steps in the process (follow-up audit, additional evidence-gathering, etc.), and clarify who is responsible for performing those steps. (Apply)

C. Audit reporting

1. Report development and content

Group observations into actionable findings of significance, and identify the severity and risk to the client and the auditee. Use appropriate steps to generate the audit report: organize and summarize details, review and finalize results, emphasize critical issues, establish unique identifiers or codes for critical issues to facilitate tracking and monitoring, etc. (Create)

2. Effective reports

Develop and evaluate components of effective audit reports, including background information, executive summary, prioritized results (observations, findings, opportunities for improvement, etc.). Use graphical tools or other means of emphasizing conclusions, and develop a timeline for auditee response and/or corrections. (Create)

3. Final audit report steps

Obtain necessary approvals for the audit report and distribute it according to established procedures. Identify the contents of the audit file and retain the file in accordance with established policies and procedures. (Apply)

D. Audit follow-up and closure

1. Elements of the corrective action process

Identify and evaluate various elements: assignment of responsibility for problem identification; the performance of root cause analysis and recurrence prevention. (Evaluate)

2. Review of corrective action plan

Evaluate the acceptability of proposed corrective actions and schedule for completion. Identify and apply strategies for negotiating changes to unacceptable plans. (Evaluate)

3. Verification of corrective action

Determine the adequacy of corrective actions taken by verifying and evaluating new or updated procedures, observing revised processes, conducting follow-up audits, etc. (Evaluate)

4. Follow-up on ineffective corrective action

Develop strategies to use when corrective actions are not implemented or are not effective, such as communicating to the next level of management, reissuing the corrective action request, and re-auditing. (Create)

5. Audit closure

Identify and apply various elements of, and criteria for, audit closure. (Apply)

III. Auditor Competencies (25 Questions)

A. Auditor characteristics

Identify characteristics that make auditors effective: interpersonal skills, problem-solving skills, attention to detail, cultural awareness and sensitivity, ability to work independently as well as in a group or on a team, etc. (Apply)

B. On-site audit resource management

Identify and apply techniques for managing audit teams, scheduling audit meetings and activities, making logistical adjustments, etc. (Apply)

C. Conflict resolution

Identify typical conflict situations (mild to vehement disagreements, auditee delaying tactics, interruptions, etc.) and determine appropriate techniques for resolving them: clarifying the question or request, reiterating ground rules, intervention by another authority, cool-down periods, etc. (Analyze)

D. Communication and presentation techniques

Select and use written, oral, and electronic communication techniques for presentations made during audits for opening, closing, ad hoc meetings, etc. Use technical and managerial reporting techniques, including graphs, charts, diagrams, multimedia aids, etc., in various situations: domestic, global, in-person, virtual (e-audits), multiple sites simultaneously, etc. (Evaluate)

E. Interviewing techniques

Select and use appropriate interviewing techniques and methodologies. (Apply)

1. Use open-ended or closed question types

2. Use active listening, paraphrasing, empathy, etc.

3. Recognize and respond to non-verbal cues: body language, the significance of pauses and their length, etc.

4. Determine when and how to prompt a response: when supervisors are present, when interviewing a group of workers, when using a translator, etc.

F. Team dynamics

Define, describe, and apply various aspects of team dynamics. (Apply)

1. Team-building: clarifying roles and responsibilities for participants and leaders to ensure equitable treatment for all team members, providing clear direction for deliverables, identifying necessary resources and ensuring their availability, etc.

2. Team facilitation: providing coaching and guidance, defusing clashes between members, eliciting input from all, cultivating objectivity, overseeing progress, encouraging diverse views and consensus, etc.

3. Stages of team development: forming, storming, norming, and performing

IV. Audit Program Management and Business Applications (30 Questions)

A. Audit program management

1. Senior management support

   Identify and explain management's role in creating and supporting the audit function. (Understand)

2. Staffing and resource management

   Develop staffing budgets that provide adequate time for auditors to plan, conduct, and respond to scheduled audits, including time and resources that internal auditees need to participate. Identify any special equipment resources needed and ensure their adequacy and availability. Consider the use of and requirements for special audits (outsourced or contracted audits, virtual or e-audits, shared audits, etc.) as driven by costs, geography, etc. Evaluate results and adjust resources as needed on a regular basis. (Evaluate)

3. Auditor training and development

   Identify minimum audit knowledge and skill requirements for auditors. Provide training on various aspects of the audit process such as relevant standards, regulatory influences, facilitation techniques, etc. Provide training on diversity and cultural influences (ethnicity, gender, age, organized labor, etc.) and how such factors can affect communications and other interactions among audit participants. (Create)

4. Audit program evaluation

   Select the correct metric to evaluate the audit program, including tracking its effect on the bottom line and the risk to the organization. (Evaluate)

5. Internal audit program management

   Develop procedures, policies, and schedules to support the organization's objectives. Review internal audit results to identify systemic trends. (Create)

6. External audit program management

   Develop procedures, policies, and schedules in support of the supplier management program, including supplier qualification surveys, surveillance audits, supplier improvement, etc. (Create)

7. Best practices

   Analyze audit results to standardize best practices and lessons learned across the organization. (Analyze)

8. Organizational risk management

   Analyze how the audit program affects an organization's risk level and how the risk level can influence the number and frequency of audits performed. (Analyze) [Note: Tools and techniques for managing risk are covered in BOK area V.H.]

9. Management review input

Examine and summarize audit program results, trends, and changes in risk to provide input to management reviews. (Evaluate)

B. Business and financial impact

1. Auditing as a management tool

Use audit results to monitor continuous improvement, supplier management, customer satisfaction, etc., and to provide management with an independent view of the strategic plan's effectiveness and how well it is deployed. (Analyze)

2. Interrelationships of business processes

Identify how business units (receiving, product and process design, production, engineering, sales, marketing, field support, etc.) and multiple sites are interrelated, and recognize how their unique metrics and goals can be in conflict with one another. (Understand)

3. Cost of quality (COQ) principles

Identify, describe, and analyze the audit program's effect on the four COQ categories: prevention, appraisal, internal failure, external failure. (Analyze)

4. Emerging roles of the auditor

Recognize new roles and responsibilities for auditors, such as being process consultants and facilitators who can help resolve internal issues, improve processes, and add value to the organization. (Understand)

V. Quality Tools and Techniques (26 Questions)

A. Basic quality and problem-solving tools

Identify, interpret, and analyze: 1) Pareto charts, 2) cause and effect diagrams, 3) flowcharts, 4) statistical process control (SPC) charts, 5) check sheets, 6) scatter diagrams, 7) histograms, 8) root cause analysis, 9) plan-do-check-act (PDCA). (Analyze)

B. Process improvement techniques

1. Six sigma

Identify, interpret, and apply the six sigma DMAIC phases: define, measure, analyze, improve, control. (Apply)

2. Lean

Identify, interpret, and apply lean tools: 5S, standard operations, kanban (pull), error-proofing, value-stream mapping, etc. (Apply)

C. Basic statistics

1. Measures of central tendency

    Identify, interpret, and use mean, median, and mode. (Apply)

2. Measures of dispersion

    Identify, interpret, and use standard deviation and frequency distribution. (Apply)

3. Qualitative and quantitative analysis

    Describe qualitative data in terms of the nature, type, or attribute of an observation or condition. Describe how quantitative data is used to detect patterns or trends and how such analysis can indicate whether a problem is systemic or isolated. (Understand)

D. Process variation

1. Common and special cause

    Identify and distinguish between common and special cause variation. (Apply)

2. Process performance metrics

    Describe elements of C_p and C_{pk} process capability studies (process centering and stability, specification limits, underlying distribution, etc.), and how these studies and other performance metrics are used in relation to established goals. (Understand)

3. Outliers

    Describe their significance and impact. (Understand)

E. Sampling methods

1. Acceptance sampling plans

    Identify and interpret these plans for attributes and variables data. (Understand)

2. Types of sampling

    Describe and distinguish between random, stratified, and cluster sampling, and identify the uses and potential problems of non-statistical sampling. (Understand)

3. Sampling terms

    Define related terms including consumer and producer risk, confidence level, etc. (Understand)

F. Change control and configuration management

    Identify the principles of change control and configuration management systems as used in various applications: hardware, software (including security considerations), product, process, and service. (Understand)

G. Verification and validation

Define, distinguish between, and use various methods of verifying and validating processes. (Analyze)

H. Risk management tools

Identify methods for managing risk, including risk avoidance, mitigation, tradeoffs, etc., and describe tools and methods for estimating and controlling risk: failure mode and effects analysis (FMEA), hazard analysis and critical control points (HACCP), critical to quality (CTQ) analysis, health hazard analysis (HHA), etc. (Understand) [Note: Organizational risk management is covered in BOK area IV.A.8.]

SIX LEVELS OF COGNITION BASED ON BLOOM'S TAXONOMY (REVISED)

In addition to *content* specifics, the subtext detail also indicates the intended *complexity level* of the test questions for that topic. These levels are based on the Revised "Levels of Cognition" (from Bloom's Taxonomy, 2001) and are presented below in rank order, from least complex to most complex.

Remember

(Also commonly referred to as recognition, recall, or rote knowledge.) Be able to remember or recognize terminology, definitions, facts, ideas, materials, patterns, sequences, methodologies, principles, etc.

Understand

Be able to read and understand descriptions, communications, reports, tables, diagrams, directions, regulations, etc.

Apply

Be able to apply ideas, procedures, methods, formulas, principles, theories, etc., in job-related situations.

Analyze

Be able to break down information into its constituent parts and recognize the parts' relationship to one another and how they are organized; identify sublevel factors or salient data from a complex scenario.

Evaluate

Be able to make judgments regarding the value of proposed ideas, solutions, methodologies, etc., by using appropriate criteria or standards to estimate accuracy, effectiveness, economic benefits, etc.

Create

Be able to put parts or elements together in such a way as to show a pattern or structure not clearly there before; be able to identify which data or information from a complex set is appropriate to examine further or from which supported conclusions can be drawn.

Appendix G
Example Audit Program Schedule

Provided by handbook reviewer Buddy M. Smith.

Facility Audits (FAA/AEAs)		Auditor and Time Management			Year: 20XX											
Area/Subject/Procedure Audited	Reference	Auditor(s)	Actual Date(s)	Time Required (hrs)	January	February	March	April	May	June	July	August	September	October	November	December
Quality Management System	**145**															
Repair station inspection procedure manual	145.207 & 9	Any auditor's name	11/25/XX	2											X	
Quality control system	145.211			2											X	
Insp. of maint., preventive maint., or alterations	145.213			2											X	
Capabilities list	145.215			2											X	
Contract maintenance	145.217			2											X	
Record keeping	145.219			2											X	
Privileges and limitations of repair station cert.	145.20X			2											X	
Reports of failures, malfunctions, or defects	145.221			2											X	
FAA inspection of subcontractor product	145.223			2											X	
Other misc. quality areas				2											X	

Total hrs.   20

Facility Audits (FAA/AEAs)

Auditor and Time Management — **Year: 20XX**

Area/Subject/Procedure Audited	Reference	Auditor(s)	Actual Date(s)	Time Required (hrs)	January	February	March	April	May	June	July	August	September	October	November	December
Resources																
Housing, facilities, equipment, and data	145.10X			2											X	
Personnel requirements	145.15X			2											X	
Records of management, sup., and inspectors	145.161			2											X	
Training requirements	145.163			2											X	

Total hrs. 8

Shop Audits — **EASA**

	Reference	Auditor(s)	Actual Date(s)	Time Required (hrs)	January	February	March	April	May	June	July	August	September	October	November	December
Airframe shop	MIP-G			7										X		
Blade shop	MIP-G			4									X			
Electric shop	MIP-G			4									X			
Engine shop	MIP-G			12									X			
Finishes shop	MIP-G			5										X		
Fixed light aircraft (FLA)	MIP-G			5											X	
Hydraulic shop	MIP-G			5										X		
Instrument shop	MIP-G			5									X			
Machine shop	MIP-G			4										X		
Nondestructive test shop	MIP-G			5										X		
Parts department	MIP-G			4.5											X	
Radio shop	MIP-G			4									X			
Rotor shop	MIP-G			5.5									X			
Sheetmetal shop	MIP-G			7										X		
Transmission shop	MIP-G			4										X		

Total hrs. 81

Maintenance Repair Organization

		Auditor and Time Management			Year: 20XX											
Area/Subject/Procedure Audited	**Reference**	**Auditor(s)**	**Actual Date(s)**	**Time Required (hrs)**	**January**	**February**	**March**	**April**	**May**	**June**	**July**	**August**	**September**	**October**	**November**	**December**

Quality Management System

Area/Subject/Procedure Audited	Reference	Auditor(s)	Actual Date(s)	Time Required (hrs)	Jan	Feb	Mar	Apr	May	Jun	Jul	Aug	Sep	Oct	Nov	Dec
Quality management system manual	QM-001					X						X				
Control of documents [4.2.3]	QMSP-03					X						X				
Control of records [4.2.4]	QMSP-12					X						X				
Associated QCPs	Various					X						X				

Total hrs. 0

Management Responsibility Processes

Area/Subject/Procedure Audited	Reference	Auditor(s)	Actual Date(s)	Time Required (hrs)	Jan	Feb	Mar	Apr	May	Jun	Jul	Aug	Sep	Oct	Nov	Dec
Management review [5.6]	QMSP-09					X			X			X			X	

Total hrs. 0

Resources

Area/Subject/Procedure Audited	Reference	Auditor(s)	Actual Date(s)	Time Required (hrs)	Jan	Feb	Mar	Apr	May	Jun	Jul	Aug	Sep	Oct	Nov	Dec
Competence, awareness [6.2.2]	QMSP-04						X				X					
Associated QCPs	Various						X									

Total hrs. 0

Maintenance Repair Organization

Auditor and Time Management

Year: 20XX

Product Realization Processes

Area/Subject/Procedure Audited	Reference	Auditor(s)	Actual Date(s)	Time Required (hrs)	January	February	March	April	May	June	July	August	September	October	November	December
Planning for product realization [7.1 & 8.2.4]	QMSP-15							X					X			
Order/contract review [7.2]	QMSP-08							X					X			
Purchase orders [7.4]	QMSP-01							X								
Vendor evaluation [7.4]	QMSP-02							X								
Customer property [7.5.4]	QMSP-18								X				X			
Identification and traceability [7.5.3]	QMSP-19								X				X			
Preservation of product [7.5.5]	QMSP-20							X	X				X			
Monitoring and measuring devices [7.6]	QMSP-11							X								
Associated QCPs	Various							X								

Total hrs.   0

Improvement Processes

Area/Subject/Procedure Audited	Reference	Auditor(s)	Actual Date(s)	Time Required (hrs)	January	February	March	April	May	June	July	August	September	October	November	December
Customer satisfaction measure [8.2.1]	QMSP-14			8	X											
Internal quality audits [8.2.2]	QMSP-05															X
Control of nonconforming product [8.3]	QMSP-13							X		X						
Corrective action [8.5.2]	QMSP-06						X				X					
Preventive action [8.5.3]	QMSP-07						X				X					
Associated QCPs	Various						X				X					

Total hrs.   8

Product Line Audits		Auditor and Time Management			Year: 20XX											
Product Line Audited	Reference	Auditor(s)	Actual Date(s)	Time Required (hrs)	January	February	March	April	May	June	July	August	September	October	November	December
Shop	Work Order															
Engine: Fuel Pump—Bristow	P1462			3						X						
Engine:																
Fuel control: Fuel control—Shell Oil	P2725			4							X					
Fuel Control:																
Hydraulic:																
Hydraulic:																
Hydraulic:																
Other:																
Other:																
Other:																

Total hrs. 7

Appendix H
Example Third-Party Audit Organization Forms

Provided by handbook reviewer Charles N. Howell, of AQA International, LLC.

Process Audit Plan

(Client information sheet and xxF-019 contain additional supporting information)

Company Information	
Site: Address: Shifts:	Support locations:

8:00–8:15	Opening Meeting	
* Time	Management processes (top management must be present)	
	Policy and objectives Management review, including overview of • Internal audit • Continual improvement • Corrective and preventive action	Customer focus/satisfaction including • Surveys/customer metrics • Delivered part or service quality • On-time delivery • Returns, stop-shipment complaints, disruptions, warranty issues Prior audit issues Use of certificate and logo
The audit plan will focus on core processes. Support processes will be audited as audit trails develop. The plan may change based on information noted above or during the audit. Special items/issues (based on preaudit information—performance issues, new products/projects, concerns/complaints, ownership/management changes) will be assessed.		

Time	Processes audited by Auditor A	Time	Processes audited by Auditor B
All shifts must be audited for QS-9000 and TS 16949. Those with significant activity should be audited for all other conformance audits.			
	Auditor debrief and caucus		
	Closing Meeting (top management must be present)		

* It is expected that management processes will involve the audit team for 1–2 hours. Detailed assessment of internal audit, continual improvement, and corrective/preventive action should be planned to occur later.

Documentation Review

ISO 9001:2008

Client name:	Client rep. submitting form:
Client location(s):	Date submitted:

I. Quality Manual (4.2.2)   To be completed by the client and verified by assessor

Requirement	Reference	Comment
a. Scope, including justification for any exclusions. *The client must state each exclusion and its justification to the right under "Comment."*		
b. Documented procedures (included or referenced in manual). *Required procedures are identified in section II of this form.*		
c. Description of sequence and interaction between client processes. *Control of outsourced processes must also be addressed.* *Processes include core, support, and management processes.* *Sequence and interaction may be shown by a process map, flow diagram, or other means.* *Assessor analysis of the sequence and interactions processes is required to ensure they operate as a network.*		

II. Process—Requirement Matrix

To be completed by client and verified by assessor

A = clause addressed by process
C# = reference to comment in part VI

Clause	Required documented procedure	Mandatory assessment E = every audit; Y = yearly
4.1 General		
4.2 Documentation		
4.2.3 Document control	(required)	
4.2.4 Records control	(required)	
5.1 Manage. commit		E
5.2 Cust. focus		E
5.3 Quality policy		E
5.4 Planning		E
5.5 Res., auth., & comm		E
5.6 Manage. review		E
6.1 Provision of res.		
6.2 Human res.		
6.2.2 Training		
6.3 Infrastructure		
6.4 Work environment		
7.1 Plan. prod. real.		
7.2 Cust-rel. process		
7.3 Design and devel		Y
7.4 Purchasing		
7.4.3 Ver of pur. prod.		
7.5 Prod. & serv. prov.		
7.6 Cont. of mon. & mea.		
8.1 Mea., anal., & improve		
8.2.1 Cust. sat.		E
8.2.2 Internal audit	(required)	E
8.2.3 M&M—process		
8.2.4 M&M—product		
8.3 Cont. nonconf.	(required)	
8.4 Anal. of data		E
8.5 Improvement		E
8.5.1 Cont. improve		E
8.5.2 Corrective action	(required)	E
8.5.3 Preventive action	(required)	E

A. Core Processes (sometimes referred to as Customer Oriented Processes):

Process:
Owner:
Procedure:

Process:
Owner:
Procedure:

Etc.

B. Support Processes:

Process:
Owner:
Procedure:

Process:
Owner:
Procedure:

Etc.

C. Management Processes:

Process:
Owner:
Procedure:

Process:
Owner:
Procedure:

Etc.

III. Quality Records *Client to reference specific record(s) and/or form number(s). Assessor to verify all records are referenced and will verify content and use of records during the assessment*

Requirement	Reference	Comment
Management reviews (5.6.1)		
Education, training, skills, and experience (6.2.2 e)		
Evidence that realization process and product meet requirements (7.1 d)		
Requirements review results (7.2.2)		
Design inputs (7.3.2)		
Design review results (7.3.4)		
Design verification results (7.3.5)		
Design validation results (7.3.6)		
Design change reviews (7.3.7)		
Supplier evaluations (7.4.1)		
Validation of (special) processes (7.5.2 d)		
Product identification (where traceability is required) (7.5.3)		
Lost and/or damaged customer property (7.5.4)		
Basis for calibration (where not traceable to standards) (7.6 a)		
Calibration results (7.6)		
Validity of previous measurements when equipment found out of calibration (7.6)		
Audit results (8.2.2)		
Evidence of product conformity, acceptance criteria, and release authority (8.2.4)		
Nature of nonconformities, subsequent actions—including concession (8.3)		
Results of corrective actions (8.5.2 e)		
Results of preventive actions (8.5.3 d)		

IV. Multiple Site Sampling Plan (if applicable) *Client must submit results of internal audits for all sites. Assessor to review results.*

Requirement	Reference	Comment
Internal audits must be performed for all sites prior to registration		

VI. Results and Additional Comments *To be completed by assessor and updated as comments are responded to.*

Additional comments:

The documentation reviewed and scope as described are appropriate for proceeding to conformance audit.   Yes _____   No _____

All documentation reviews are subject to on-site verification.
Addressed (A) = Documentation appears to meet the standard; no documentation changes are needed at this time.
"Note" = Notes are for information only; no documentation changes are required at this time.
All other comments (C#) specify a requirement that must be addressed.

Document assessor signature: _____   **Date:** _____

Nonconformance Report

Report no:	Number:	❏ Major ❏ Minor
		Has this nonconformance occurred in the recent past? yes___ no___

Requirement (Statement of or reference to specific requirement in standard and/or customer document):

Nonconformance (Statement of nonconformance to above requirement):

Objective evidence (Statement of or reference to examples/evidence):

Management representative:_____ Date: _____

Assessor: _____ Date: _____

Lead assessor: _____ Date: _____

Response due date: _____ (Typically 30 days, maximum of 60 days)

Clients are required to transfer this nonconformance to their internal corrective action form and system

Corrective action form must be submitted by the response due date and contain:
1. Restatement of nonconformance, including reference to AQA nonconformance number.
2. Actions taken to determine the extent of and contain the specific nonconformance.
3. Root cause (results of an investigation to determine the most basic cause(s) of the nonconformance).
4. Actions taken to correct the nonconformance and, in response to the root cause, to eliminate recurrence of the nonconformance.
5. Verification of corrective action implementation. Longer-range plans that cannot be verified by the due date must be justified and have a target date for completion (plans are not acceptable for QS/TS).
6. Objective evidence (revised portion of procedures, training records, calibration record, etc.) of corrective action implementation must be listed and attached.

Client corrective action records, including objective evidence, must be maintained for at least three (3) years.

AQA/Client managers are required to complete this section:
Client CAR: _____

Root cause/corrective action plan: Accepted: _____ **Rejected:** _____
Root cause must be specific and resulting from an investigation to determine the most basic cause(s) of the nonconformance. Corrective actions to correct or contain the nonconformance and to address the root cause to prevent recurrence of the nonconformance must be established in a reasonable time frame.

Verification of corrective action implementation: Verified: _____ **Rejected:** _____
Verification of corrective action implementation should be accomplished to support closure of the nonconformance. Verification may be performed at the client site or remotely by review of sufficient evidence. Plans with specific actions and target dates to prevent recurrence that, by nature, require more time to implement may be accepted but must be justified and have a target date for completion.

Comments:

AQA Assessor: _____ **Date:** _____

All corrective actions will be verified for continuing effectiveness during the next audit.

Auditor Feedback
(Return to headquarters only if you have something to report)

Auditor name: _____   Report number: _____

Customer name: _____   Audit type: _____

Audit date: _____

_____ Missing information in packet   _____ Schedule/directions/coordination problems

_____ Document review problems   _____ Incorrect/incomplete forms and/or
                                                        overheads
_____ Customer concern
                                                _____ Other
_____ Auditor conduct

Problem description:

Action taken during audit in response to problem:

Recommendation to prevent problem from recurring:

Action taken to prevent problem from recurring (to be completed by AQA Home Office):

Appendix I
Example Audit Reports

Provided by handbook reviewer Nancy Boudreau, of Total Logical Concepts, Inc.

Acme Electronics Inc. Internal Audit Report

Audit#: 04-04	**Location:** Acme Electronics Inc., Anytown, UN
Date of Audit: 11/12/20XX	**Auditor:** Nancy Anybody, Audit Company Inc.
	Report issued to: Bob Smith, Management Representative, Acme Electronics Inc.

Description: Internal audit of Acme Electronics Inc. to determine compliance to and effective implementation of ISO 9001:2008, sections 4.2.3, Control of documents, and 4.2.4, Control of records.

Scope: All areas of AEI's facility in Anytown, UN, necessary to determine compliance to and effective implementation of ISO 9001:2008, section 4.2.3, Control of documents; 4.2.4, Control of records; and all related procedures and policies.

Audit Summary: This summary indicates the audit team's judgment as to the extent of the auditee's compliance with the applicable quality system standard and related documentation, and opportunities for improvement.

Based on objective evidence found, it is this auditor's opinion that AEI is not compliant with either of these requirements of the International Standard.

The standard requires a documented procedure to define the controls needed for documents required by the quality management system (QMS). Although there is a documented process map defining the controls for forms and work instructions, the production traveler and engineering document, which are clearly documents required by the QMS, do not fall under this process and do not have a documented procedure of their own that fulfills the requirements of the standard. External documents are another type of document whose requirements fall under this section.

Records are a special type of document and have their own requirements, which must also be defined in a documented procedure. Additionally, record retentions are not generally known, and the responsibility for disposition is unknown and not documented.

An additional opportunity for improvement in this area would be to reduce the number of hard copies that are required. If a database is available to those that require access to the documents, use this as the repository for documents (including internal audit reports) and forget the hard copies, which saves time (and copy costs) and allows resources to be redirected to more value-added tasks. Documents should be used as a tool and not take on a life of their own.

Signed: **Nancy Anybody**

    Nancy Anybody, CQA, Lead Auditor
    Audit Company, Inc.

R/F-17.5 last revised 4/19/20XX

Acme Electronics Inc. Internal Audit Report—Summary of Corrective Action Requests

Audit#: 04-04	Location: Acme Electronics Inc., Anytown, UN
Date of Audit: 11/12/20XX	Auditor: Nancy Anybody, Audit Company
	Report issued to: Bob Smith, Management Representative, Acme Electronics Inc.

CAR#	Requirement	Severity A B C, A = Major
04-04C1	ISO 9001:2008, section 4.2.3, Control of documents, states, "Documents required by the quality management system shall be controlled. A documented procedure shall be established to define the controls needed for a) through g)."	A
04-04C2	ISO 9001:2008, section 4.2.4, Control of records, states, "A documented procedure shall be established to define the controls needed for the identification, storage, protection, retrieval, retention time and disposition of records."	A

Acme Electronics Inc. Internal Audit Report—Audit Notes

Audit#: 04-04	**Location:** Acme Electronics Inc., Anytown, UN
Date of Audit: 11/12/20XX	**Auditor:** Nancy Anybody, Audit Company
	Report issued to: Bob Smith, Management Representative, Acme Electronics Inc.

Include objective evidence:

Spoke with document control coordinator and reviewed process map 14.2.P01 Rev: 2, Internal Documentation Control. Most requirements for a documented procedure are being met by the process map, but there is no reference to external documents even though there is an external documents list and no reference to production travelers. It was stated that this process does not apply to engineering documents either. When asked about documented procedures for these three items since they were not covered by the existing map, it was stated that there are none, and different individuals have the responsibility for controlling travelers and engineering documents. It was also observed from the process map that five copies of any newly released document are printed and put into five different locations, even though documents reside on the computer, which everyone has access to.

Observed a list of external documents including the 2008 version of this International Standard. When asked how distribution was controlled, the auditor was shown a distribution list for each external document, 14.2.M05 Rev 0. This is an excellent way to control distribution, although there was no distribution list for the standard.

Observed a Business Records Matrix, Ref 14.2.M02, including the map name, reference number, type of record, description, location, retention, disposition, and length of archive if applicable. Noted that the purchase order record was listed as being kept "permanently" and never archived, but the owner of this process could not produce a 26-year-old purchase order. I did, however, observe PO 14312 from 8/21/07 and PO 115790 from 10/05/10. The owner of the process stated that she was unaware of the record retention or what she needed to do when the retention time was reached. Observed the record of nonconforming product, which is a record required by the standard, with no retention date. Even though records are kept on a database, they still could be purged periodically to make more disk space for current information. Was unable to observe audit records for 20XX, although the retention time is three years, with a four-year archive period. Observed a supplier evaluation record for A1 Instrument, a calibration vendor from 6/05/11. Because there is no documented procedure defining responsibility and control, it is not known how to dispose of old records. Can they be thrown away or must they be shredded? Can they be recycled?

Acme Electronics Inc. Internal Audit Report

Audit#: 04-05	Location: Acme Electronics Inc., Anytown, UN
Date of Audit: 11/12/20XX	Auditor: Nancy Anybody, Audit Company Inc.
	Report issued to: Bob Smith, Management Representative, Acme Electronics Inc.

Description: Internal audit of Acme Electronics Inc. to determine compliance to and effective implementation of ISO 9001:2008, section 7.6, Control of monitoring and measuring devices.

Scope: All areas of AEI's facility in Anytown, UN, necessary to determine compliance to and effective implementation of ISO 9001:2008, section 7.6, Control of monitoring and measuring devices and all related procedures and policies.

Audit Summary: This summary indicates the audit team's judgment as to the extent of the auditee's compliance with the applicable quality system standard and related documentation, and opportunities for improvement.

Based on objective evidence found, it is this auditor's opinion that AEI is not fully compliant with this requirement of the International Standard.

One outstanding feature of AEI's calibration program is that when new pieces of equipment are purchased by AEI, they arrive via the receiving process and are taken to the manufacturing engineering technician for calibration before initially being put into use. This process ensures that measuring equipment is capable of providing evidence of conformity of product to determined requirements.

Since all calibration is done by an outside firm once a year, it makes it easier to perform calibrations when due. However, the method used to retrieve the equipment from the floor to be calibrated has a certain element of risk, since the process is to inform the departments of the pieces of equipment that need to be moved to the calibration area, but not verify from the calibration list that all pieces have been brought forward. An opportunity for improvement exists here.

An area of concern exists regarding monitoring and measuring equipment that was found to be out of calibration when checked. Process map 7.6.P01 Rev: 2 addresses this situation as required by the standard, which is to verify all product that has been measured since the last known calibration and take appropriate action; however, calibration records do not indicate the status of the equipment when it was measured. Therefore, how does AEI know whether the equipment was out of calibration when checked?

A second area of concern is measuring and testing software. Where software is used to monitor and/or measure specified requirements, the ability of the software to satisfy the intended requirements has to be confirmed before use and reconfirmed as necessary. There is no program in place for doing this.

Signed: **Nancy Anybody**

Nancy Anybody, CQA, Lead Auditor
Audit Company, Inc.

Acme Electronics Inc. Internal Audit Report—Summary of Corrective Action Requests

Audit#: 04-05	Location: Acme Electronics Inc., Anytown, UN
Date of Audit: 11/12/20XX	Auditor: Nancy Anybody, Audit Company Inc.
	Report issued to: Bob Smith, Management Representative, Acme Electronics Inc.

CAR#	Requirement	Severity A B C, A = Major
04-05C1	ISO 9001:2008, section 7.6, Control of monitoring and measuring devices, states, "In addition, the organization shall assess and record the validity of the previous measuring results when the equipment is found not to conform to requirements. The organization shall take appropriate action on the equipment and any product affected. Records of the results of calibration and verification shall be maintained."	A
04-05C2	ISO 9001:2008, section 7.6, Control of monitoring and measuring devices, states, "When used in the monitoring and measurement of specified requirements, the ability of computer software to satisfy the intended application shall be confirmed. This shall be undertaken prior to initial use and reconfirmed as necessary."	A
04-05C3	ISO 9001:2008, section 7.6, Control of monitoring and measuring devices, states, "When necessary to ensure valid results, measuring equipment shall a) be calibrated or verified at specified intervals . . ."	B
04-05C4	ISO 9001:2008, section 7.6, Control of monitoring and measuring devices, states, "The organization shall determine the monitoring and measurement to be undertaken and the monitoring and measuring devices needed to provide evidence of conformity of product to determined requirements."	C

Acme Electronics Inc. Internal Audit Report—Audit Notes

Audit#: 04-05	**Location:** Acme Electronics Inc., Anytown, UN
Date of Audit: 11/12/20XX	**Auditor:** Nancy Anybody, Audit Company Inc.
	Report issued to: Bob Smith, Management Representative, Acme Electronics Inc.

Include objective evidence:

Spoke with the manufacturing engineering technician and reviewed with him process map 17.6.P01 Rev: 2, Calibration.

The technician stated that all calibrations are done outside annually. I observed several calibration records from A1 Instruments, including but not limited to #1369240, oscilloscope; 2369293 ESD Strap tester; 336913, 336914, 336915, 336916, 336917, 336918, 336919, calipers; and 4369274, 5369286, 6369285, weights; all done in March 2004. Records contained the NIST standard to which the calibration was performed, the date done, and the next date due. The records did not show what the status of the equipment was when checked. Was it in or out of calibration? This information is needed since the standard requires that when measuring and monitoring equipment is found to be out of calibration, all product measured since the last time it was in calibration must be reassessed to determine the validity of previous measurements. Also,observed the calibration record for caliper 336917, a new caliper purchased 10/13/2004, but did not find it on the calibration master list.

While observing monitoring and measuring equipment that was in use on the production floor, observed device number 7369243, calibrated 3/18/04; 8369258, calibrated 3/15/04; and 9369227, calibrated 3/18/04. Observed device 1347548, DC Power Supply due 3/20/04, NOT calibrated and in use. It was stated that when A1 Instruments came in to calibrate, it was probably hidden under the counter and missed the calibration. The operator was not aware that he should only be using equipment that is calibrated. All equipment had the appropriate calibration stickers.

Spoke with the manufacturing engineer to find out about software calibration since no software was on the calibration schedule. He stated that he didn't realize that had to be done, and he knew there was no program in place for doing it.

Acme Electronics Inc. Internal Audit Report

Audit#: 04-10	Location: Acme Electronics Inc., Anytown, UN
Date of Audit: 11/12/20XX	Auditor: Nancy Anybody, Audit Company Inc.
	Report issued to: Bob Smith, Management Representative, Acme Electronics Inc.

Description: Internal audit of Acme Electronics Inc. to determine compliance to and effective implementation of ISO 9001:2008, section 8.2.1, Customer satisfaction.

Scope: All areas of AEI's facility in Anytown, UN, necessary to determine compliance to and effective implementation of ISO 9001:2008, section 8.2.1, Customer satisfaction and all related procedures and policies.

Audit Summary: This summary indicates the audit team's judgment as to the extent of the auditee's compliance with the applicable quality system standard and related documentation, and opportunities for improvement.

Based on objective evidence found, it is this auditor's opinion that AEI is compliant with the requirements of this section.

The requirement for customer focus and resulting satisfaction are stated in the new version of the standard and no longer just implied. The requirement is to proactively solicit feedback from customers regarding their perception as to whether the organization has met their requirements. Customer complaints are no longer enough since they are considered reactive.

The new process owner of the customer satisfaction process reviewed several excellent ideas he has for soliciting this feedback. The next audit should review the output from these plans to ensure that they are being effectively implemented, that the process map has been updated to reflect the new process, and that the results are being used as input to management review.

This is an example of a process owner actually taking ownership of a process and doing what it takes to make it successful.

Signed: **Nancy Anybody**

      Nancy Anybody, CQA, Lead Auditor
      Audit Company, Inc.

R/F-17.5 last revised 4/19/20XX

Acme Electronics Inc. Internal Audit Report—Summary of Corrective Action Requests

Audit#: 04-10	**Location:** Acme Electronics Inc., Anytown, UN
Date of Audit: 11/12/20XX	**Auditor:** Nancy Anybody, Audit Company Inc.
	Report issued to: Bob Smith, Management Representative, Acme Electronics Inc.

CAR#	Requirement	Severity A B C, A = Major
	No nonconformances found.	

Acme Electronics Inc. Internal Audit Report—Audit Notes

Audit#: 04-10	**Location:** Acme Electronics Inc., Anytown, UN
Date of Audit: 11/12/20XX	**Auditor:** Nancy Anybody, Audit Company Inc.
	Report issued to: Bob Smith, Management Representative, Acme Electronics Inc.

Include objective evidence:

Spoke with the owner of process map 18.2.P02 Rev 0. The process owner stated that he had recently taken over this process and was implementing several new ideas for soliciting customer feedback. He spoke of a short list of questions being added to the end of a phone call to "help improve our service," changes to the website planned for January and February, and doing daily, weekly, and monthly reporting. He stated that this will be input to the management review meeting. He will also be implementing "monitoring for quality" on some customer phone calls and include monthly training sessions.

Currently, the process map does not reflect what he is doing and needs to be changed. The requirement of the standard is to define methods for collection, which he is doing.

Appendix J
Product Line Audit Flowchart

Provided by handbook reviewer Buddy M. Smith.

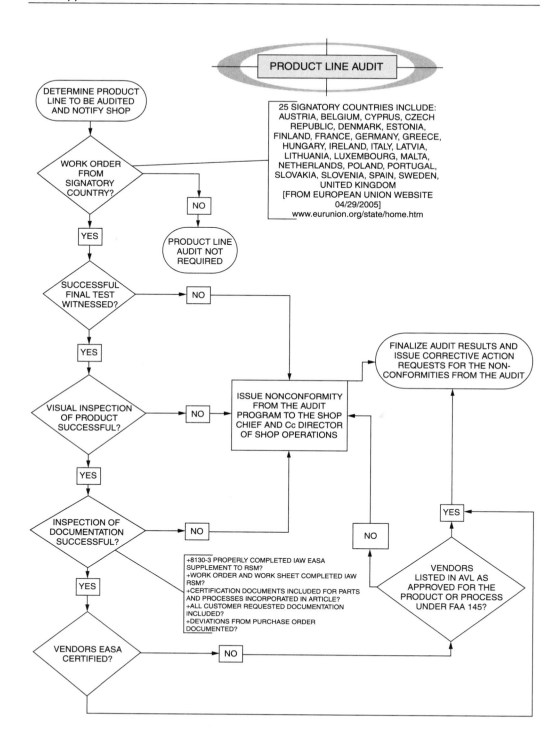

PRODUCT LINE AUDIT

DETERMINE PRODUCT LINE TO BE AUDITED AND NOTIFY SHOP

25 SIGNATORY COUNTRIES INCLUDE: AUSTRIA, BELGIUM, CYPRUS, CZECH REPUBLIC, DENMARK, ESTONIA, FINLAND, FRANCE, GERMANY, GREECE, HUNGARY, IRELAND, ITALY, LATVIA, LITHUANIA, LUXEMBOURG, MALTA, NETHERLANDS, POLAND, PORTUGAL, SLOVAKIA, SLOVENIA, SPAIN, SWEDEN, UNITED KINGDOM [FROM EUROPEAN UNION WEBSITE 04/29/2005] www.eurunion.org/state/home.htm

WORK ORDER FROM SIGNATORY COUNTRY?

NO

YES

PRODUCT LINE AUDIT NOT REQUIRED

SUCCESSFUL FINAL TEST WITNESSED?

NO

YES

FINALIZE AUDIT RESULTS AND ISSUE CORRECTIVE ACTION REQUESTS FOR THE NON-CONFORMITIES FROM THE AUDIT

VISUAL INSPECTION OF PRODUCT SUCCESSFUL?

NO

ISSUE NONCONFORMITY FROM THE AUDIT PROGRAM TO THE SHOP CHIEF AND Cc DIRECTOR OF SHOP OPERATIONS

YES

INSPECTION OF DOCUMENTATION SUCCESSFUL?

NO

YES

+8130-3 PROPERLY COMPLETED IAW EASA SUPPLEMENT TO RSM?
+WORK ORDER AND WORK SHEET COMPLETED IAW RSM?
+CERTIFICATION DOCUMENTS INCLUDED FOR PARTS AND PROCESSES INCORPORATED IN ARTICLE?
+ALL CUSTOMER REQUESTED DOCUMENTATION INCLUDED?
+DEVIATIONS FROM PURCHASE ORDER DOCUMENTED?

NO

YES

NO

VENDORS LISTED IN AVL AS APPROVED FOR THE PRODUCT OR PROCESS UNDER FAA 145?

VENDORS EASA CERTIFIED?

NO

Appendix K
First, Second, and Third Edition Contributors and Reviewers

The acknowledgments for the first and second editions are in chronological order of involvement of project by teams and do not reflect the significance of individual contributions.

EARLY PROJECT PARTICIPATION (OUR VISIONARIES)

Norman C. Frank

Barbara Houlihan

John C. Dronkers

FIRST EDITION

Topical Paper Contributions

Early in the development of the handbook, division members provided new or existing papers for consideration for the proposed handbook. Some papers were not selected, because they simply did not fit our needs. Putting together a creditable paper is very difficult, and the importance of the contributions cannot be overstated. We wish to thank all those who prepared and submitted papers to support the development of the handbook. Here are the authors whose papers were used:

Glena G. Anger and co-authors Robert Cofer, Tom Feyerabend, Joyce Ford, Marti Levy, Patti McGuire, and Betty Wims

Shyam Banik

Rudolph C. Hirzel

Kathryn E. Jackson and Thomas B. Tucker

Joseph H. Maday, Jr.

Larry McArthur

Jerry Nation

Writer Organization

Dorinda Clippinger (owner of Penworthy, Inc., of Cincinnati) and Janice Smith (writer) worked well with the members of the Quality Audit Division. Their professional approach and can-do attitude made the development of the handbook run smoothly. They provided us with a great first edition of the handbook.

Interviews with the Writer

Some of the necessary material was not initially available. Additionally, some of the material from the referenced texts was conflicting. We therefore found it necessary to query some of our members by telephone about certain topics within the quality audit Body of Knowledge. They provided supplemental information and examples for us to use. They helped fill in the missing pieces of information needed to complete the work. The members who participated in the interviews are listed here, along with their credentials at that time:

Dennis R. Arter, PE, FASQ, ASQ CQA

John Barrett, ASQ CQA, ASQ CRE, RAB QSA

Don Beckwith, ASQ CQA, Ball State University CTC

Mary Carter Berrios, ASQ CQA, ASQ CQE, ASQ CQM

Cheryl A. Boyce, ASQ CQA and RAB QSLA

John J. Boyle, ASQ CQA

Bruce H. Campbell, PE, FASQ, ASQ CQA, ASQ CQE

Mike Coughlin, ASQ CQA, ASQ CQE

Traci V. A. Edwards, ASQ CQA, ASQ CQE, ASQ CQM

Norman C. Frank, PE, ASQ CQA, ASQ CQE

Marvin C. Gabalski, ASQ CQA, ASQ CQE, ASQ CRE, RAB QSLA

David A. Kelly, PhD, ASQ CQA, ASQ CQE, RAB QSLA

Judith Ann Malsbury, ASQ CQA, ASQ CQE, ASQ CQM

George Mouradian, PE, FASQ, ASQ CQA, ASQ CQE, ASQ CRE

Robert J. Nash, PhD, ASQ CQA, ASQ CQM

Terry Regel, ASQ CQA, ASQ CQE, RAB QSLA, IRCA LA

Charles Robinson, FASQ, ASQ CQA, RAB QSLA

Haakon Rud, DnV Certified Lead Auditor

Douglas Stimson, ASQ CQE, RAB QSLA

Steven Wilson, ASQ CQA

Manuscript Reviewers

It was the job of the reviewers to review text for technical correctness. The many reviewers provided feedback, ideas for developing the work, and examples for inclusion in the handbook.

United States Reviewers

Ronald L. Ackers, PE, FASQ, ASQ CQA, ASQ CQE, ASQ CRE, ASQ CQM, IIE-CST, RAB QSLA

Douglas G. Anderson, ASQ CQA

Richard M. Baehr, ASQ CQA, RAB QALA

Lon L. Barrett, ASQ CQA

Jimmy Bell, ASQ CQA

Bernard Carpenter, ASQ CQA, ASQ CQM, MSQA

Ariel Castro, ASQ CQA

Robert G. Chadwick, FASQ, ASQ CQA, ASQ CQE, ASQ CMI

Robert G. Chisholm, Sr., ASQ CQA, ASQ CQE, ASQ CMI, RAB QSLA, QS-9000 Auditor

Jim Coley, ASQ CQA

Peter R. Corradi, ASQ CQA, ASQ CQE, RAB QSA

Harold Crotts, ASQ CQA, ASQ CQE, ASQ CMI, AAS, Ind. Eng.

Jeffrey A. Deeds, ASQ CQA

Kathleen L. Eaves, ASQ CQA

Cheryl A. Hadley, ASQ CQA

Rudolph C. Hirzel, ASQ CQA, ASQ CQE, ASQ CQM

David Kildahl, ASQ CQA

Ramesh Konda, ASQ CQA, ASQ CQE

Jim Lamar, ASQ CQA

James (Rusty) Lusk, ASQ CQA, ASQ CQE, ASQ CQM, RAB QSLA

Donald Mason, ASQ CQA

Jerry T. Nation, PE, ASQ CQA, ASQ CQE, ASQ CQM, RAB QSLA

Chris Newcomer, ASQ CQA

Martin F. Patton, ASQ CQA, RAB QSLA, IRCA LA

Steven L. Pearson, ASQ CQA, RAB QSLA, AIAG Cert, QS-9000 LA

David Prins, ASQ CQA, ASQ CMI, ASQ CQE, ASQ CQT, ASQ CRE, NAPM-CPM

Terry Regel, ASQ CQA, ASQ CQE, RAB QSLA, IRCA LA

John Rinaldi, ASQ CQA

Gwen E. Sampson, ASQ CQA

Stephen Sheng, ASQ CQA, RAB QSLA

Ron Spring, ASQ CQA

David L. Thibault, ASQ CQA, ASQ CQE

Alfred F. Wales, ASQ CQA, ASQ CQE

Stoney F. Walker, ASQ CQA

Worldwide Reviewers

Steven Britton (Canada), PE, ASQC CQE, ASQC CQA

Chui Karson (Hong Kong), ASQC CQA, ASQC CQE

Darren Kent (Canada), ASQC CQA

Ian A. MacNab (Canada)

Akhilesh Singh (India), IRCA LA

Peter Wright (Canada), ASQC CQA, IRCA, AOQ CQT

Jorge Xavier (Brazil)

Roger Zigmond (Canada), ASQC CQA, ASQC CQE

Tiebreaker Committee

The tiebreaker committee resolved differences that surfaced in the review process. It provided guidance to the editor and the writer. The tiebreaker committee helped to ensure that various views were considered. It also kept the project focused on the quality audit Body of Knowledge.

Norman C. Frank, PE, ASQ CQA, ASQ CQE

Linda Reinhart, ASQ CQA

Gerry Sherman, ASQ CQA, ASQ CQE, ASQ CQM

SECOND EDITION

For the second edition, a group of ASQ Quality Audit Division members formed the handbook subcommittee and volunteered to be responsible for updating one part of the quality audit Body of Knowledge. Updating included adding examples and addressing new topics introduced by the August 1997 revised Body of Knowledge. Committee contributors and their assigned part of the Body of Knowledge are as follows:

Richard M. Baehr, Part VI: Audit Program Management

Wallace (Chuck) Carlson, Jr., Part IV: Audit Reporting

Bernie Carpenter, Part II: Audit Preparation

Norman C. Frank, Part I: Ethics, Professional Conduct, and Liability; Audit Sampling Appendix

Rudolph C. Hirzel, Part VII: General Knowledge and Skills

Baskar Kotte, Part III: Audit Performance

Jim Maiden, Part VI: Audit Program Management

Terry Regel, Part V: Corrective Action Follow-up and Closure

J. P. Russell, Handbook Committee Chair

Second Edition Manuscript Reviewers

The reviewers provided feedback on the updated information from the committee members and the editor. It is obvious from the quality of the review comments and the examples provided that many reviewers spent long hours carefully reviewing the manuscript.

Robert A. Abbott, FASQ, ASQ CQE, RAB QSLA

Ronald L. Ackers, PE, FASQ, ASQ CQE, ASQ CQA, ASQ CRE, ASQ CQM, IIE-CSI, RAB QSLA

Judith J. Akers, RAB QSLA

Ralph W. Arnott, Principal, ASQ CQA, ASQ CQE

Dennis R. Arter, PE, FASQ, ASQ CQA

Richard M. Baehr, ASQ CQA, RAB QSLA

Shyam Banik, ASQ CQA, ASQ CQE, RAB QSLA

John Barrett, ASQ CQA, ASQ CQE, ASQ CRE, ASQ CQM, RAB QSA

John J. Boyle, Principal Quality Eng., ASQ CQA

James M. Coley, ASQ CQA, RAB QSPA

Linda L. Feaster, ASQ CQA

Wendy Finnerty, ASQ CQA

Norman C. Frank, ASQ CQA, ASQ CQE

Peter J. Gauthier, ASQ CQA

Milad R. Matthias, PhD, PE

A. B. (Gus) Mundel, Chair of TAG 69, FASQ, ASQ Edwards Medalist

Jay Michael Pratt, RAB QSLA, Institution of Nuclear Engineers Fellow

Alfred F. Wales, ASQ CQA, ASQ CQE

Daniel S. Whelan, ASQ CQA, ASQ CQM

The final acknowledgment is for the QAD officers, especially Norman Frank (Vice Chair Technical) and Terry Regel (Technical Publications Chair), for their help and leadership. Many times they were asked for their assistance on certain topics and the direction the handbook needed to take.

THIRD EDITION

Contributors and reviewers of the third edition of the handbook are listed in alphabetical order. It was too difficult to separate the list into contributors and reviewers because many reviewers made significant contributions. Reviewers shared insights and knowledge. Sometimes I was overwhelmed by their generosity.

Dennis Arter, ASQ Fellow, CQA

Douglas Berg, ASQ CQE, CRE, CQA, CQMgr, RAB QS-LA, IATCA Sr. Auditor, IRCA LA

Nancy Boudreau, ASQ CQA

Lois Y. Cowden, ASQ CQA

Mark Crossley, ASQ CQE, ASQ CRE, ASQ CQA, ASQ CQMgr, ASQ CSSBB

Norman Frank, PE

William M. Harral, ASQ Fellow, ASQ CQA, ASQ CQE, ASQ CQMgr, ASQ CRE, RAB QS-LA, PEIT

Charles N. Howell, RAB QSLA, IATF International Qualified Automotive Auditor

Mark Kempf, ASQ CQA, ESDS 2020 Certified Auditor, TL9000 Registrar Auditor

Jerald Marmon, CQA

Akio Miura, ASQ Fellow, ASQ CQA, ASQ CBA, ASQ CHA, ASQ CQE, ASQ CQMgr, ASQ CRE, ASQ CSQE, ASQ CSSBB, RAB IATCA approved Auditor Trainer

Lawrence Mossman, ASQ CQA

Terry Regel, ASQ CQA, ASQ CQE

Linda D. Sickles, ASQ CQA

Buddy M. Smith, ASQ CQA, FAA A&P, AAS AMT

Dennis Welch, ASQ CQA, ASQ CQMgr

Larry Whittington, ASQ CSQE, ASQ CQA, RAB QSA-QMS Lead Auditor, IRCA-QMS 2000 Principal Auditor

It was the job of the reviewers to review text for technical correctness. The many reviewers provided feedback, ideas for developing the work, and examples for inclusion in the handbook.

The final acknowledgment is to the QAD officers for their help and leadership. They provided assistance on certain topics and the direction the handbook needed to take.

Notes

CHAPTER 1

1. ISO 19011:2011, *Guidelines for Auditing Management Systems* (Milwaukee, WI: ASQ Quality Press, 2011), p. 16.
2. Akio Miura, taken from auditor training materials, provided July 11, 2005.
3. Dennis R. Arter, *Quality Audits for Improved Performance*, 3rd ed. (Milwaukee, WI: ASQ Quality Press, 2003), p. 15.
4. ASQC Energy Division, *Nuclear Quality Systems Auditor Training Handbook*, 2nd ed. (Milwaukee, WI: ASQC Quality Press, 1986), p. 2.
5. Arter, p. 6.
6. ANSI-ASQ National Accreditation Board, "ANAB Frequently Asked Questions," http://www.anab.org (accessed July 7, 2005).

CHAPTER 2

1. Allan J. Sayle, *Management Audits: The Assessment of Quality Management Systems*, 3rd ed. (Brighton, MI: Allan Sayle Associates, 1997), p. 8. Reproduced with permission of Allan J. Sayle.
2. J. P. Russell, *Continual Improvement Assessment Guide: Performing and Sustaining Business Results* (Milwaukee, WI: ASQ Quality Press, 2004), p. 59.

CHAPTER 3

1. Charles A. Mills, *The Quality Audit: A Management Evaluation Tool* (New York: McGraw-Hill, 1988), p. 89.

CHAPTER 4

1. Walter Willborn, *Audit Standards: A Comparative Analysis* (Milwaukee, WI: ASQC Quality Press, 1993), p. 31.
2. Charles A. Mills, *The Quality Audit: A Management Evaluation Tool* (New York: McGraw-Hill, 1988), pp. 36–40.
3. Mills, pp. 43–46.
4. J. P. Russell, portions taken from QualityWBT Center for Education training materials for the Auditing (CQA) Fundamentals II e-learning class, 2001, http://www.QualityWBT.com.

CHAPTER 5

1. Charles A. Mills, *The Quality Audit: A Management Evaluation Tool* (New York: McGraw-Hill, 1988), p. 87.

2. American Society for Quality, *ASQ's Foundations in Quality: Certified Quality Auditor, Module 1: Ethics, Professional Conduct, and Liability Issues* (Milwaukee, WI: ASQ Quality Press, 1998), pp. 1–19.

3. Harold L. Federow, *Quality Practices and the Law*, 3rd ed. (New York: Quality Resources, 1997), p. 179.

4. Henry Campbell Black, *Black's Law Dictionary* (St. Paul, MN: West Publishing Co., 1990), p. 466.

5. Walter Willborn, *Audit Standards: A Comparative Analysis* (Milwaukee, WI: ASQC Quality Press, 1993), p. 15.

6. *Standards for the Professional Practice of Internal Auditing* (Altamonte Springs, FL: Institute of Internal Auditors, 1978).

7. ISO 19011:2011, *Guidelines for Auditing Management Systems* (Milwaukee, WI: ASQ Quality Press, 2011), clause 4, p. 4.

8. ISO 19011:2011, p. 4.

CHAPTER 6

1. Dennis R. Arter, *Quality Audits for Improved Performance*, 3rd ed. (Milwaukee, WI: ASQ Quality Press, 2003), p. 40.

2. J. P. Russell and Terry Regel, *After the Quality Audit*, 2nd ed. (Milwaukee, WI: ASQ Quality Press, 2000).

3. Dennis R. Arter, Charles A. Cianfrani, and John E. West, *How to Audit the Process-Based QMS* (Milwaukee, WI: ASQ Quality Press, 2003), p. 81.

4. J. P. Russell, *The Process Auditing Techniques Guide* (Milwaukee, WI: ASQ Quality Press, 2003), p. 16.

5. Arter, Cianfrani, and West, p. 86.

6. ASQC Energy Division, *Nuclear Quality Systems Auditor Training Handbook*, 2nd ed. (Milwaukee, WI: ASQC Quality Press, 1986), p. 26.

7. IAF MD 5:2009 Duration of QMS and EMS Audits, http://www.iaf.nu/articles/Mandatory_Documents_/38, issued February 1, 2009.

8. Russell and Regel, p. 144.

9. Arter, Cianfrani, and West, p. 85.

10. ASQC Energy Division, p. 40.

11. ASQC Energy Division, p. 25.

12. Scott Parsowith, *Fundamentals of Quality Auditing* (Milwaukee, WI: ASQC Quality Press, 1995), p. 24.

13. J. P. Russell, "Audit Planning: Audit Logistics," *Quality Auditor Review* 1, no. 4 (1997): 3.

14. Russell, "Audit Planning: Audit Logistics."

15. Arter, p. 47.

16. Russell, *The Process Auditing Techniques Guide*, p. 47.

17. ASQC Energy Division, p. 26.

18. J. P. Russell, *The Internal Auditing Pocket Guide* (Milwaukee, WI: ASQ Quality Press, 2003), p. 45.

19. ASQC Energy Division, p. 26.
20. ASQC Energy Division, p. 26.
21. Arter, p. 71.
22. Whittington and Associates, "Audit by Process Instead of by Clause," July 2004, http://www.WhittingtonAssociates.com (accessed July 14, 2005).
23. Russell, *The Internal Auditing Pocket Guide*, p. 60.
24. Parsowith, p. 23.
25. Arter, p. 48.

CHAPTER 7

1. Dennis R. Arter, *Quality Audits for Improved Performance*, 3rd ed. (Milwaukee, WI: ASQ Quality Press, 2003), p. 67.
2. ASQC Energy Division, *Nuclear Quality Systems Auditor Training Handbook*, 2nd ed. (Milwaukee, WI: ASQ Quality Press, 1986), p. 42.
3. Charles A. Mills, *The Quality Audit: A Management Evaluation Tool* (New York: McGraw-Hill, 1988), p. 185.
4. Arter, pp. 39–40.
5. Arter, p. 73.
6. Walter Willborn, *Audit Standards: A Comparative Analysis* (Milwaukee, WI: ASQC Quality Press, 1993), pp. 52–53.
7. Arter, p. 73.
8. J. P. Russell, *The Internal Auditing Pocket Guide* (Milwaukee, WI: ASQ Quality Press, 2003), p. 95.
9. Arter, p. 86.
10. ASQC Energy Division, p. 45.
11. J. P. Russell, *The Process Auditing Techniques Guide* (Milwaukee, WI: ASQ Quality Press, 2003), p. 112.
12. J. P. Russell and Shauna Wilson, *eAuditing Fundamentals: Virtual Communication and Remote Auditing* (Milwaukee, WI: ASQ Quality Press, 2012).
13. "Closing Meeting: Record Keeping," *QAR Newsletter* 1, no. 1 (1997), http://www.JP-Russell.com (accessed May 11, 2005).
14. Scott Parsowith, *Fundamentals of Quality Auditing* (Milwaukee, WI: ASQC Quality Press, 1995), p. 30.
15. Russell and Wilson.
16. Parsowith, p. 30.

CHAPTER 8

1. J. P. Russell and Terry Regel, *After the Quality Audit*, 2nd ed. (Milwaukee, WI: ASQ Quality Press, 2000), p. 9.
2. Charles B. Robinson, *How to Make the Most of Every Audit* (Milwaukee, WI: ASQC Quality Press, 1992), p. 94.
3. Dennis R. Arter, *Quality Audits for Improved Performance*, 3rd ed. (Milwaukee, WI: ASQ Quality Press, 2003), p. 98.
4. J. P. Russell, *The Process Auditing Techniques Guide* (Milwaukee, WI: ASQ Quality Press, 2003), pp. 108, 109.

5. Russell and Regel, p. 5.

6. Russell and Regel, p. 114.

7. Arter.

8. Arter, p. 105.

9. QualityWBT Center for Education training materials, http://www.QualityWBT.com (accessed May 13, 2005).

10. Russell and Regel, p. 17.

11. Russell and Regel, pp. 9–14.

12. Russell and Regel, pp. 14–16.

13. Arter.

14. "Update: Nonfinancial Monitor Falls Short," *Internal Auditor*, February 2005, p. 16.

15. J. P. Russell, "Standards Outlook," *Quality Progress Magazine*, June 2005.

CHAPTER 9

1. J. P. Russell and Shauna Wilson, *eAuditing Fundamentals: Virtual Communication and Remote Auditing* (Milwaukee, WI: ASQ Quality Press, 2012).

2. American Society for Quality, *ASQ's Foundations in Quality, Audit Process, Module 2* (Milwaukee, WI: ASQ Quality Press, 2004).

CHAPTER 10

1. ISO 19011:2011, Guidelines for auditing management systems, clause 7.1, p. 28.

CHAPTER 12

1. Peter R. Scholtes, Brian L. Joiner, and Barbara J. Streibel, *The Team Handbook*, 3rd ed. (Madison, WI: Oriel, 2003), p. 74.

CHAPTER 13

1. *Certified Quality Auditor: ASQ Foundations in Quality, Module 7* (Milwaukee, WI: ASQ Quality Press, 1998), pp. 7–54.

2. *Certified Quality Auditor: ASQ Foundations in Quality, Module 7*, pp. 7–55.

3. J. P. Russell and Terry Regel, *After the Quality Audit*, 2nd ed. (Milwaukee, WI: ASQ Quality Press, 2000), p. 171.

CHAPTER 15

1. B. W. Tuchman, "Development Sequence in Small Groups," *Psychological Bulletin* 63 (1965).

CHAPTER 16

1. Scott Parsowith, *Fundamentals of Quality Auditing* (Milwaukee, WI: ASQC Quality Press, 1995), p. 14.

2. Walter Willborn, *Audit Standards: A Comparative Analysis* (Milwaukee, WI: ASQC Quality Press, 1993), p. 13.

3. Charles B. Robinson, *How to Make the Most of Every Audit* (Milwaukee, WI: ASQC Quality Press, 1992), p. 12.

4. Don Benbow, "Distance Learning in a Cyber Classroom," ASQ *Quality Progress*, July 1998, pp. 43–45.

5. J. P. Russell and Terry Regel, *After the Quality Audit*, 2nd ed. (Milwaukee, WI: ASQ Quality Press, 2000), p. 139.

6. Russell and Regel, pp. 139–160.

7. Russell and Regel, p. 160.

8. Allan J. Sayle, *Management Audits: The Assessment of Quality Management Systems*, 2nd ed. (Great Britain: Allan Sayle Associates, 1988), pp. 1–8. Reproduced with permission of Allan J. Sayle.

9. Russell and Regel, p. 27.

10. Russell and Regel, p. 143.

11. Taken from J. P. Russell, "Supply Chain Management: Resourcing Organization Needs" (presentation, ASQ Audit Division Conference, Augusta, GA, October 2012).

12. Taken from Joe Kausek, *The Management System Auditor's Handbook* (Milwaukee, WI: ASQ Quality Press, 2006), pp. 364–365.

13. Taken from Kausek, p. 367.

14. Taken from J. P. Russell, ASQ *Quality Progress*, August 2012, pp. 52–54, and September 2012, pp. 52–53.

15. ISO 31000:2009, Risk management—Principles and guidelines, clause 5.1, Figure 3—Risk Management Process, p. 14.

16. ISO 19011:2011, Guidelines for auditing management systems, clause 6.4.4, Communicating during the audit.

17. ISO Guide 73:2009 Risk Management—Vocabulary, "risk," clause 1.1, p. 1.

CHAPTER 17

1. J. M. Juran, *Juran on Leadership for Quality: An Executive Handbook* (New York: Free Press, 1989), p. 7.

2. ASQ Quality Glossary, http://asq.org/glossary (accessed July 27, 2005).

3. J. P. Russell, *Continual Improvement Assessment Guide: Performing and Sustaining Business Results* (Milwaukee, WI: ASQ Quality Press, 2004), p. 2.

4. Russell.

5. Nancy Boudreau and J. P. Russell collaborated to develop these tenets (July 2012).

6. W. Edwards Deming, *The New Economics: For Industry, Government, Education* (Cambridge, MA: MIT Press, 1993), p. 51.

7. Taken from "Cost of Quality," in *The Certified Manager of Quality/Organizational Excellence Handbook*, ed. Russell T. Westcott (Milwaukee, WI: ASQ Quality Press, 2006), pp. 365–369.

CHAPTER 18

1. John T. Burr, "The Tools of Quality, Part VI: Pareto Charts," ASQC *Quality Progress*, November 1990, p. 61.

2. Charles A. Mills, *The Quality Audit: A Management Evaluation Tool* (New York: McGraw-Hill, 1988), p. 214.

3. Dennis R. Arter, Charles A. Cianfrani, and John E. West, *How to Audit the Process-Based QMS* (Milwaukee, WI: ASQ Quality Press, 2003), p. 91.

4. J. P. Russell, *The Process Auditing Techniques Guide* (Milwaukee, WI: ASQ Quality Press, 2003), p. 23.

5. Peter D. Shainin, "The Tools of Quality, Part III: Control Charts," ASQC *Quality Progress*, August 1990, pp. 79–80.

6. J. M. Juran and Frank M. Gryna, eds., *Juran's Quality Control Handbook*, 4th ed. (New York: McGraw-Hill, 1989), p. 24.8.

7. Juran and Gryna, p. 24.7.

8. Scott Parsowith, *Fundamentals of Quality Auditing* (Milwaukee, WI: ASQC Quality Press, 1995), p. 65.

9. Mark L. Crossley, *The Desk Reference of Statistical Quality Methods* (Milwaukee, WI: ASQ Quality Press, 2000), pp. 391–396.

10. Crossley.

11. This paragraph and the remainder of this section (except figures) were taken from the NIST Engineering Statistics Handbook at http://www.itl.nist.gov/div898/handbook/index.htm.

12. C. W. Champ and W. H. Woodall, "Exact Results for Shewhart Control Charts with Supplementary Runs Rules," *Technometrics* 29, no. 4 (1987): 393–399.

13. Akio Miura, taken from course materials with permission, August 2005.

14. Juran Institute, "The Tools of Quality, Part IV: Histograms," ASQC *Quality Progress*, September 1990, pp. 77–78.

15. Taken from Russell T. Westcott, ed., *The Certified Manager of Quality/Organizational Excellence Handbook* (Milwaukee, WI: ASQ Quality Press, 2006), pp. 344–346.

16. Taken from Westcott, pp. 346–347.

CHAPTER 19

1. J. P. Russell, *Continual Improvement Assessment Guide: Performing and Sustaining Business Results* (Milwaukee, WI: ASQ Quality Press, 2004).

2. W. R. Trischler, *Understanding and Applying Value-Added Assessment: Eliminating Business Process Waste* (Milwaukee, WI: ASQC Quality Press, 1996).

CHAPTER 20

1. J. M. Juran and Frank M. Gryna, eds., *Juran's Quality Control Handbook*, 4th ed. (New York: McGraw-Hill, 1989), p. 23.15.

2. Juran and Gryna, p. 23.16.

3. IIA, *Internal Auditing: Principles and Techniques*, 2nd ed. (Altamonte Springs, FL: Institute of Internal Auditors [IIA], 1996), pp. 671–749.

4. Charles A. Mills, *The Quality Audit: A Management Evaluation Tool* (New York: McGraw-Hill, 1988), p. 205.

5. Akio Miura, taken from course materials with permission, August 2005.

CHAPTER 21

1. W. E. Deming, *Out of the Crisis* (Cambridge, MA: MIT Center for Advanced Engineering Study, 1986).
2. ASQ Statistics Division, *Improving Performance through Statistical Thinking* (Milwaukee, WI: ASQ Quality Press, 2000).

CHAPTER 22

1. Taken from QualityWBT Center for Education training materials, *Quality Tools and Techniques*, Lesson 3 (2012).

CHAPTER 25

1. David Ropeik and George Gray, *Risk: A Practical Guide for Deciding What's Really Safe and What's Really Dangerous in the World Around You* (New York and Boston: Houghton Mifflin, 2002), pp. 3–5.
2. James Kolka, *ISO 9000 A Legal Perspective* (Montclair, VA: INFORM with ASQ Quality Press, 1998), pp. 77–80.
3. Taken from Russell T. Westcott, *The Certified Manager of Quality/Organizational Excellence Handbook* (Milwaukee, WI: ASQ Quality Press, 2006), pp. 450–452.
4. Taken from Westcott, pp. 419–420.
5. Taken from FAA System Safety Handbook, Chapter 8, 8.4.7, pp. 8–19, http://www.faa.gov/library/manuals/aviation/risk_management/ss_handbook/media/Chap8_1200.pdf (accessed September 5, 2012).

APPENDIX E

1. ISO 9000:2005, *Quality Management Systems—Fundamentals and Vocabulary* (Milwaukee, WI: ASQ Quality Press, 2000), clause 3.1.1, quality, p. 7.
2. J. P. Russell, *The Quality Master Plan* (Milwaukee, WI: ASQC Quality Press, 1990), p. 7.
3. ISO 9000:2005, clause 3.2.2, management system, p. 8.
4. ISO 9000:2005, clause 3.2.11, quality assurance, p. 9.
5. ISO 9000:2005, clause 3.2.10, quality control, p. 9.
6. Charles A. Mills, *The Quality Audit: A Management Evaluation Tool* (New York: McGraw-Hill, 1988), pp. 5, 6, 7.
7. Mills, p. 11.
8. Allan J. Sayle, *Management Audits: The Assessment of Quality Management Systems*, 3rd ed. (Brighton, MI: Allan Sayle Associates, 1997), p. 12. Reproduced with permission of Allan J. Sayle.
9. Dennis R. Arter, *Quality Audits for Improved Performance*, 3rd ed. (Milwaukee, WI: ASQ Quality Press, 2003), p. 11.
10. Arter, p. 7.
11. ISO 9000:2005, clause 3.8.1, objective evidence, p. 15.
12. Dorsey J. Talley, *Management Audits for Excellence* (Milwaukee, WI: ASQC Quality Press, 1988), p. 42.

Glossary

Definitions are taken from ISO 19011:2011 and ISO 9000:2005, with definitions from the former superseding the latter.

audit—Systematic, independent and documented process for obtaining audit evidence and evaluating it objectively to determine the extent to which the audit criteria are fulfilled.

audit client—Organization or person requesting an audit.

audit conclusion—Outcome of an audit, provided by the audit team after consideration of the audit objectives and all audit findings.

audit criteria—Set of policies, procedures or requirements.

audit evidence—Records, statements of fact or other information, which are relevant to the audit criteria and verifiable.

audit findings—Results of the evaluation of the collected audit evidence against audit criteria.

audit plan—Description of the activities and arrangements for an audit.

audit program—Set of one or more audits planned for a specific time frame and directed towards a specific purpose.

audit scope—Extent and boundaries of an audit.

audit team—One or more auditors conducting an audit, supported if needed by technical experts.

auditee—Organization being audited.

auditor—Person with the competence to conduct an audit.

capability—Ability of an organization, system or process to realize a product that will fulfill the requirements for that product.

characteristic—Distinguishing feature.

competence—Demonstrated personal attributes and demonstrated ability to apply knowledge and skills.

concession—Permission to use or release a product that does not conform to specified requirements.

conformity—Fulfillment of a requirement.

continual improvement—Recurring activity to increase the ability to fulfill requirements.

correction—Action to eliminate a detected nonconformity.

corrective action—Action to eliminate the cause of a detected nonconformity or other undesirable situation.

customer—Organization or person that receives a product.

customer satisfaction—Customer's perception of the degree to which the customer's requirements have been fulfilled.

defect—Non-fulfillment of a requirement related to an intended or specified use.

dependability—Collective term used to describe the availability performance and its influencing factors: reliability performance, maintainability performance and maintenance support performance.

design and development—Set of processes that transforms requirements into specified characteristics or into the specification of a product, process or system.

deviation permit—Permission to depart from the originally specified requirements of a product prior to realization.

document—Information and its supporting medium.

effectiveness—Extent to which planned activities are realized and planned results achieved.

efficiency—Relationship between the result achieved and the resources used.

grade—Category or rank given to different quality requirements for products, processes or systems having the same functional use.

information—Meaningful data.

infrastructure—System of facilities, equipment and services needed for the operation of an organization.

inspection—Conformity evaluation by observation and judgment accompanied as appropriate by measurement, testing or gauging.

interested party—Person or group having an interest in the performance or success of an organization.

management—Coordinated activities to direct and control an organization.

management system—System to establish policy and objectives and to achieve those objectives.

measurement control system—Set of interrelated or interacting elements necessary to achieve metrological confirmation and continual control of measurement processes.

measurement process—Set of operations to determine the value of a quantity.

measuring equipment—Measuring instrument, software, measurement standard, reference material or auxiliary apparatus or combination thereof necessary to realize a measurement process.

metrological characteristic—Distinguishing feature which can influence the results of measurement.

metrological confirmation—Set of operations required to ensure that measuring equipment conforms to the requirements for its intended use.

metrological function—Function with organizational responsibility for defining and implementing the measurement control system.

nonconformity—Non-fulfillment of a requirement.

objective evidence—Data supporting the existence or verity of something.

organization—Group of people and facilities with an arrangement of responsibilities, authorities and relationships.

organizational structure—Arrangement of responsibilities, authorities and relationships between people.

preventive action—Action to eliminate the cause of a potential nonconformity or other undesirable potential situation.

procedure—Specified way to carry out an activity or a process.

process—Set of interrelated or interacting activities which transforms inputs into outputs.

product—Result of a process.

project—Unique process consisting of a set of coordinated and controlled activities with start and finish dates, undertaken to achieve an objective conforming to specific requirements, including the constraints of time, cost and resources.

qualification process—Process to demonstrate the ability to fulfill specified requirements.

quality—Degree to which a set of inherent characteristics fulfills requirements.

quality assurance—Part of quality management focused on providing confidence that quality requirements will be fulfilled.

quality characteristic—Inherent characteristic of a product, process or system related to a requirement.

quality control—Part of quality management focused on fulfilling quality requirements.

quality function deployment—A customer-driven product or service planning process. It is a methodology for translating customer requirements into company requirements at each stage, from concept definition to process engineering and production and into the marketplace.

quality improvement—Part of quality management focused on increasing the ability to fulfill quality requirements.

quality management—Coordinated activities to direct and control an organization with regard to quality.

quality management system—Management system to direct and control an organization with regard to quality.

quality manual—Document specifying the quality management system of an organization.

quality objective—Something sought, or aimed for, related to quality.

quality plan—Document specifying which procedures and associated resources shall be applied by whom and when to a specific project, product, process or contract.

quality planning—Part of quality management focused on setting quality objectives and specifying necessary operational processes and related resources to fulfill the quality objectives.

quality policy—Overall intentions and direction of an organization related to quality as formally expressed by top management.

record—Document stating results achieved or providing evidence of activities performed.

regrade—Alteration of the grade of a nonconforming product in order to make it conform to requirements differing from the initial ones.

release—Permission to proceed to the next stage of a process.

repair—Action on a nonconforming product to make it acceptable for the intended use.

requirement—Need or expectation that is stated, generally implied or obligatory.

review—Activity undertaken to determine the suitability, adequacy and effectiveness of the subject matter to achieve established objectives.

rework—Action on a nonconforming product to make it conform to the requirements.

scrap—Action on a nonconforming product to preclude its originally intended use.

specification—Document stating requirement.

supplier—Organization or person that provides a product.

system—Set of interrelated or interacting elements.

technical expert—Person who provides specific knowledge or expertise to the audit team.

test—Determination of one or more characteristics according to a procedure.

top management—Person or group of people who directs and controls an organization at the highest level.

traceability—Ability to trace the history, application or location of that which is under consideration.

validation—Confirmation, through the provision of objective evidence, that the requirements for a specific intended use or application have been fulfilled.

verification—Confirmation, through the provision of objective evidence, that specified requirements have been fulfilled.

work environment—Set of conditions under which work is performed.

Index

Note: Page numbers followed by *f* refer to figures; those followed by *t* refer to tables.

A

ABC (activity-based costing), 204–205
abstract, audit report, 109
acceptable quality level (AQL), 270
acceptance sampling, 269–270
accreditation, certification and, 7
acknowledgment of nonconformities, 74
activity sequence flowchart, 212*f*
activity symbol, 211
Advanced Medical Technology Association
   (AdvaMed) standards, 53
After the Quality Audit, 55, 59, 60, 116
agent, auditor as, 38–40
American Society for Quality (ASQ)
   code of ethics, 26, 27*f*, 35
ANSI-ASQ National Accreditation Board
   (ANAB), 7
ANSI/ASQ Z1.4-2008 applicability and
   use, 271
antagonistic situations, defusing, 142
anti-gag statutes, 34
appraisal costs, 201, 202, 203
approvals, audit report, 114
arithmetic mean, 250–251
ASQ Audit Division
   certification requirements, 135*t*
   Code of Ethics, 291
   continuing education opportunities,
      168–169
   Ethics Committee, 35
   mission, 8, 22
ASQC Q3-1998 applicability and use, 271
assessments, 9
assignable causes, 218
assignable cause variation, 261
assignment considerations, 60*f*
attribute data, 216
auditable requirements, 56–57
audit basis, 19

auditee
   concerns, 84–85
   defined, 21
   responsibilities and duties, 23
   roles and responsibilities, 88
audit-like inquiries, 9
auditor-auditee relationship, 4–6
auditors
   access to legal counsel, 33
   as agent, 38–40
   certification, 134, 135*t*
   competence, 137–138
   defined, 21
   education and experience, 134–136
   emerging roles of, 205
   guidelines for, 72–73
   interpersonal skills, 136–138
   performance, 170, 172
   personal traits, 138
   responsibilities and duties, 23
   roles and responsibilities, 87
   selection of, 59–63
   skills and competencies, 46, 134–135, 136*t*
   training and development, 166–170
audit performance
   data collection and analysis, 89–97
   exit and closing meetings, 101–107
   objective evidence, establishment of,
      97–98
   objective evidence, organization of,
      98–101
   on-site management, 82–85
   opening meeting, 85–89
   problems encountered during, 105–106
audit plan
   changes to, 83–84
   common problems encountered, 81
   communication and distribution of, 79–80
   defined, 79
   purpose and content of, 49–51

The Knowledge Center
www.asq.org/knowledge-center

Learn about quality. Apply it. Share it.

ASQ's online Knowledge Center is the place to:

- Stay on top of the latest in quality with Editor's Picks and Hot Topics.

- Search ASQ's collection of articles, books, tools, training, and more.

- Connect with ASQ staff for personalized help hunting down the knowledge you need, the networking opportunities that will keep your career and organization moving forward, and the publishing opportunities that are the best fit for you.

Use the Knowledge Center Search to quickly sort through hundreds of books, articles, and other software-related publications.

www.asq.org/knowledge-center

ASQ®
The Global Voice of Quality™

TRAINING   CERTIFICATION   CONFERENCES   MEMBERSHIP   **PUBLICATIONS**

Ask a Librarian

Did you know?

- The ASQ Quality Information Center contains a wealth of knowledge and information available to ASQ members and non-members

- A librarian is available to answer research requests using ASQ's ever-expanding library of relevant, credible quality resources, including journals, conference proceedings, case studies and Quality Press publications

- ASQ members receive free internal information searches and reduced rates for article purchases

- You can also contact the Quality Information Center to request permission to reuse or reprint ASQ copyrighted material, including journal articles and book excerpts

- For more information or to submit a question, visit **http://asq.org/knowledge-center/ask-a-librarian-index**

Visit www.asq.org/qic for more information.

ASQ

The Global Voice of Quality™

Belong to the Quality Community!

Established in 1946, ASQ is a global community of quality experts in all fields and industries. ASQ is dedicated to the promotion and advancement of quality tools, principles, and practices in the workplace and in the community.

The Society also serves as an advocate for quality. Its members have informed and advised the U.S. Congress, government agencies, state legislatures, and other groups and individuals worldwide on quality-related topics.

Vision

By making quality a global priority, an organizational imperative, and a personal ethic, ASQ becomes the community of choice for everyone who seeks quality technology, concepts, or tools to improve themselves and their world.

ASQ is...

- More than 90,000 individuals and 700 companies in more than 100 countries

- The world's largest organization dedicated to promoting quality

- A community of professionals striving to bring quality to their work and their lives

- The administrator of the Malcolm Baldrige National Quality Award

- A supporter of quality in all sectors including manufacturing, service, healthcare, government, and education

- YOU

Visit www.asq.org for more information.

TRAINING   CERTIFICATION   CONFERENCES   MEMBERSHIP   **PUBLICATIONS**

The Global Voice of Quality™

ASQ Membership

Research shows that people who join associations experience increased job satisfaction, earn more, and are generally happier*. ASQ membership can help you achieve this while providing the tools you need to be successful in your industry and to distinguish yourself from your competition. So why wouldn't you want to be a part of ASQ?

Networking

Have the opportunity to meet, communicate, and collaborate with your peers within the quality community through conferences and local ASQ section meetings, ASQ forums or divisions, ASQ Communities of Quality discussion boards, and more.

Professional Development

Access a wide variety of professional development tools such as books, training, and certifications at a discounted price. Also, ASQ certifications and the ASQ Career Center help enhance your quality knowledge and take your career to the next level.

Solutions

Find answers to all your quality problems, big and small, with ASQ's Knowledge Center, mentoring program, various e-newsletters, *Quality Progress* magazine, and industry-specific products.

Access to Information

Learn classic and current quality principles and theories in ASQ's Quality Information Center (QIC), *ASQ Weekly* e-newsletter, and product offerings.

Advocacy Programs

ASQ helps create a better community, government, and world through initiatives that include social responsibility, Washington advocacy, and Community Good Works.

Visit www.asq.org/membership for more information on ASQ membership.

*2008, The William E. Smith Institute for Association Research

TRAINING   CERTIFICATION   CONFERENCES   **MEMBERSHIP**   PUBLICATIONS   The Global Voice of Quali